C. Wright Mills and the Criminological Imagination

Prospects for Creative Inquiry

Edited by

JON FRAULEY
University of Ottawa, Canada

ASHGATE

Published by
Ashgate Publishing Limited
Wey Court East
Union Road
Farnham
Surrey, GU9 7PT
England

Ashgate Publishing Company
110 Cherry Street
Suite 3-1
Burlington, VT 05401-3818
USA

www.ashgate.com

British Library Cataloguing in Publication Data
A catalogue record for this book is available from the British Library

The Library of Congress has cataloged the printed edition as follows:
C. Wright Mills and the criminological imagination : prospects for creative inquiry / [edited] by Jon Frauley.
    pages cm. – (Classical and contemporary social theory)
 Includes bibliographical references and index.
  ISBN 978-1-4724-1474-8 (hardback : alk. paper) – ISBN 978-1-4724-1475-5 (ebook) –
 ISBN 978-1-4724-1476-2 (epub) 1. Mills, C. Wright (Charles Wright), 1916–1962.
 2. Criminology. I. Frauley, Jon, 1972– editor.
  HV6025.W75 2015
  364–dc23
                                                                      2015014522

ISBN: 9781472414748 (hbk)
ISBN: 9781472414755 (ebk – PDF)
ISBN: 9781472414762 (ebk – ePUB)

MIX
Paper from
responsible sources
FSC   FSC® C013985
www.fsc.org

Printed in the United Kingdom by Henry Ling Limited,
at the Dorset Press, Dorchester, DT1 1HD

summa experimenti sumus

For Isobel and Amelia, with love

Contents

Notes on Contributors

Alana Barton is Senior Lecturer in Criminology at Edge Hill University (United Kingdom).

Eamonn Carrabine is Professor and former Head of Sociology at the University of Essex (United Kingdom).

Nicolas Carrier is Associate Professor of Criminology at Carleton University (Canada).

Howard Davis is Senior Lecturer in Criminology at Edge Hill University (United Kingdom).

Jon Frauley is Associate Professor of Criminology at the University of Ottawa (Canada) and for 2014–2015 was Visiting Professor of Law and Legal Studies, Criminology and Criminal Justice at Carleton University (Canada).

David Nelken is Professor of Comparative and Transnational Law and Associate Dean and Head of Research at the Dickson Poon School of Law, King's College London (UK). Since 2010 he has been Visiting Professor of Criminology at Oxford University (UK). In 2014 he was Global Law Professor at Tilburg Law School, the Netherlands. Previous appointments include Distinguished Professor of Legal Institutions and Social Change at the University of Macerata (Italy) and Distinguished Research Professor of Law at Cardiff University (Wales).

Stephen Pfohl is Professor of Sociology at Boston College (United States).

Stephanie Piamonte is a PhD Candidate in Criminology at the University of Ottawa (Canada).

Joseph A. Scimecca is Professor of Sociology at George Mason University (United States).

David Scott is Senior Lecturer in Criminology at Liverpool John Moores University (United Kingdom).

Melanie White is Senior Lecturer in Social Theory in the School of Social Sciences at the University of New South Wales, Australia.

Rob White is Professor of Criminology in the School of Social Sciences at the University of Tasmania (Australia).

Frank P. Williams III is Professor Emeritus of Criminal Justice at California State University, San Bernardino (United States).

Foreword

This book comes at a pivotal moment for the field of criminology. That may seem like something of a cliché, but I believe it's true. As some of the contributors to this volume point out, criticism of a dearth of imagination in academic criminology isn't new: in fact, some of these authors themselves first made that critique decades ago. What is new, to me, is the vibrancy of some trends within criminology that could revitalize the field and restore that lost imagination.

There are (at least) two 'criminologies' today. One is the rather soulless variant of the 'scientism' that C. Wright Mills lambasted at the end of the 1950s – whose ascendancy is the target of many of this book's authors. But that isn't the whole story. Indeed, it probably never was. Creative, boundary-pushing work has always coexisted with more timid and narrow variants, for at least as long as I've been at this work, which is, by now, longer than I want to think about. But I think that kind of creative work is more common today than it was twenty years ago, or even back in the day when I began.

There are several reasons for that blooming of new and creative perspectives in the field. One is the changing face of the people who work in it. Increasing diversity of gender, race and ethnicity, the growing presence in the field of scholars with experience behind bars – a consequence in part of the breadth and scope of America's incarceration binge – have all begun to reshape what we talk about in the field, and how we talk about it: not always easily, but still to a degree that has already begun to transform the discipline and that's unlikely to be rolled back. Another force is the shift away from the American dominance of criminology. I think it's safe to say that the United States was historically the bastion of the kind of criminology – and social science generally – that Mills would have derided: as home-grown criminology has blossomed in countries around the world with broader and more inclusive intellectual traditions, the hegemony of that kind of criminology has necessarily weakened. Deepening environmental crises and intensified global economic predation have forced green criminology onto the agenda and highlighted the importance of the study of corporate crime. An explosion of immigration around the world has stimulated fresh new thinking on the impact of migration and the criminalization of immigrant communities. The scourges of mass atrocities and global terrorism have – if belatedly – put those issues into the frame of the discipline and sparked genuinely imaginative scholarship.

All of these changes, and others, have brought an encouraging surge of new or newly revitalized criminologies and the emergence of a new crop of younger scholars who are doing creative, boundary-nudging work every day – and getting it published. But that's the good news. Paradoxically, that growth of new and creative criminology has coexisted with the solidification and entrenchment, in some places, of the narrower, more constrained and more troubling criminology that this book powerfully challenges. We see this in the increasing obscurity and decreasing relevance of too many of the 'official' journals in the field; we see it in the steady 'hardening' of some academic departments into stultifying incubators of the least imaginative work imaginable; we see it in the continuing influence of that kind of criminology over some funding agencies and professional associations.

Personally, I see it most immediately, and most painfully, in its impact on my own students, some of whom feel bullied and oppressed by what they perceive to be the dominant drift of the field – one that, far from rewarding imaginative work, actively penalizes it and works to marginalize it. They feel themselves caught in an intellectual culture that demands fidelity to a narrow, uniform and uncongenial way of thinking and working that just doesn't feel like *them*. I often think that a huge part of what I do as a teacher and mentor is to simply to give smart, creative students permission to do the kind of work they came into the field to do – and to convince them that they can do that work and still be employed.

So the obstacles to doing creative and engaged criminology are very real, and I don't want to minimize them. But I think it's crucial to recognize that, increasingly, the old criminology is not the only game in town. That recognition can help us avoid the kind of fatalism and even desperation that can afflict those of us who are more than a little appalled by some of what passes for 'mainstream' work in our field. Here, as in much else in life, Franklin D. Roosevelt's declaration that 'the only thing we have to fear is fear itself' is apposite. We do ourselves, and our students (and their students farther down the road), a disservice if we crawl into a hole and assume we have less professional heft and less opportunity for impact on the discipline than we actually do. Narrow 'scientism' may hold sway in some academic departments and in some mainstream journals. But it is by no means the only way, or even the normal way, that you make a name for yourself in this field – or produce work that gets widely disseminated and widely talked about, or land a good job. We have only to look at the stream of fine, imaginative historical, qualitative and theoretical work that has enriched the way we think about crime and punishment in the last twenty years to see that.

But this isn't a call for complacency. Which kind of criminology will prevail in the coming years will depend very much on our ability to build a strong infrastructure to support and nurture the criminological imagination in the face of the still formidable forces arrayed against it. That means, for example, launching new, bolder and more inclusive journals to provide ample venues for publishing; building strong networks of scholars committed to a diverse, 'big tent' vision of engaged and creative work – networks that can offer an intellectual home for imaginative scholarship and also nurture opportunities for jobs and funding; sponsoring new kinds of conferences and taking a more assertive role in shaping the content of the ones we already go to, and challenging the creep towards uniformity and timidity in graduate education – through new kinds of student funding that reward unconventional work, new curricular configurations that allow students and faculty to jointly explore emerging and under-studied issues, and much more.

That's a big agenda, but I think it's one worth fighting for. And I believe we are already moving in these directions, in real and important ways. I doubt that everyone in this volume would share my cautious optimism about the future of criminology. But I am sure that their own exemplary work will help us get there.

Elliott Currie
University of California, Irvine

Acknowledgements

There are a great many people to thank, and I will inevitably forget at least one name. Please accept my apologies for this.

To all the contributors, I owe my gratitude for entrusting me with your work and for staying with the project despite its being more than a year overdue. For this I am grateful. The work turned over to me was extremely fine-tuned, and so made my job much easier. It was a pleasure reading each chapter, and an even greater pleasure to find everyone so receptive and committed to the project.

Thank you to Neil Jordan at Ashgate Publishing for his patience and commitment to the project. I want to thank David Nelken for his very early commitment to the project and for his 'sleep-writing' – something I aspire to. I thank George Rigakos, Nicolas Carrier, Ron Saunders and the Department of Law and Legal Studies at Carleton University for generously providing office space. A special thank you to Elliott Currie for taking the time to contribute his foreword.

As always, I thank my colleagues at the University of Ottawa for supporting my work and for offering intellectual stimulation. Thank you to Dana Burke, for supporting and inspiring me.

Jon Frauley

C. Wright Mills and the Criminological Imagination: Introductory Remarks

Jon Frauley

No social study that does not come back to the problems of biography, history and of their intersections within a society has completed its intellectual journey.
(Mills 1959, 6)

In 1959 Mills offered a trenchant and still relevant critique of what he viewed as the growth of an applied and technique-driven industrialized science indebted to the problems and questions of the post-war expansion of bureaucracy (see Frauley, Chapter 1 in this volume). His most influential book, *The Sociological Imagination*, is concerned to illustrate the rise of a 'bureaucratic ethos' and the implication of this for social life, the process and objectives of social science, and for knowledge production. The text offers us a framework for understanding how criminology and justice studies do contribute to the reproduction of bureaucratic domination and the production of what Mills termed the 'cheerful robot' (see Chapter 1 in this volume). Cheerful robots – the uninformed, alienated, and politically disengaged (Scimecca 1977; Kerr 2009; Trevino 2012) – abound today, especially with the specialized division of labour and commercial model of social life that is characteristic of the enterprise culture of market capitalism. Market-driven and private–public partnering in public service delivery and the shift from a manufacturing, industrial economy to one built on high consumer debt, over-consumption of junk and what Bruns (2008) has called 'produsage' (which emphasizes 'soft' or virtual commodity production, collective commodity fetishism and crowdsourcing) has left criminology with new puzzles and challenges, but without the necessary theoretical or methodological tools to deal with these (see Carrabine, Chapter 3, and Pfohl, Chapter 4 in this volume; Garland and Sparks 2000). The neglected work of Mills offers one possible way forward and one possible way to renew criminology's relevance in the face of new intellectual challenges posed by relatively recent technological and political developments (Braithwaite 2000; Garland and Sparks 2000; Haggerty 2004a; Currie 2007; Pfohl, Chapter 4 in this volume).

Much has been written on the demise of the liberal arts and the incremental marketizing and commercializing of the university. Criminologists and justice studies scholars, as well, have reflected on this issue and on the changing political and economic landscape that has nourished what Williams (Chapter 2 in this volume; 1984) refers to as the 'demise of the criminological imagination' (see also Carrabine, Chapter 3, Pfohl, Chapter 4, and Barton and Davis, Chapter 9 in this volume). As with certain aspects of crime control today, the production and appropriation of criminological knowledge has been increasingly subject to technocratic ends and commercialization (Tombs and Whyte 2002, 2003; Walters 2003; White 2001; O'Malley 1996; Garland and Sparks 2000; Barton and Davis, Chapter 9 in this volume). Indeed, much of the production of criminological knowledge is fuelled and in many ways constrained by images of reality that reflect a widespread fear and fascination with crime and its control (see Carrabine, Chapter 3, and Pfohl, Chapter 4 in this volume). This has contributed to the mounting pressure on academics to concentrate on applied research that will yield tangible and immediate benefits for industry and government. Indeed, as research on ethics review boards within universities has demonstrated, it is more difficult today than in the past for non-positivistic and less structured research designs – those which deviate from applied or industrial science models – to gain approval (Palys 2003; Hammersly 2009; Haggerty 2004b).

Conditions contributing to the demise of the criminological imagination, or perhaps simply its perpetual underdevelopment, have also had an impact on the transmission of criminological knowledge in the classroom (White 2001; Frauley 2005; Barton et al. 2010; Barton and Davis, Chapter 9 in this volume). For instance, more pressure has been placed on scholars to identify and list the skills students will obtain from their courses and, in some instances, to adopt new teaching and/ or evaluation techniques such as 'clickers' or multiple-choice testing to cope with expanding class sizes and the increasingly difficult task of failing or ranking low the 'clients' of the university. Overall, the use of the criminological imagination for teaching and research has been minimized and undermined.

Related to this underdevelopment of the criminological imagination, criminologists and justice studies scholars, albeit with exceptions, have in the main long displayed theoretical and political timidity and a lack of curiosity concerning 'big' theoretical and substantive questions pertaining to politics, power, the state and, especially, the changing forms of domination in Western societies and how these relate to the decline of social democracy.[1] This widespread timidity – manifested in narrow empirical studies of little theoretical depth or significance and in very broad theoretically eclectic work of little substantive import – has cast criminologists and their respective disciplines invariably as empiricist, ahistorical and vocationally oriented (see Williams, Chapter 2, Carrabine, Chapter 3, and Pfohl, Chapter 4 in this volume).

Criminology and justice studies are in need of renewal, or as Carrabine (Chapter 3 in this volume) has put it, 'rediscovery' toward regaining 'intellectual energy and vitality'. We might begin this renewal by asking ourselves: 'Are

---

1   Many sociological criminologists might find this statement puzzling, but not all criminologists or justice studies scholars are sociologists, and there exist ample non-sociological journals devoted to the study of crime and delinquency to demonstrate this.

criminology and justice studies social sciences capable of producing illuminating description and explanation of the pressing political and economic conditions that prop up and reproduce social problems as problems of control?' 'Can they operate independently of state and official definitions of crime?' 'Can they offer critical scrutiny of themselves as well as systems of power and control at work within contemporary societies?' In a sea of textbooks it is challenging to find those that do not align criminology and justice studies with the criminal law and its administration (and in doing so with state definitions of its subject matter). Many are replete with misleading descriptions of the crime control apparatus as a unified 'system' that stems from societal consensus about the values and norms embedded in and enforced by its practices. In addition, there is an almost total negation of criminal justice administration and criminalization as a complex and contradictory political apparatus and process that serves to reproduce privilege and widespread deprivation.

There is a need today to forge a criminology that is more than simply a 'rendezvous subject' (Downes 1988), 'hybrid field' (Fattah 1997) or an 'inter-institutional' discipline (Ericson 1996). As Carrabine argues in Chapter 3 in this volume: 'it is the traffic in multidisciplinary approaches that has sustained post-war British criminology, but which has also left it prone to a bewildering eclecticism and disorganized fragmentation'. On the North American front its growth owes in large part to its pseudo-professional 'protective service' orientation and the expansion and problems of the carceral complex (Williams, Chapter 2 in this volume; Morn 1995; Frauley 2005). As social sciences, criminology and justice studies will benefit from the analytic tools, model of society and methodological approach found in the work of Mills. Advocating synthesis through systematic engagement with viewpoints within and beyond one's own field, a Millsian-inspired criminology would have us move between these insights as well as alternating our focus between the specific and the remote aspects of our society.

Although those working within sociology have long debated and built upon the work of Mills, his radical sociology has had virtually no impact on criminology or justice studies (see Scimecca, Chapter 5 in this volume). Contributors to this volume make a concerted effort to rectify this unfortunate state of affairs by putting forth criminological interpretations, theorizations and applications of Mills' ideas, offering insights, extensions and reformulations of his work for criminological enquiry, while at the same time examining the intersection of 'criminological enquiry' and 'criminological imagination'.

Although Figure 1 is overly schematic, it attempts only to illustrate the breadth and scope of Mills' ideas to suggest an affinity with criminology. Although Mills did not specifically tackle crime or its control, his overall model is, as Scimecca (1975; Chapter 5 in this volume) has shown, amenable to developing criminological theory, and as Krisberg (1974) has argued, it is compatible with the study of crime control as a political enterprise. As Mills had a keen interest in political institutions, personality structure and formation, and their interconnection, his work can be drawn upon to illuminate and further understand connexions between

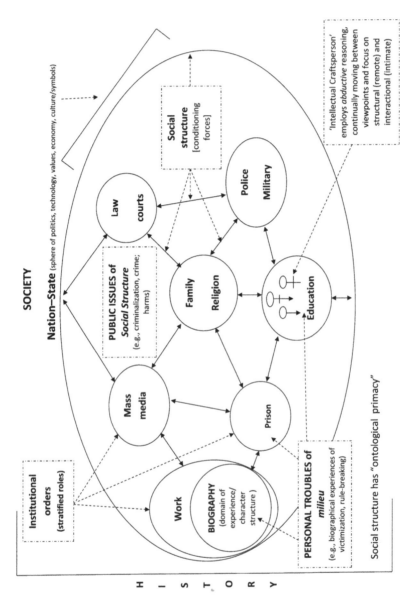

SOCIETY

Nation–State (sphere of politics, technology, values, economy, culture/symbols)

Social structure [conditioning forces]

Law courts

Police Military

PUBLIC ISSUES of *Social Structure* (e.g., criminalization, crime; harms)

Family Religion

Education

Mass media

Prison

'Intellectual Craftsperson' employs *abductive* reasoning, continually moving between viewpoints and focus on structural (remote) and interactional (intimate)

Institutional orders (stratified roles)

Work

BIOGRAPHY (domain of experience/ character structure)

PERSONAL TROUBLES of *milieu* (e.g., biographical experiences of victimization, rule-breaking)

Social structure has "ontological primacy"

H I S T O R Y

Figure 1   The criminological imagination

crime control practices and ideologies as well as actors' changing experiences and understandings of the dynamics of criminalization, victimization and the administration of the criminal law. Moreover, it will help us clearly connect the criminal justice apparatus to other institutions that are typically not thought of as falling within the purview of criminology or as being integrated with crime and its control, institutions such as education, labour, mass media and types of law other than the criminal law.

Mills' work offers great promise for those interested in more adequate and holistic criminologies because his work offers a metatheoretical framing that can be harnessed to formulate a criminology that is sensitive to interactional and structural dynamics and the relationship between these two aspects of any society within, importantly, their historical context. It provides an 'umbrella', if you will, for situating and evaluating criminological work, the criminologist, as well as for producing new criminological insights. As a general or 'meta' framework it can guide the operating of criminology's analytic languages, assessing these languages, producing new ones or reformulating old ones. His work is sensitive to the structural basis of power, domination and alienation that is inherent to liberal democracies. His work offers a critical humanism that is critical of (neo-)liberalism, scientism, and abuses of power and authority and which can be employed to compare explanatory frameworks and empirical claims and, ultimately, produce non-eclectic syntheses that can be deployed to engage public debate and promote scholarly research, especially on the production, reproduction and transformation of crime and its control.

The importance and benefit of Mills for criminology should not be underestimated. With the waning of one of criminology's most formidable 'big picture' approaches, namely Marxism, Mills' importance takes on new significance. Although Marxism has its limitations, as Mills and others have noted, it offered a formidable challenge to apolitical conflict theory and to functionalism – approaches that neglected the dynamism of social structure, political economy and the endemic and multifaceted nature of change. With its passing, or at least given its decline, we have yet to encounter a formidable alternative. As Stuart Russell (2002, 113) has discussed, 'new directions' in critical criminology today have 'consciously excluded Marxism as being out-dated' and have abandoned or downplayed the importance of political economy and 'big' picture analysis. As Barton et al note:

> [S]ome criminologists have sought to imagine new ways in which the discipline can challenge intellectually and practically the agendas of the powerful. Given the ascendancy and consolidation of a state-driven agenda within and outside criminology, a critical and creative imagination is necessary now more than ever. It is time for criminologists to reflect upon the utility of the discipline in order to reawaken, revive and expand a criminological imagination. ... Current developments in mainstream and administrative criminology have presented us with an unimaginative and individualized discourse that has displaced criminal

actors from their broader structural, economic and political contexts. (Barton et
al. 2007, 2; see also O'Malley 1996)

The void left with the decline of one of criminology's most formidable 'big
picture' frameworks affects not only those working within a Marxist tradition or
those committed to a sociological criminology, but those working in a critical and
democratic tradition:

> In the period from the late 1960s to the early 1980s, when critical scholarship
> was strong in the social sciences, and when Marxism played a significant role
> within this, critique meant engaging seriously with the positions held by one's
> opponents. In general, there was an expectation that positions with which
> one disagreed should be represented accurately and challenged conceptually,
> epistemologically, and empirically; it was also anticipated that an exchange
> might develop subject to the same 'rules'. While this was not always achieved
> in practice, it nevertheless constituted a regulative ideal. However passionately
> a position was held, there existed a real possibility of its modification, its
> development, its abandonment, and, sometimes, the development of surprising,
> and non-eclectic, syntheses. A disturbing aspect of current academic practice is
> that differing but rigorous interpretations of the nature of the social world and
> of theories and theorists are often simply ignored, at times crudely parodied,
> or simply, and contemptuously, dismissed. This is to no one's benefit and it
> seems important to find different ways of dealing with such disagreements.
> (Pearce 2003, xi)

Without lamenting the waning of Marxism, it can be said that this decline or
waning of 'big picture' analysis has left a void within criminology. However,
as Rosenfeld (2011) has recently argued, although criminology today lacks 'big
picture' thinking, Millsian sociology can provide this, especially for looking at
the 'particular types and levels of crime' which today is 'largely absent from
contemporary criminology' (Rosenfeld 2011, 2; Williams, Chapter 2 in this
volume). Scimecca (1976) long ago argued that Mills offered an alternative to
Marxian critical social science and thus offers today an as yet unrealized promise
for critical criminology. It is in this light – of being able to challenge intellectually
and practically the agendas of the powerful, place emphasis on critical and
imaginative enquiry and on big picture analysis without neglecting agency and
social action, and in attending to power and domination while escaping vulgar
instrumentalist and determinist analyses – that Mills' work holds much theoretical
and methodological promise for criminology and justice studies.

Although Mills' work has been important and profoundly influential within
sociology, his presence has not been felt to any substantial degree within

criminology.[2] Mills' absence from criminology is strange given the space created for heterodox and politically oriented scholarship from the 1960s onward. Initially, the space of heterodox criminology was filled by liberal conflict theory (i.e., especially that of symbolic interactionism) and, on the other hand, a Marxist critique of positivism and liberalism (which gave birth to 'radical' criminology and paved the way for feminist, postmodernist, criminological realism, peacemaking and other approaches). Although there was some appetite for Mills' scholarship (Krisberg 1974; Scimecca 1975; Williams 1984), his work did not catch on or mobilize a school of thought within criminology.[3] This anthology is explicitly geared toward a criminological contemplation of Mills' work for both empirical analysis and theorizing, and for bridging the unfortunate divide that often separates the two.

Criminology today is popular and growing as an academic field, but it is not yet a theoretically or methodologically robust field, as Jock Young (2011) and others have contended, and this is precisely why we must work to develop a criminological imagination. Imagination for Mills 'is the capacity to shift from one perspective to another – from the political to the psychological; .... It is the capacity to range from the most impersonal and remote transformations to the most intimate features of the human self – and to see the relations between the two' (1959, 7). Imagination enables one to construct a fuller, more robust picture of what is observed and to speculate about what cannot be seen directly. Bringing together or synthesizing different viewpoints and imagining questions based on these different points of view and how these can illuminate connections between the level of action and structure requires creativity. An imaginative criminology, therefore, is the outcome of a continual synthesis of thought and combinatory movement between different substantive and conceptual vantage points whilst explicitly maintaining an awareness of historical and political context.

The criminological imagination is what Woodiwiss (2001, 3) has called a 'system of visualisation'. Frauley in Chapter 1 in this volume discusses this visual metaphor in Mills in terms of the optical processes of refraction and parallax. Kemple and Mawani (2009) pick up on this theme as well, emphasizing the 'bi-focal' nature of Mills' quality of mind as it helps us visualize within the same frame what is close up and what is remote. It is a system for 'making things and actions visible' and for producing 'visualities' (Woodiwiss 2001, 3; see also Woodiwiss 1990). Visualities are pictures of social reality that social scientists fabricate using theoretical and methodological tools imaginatively. They are outcomes of systematic and rigorous analysis. Scott in Chapter 8 in this volume, for example, offers an illustration of this as he deploys Mills to not only challenge existing and dominant ways of

---

2   *The Sociological Imagination* has been ranked the second most influential book of the twentieth century by the International Sociological Association: 'Books of the Century', ISA, http://www.isa-sociology.org/books/books10.htm (accessed 6 June 2015).

3   Contemporary criminological works that draw on Mills are limited: Carrier (2011); Frauley (2011); Simon (1985, 1988, 1991); White (2003); Wozniak (2009); Young (2011).

thinking about prison life, but also to delineate critical research values for future prison ethnographies. Likewise Rob White in Chapter 10 in this volume constructs a visuality about the potential impact that the 'ecocide' by government and business, through their collective failure to systematically address the causes and consequences of global warming, has on children. Visualities are not unlike the 'theoretical stories' discussed by Pfohl (1994, 7) or the 'criminological narratives' produced by Ruggiero (2003). They are the products of creative and imaginative conceptualizing, but one that is constrained by disciplinary training and historical standpoint. As it is inevitable that such pictures of social reality will highlight some aspects and exclude others (Pfohl 1994, 7), it stands to reason that better-quality pictures can be produced with better-quality frameworks, especially ones that are designed for increased scope.

Williams (1984, 91) argued that 'useful and insightful theories are products of imagination and speculation', but that such work was rarely valued within criminology – a point made by Ruggiero (2003, vii) in his remarks on the low value many of his colleagues attached to his efforts to bring literature to criminology and criminology to the study of fiction. The erosion of value within criminology of imagination and speculation, continues Williams (1984), left it to become theoretically bereft and to gradually become characterized by low- and poor-quality conceptualizing. As a consequence criminology had become stunted, and was no longer expanding its knowledge base or growing as a social science. Instead it had moved in the direction of applied study, adopting what I have described elsewhere as a 'protective service' orientation (Frauley 2005). Criminology, Williams argued, had become too 'empiricist' and bereft of imagination, for two reasons. The first was the rise of 'scientism', the appearance or mimicking of natural science through a reliance on a positivist epistemology, use of statistical techniques and production of so-called 'hard' data. This was made all the more attractive by the convenience of computer assisted data processing. Second, criminology had begun to take its problems from the professional domain of criminal justice with its focus on 'the system', increasingly narrowing in scope and driven by external interests that had little or no stake in social science.

Williams argued that within criminology there developed a concern with the application of knowledge without explicit concern for the process of knowledge production. This, he argued, stemmed from the preoccupation with mimicking a natural science approach without generating new knowledge (on this more generally, see Sayer [1992]). 'Major breakthroughs', Williams argued, 'have resulted from changing perceptions of data, not from the accumulation of evidence which then commands a new form of understanding' (Williams 1984, 96). It is the quality of our concepts, the continual development and refinement of criminological ideas and improvement of the craft of social science that enable the extraction of new meaning and allow us to visualize new criminological significance within our data. By implication, Williams argued that the dominant but quite erroneous idea that new knowledge is created incrementally through accumulating more and more data was due to a turn within criminology toward quantification, statistical measurement and applied science: 'We have followed the "hard" sciences into an alley where we are more concerned with measurement itself than with speculation about the substance being measured.' This is the 'fetishism of method' Mills attributed to what he called 'abstracted empiricism'. The result was to remove the qualitative 'essence of social life' which amounted to a 'reification of scientism' (Williams 1984, 7).

We can take from this the view that although criminologists might be very good at applying already existing concrete (and not too abstract) ideas, producing information in the context of very narrow problems or quite competent in manipulating and processing data, this is not, following Mills, social science at all, but technical, bureaucratic work. Simply put, Williams, following Mills, argued that criminology had become technocratic. This slide toward the technocratic was largely the result of changing needs of industry and government, uncritical acceptance of the problems of the justice system as the problems of criminology, and the belief that social science should look like natural science (i.e., scientism), resulting in a devaluing of creative and speculative conceptualizing. By contrast, the quality of mind Mills outlined was inquisitive, imaginative and critical: 'It is this imagination, of course, that sets off the social scientist from the mere technician. Adequate technicians can be trained in a few years. The sociological imagination can also be cultivated; .... There is a playfulness of mind ... which the technician as such usually lacks' (1959, 211).

The issue that is important for us is that although imagination and speculation are necessary for the social scientific production of knowledge, these are regarded by the bulk of criminologists as external to science in the same way that reading and writing fiction might be conceived to be external or even antithetical to science. This problem of where imagination and science meet, of what constitutes the 'proper' domain of objects for criminology and justice studies, of how speculation and observation intersect, is also one that can be found within cultural criminology (Ferrell et al. 2008), the work of Rafter (2006) and Ruggiero (2003), and other attempts to produce imaginative criminologies (see Piamonte, Chapter 11 in this volume; Frauley 2015).

Importantly, Williams points out that the great and foundational works of criminology and sociology were not devoid of imagination and speculation: 'The great works of criminology, such as those of Emile Durkheim, Edwin Sutherland, and Robert Merton, have great value to us because they are an exemplary display of intuition and speculative logic. These works are still useful today because they have this explanatory power' (1984, 102; references omitted).

Influential 'intellectual universes', as Mills (1959, 13) referred to them – those bequeathed by Durkheim, Sutherland, Merton, Newton, Darwin and others – have left traces on the social sciences because they have been taken up widely. This is due to their value, which does not rest on the deriving of truths from facts, but on the powerful analytic concepts produced from an engagement with a historically situated and significant empirical or theoretical puzzle (see examples in M. White, Chapter 6, and Carrier, Chapter 7 in this volume). Because these widely regarded (social) scientists attempted to think about broad, general problems and issues *through* their particular object, their work was 'double-sided'. In turn, because of this scope their work is still useful for contemplating and analysing a broad range of phenomena today.

Explanatory power and longevity derive from an exploration of empirical phenomena in order to not only produce information about that particular problem (e.g., gangs, youth delinquency, domestic violence), but to also craft or refine analytic lenses that can be used in the formulation of general and somewhat speculative theoretical statements (see Layder 1993). For example, Robert Merton (1938) took youth delinquency as a vehicle to study social integration. He was interested in how youth delinquency offered a way to think more broadly about integration in terms of the conflict between widely diffused 'culture goals' that youth are socialized to aspire to and the relative lack of 'legitimate means' available to some to realize these aspirations. This mismatch of goals and legitimate means, he surmised, caused some individuals, particularly youth, to experience 'strain' and to 'adapt' in various ways. Rather than view strain as only a problem of individual failure or frustration, Merton formulated his ideas about delinquency to denote 'structural strain' in order to capture two opposing forces that could pull the individual in different directions. With youth caught in the middle – between socialized aspirations to attain dominant culture goals and limited legitimate means for doing so – strain resulted in delinquent behaviour.

Whether or not we agree with Merton's theorization, we cannot deny that his work serves as a good example of the explanatory power and longevity of double-sided conceptual tools. This power and longevity does not derive from whether or not theories or concepts offer 'true descriptions', but with how well they help us produce plausible, defensible, robust and holistic descriptions and explanations. That is, can we say more or less with their help. If we can say more, then this demonstrates their value. 'In terms of them, or in terms derived from them,' Mills stipulates, 'unknown scholars as well as fashionable commentators came to re-focus their observations and re-formulate their concerns' (1959, 13–14). Some of these 'terms', the concepts and analytic languages of the social sciences, have proven to be transformative for thought and action. Thus, some 'intellectual universes' have staying power because of the strength of the analytic categories offered for working on empirical and theoretical problems and issues. They enable us – even require us – to formulate or visualize differently the problem at hand and to see that empirical problems always have a conceptual side and conceptual problems have an empirical dimension. Concepts enable sharper but also sometimes blurry imaginings; it is *through* them that we come to understand and act on the world in particular ways. It is by operating and refining these lenses that we can produce systematic and rigorous descriptions, explanations, understandings and interpretations, and this is why we need to attend to the 'criminological imagination' because it will allow us to 'see' with more clarity. When Krisberg (1974, 148) invited us to participate in an 'interchange which [perhaps] will improve the methodology of critical research', this is what he was alluding to. For Krisberg, Mills' project was aligned with a sociology of knowledge or philosophy of science (see also Scimecca 1976, 148), and in advocating a 'rediscovery of C. Wright Mills and his conception of the sociological imagination' (Krisberg 1974, 159), he, not unlike the contributors to this volume, advocated a Millsian metatheory to inform substantive theory production and empirical research.

In rediscovering Mills and for realizing the theoretical and methodological promise of the sociological imagination for criminology, we must take note of *three basic types of questions* that concern imaginative and critically aware enquiry. Mills (1959, 6–7) called these questions the 'intellectual pivots' of thought-provoking, useful and insightful social science. As the sociological imagination is a framework for critical and imaginative social scientific practice (Frauley 2011; Chapter 1 in this volume), it has our enquiry turn on these questions in order to move between different intellectual universes and different levels of social reality as we make sense of our substantive problem.

Pfohl (Chapter 4 in this volume; references omitted) stipulates that these questions reflect Mills' core concerns, but that these are glaringly absent from much of contemporary criminology, where there exists 'an unspoken norm' to neglect such matters and, perhaps inadvertently, 'divert attention from structures of power'. The problem is not simply that Mills has been neglected within criminology, but that this unspoken normative commitment to the role of 'expert technician' devoid of passion or interest in how the particular issues studied link up with the broader context of power and politics hinders the reproduction of criminology as a relevant social science. This is because '[c]rime and punishment are bound up with wider social processes', making one of criminology's chief aims the identifying of 'these links and the problems that flow from them, even as the relationships change and become more obscure' (Carrabine, Chapter 3 in this volume). Neglecting these broader historical and structural dynamics restricts the adequacy of any description or explanation produced while making it all but impossible to 'translate' personal experiences and problems 'into issues in terms of presenting the individual with a new and plausible "bigger picture" of his or her social world, one that offered new orienting values, feelings, motives, understandings and meanings' (Barton et al. 2007, 4; see also M. White, Chapter 6 in this volume). Taking the troubles of individuals and showing their connection to public issues (i.e., the remote, impersonal political realm of institutional conflict and contradiction) is one of the strengths of the sociological imagination. With respect to criminology, according to Melanie White in Chapter 6 in this volume, one must pay 'particular attention to conduct that challenges accepted norms' to see 'order in disorder and innovation in disobedience'. The orientation, she continues, is 'toward the task of viewing the "present in history" and the "future as responsibility" by considering how so-called "crimes" vary historically from the perspective of the individual and of society'. This goes beyond claiming that crime is historically relative; rather, it is emergent and cannot be made sense of without undertaking some examination of the institutional order at work at that time, including the collective sensibilities that enable a division of the 'normal and appropriate' from the 'abnormal and inappropriate' (M. White, Chapter 6 in this volume). Thus, for those advocating a rediscovery, expansion and adaptation of the sociological imagination for criminology, any criminological practice employing the quality of mind envisioned by Mills would only be possible if the normative bias of criminology against identifying and critiquing structures of power and domination, including criminology itself, were acknowledged and purged. In addition, we must acknowledge our political and ethical responsibility to 'bring our history to bear on the choice of our problems and the nature of the work we undertake' as we engage in a 'sympathetic translation of personal troubles into public issues' to 'demonstrate that criminality is an important facet of social life, and can be the basis of politically and morally meaningful problems' (M. White, Chapter 6 in this volume):

> To understand the problem of 'crime' ... criminologists must use their imagination to provide clear connections between the actor, the event and location of the criminalized incident and the structural, spatial and historical determinants shaping definitions and applications of the label of 'crime', deviance and illegality at that particular time. (Barton et al. 2007, 3–4; reference omitted)

The pivots for a *criminological* imagination essentially force us to engage in conceptualizing and empirical observation, moving: 'from the political to the psychological; from examination of a single family to comparative assessment of the national budgets of the world ... from the most impersonal and remote transformations to the most intimate features of the human self – and to see the relations between the two' (Mills 1959, 7).

First we must ask: *What is the structure of this particular society as a whole?* For Mills, the institutional order of our society is characterized by the production of what I refer to in Chapter 1 as 'structural ignorance' Structural ignorance serves and is organized under a 'bureaucratic ethos' characterized by practices animated by what Mills has termed an 'engineering imagination'. This has helped transform social science into a set of bureaucratic techniques serving industrial capitalism and turn social scientists into research technicians. This question of the structure and organization of a particular society concerns the impersonal and remote aspects of social reality (that, in turn, shape individual and collective experience, understanding and action). Our concern here would include identifying and connecting 'roles' that transmit values, expectations and experiences. A criminological imagination would have us pose such questions as, 'What is the political, economic and moral context of punishment today?' 'How is the for-profit commercial sector connected to or tied into state delivery of safety and security?' 'What values are expressed in distributing safety, security, health and welfare according to user-pay and market driven models?' 'What does this signify about the general value of human life and dignity? 'Which institutions or milieu are directly and/or indirectly connected to state punishment (e.g., the police, courts, religion, law, markets, education, workplaces, mass media)?' 'What do state-sanctioned torture and mass incarceration indicate about our collective "cherished values"?' 'How does this present "institutional order" differ from others?'

Second, we must pose the question: *Where does this society stand in human history?* For Mills, US society was politically disengaged and in decline, but he was hopeful of turnaround. To Mills, apathy, specialized division of labour and fragmentation were characteristic of post-war America. This question of the place of societal organization, including its dominant institutions, ideologies and cultural practices in history, draws attention to social change and the importance of a comparative-historical approach to enquiry: 'What are the features of punishment today?' 'What justifications are given for our current practices of punishment'? 'How have the institutions, practices, and justifications of punishment changed over time?' 'What values are expressed in this?' 'How is punishment culturally significant? Does it define our society in some way that makes it and ourselves different from others?' 'How have the practices and justifications of punishment been shaped by capitalism?' 'Where might we be headed if we continue our current practices and/or continue to ignore contradictory rationales and the practical problems these generate?'

Third, *What varieties of men and women now prevail in this society and in this period?* This question concerns biographical and experiential aspects of social life – intimate and interpersonal relations (as shaped and moulded within a broader political and institutional context). Here we see also a concern with identifying the emergent categories of person that have become dominant, subordinate, free or enslaved. 'Research technicians' and 'cheerful robots' spring to mind as dominant and prevalent varieties of men and women. This question concerns the practices that characterize our society, significant and meaningful for what they signify about our 'human nature' (and for how emergent social roles in part constitute this nature). The criminological imagination would have us pose questions such as: 'What experiences do punitive sanctions produce within particular milieux?' 'What sorts of men and women are produced within capitalist market societies?' 'What of their character and values?' 'What sorts of "human kinds" are needed to reproduce the values embedded in the carceral complex?' 'What character and conduct is required for positive social transformation'? 'What constitutes an "educated citizen" within a technocracy?' 'What is the prevalent experience and understanding of punishment today?' 'What is the level of malaise or apathy exhibited by publics regarding punishment today?'

These intellectual pivots represent the central concerns around which criminological enquiry should be organized. They are the basis for adequate enquiry, whether for research or teaching. They help us formulate more specific sets of questions for revealing naturalized ideologies that underpin taken-for-granted practices that inform and shape our experiences of being human. The contributors to this volume attempt to rediscover Mills and these pivots, and to pursue an adaptation of his work for criminological enquiry. This anthology brings together scholars who illustrate the usefulness and innovative nature of Mills' ideas for criminological enquiry. If nothing else, the main argument is that criminology has much to gain from Mills, and that the realization of the theoretical and methodological promise of the sociological imagination will play significantly into the renewal of criminological theorizing and empirical enquiry. The chapters collected here demonstrate this promise by employing and showing the usefulness and innovative nature of Mills' ideas for contemplating a wide variety of criminological issues, including power and domination, incarceration, environmental justice, transnational security, values and ethics in research, emotional and conceptual awareness for enquiry, theorizing social control, critical pedagogy, and new objects of criminological analysis such as fictional worlds.

The anthology invites readers to contemplate not only the multifaceted and dynamic nature of the 'criminological imagination', but also what such a concept can offer to criminological enquiry and analysis. What is of interest is the emergence of a criminological imagination indebted to Mills' work. Some contributors offer theoretical reflection on the different facets of the criminological imagination and its value for creative enquiry, others are empirically focused and put some idea of the criminological imagination to work to illustrate its value through application (wherein the case study offered provides a good empirical illustration of the concept). Collectively the chapters advance a conception of the criminological imagination, one that is the product of collective effort and one that emerges from the contributions themselves taken together as a set. Readers are invited to contemplate each chapter on its own, but to also take them together, reading them intertextually to produce an emergent conception of 'criminological imagination', a strategy that follows from Mills' notion of 'intellectual craftsmanship': 'Imagination is often successfully invited by putting together hitherto isolated items, by finding unsuspected connections' (Mills 1959, 201). The chapters in this book can be used to reflect systematically on one's own experiences, and one's own experience can be drawn on to reflect on these materials. This is to encourage systematic (self-) reflection, comparison and contrasting of the themes and ideas. The more we can rearrange the ideas we encounter, play them off one another, the more we can produce differing points of view and the more we can play the points of view from one encounter against another. This is to engage the reader in his or her own intellectual production, and not to accept in a passive manner the world of experiences or the categories that we use in our thinking (or in this volume). Readers are encouraged to:

> make an inventory of everything that seems involved in whatever you are trying to understand ... pare it down to the essentials; then carefully and systematically you will relate these items to one another in order to form a sort of working model. And then you will relate this model to whatever it is you are trying to explain. (Mills 1959, 223; for a discussion, see Kaufman and Schoepflin 2009)

References

Barton, Alana, Karen Corteen, Julie Davies and Anita Hobson. 2010. 'Reading the Word and Reading the World: The Impact of a Critical Pedagogical Approach to the Teaching of Criminology in Higher Education.' *Journal of Criminal Justice Education* 21(1): 24–41.

Barton, Alana, David Scott, Karen Corteen and Dave Whyte, eds. 2007. *Expanding the Criminological Imagination: Critical Readings in Criminology*. Portland, OR: Willan Publishing.

Braithwaite, John 2000. 'The New Regulatory State and the Transformation of Criminology.' *British Journal of Criminology* 40(2): 222–38.

Bruns, Axel. 2008. *Blogs, Wikipedia, Second Life, and Beyond: From Production to Produsage*. New York: Peter Lang.

Carrier, Nicolas. 2011. 'Critical Criminology Meets Radical Constructivism.' *Critical Criminology* 19(4): 331–50.

Currie, Elliott. 2007. 'Against Marginality: Arguments for a Public Criminology.' *Theoretical Criminology* 11(2): 175–90.

Downes, David. 1988. 'The Sociology of Crime and Social Control in Britain, 1960–1987.' *British Journal of Criminology* 28(2): 45–57.

Ericson, Richard. 1996. 'Making Criminology.' *Current Issues in Criminal Justice* 8(1): 14–25.

Fattah, Ezzat. 1997. *Criminology: Past, Present, and Future: A Critical Overview*. New York: Macmillan.

Ferrell, Jeff, Keith Hayward and Jock Young. 2008. *Cultural Criminology: An Invitation*. London: Sage.

Frauley, Jon. 2005. 'Representing Theory and Theorising in Criminal Justice Studies: Practising Theory Considered.' *Critical Criminology: An International Journal* 13(3): 245–65.

———. 2011. *Criminology, Deviance and the Silver Screen: The Fictional Reality and the Criminological Imagination*. New York: Palgrave Macmillan.

———. 2015. 'On Imaginative Criminology and It's Significance.' *Societies* 5(2) (forthcoming).

Garland, David and Richard Sparks. 2000. 'Criminology, Social Theory and the Challenge of Our Times.' *British Journal of Criminology* 40: 189–204.

Goode, Erich. 2008. 'From the Western to the Murder Mystery: The Sociological Imagination of C. Wright Mills.' *Sociological Spectrum* 28(3): 237–53.

Haggerty, Kevin. 2004a. 'Displaced Expertise: Three Constraints on the Policy Relevance of Criminological Thought.' *Theoretical Criminology* 8(2): 211–31.

———. 2004b. 'Ethics Creep: Governing Social Science Research in the Name of Ethics.' *Qualitative Sociology* 27(4): 391–414.

Hammersly, Martyn. 2009. 'Against the Ethicists: On the Evils of Ethical Regulation.' *International Journal of Social Research Methodology* 12(3): 211–25.

Kaufman, P. and T. Schoepflin. 2009. 'Last but Not Least the Pedagogical Insights of "Intellectual Craftsmanship."' *Teaching Sociology* 37(1): 20–30.

Kemple, Thomas and Renisa Mawani. 2009. 'The Sociological Imagination and its Imperial Shadows.' *Theory, Culture & Society* 26(7/8): 228–49.

Kerr, Keith. 2009. *Postmodern Cowboy: C. Wright Mills and a New 21st-Century Sociology*. Boulder, CO: Paradigm.

Krisberg, Barry. 1974. 'The Sociological Imagination Revisited.' *Canadian Journal of Criminology & Corrections* 16: 145–61.

Layder, Derek. 1993. *New Strategies in Social Research*. Cambridge: Polity Press.

Merton, Robert. K. 1938. 'Social Structure and Anomie.' *American Sociological Review* 3(5): 672–82.

Messner, Steven. 2012. 'Morality, Markets, and the ASC: 2011 Presidential Address to the American Society of Criminology.' *Criminology* 50(1): 5–25.

Mills, C. Wright. 1959. *The Sociological Imagination*. New York: Oxford University Press.

Morn, Frank. 1995. *Academic Politics and the History of Criminal Justice Education*. Westport, CT: Greenwood Publishing.

O'Malley, Pat. 1996. 'Post-social Criminologies: Some Implications of Current Political Trends for Criminological Theory and Practice.' *Current Issues in Criminal Justice* 8(1): 26–38.

Palys, Ted. 2003. 'Ethics in Social Research.' In *Research Decisions*, 80–120. Toronto, ON: Thomson Nelson.

Pearce, Frank. 2003. 'Holy Wars and Spiritual Revitalization.' In *Unmasking the Crimes of the Powerful: Scrutinizing States and Corporations*, edited by Tombs and White, ix–xiv. New York: Peter Lang.

Pfohl, Steven. 1994. *Images of Deviance and Social Control*. Upper Saddle River, NJ: Prentice-Hall.

Rafter, Nicole. 2006. *Shots in the Mirror: Crime Films and Society*, 2nd edn. New York: Oxford University Press.

Rosenfeld, Richard. 2011. 'The Big Picture: 2010 Presidential Address to the American Society of Criminology.' *Criminology* 29(1): 1–26.

Ruggiero, Vincenzo. 2003. *Crime in Literature: Sociology of Deviance and Fiction*. New York: Verso.

Russell, Stuart. 2002. 'The Continuing Relevance of Marxism to Critical Criminology.' *Critical Criminology* 11(2): 113–35.

Sayer, Andrew. 1992. *Method in Social Science: A Realist Approach*. New York: Routledge.

Scimecca, Joseph. 1975. 'The Implications of the Sociology of C. Wright Mills for Modern Criminological Theory.' *International Journal of Criminology and Penology* 3: 145–53.

———. 1976. 'Paying Homage to the Father: C. Wright Mills and Radical Sociology.' *The Sociological Quarterly* 17(2): 180–86.

———. 1977. *The Sociological Theory of C. Wright Mills*. London: Kennikat Press.

Simon, David. 1985. 'Organizational Deviance: A Humanist View.' *Journal of Society and Social Welfare* 12: 521–51.

———. 1988. 'Liberalism and White Collar Crime: Toward Resolving and Crisis.' *Quarterly Journal of Ideology* 12(1): 19–30.

———. 1991. 'White Collar Crime, Dehumanization and Inauthenticity: Towards a Millsian Theory of Elite Wrongdoing.' *International Review of Modern Sociology* 21(1): 93–107.

Tombs, Steve and David Whyte. 2002. 'Unmasking the Crimes of the Powerful.' *Critical Criminology* 11: 217–36.

———. 2003. 'Scrutinizing the Powerful: Crime, Contemporary Political Economy, and Critical Social Research.' In *Unmasking the Crimes of the Powerful: Scrutinizing States and Corporations,* edited by Steve Tombs and David Whyte, 3–45. New York: Peter Lang.

Trevino, Javier. 2012. *The Social Thought of C. Wright Mills.* Thousand Oaks, CA: Sage.

Walters, Reece. 2003. 'New Modes of Governance and the Commodification of Criminological Knowledge.' *Social & Legal Studies* 12(1): 5–26.

White, Rob. 2001. 'Criminology for Sale: Institutional Change and the Intellectual Field.' *Current Issues in Criminal Justice* 13(1): 123–42.

———. 2003. 'Environmental Issues and the Criminological Imagination.' *Theoretical Criminology* 7(4): 483–506.

Whitehead, John T. 1985. 'The Criminological Imagination: Another View.' *Criminal Justice Review* 10(2): 22–6.

Williams, Frank. 1984. 'The Demise of the Criminological Imagination.' *Justice Quarterly* 1(1): 91–106.

Woodiwiss, Anthony. 1990. *Social Theory after Post-modernism: Rethinking Production, Law, and Class.* London: Pluto Press.

———. 2001. *The Visual in Social Theory.* New York: Athlone Press/Continuum.

Wozniak, John. 2009. 'C. Wright Mills and Higher Immorality: Implications for Corporate Crime, Ethics, and Peacemaking Criminology.' *Crime, Law, and Social Change* 51: 189–203.

Young, Jock. 2011. *The Criminological Imagination.* New York: Blackwell.

PART I
C. Wright Mills,
the Criminological Imagination and
the Criminological Field

Chapter 1

For a Refractive Criminology: Against Science Machines and Cheerful Robots

Jon Frauley

... let your mind become a moving prism catching light from as many angles as possible. (Mills 1959, 214)

Serious differences among social scientists ... have rather to do with what kinds of thinking, what kinds of observing, and what kinds of links, if any, there are between the two. (Mills 1959, 33)

In 1959 sociologist C. Wright Mills offered a trenchant (and still relevant) critique of empiricist and theoreticist social science, outlining a strategy for rejecting what he thought had become a mainly reductionist and technique-driven bureaucratic enterprise. His path-breaking book *The Sociological Imagination* is concerned to illustrate the rise of a 'bureaucratic ethos' and the implication of this for social life as well as the impact this ethos was having on the process, objectives and organization of social science and knowledge production. Mills argued for a particular 'quality of mind' that he believed necessary for the production of holistic and politically engaging descriptions and understandings of social reality. To understand experiences of unrest and apathy, he maintained, it was necessary to identify and then connect two fundamental aspects of social life: 'personal troubles of milieu' and 'public issues of social structure':

Troubles occur within the character of the individual and within the range of his immediate relations with others; they have to do with his self and with those limited areas of social life of which he is directly and personally aware. Accordingly, the statement and the resolution of troubles properly lie within the individual as a biographical entity and within the scope of his immediate milieu – the social setting that is directly open to his personal experience and to some extent his willful activity. A trouble is a private matter: values cherished by an individual are felt by him to be threatened .... *Issues* have to do with matters that transcend these local environments of the individual and the range of his inner life. They have to do with the organization of many such milieux into the institutions of an historical society as a whole, with the ways in which various milieux overlap and interpenetrate to form the larger structure of social and historical life. An issue is a public matter: some value cherished by publics is felt to be threatened. Often there is a debate about what that value really is and about what it is that really threatens it. This debate is often without focus if only because it is the very nature of an issue, unlike even widespread trouble, that it cannot very well be defined in terms of the immediate and everyday environments of ordinary men. An issue, in fact, often involves a crisis in institutional arrangements, and often too it involves what Marxists call 'contradictions' or 'antagonisms'. (Mills 1959, 8–9)

The imaginative and speculative quality of mind envisioned by Mills was needed, he believed: (1) to adequately clarify how human beings and their experiences were situated and shaped within the political, economic, institutional, discursive, and importantly, historical constraints of their society, and (2) to contribute to personal and social transformation and thus use this knowledge of our contemporary societal constraints to live a more authentic and meaningful life. Employing a sociological imagination could lead to a citizenry actively and politically engaged in issues of consequence.

As a methodology,[1] the sociological imagination sought to bridge what Mills considered to be a detrimental gap between studies of social action, on the one hand, and studies of social structure on the other, as well as a division between abstract theorizing (i.e., the theoreticism of 'grand theory') and atheoretical empirical research (i.e., the empiricism and methodological individualism of 'abstracted empiricism').[2] In chastising 'research technicians' for self-identifying

---

1   To clarify my usage, 'method' is used to refer to the *technique* of data collection, analysis and interpretation; 'methodology' is used to refer to the *study* of these techniques as well as modes of reasoning and knowledge-production and the broader philosophical or meta-theoretical principles that subtend social enquiry. See Blaikie (2000), Mouton (1996) and Mills (1959, 57–8).

2   *Empiricism* holds that what we can experience directly through our senses is all there is and all that is worthy of knowing. It also assumes that we can experience reality directly apart from any kind of theoretical or conceptual intermediary. A variation of this is the use of theoretical concepts to order data or the search within data for examples of 'variables' without any attempt to utilize the concepts to fabricate a description and explanation or to say what is of significance in the data and why this is. Abstracted empiricism is empiricist because it is atheoretical and strips observations from their larger context. With abstracted empiricism, social theories become collections of variables (Mills 1959, 63, 69). *Theoreticism*, according to Pearce (1989, 14), occurs when theories are developed in a manner apart from any reference to an empirical referent; in turn, empirical examples are marshalled only to illustrate concepts. The problem, according to Pearce, is that this form of theory-construction and subsequent manner of illustrating concepts amounts to a substitute for investigating or exploring the complexity of social phenomena. Grand theory was theoreticist because it proceeded without observations or simply held that what was observed was an illustration of theoretical concepts without regard for specific empirical differences. Of grand theory Mills wrote: 'The magical elimination of conflict, and the wondrous achievement of harmony, remove from this "systematic" and "general" theory

as (social) scientists and ridiculing 'science machines' for masquerading as (social) sciences, he advocated a 'creative ethos' and the practice of 'intellectual craftsmanship' as a counter to technocracy.[3] Thus the book is a methodological and political call for a reflective and self-critical practice of knowledge production, one that can illuminate structural and ideational constraints on freedom as well as the possible points of intervention for fostering positive social transformation and strengthening social democracy (Scimecca 1976, 194; Krisberg 1974; Frauley 2010). As a methodology it offers a hopeful and humanist sociological practice, and as a politics it denigrates liberalism and liberal social science as being ahistorical and blind to its own oppressive conditions of existence.

The sociological imagination promises empirically informed theorizing and theoretically informed empirics for speculation, perspectivalism and synthesis. What are produced are robust and holistic understandings and explanations of the 'threats' to a society's 'cherished values' – threats often experienced existentially as 'uneasiness' and 'indifference' and politically as 'malaise' and 'apathy'. Thus this quality of mind has just as much to do with battling ant-intellectualism in the classroom and beyond as it does the empiricist and theoreticist research that contributes little to the production or expansion of an intellectual stock of knowledge. If we are to continue to develop, test and reformulate the criminological stock of *knowledge*[4] that informs, frames, and guides research and teaching and which enables us to produce criminological descriptions, interpretations, understandings and explanations, we must take the empirical element (e.g., justice programming, public policy, punishment, law enforcement, criminalization, victimization or what have you) as a *fecund stimulus* for advancing conceptual mappings and framings to develop multidimensional conceptual frameworks that will help us access the various dimensions and facets of our objects of study so that we might better understand them, their reproduction and transformation over time (see Layder 1993). Accumulating *information* on the distribution of various incidences of crime across different regions, for instance, does not necessarily help social scientists expand their stock of knowledge or tackle problems within social science that pertain to theory construction, analysis or methodology. Of course, such information may be very important for crime prevention programs

---

the possibilities of dealing with social change, with history. ... Virtually any problem of substance that is taken up in the terms of grand theory is incapable of being clearly stated' because it is loaded with 'sponge words' (1959, 42–3). Grand theory involves the 'fetishism of the Concept', whereas abstracted empiricism has to do with the fetishism of method. Both of these schools 'represent abdications of classic social science. The vehicle of their abdication is pretentious over-elaboration of "method" and "theory"; the main reason for it is their lack of firm connection with substantive problems' (Mills 1959, 74–75).

   3   On 'technocracy', see Postman (2011) and Lyotard (1979).

   4   The 'criminological stock of knowledge' refers to the ideas, interpretive frameworks and methodologies of criminology, and not the accumulation of *information* on crime, criminals and so on.

and strategic policing initiatives – and this is work criminologists should be engaged in, if for no other reason than to question and critique existing models and methods of social control and highlight the implications of said models – but the objective cannot be to only produce information for social control strategies.

The quality of mind advanced by Mills facilitates 'refractive thinking'. It is beneficial and necessary to reflect on the place and role of this type of thinking for criminal justice studies and criminological enquiry, especially if we are to defend them as rigorous and insightful fields of enquiry that can produce new or deeper understandings, more adequate explanations, and holistic descriptions of social issues of consequence stemming from criminalization and criminal justice administration as well as related practices. Importantly, we must identify and then reject the organizational features of these criminology and criminal justice studies that impugn refractive thinking and the development of what Mills termed 'intellectual craftsmanship'. In short, we must identify and be wary of what he called an 'engineering imagination' (i.e., bureaucratic ethos) because it acts to interpellate its user, to borrow from Althusser (1971), as a 'cheerful and willing robot' (Mills 1959, 71, 72; 1951, 233). The cheerful robot is not only a subjectivity that is characterized by the experience of alienation and dehumanization, it is also an institutional role within the 'bureaucratic machines' of technocracies – 'The society in which this man, this cheerful robot, flourishes is the antithesis of the free society – or in the literal and plain meaning of the word, of a democratic society' (Mills 1959, 171, 172) – and it views intelligence 'as a kind of skilled gadget that they hope to market successfully' (Mills 1959, 106, *passim*). The cheerful robot is characteristically 'disengaged' and: 'inattentive to political concerns of any kind. They are neither radical nor reactionary. They are inactionary. If we accept the Greek's definition of the idiot as an altogether private man, then we must conclude that many citizens of many societies are indeed idiots' (Mills 1959, 41).

We must ask ourselves: 'Are criminal justice studies and criminology in the business of producing idiots?' 'Are criminology and justice studies "science machines"?' 'Do justice studies and criminology produce symbols of power that legitimate domination or do they strive to identify and deconstruct such symbols?' 'Do justice studies and criminology help to reproduce contemporary forms of domination by producing cheerful robots to take up positions in the crime control industry, or do they help thwart their reproduction from the inside by graduating "intellectual craftspersons" to fill those positions?' These questions would have us confront the dominance within criminology and justice studies of an engineering imagination that promotes technocratic practice, intellectual and political disengagement, and which thwarts – or rather involves scholars in thwarting – the realization of the methodological and theoretical promise of the sociological imagination for studies of crime, criminalization and crime control.

A criminological imagination would see scholars aim for a 'unity of trouble and issue' (Krisberg 1974, 150). It can offer a vantage point on the ways crimes and harms are connected to social institutions as an alternative to the great majority of one-sided or 'post-social' criminological theories currently employed which inadequately guide empirical research (Wozniak 2009; Simon 1985, 1988, 1991; Barton et al., 2007; Williams 1984; O'Malley 1996). The desire to produce such a meta-view or big picture is to install imagination, speculation and intuition as guiding forces behind the production of criminological insight (Williams 1984, 96, 97 *passim*; Williams 1999; McShane and Williams 1989, 563). Such a meta-view will, according to the few criminological scholars who have taken up Mills, aid in challenging both intellectually and practically the agendas of those who engage in elite deviance, corporate and white-collar crime (Barton et al. 2007; Simon 1985, 1988, 1991; Wozniak 2009). It will also help criminologists meet new intellectual challenges and clarify and strengthen criminology's relevance where today this is questioned (Braithwaite 2000; Garland and Sparks 2000; Haggerty 2004a; Currie 2007; Nelken 1994).

A creative, imaginative and speculative criminology is one that we must build; it will not simply emerge without us first identifying and then attempting to develop and implement a conceptual and methodological architecture by which we can strive for more robust explanations and descriptions and thereby create the possibility for inducing positive social transformation (Goode 2008). To employ the criminological imagination is to think in a refractive way, and this refractive thinking is one of the greatest promises of the sociological imagination. To understand the value of refractive thinking as an insightful and imaginative form of thought and practice and why this is not widespread within criminology or justice studies today, it is necessary to outline its main obstacle: scientism.

Scientism and the Bureaucratic Ethos

> The opposition between empty theoreticism and blind empiricism, however, is but one of the many antagonistic pairs (*couples ennemis*), or antinomies, which structure sociological thought and practice and hinder the development of a science of society capable of truly cumulating its already immense achievements. (Bourdieu 1988, 777)

It is uncanny the degree to which Mills anticipated views by contemporary thinkers. For instance, Mills anticipates Pierre Bourdieu's (1988) criticism of the perpetuation in social science of the false division between theory and method as well as the fiction of the autonomous nature of the various social sciences. Likewise, his view on technocracy pre-dates Jean-François Lyotard's (1979) monumentally influential analysis of the 'postmodern condition' wherein intellectual culture is reduced to a technical and pragmatic enterprise devoid of meta-theoretical justification.[5] In addition, his diagnosis of the problem of how

---

5   Just as science was no longer 'organized around the role of the scientist' as it had been for nearly five hundred years (Restivo 1988, 201), social science was becoming industrialized and bureaucratized and moving away from the organising role of the 'intellectual craftsman'.

social science was implicated in the reproduction of state power and domination pre-dates criminological critiques of how criminology had become complicit in serving the state apparatus (Taylor et al. 1973; Ratner 1984; O'Malley 1996; White 2001; Walters 2003; Tombs and Whyte 2003; Wood and Shearing 1989; Ferrell et al. 2008; Young 2011).

Critical of the university and politics of his day, Mills lamented that social science had succumbed to an advanced technical division of labour, the pressures of the modern bureaucracy, the false promises of industrial science, as well as a blind faith in the latter's organizational model. As we are still in the midst of many of the changes he observed in the 1950s (such as the transformation of the objectives and process of scholarly enquiry), much of what Mills had to say is still highly relevant, especially for criminologists and justice studies scholars interested in social justice and the possibility of positive social transformation (see also Scimecca, Chapter 5 in this volume). An example of this continued relevance is found in his critique of *scientism*, which is framed by a discussion of what he called the *new practicality*.[6]

According to Mills (1959, 95), emerging from a post-war *new practicality* were the images of science as a 'machine' and the social scientist as a 'research technician'. The new practicality was an ethos that valued utility and the bureaucratic usefulness of knowledge. 'Nowadays,' Mills exclaimed, 'social research is often of direct service to army generals and social workers, corporation managers and prison wardens. Such bureaucratic use has been increasing; no doubt it will continue to increase' (1959, 80). For Mills (1959, 166) this new practicality signalled a transition from the 'modern era' to a 'postmodern period'. The term 'postmodern' was used to designate a bureaucratic epoch wherein we find 'new kinds of social structure' that facilitate the displacement of 'reason and freedom' as central societal values. What was generated with this structural displacement of core values was a form of structural ignorance: 'A high level of bureaucratic rationality and of technology,' Mills argued, 'does not mean a high level of either individual or social intelligence. … Universal education may lead to technological idiocy and nationalist provinciality – rather than to the informed and independent intelligence' (1959, 168).

Mills believed that this new practicality, this 'illiberal practicality', was having a profound and negative impact not only on societal values and political engagement generally speaking, but also on the positioning and practice of social scientists:

> from academic to the bureaucratic; their publics [audiences] change – from movements of reformers to circles of decision makers; and their problems change – from those of their own choice to those of their new clients. The scholars themselves tend to become less intellectually insurgent and more administratively practical. Generally accepting the status quo, they tend to

---

6   On Mills and scientism, see Krisberg (1974, 151–2), Williams (1984, 93–8; Chapter 2 in this volume) and Kemple and Mawani (2009). On Mills' continued relevance, see Scimecca (Chapter 5 in this volume), Gane and Back (2012) and Kemple and Mawani (2009).

formulate problems out of the troubles and issues that administrators believe
they face. (Mills 1959, 96)

Although this statement pre-dates the arrival of criminology and criminal justice
studies, Mills here captures the very problems that critical criminologists have
long railed against, namely taking the problems and official definitions of the
'system' as criminological. As this new division of labour and new practicality
'sets up more and more spheres of life, work, and leisure, in which reasoning is
difficult or impossible' (Mills 1959, 168), the holistic pictures that intellectual
craftsmen strive to produce of personal troubles, social issues and the relation
between the two within the context of ongoing cultural change are structurally
excluded. That is, they are not outcomes of the specifically technocratic practices
that characterize complex bureaucratic machines such as the criminal justice and
legal systems and higher education.

This 'bureaucratic ethos' was manifested in, among other things, careerism
and the professionalization of the professoriate. These two things Mills (1959, 97,
98, ch. 5) thought had a profound impact on intellectual work. The university, as
one of the many massive centralized institutions that make up Western society,
was slowing becoming modernized, and along with it so too were intellectual
workers. The social sciences were not autonomous from those same modernizing
forces that swept across the university and other institutions, and the burgeoning
careerism and professionalization Mills witnessed can be thought of as outcomes of
adjustment to the overwhelming dehumanization and alienation that characterizes
'postmodern' social organization and related technological developments (Simon
1991, 101). Careerism and professionalization, according to Mills, were 'an
academic response to a greatly increased demand for administrative technicians
who will deal with "human relations" and for new justifications of corporate
business as a system of power' (Mills 1959, 96, 114). As the images and the ideas
communicated through the restructuring of social research as well as the new
outcomes of scientific practice were often used to buttress existing structures of
power by providing the 'ideologies' and 'symbols' to justify post-war forms of
domination, Mills surmised that simply by working as a social scientist one is
'enacting a bureaucratic or an ideological role' (1959, 81) and is thus involved in
a 'politics of truth' (1959, 178; Krisberg 1974, 152, 155, 156).

Having struggled since their inception with their identity (i.e., handmaiden
to the state or autonomous scholarly field; science machine or social science),
criminology and justice studies are especially prone to the technocratic pressures
of the related and updated new practicality in neo-liberalism. An extension
of the postmodern epoch discussed by Mills, or perhaps as a step beyond this,
criminologists such as O'Malley (1996) have discussed the 'post-social' state as
one in which the technocracy observed by Mills has ramped up and where the
post-war welfare capitalism of Mills' time has given way to monetarist economic
policy (see Pearce and Snider 1995; see also Rose 1996) and wherein, as Pfohl
(Chapter 4 in this volume) argues, new realities are being forged via an almost

compulsory participation in the massive and hegemonic electronic communication network that is now characteristic of such post-social or 'ultramodern' societies. These new developments have had a profound impact on the production of criminological knowledge (see O'Malley 1996; Walters 2003; White 2001; Taylor 1999). Moreover, the 'triangle of power' Mills described in *The Power Elite* – the hegemonic interlocking of the political, economic, and military institutional orders – has been further entrenched as we witness the unprecedented growth today of the prison-industrial complex (Shichor 1998; Schlosser 1998; Shelden and Brown 2000; Pfohl, Chapter 4 in this volume) and blatant abuse of power and law by powerful corporations and states (Michalowski and Kramer 2006; Bittle 2012; Pearce and Tombs 1998; Coleman et al. 2009; Tombs and Whyte 2003).

Despite these developments, however, and perhaps counter-intuitively, it is not with the 'illiberal practicality' that Mills described or with the more contemporary 'neo-liberalism' that we should be concerned. It is not the decline of welfarism or only the erosion of social democracy (see Teeple 2000) that criminologists should take issue with. These ideologies and substantive changes in governing certainly have had an impact on institutions, policy and practice, and they have introduced an idiom by which problems, issues and solutions are made sense of, but it is *scientism* that underlies these. It is scientism that underlies contemporary 'criminologies of everyday life' (Garland 2001) and the 'post social criminologies' (O'Malley 1996) that embrace what is an anti-social conceptualization of crime and its control, rooting causes of crime in the rational choices of the individual and holding that community is nothing more than a collection of self-interested individuals. Mills' notion to connect personal troubles of milieu with public issues of social structure to forge communities rooted in lived experiences of public issues is a call to reject such illiberal and anti-democratic conceptualizations of community, social life and science and the practices that follow from these:

> The modern esteem for science has long been merely assumed, but now the technological ethos and the kind of engineering imagination associated with science are more likely to be frightening and ambiguous than hopeful and progressive .... Much that has passed for 'science' is now felt to be dubious philosophy; much that is held to be 'real science' is often felt to provide only confused fragments of the realities among which men live. Men of science, it is widely felt, no longer try to picture reality as a whole or to present a true outline of human destiny. Moreover, 'science' seems to many less a creative ethos and a manner of orientation than a set of Science Machines, operated by technicians and controlled by economic and military men who neither embody nor understand science as ethos and orientation. In the meantime, philosophers who speak in the name of science often transform it into 'scientism', making out its experience to be identical with human experience, and claiming that only by its method can the problems of life be solved. With all this, many cultural workmen [who exercise intellectual craftsmanship] have come to feel that 'science' is a

false and pretentious Messiah, or at the very least a highly ambiguous element in modern civilization. (Mills 1959, 15–16)

It was against scientism as an ideological rendering of scientific logic, as a logic of justification for forms of political domination, and against the shifting objectives and practices of social scientific enquiry that Mills launched his trenchant critique of empiricism and theoreticism. Scientism, following from Mills and from Manicas (1987), constituted the ideological condition for the emergence of both criminology and criminal justice studies, so it is unsurprising that this would continue to underwrite at least in part some degree of the criminological common sense today. The preoccupations of many criminologists critical of administrative criminology, the state and persistent forms of domination have, perhaps unknowingly, taken issue with the bewildering dominance of scientism.[7] It was this critique of scientism, I believe, that early proponents of a Millsian criminology found valuable (Krisberg 1974; Scimecca 1975; Scimecca, Chapter 5 in this volume; Williams 1984; Williams, Chapter 2 in this volume).

Krisberg (1974), in an early attempt to explicitly bring Mills' analytic strategies and research techniques to the attention of a criminological audience (or 'public', as Mills might say), emphasized the methodological insights that could be harnessed for a reflexive, compassionate, politically engaged, humanist and heterodox criminology. A valuable aspect of this new methodological programme for criminology is found in how it helps us alter and intensify our vision (Krisberg 1974, 148). One major obstacle, however, to the realization of the sociological imagination in Mills' day, according to Krisberg, was scientism: 'the pretension of natural science methods which (1) does not correctly apply this philosophy of the natural sciences and (2) in fact, substitutes the questionable pursuit of the perfect method for the important goal of interpreting social life' (1974, 151). Picking up on this theme, Williams (1984) argued that in the 1970s the fetishism of method and 'measurement' to the detriment of speculation, especially with the advent of micro-computing and the statistical movement, had a profoundly negative and regressive impact on criminological conceptualizing. There was a move away from speculation toward description of observable facts. Thus 'descriptive empiricism', 'empirical theory' or what Williams called 'empirical scientism' became the *de facto* approach to criminological knowledge production. This helped thwart theory construction and efforts to integrate concepts, resulting in a theory-testing paradigm becoming prominent. In addition, with this emphasis

---

7 Scientism and its transformative capacity for social, political and economic practice have not been given explicit consideration by criminologists or justice studies scholars. Certainly those working in the areas of the philosophy of science, sociology of science as well as the sociology of health and illness and medicalization have hit on this, but criminologists have made little of the developments in these aligned fields. Recently Edwards and Sheptycki (2009) have explored scientism for how it has played into gun control debates and how recent sociology of science can be useful for producing a 'third wave criminology' that is empirical but not scientistic.

on the recording of observations and theory-testing, rise of machine logic and changing political tides, the conditions were right for the emergence of criminal justice studies (a great example of what Mills called a 'science machine'). Most recently, as criminologists have not yet realized the promise of the criminological imagination, Young (2011, 7, 25) pointed out Mills' admonishing of the 'physics envy' of research technicians in order to set up his critique of the *datasaur* who eats 'ravenously but rarely thinks about the actual process of statistical digestion …'. The point raised by Young's survey of contemporary criminology is not only that scientism remains dominant, but that as an epistemology it is wholly inadequate to producing thoughtful, imaginative, speculative knowledge about meaningful and consequential issues that resonate with people's lived experiences. When social scientists suffer from physics envy, 'social science itself often tends to become a functionally rational machine' (Mills 1959, 180).

Just as Mills believed that scientism had gained traction as a dominant idiom and ideology for rendering intelligible personal troubles and public issues, whilst obfuscating their interrelation and sequestering public debate, it has had a profound impact on criminological enquiry as criminologists, especially those working in criminal justice studies, have attempted to follow its ideological rendering of scientific logic and procedure. Human suffering and political apathy, Mills argued, could not be adequately addressed as mere technological problems, however. Rather, what was required was a 'creative ethos' and compassionate enquiry that was holistic, perspectivalist and offered a deep understanding of how institutional issues – the problems and contradictions of the economy, politics, the military, family, religion, education and mass media – are often manifested at a distance from the corridors of power in various ways at the experiential level as personal troubles. The point is to reveal that the problems suffered by individuals are hardly ever only individual in nature or solvable at that level. Individualizing societal problems furthers the mythology that societies are merely collections of individuals and that structural factors do not play a significant role in causing suffering for individuals or in constraining their freedom. Importantly, if we are to exercise a 'criminological imagination' and realize its promise we must identify and break with the 'engineering imagination' and 'technological ethos' that fuels the individualizing effects of scientistic endeavours because these threaten to obscure the structural relation between personal experiences and institutional conflict whilst also reducing social scientists to technicians and social science to information processing.

For Mills there was an important aesthetic or imaginative as well as speculative dimension missing from science. Mills argued that the social sciences were producing 'cheerful robots' for industry. The social sciences were not imparting 'passionate curiosity' or 'genuine intellectual puzzlement' to students, academics or community members (Mills 1959, 105). This was a problem for Mills because it is through the sociological imagination that people's 'capacity for astonishment is made lively again' (1959, 8). As he suggested, there was growing scepticism that what was called science in the post-war period could not resolve societal problems and that no amount of posturing could change the fact that it had become a 'false and pretentious messiah'. Important dimensions of human experience and human capacity were excluded from industrialized science. As Sayer has argued: 'Scientific practice embraces several types of knowledge, including some which are generally excluded as non-science or even anti-science by scientism. ... [S]cientific knowledge presupposes among its very foundation a kind of knowledge which 'scientism' has sought to deny, exclude, or derogate' (1992, 17).

Thus, as science strives to embrace various types of knowledge through systematic and reasoned assessment, the post-war developments whereby speculation and intuition were excluded were not in keeping with the spirit of scientific enquiry: 'One of the major obstacles to progress in the social sciences no doubt resides in this formidable *gap* between strict compliance with the rules of proper scientific conduct, as they are defined by the methodological doxa taught in universities, and true scientific virtues' (Bourdieu 1988, 777; emphasis added).

Today the still-dominant place of empiricism within criminology and justice studies suggests that these fields have a ways to go before they realize the theoretical and methodological promise of a criminological imagination. As Mills argued: 'No social study that does not come back to the problems of biography, history and of their intersections within a society has completed its intellectual journey' (1959, 6).

According to Mills, it was in the nineteenth century that the poetic dimension of scientific enquiry had been neglected and allowed to wither with the 'zealous search for "laws" presumably comparable to those imagined to be found by natural scientists' (1959, 17; see also Restivo 1988, 210). 'By the mid-nineteenth century,' Restivo recounts, 'science had crystallized as a social institution. Since then it has undergone transformations in scale and power coincident with processes of professionalization and bureaucratization internally and changes in its relationship with the state externally' (Restivo 1988, 210; references omitted). It is this context that frames Mills' (1959, 180) critique of industrial science as scientistic. This era of 'industrialized science' or 'technocratic science' began in Germany in the late 1800s with the emphasis on 'purposive research' (Manicas 1987, 203). To understand the constitution of the modern social sciences and their 'Americanization', Manicas argues, we must consider three interrelated issues. First, there is the development of industrial capitalism, which led to the emergence of the 'social question' and various reactions of Western states to this problem (see Castel 2003). Second, within this context of the social question we see the development and expansion of higher education. Although the university has medieval roots, the modern university was born primarily in the nineteenth century, at a time when Western societies were undergoing great political, economic and moral upheaval. Hence, Manicas argues, modern higher education is intimately linked with the state's reaction to the growth of the new and unprecedented social problems of industrial capitalism.[8] Third, he argues that the development,

---

8   The following provide accounts of the impact of structural transformation on higher education in Canada and the USA: Clark et al. (2009); Clark et al. (2011); Axelrod (2002);

industrialization and specialization of the natural sciences were significant for the organizational model that would eventually be followed in the social sciences, leading to the compartmentalization of the latter (see Carroll 2013). As Mills (1959, 84) noted, the social sciences split into academic specialties in the early twentieth century, and this 'curious division of academic departments may have helped social scientists fragment their problems', 'scattering' the attention of social scientists and narrowing their vision (1959, 85, 87).

Such a scattering of attention through fragmentation has become an important feature of the professionalization, bureaucratization and organization of the university today, including studies of crime and its control. Many (Carrabine, Chapter 3 in this volume; Ericson and Carriere 1994; Ericson 1996; Fattah 1997; Simon 1988) have remarked on this characteristic aspect of criminology, and Carroll (2013) has recently commented on this development for social science more generally, arguing that fragmentation makes little sense from a knowledge-production point of view, but that it makes political sense in relation to the growth of capitalist states that require specialized knowledges of utility within an increasingly complex division of labour. Indeed, the increasing numbers of specialisms today that look at crime, criminality and crime control have displaced criminological expertise and threaten criminology's policy relevance (Haggerty 2004a; Currie 2007).

Criminal justice studies and criminology, born of this fragmentation at a time when higher education was moving away from training in classics and philosophy toward vocational training (see Morn 1995), appeared as useful information-producing fields that could help with new problems of state governance. They both were instituted with the idea of 'industrial science' in mind. Thus within each field a scientistic view of science was entrenched to inform the model of knowledge-production (challenged to some extent, but not defeated, in the 1960s with the rebirth of interactionist social science, in the 1970s with advances in Marxist and feminist scholarship, and in the 1980s with the rise of postmodernism). My point here is that the North American origins of criminal justice studies and criminology (as well as psychology, sociology and other fields) follow the fragmentation and compartmentalization of industrial science, contain within them orthodoxies and practices that are scientistic, and are deeply political (see Manicas 1987; Morn 1995; Foucault 1977/1980, 1974/1997, 1970/1998, 1976/1980; Williams 1984). Crucially, criminology and criminal justice developed in strong relation to a technocratic orientation that views knowledge-production as ultimately having the goal of application within business, industry and the state (Manicas 1987, 200–201). Thus an interest in 'usable knowledge' characterizes the development of higher education generally and criminal justice more specifically, especially in the USA (Morn 1995, 2). '[I]n critical ways,' states Manicas (1987, 207), 'this is a fundamental problem of our time'. It is the very problem Mills grappled with

---

Côté and Allahar (2007); Guppy and Davies (1998); Sears (2000, 2003); Slaughter and Leslie (1997); Tudiver (1999); Rhoades and Slaughter (1997).

and why he advocated intellectual craftsmanship as a practical way to make social science more relevant and meaningful.

It is against the neglect of the poetic and speculative dimension of knowledge production within sociology that Mills launched his critique of scientism and theoreticism. It is this same neglect within criminology and justice studies that concerned Williams (1984), Scimecca (1975) and Krisberg (1974), and it is this which remains today a problem for many (see Ferrell et al. 2008; Jacobsen 2014; Rafter 2006; Rosenfeld 2011; Ruggiero 2003; Williams 1999; Young 2011). It is with the role and subjectivity of the cheerful robot and the connection of this to scientism and scientistic practice that criminologists ought to be concerned: 'What is it about the contemporary organizational structure of the university and our specific scholarly field that facilitates or impugns efforts to instil intellectual craftsmanship?' 'How do criminology and criminal justice studies operate as a mode of governance that reproduces or disrupts the production of cheerful robots?'[9] Criminology and justice studies must reject scientism and its bureaucratic ethos and embrace intellectual craftsmanship, and it is our task to find ways to impugn the reproduction of the cheerful robot and become cognizant of our own participation in the reproduction of our respective fields as 'science machines'. We must 'help the individual become a self-educating' person as well as make a contribution to 'build and to strengthen self-cultivating publics' (Mills 1959, 186). The sociological imagination, according to Mills, has the ability to move our 'mentalities' beyond 'a series of limited orbits' (Mills 1959, 8) to enrich our understanding of the significance of how 'public issues' (such as crime and its control) are entwined with 'personal troubles' (such as victimization, exploitation and alienation) as these latter are experiential manifestations of the former. Thus, embracing and transmitting in practical ways 'refractive thinking' for criminology has much value.

Refractive Thinking and Intellectual Craftsmanship

Mills (1959, 20) unequivocally rejected the idea that social science was simply a compilation of 'a set of bureaucratic techniques'. Mills viewed social scientists not as technicians who 'split their work from their lives', but as 'intellectual craftsmen' (1959, 195, 196, 211) who were engaged in 'the practice of a craft' (Mills 1959, 195), and like any craft it was subject to refinement and improvement.[10] Thus one of Mills' main concerns was with *how* social enquiry should be carried out and its usefulness for sparking and informing public, political debate on timely and important issues of consequence. The serious differences among social scientists,

---

9   Jochelson et al. (2013) have contemplated these issues, although from a different perspective.

10   Mills later came to prefer the term 'cultural workmen' to 'intellectual craftsmen', and included academics as one of many different types of cultural workmen contributing to the 'cultural apparatus' (see Sawchuck 2001).

Mills argued, had to do with 'what kinds of thinking, what kinds of observing, and what kinds of links, if any, there are between the two' (1959, 33). The focal concern was with the one-sidedness and narrowness of theory and research, and indeed public discourse, that was predominantly underpinned by an engineering imagination. His critique of empiricism was not only a critique of a one-sided 'style' of social science, but as discussed above, a critique of scientism which is certainly prominent today, especially as research review boards are primarily oriented to the norms of positivistic, experimental and quantitative enquiry (see Palys 2003; Haggerty 2004b; Hammersly 2009). Likewise, his critique of theoreticism ruminated on the lack of empirical observation and the dearth of creative and innovative thinking.

Mills' antidote to scientistic and theoreticist enquiry and the engineering imagination that underwrites this technician's enterprise was the practice of intellectual craftsmanship, a practice animated by the creative ethos of the sociological imagination:

> Craftsmanship as a fully idealized model of work gratification involves six major features: There is no ulterior motive in work other than the product being made and the processes of its creation. The details of daily work are meaningful because they are not detached in the worker's mind from the product of the work. The worker is free to control his own working action. The craftsman is thus able to learn from his work; and to use and develop his capacities and skills in its prosecution. There is no split of his work and play, or work and culture. The craftsman's way of livelihood determines and infuses his entire mode of living. (Mills 1951, 220)

The sociological imagination entails what I call 'refractive thinking', and a poetic, speculative and multidimensional way of thinking and doing to get beyond the immediate context for how our experiences may be shaped by and derived from broader features of social life and for how our actions are implicated in reproducing (but are also capable of altering) these broader societal features. The criminological imagination fosters a type of sense-making that facilitates political engagement, positive social transformation and social justice through a concerted effort to trace and connect the structured domains of personal milieu (within which human beings experience social reality) with the institutions and politics that shape this experience (within the process of ongoing social change).

Mills (1959, 14, 17) held out literary work, journalism and artistic endeavours as exemplars of the sociological imagination (see Piamonte, Chapter 11 in this volume), and criminology has benefited greatly from those few who have turned their attention toward literature, film and popular culture. As Mills suggested:

> Novelists – whose serious work embodies the most widespread definitions of human reality – frequently possess this [sociological] imagination, and do much to meet the demand for it. … In the absence of an adequate social science, critics

and novelists, dramatists and poets have been the major, and often the only, formulators of private troubles and even of public issues. (Mills 1959, 14, 18)

Ruggiero (2002, 2003) has illustrated the usefulness of imaginative and speculative thinking for criminology through his criminological examination of classic works of fiction. Here he reveals the criminological insights embedded in fiction, insights on the nature of public issues that the authors did not necessarily intend, but were nevertheless present. For example, in looking at Herman Melville's *Moby-Dick* as an allegory for economic crime (see Frauley 2011), he was able to clarify, reformulate and extend currently utilized criminological theories and concepts. By examining these in a different way against a different empirical referent and then bringing these reformulated ideas into use to examine more traditional criminological phenomena he shows the value of thinking in a refractive way (see Frauley 2010, 2011).

Potter (1998), writing about the 'potential scientificity' of literary criticism and fiction's value for social science, captures sentiments expressed by Mills and intimated by Ruggiero:

> Writers, good writers, as well as possessing a creative facility with language, have insights into the human condition, insights into the dynamics of social grouping, ... the sort of knowledges achieved through other, through actually sometimes very similar, means, by psychologists, sociologists, historians, philosophers. ... [W]hen crafting a work of fiction they do not attempt these insights in a formalised analytical form. Rather they utilise their insight in their creation of fictional universes. (Potter 1998, 185)

Mills (1959, 17) recognized that such work contained analytical insights and that 'literary men' operated as intellectual craftsmen, often trying to 'characterize societies as wholes, and to discern their moral meanings', but that the growth of scientism relegated the cultural artefacts of 'artisans', 'novelists' or 'journalists' to a different, non-scientific realm than those of 'social scientists' and furthered the split between fact and fiction or science and the creative (see also Frauley 2015). Within the social sciences there was dwindling space for intellectual craftsmen, but within 'culture' this space was available (Mills 1959, 137). Just as Mills had argued that 'personal problems of milieu' were manifestations of broader structural problems (1959, ch. 1),[11] owing to the organization and restructuring of institutional fields the problem of the decline of intellectual craftsmanship was in part a feature of the re-organization of science, higher education and the

---

11 'We have come to see that the biographies of men and women, the kinds of individuals they variously become, cannot be understood without reference to the historical structures in which the milieu of their everyday life are organized' (Mills 1959, 158). 'The life of an individual cannot be adequately understood without references to the institutions within which his biography is enacted' (Mills 1959, 161).

'lazy safety of specialization' (1959, 21) within capitalist societies plagued by 'illiberal practicality'.

Despite this persistence of intellectual craftsmen predominantly outside social science, their insights were not formalized in analytical form. This for Mills was a problem, because although art and literature can express sociological insights, they cannot do so 'with the intellectual clarity required' for understanding or ameliorating private troubles or public issues (1959, 18). Again, Potter's remarks prove insightful:

> Art, literature, celebrates, consoles and entertains. It pleases us with its beauty. It haunts us with its emotional force. It does produce knowledges. But these knowledges are in a different form and were produced (mainly) through different means than scientific knowledges. However, once produced in literary form, such knowledges can later be accessed by different means – the particular methodologies of literary criticism. (Potter 1998, 187)

The fictional worlds of literature and film include traces of practices and social structural elements that played a role in positioning authors and in constituting the conditions for these worlds to emerge. The insights into the human condition that good novelists succeed in producing can be unlocked by the sociological imagination because it is adept at identifying biographical and structural elements and then clarifying the relationship between these: it entails '[t]he capacity to shuttle between levels of abstraction, with ease and with clarity' (Mills 1959, 34). This movement 'is a signal mark of the imaginative and systematic thinker' (Mills 1959, 34). This imagination, Mills states: 'is the capacity to shift from one perspective to another – from the political to the psychological; …. It is the capacity to range from the most impersonal and remote transformations to the most intimate features of the human self – and to see the relations between the two' (1959, 7).

Practices animated by the criminological imagination – such as criminological research practice, theoretic practice or pedagogical practice – proceed via a *combinatory movement between* different conceptual and substantive vantage points that is *synthesizing, perspectival, holistic* and *comparative*. This *continual movement between vantage points* (i.e., perspectives; frameworks, perspectivalism) and *between societal levels* (i.e., from the personal to the remote, relationships to relations) enables one to construct a fuller, more complete picture of what is observed: 'It is commonly recognized that any systematic attempt to understand involves some kind of alternation between (empirical) intake and (theoretical) assimilation, that concepts and ideas ought to guide factual investigation, and that detailed investigations ought to be used to check up on and re-shape ideas' (Mills 1959, 74).

Applying a Criminological Imagination

What is most valuable about this continual movement between vantage points (perspectives) and between societal levels (personal to the remote) is the perspectivalism enabled. This requires one to avoid both a theoreticist 'fetishism of the Concept' (Mills 1959, 35) and empiricist 'methodological inhibition' (Mills 1959, 50) which promotes refractive thinking and engenders a parallax view, an apparent shift or change in the object or its position and, consequently, what appears as a different picture as well as a different understanding of the object (see Kemple and Mawani [2009], who, coincidentally, also discuss parallax and Mills). This parallax view is ultimately what is most valuable about Mills' sociological imagination and what, then, will prove most valuable about the criminological imagination. It is the generating of this parallax that is the theoretical and methodological promise of the sociological imagination.

Refraction and Parallax

When Mills (1959, 214) stated 'let your mind become a moving prism catching light from as many angles as possible', he introduced, but never developed, the metaphor of the prism to highlight the workings of the sociological imagination. The prism is an optical device that affects the way we see and understand that which it filters. Like a triangular prism, the sociological imagination is a filter through which white light (i.e., complex relations) is separated into its various colourful wavelengths and in the process unravels and exposes the complex layering of our object of analysis. What may appear to the naked eye as coherent and uniform is untangled to reveal complexity in its constitutive strands. In this way the sociological imagination is a multifaceted platform for enquiry that can help us reveal complexity (i.e., the whole is broken down) in order to produce more complex or synthetic descriptions and understandings of things. It aids in combining or synthesizing multiple strands of thought and forces us to shift our perspective between impersonal social relations and interpersonal relationships; at the same time it aids in identifying and describing parts of a more complex whole.

In utilizing the prism as a metaphor for the sociological imagination Mills invokes the broader context of optics. This metaphor, especially the process of *refraction* (as it is understood both in physics and ophthalmology) and the outcome of *parallax* are useful for criminologists to help them visualize refractive thinking and its benefits. Criminology, it is argued, can benefit from and produce a benefit for others in producing parallax views of the politics of crime and criminalization as well as the practices, discourses and structuring of crime control.

Optical Physics and Refraction: Dispersion and Complexity Revealed

We are probably most familiar with the notion of refraction that stems from optical physics. According to the *American Heritage Science Dictionary*:

> Light passing through a prism is mostly refracted, or bent, when it enters the prism and again when it leaves the prism. Since the index of refraction in most substances depends on the frequency of the wave, light of different colors is refracted by different amounts – hence the colorful rainbow effect of prisms.[12]

Because the white light that surrounds us is made up of different 'strands' of light or different wavelengths of energy (each resonating at a different frequency) and because each wavelength bends or moves differently when entering and exiting a prism, the white light separates or is dispersed 'into a spectrum of colors' (Barnes-Svarney 1995, 289). Thus the bending or distortion of white light separates it into distinct wavelengths which appear to us as different-coloured light. So a uniform image which is carried by white light will be dispersed into its constitutive strands as these are 'detangled' by the prism.[13] This dispersion of white light illustrates this first meaning of refraction: 'to break up'[14] or to separate. But there is a second understanding of refraction that has not to do with dispersion, but with concentration or focus.

Ophthalmological Refraction: Focal Power

To 'see' any object, white light must be reflected from that object and travel to our eyes, where it passes through, first, our cornea, second, something called a crystalline lens, and then it is received by our retina. This process is known as *refraction*. In ophthalmology, the branch of medicine dealing with the science of eyes, refraction refers to the eye assembling light from an object into an image.[15] Thus what we have with this form of refraction is a reassembly of the strands of light reflected from an object to produce an image. Thus we have a *reduction*

---

    12   'Refraction', *The American Heritage Science Dictionary*, http://dictionary. reference.com/browse/refraction (accessed 6 June 2015).
    13   Dispersion, according to Gibilisco (2002, 507), 'is the principle by which a prism works'. It is not simply the prism that produces this dispersion, but the light striking the boundary separating the density of the medium of the prism and that of the adjoining medium (see Gibilisco 2002, ch. 19, 'Optics').
    14   'Refraction', *Online Etymology Dictionary*, http://dictionary.reference.com/ browse/refraction (accessed 6 June 2015); 'Refraction', *Oxford English Dictionary*, http:// www.oed.com/view/Entry/161038 (accessed 6 June 2015).
    15   'Refraction', *Dictionary.com Unabridged*, http://dictionary.reference.com/browse/ refraction (accessed 6 June 2015); 'Human Eye', *Encyclopaedia Britannica: Academic Edition*,   http://www.britannica.com/EBchecked/topic/1688997/human-eye/64898/The-work-of-the-optical-lens-system (accessed 6 June 2015).

of complexity through refraction: strands of light are captured, if you will, and condensed into an image of the object we are looking at.[16]

However, as anyone who wears contact lenses or glasses knows, our anatomical lenses are sometimes in need of correction, and with corrective lenses one might better see, but also better understand, describe and interpret what one is seeing. This need for corrective lenses stems from some deficiency in one's anatomical lenses. This has to do with what is called *refractive error*. The structure of what are called *ametropic* or abnormal eyes produces refractive error, meaning the structure of these eyes constrains their ability to focus well or to clearly present the image of nearby (*hyperopia*) or distant (*myopia*) objects.[17] If the image is focused in front of the retina (myopia or near-sightedness) or behind it (hyperopia or far-sightedness), the object will appear blurry. To gain clarity, the media through which light passes – the cornea and crystalline lens – must be corrected. The ametropic or abnormal lenses are in need of correction because they have diminished *focal power*.[18] The *emmetropic* or normal eye, on the other hand, produces a sharper image because its lenses have greater focal power (and a lower degree of refractive error). The emmetropic eye – *as an apparatus* – allows us to see more clearly.

Just as our eyes may be in need of corrective lenses, and those corrective lenses may need periodic adjustment, our conceptual lenses may produce varying degrees of clarity, and may also require correction and periodic adjustment. Thus lenses – whether conceptual or anatomical – have an impact on the quality of visualization that can be produced due to their focal power. In a sense, the quality of mind envisioned by Mills was a corrective to an *ametropic social science* that contained a great degree of refractive error and had weak or low focal power. The sociological imagination is offered as an emmetropic eye for social enquiry that can correct refractive errors within social science, specifically those errors produced by styles of enquiry that are either *short-sighted* (such as 'abstracted empiricism') or *far-sighted* (such as 'grand theory') – two differing but dominant styles of social science during Mills' time.

Focal power has to do with our scope and ability to move between what is immediate and what is distant. What is of concern is the *depth* and *scope* of our criminological vision. We do not want to be only far-sighted or near-sighted,

---

16 Of course, part of this image-reconstruction has to do with our *knowledge* and the *meaning* and *significance* we attach to what we observe. As post-structuralists and critical realists, among others, have argued, our observations are 'theory-laden'. Our understandings of the images that are reconstructed have to do with our *ability to conceptualize* and the *range* of analytic tools available to us for this work of conceptualizing and imagining, but also to how our eyes distort light.

17 Rosa M. García Hdez, 'Refractive Visual Disorders: Some Clarifications', *Exploring the World of Vision*, 11 December 2008, http://rosavisionenglish.blogspot.ca/2008/12/refractive-visual-disorders-some.html (accessed 6 June 2015).

18 'Human Eye', *Encyclopaedia Britannica: Academic Edition*, http://www.britannica.com/EBchecked/topic/1688997/human-eye/64898/The-work-of-the-optical-lens-system (accessed 6 June 2015).

but want to come somewhere in between. This depends on the quality of our conceptual apparatus, not simply on how much information we accumulate. In this sense, analytic concepts can be *made* to have more focal power to allow us to produce fuller and clearer pictures of social reality. This is what Ruggiero attempts in his analyses of classic works of fiction. Thus an important endeavour for social scientists is the clarifying and refining of analytic lenses as these are put to work in empirical enquiry. Thus it is not simply beneficial but necessary to view social enquiry as requiring both empirically informed theorizing and theoretically informed empirics. Empirical enquiry must play a strong role in the production and refinement of our conceptual lenses. If it does not, then it will be difficult to contribute to or advance criminological *knowledge* (bearing in mind that *information* on administrative practice and crime rates and so on is descriptive of particular political and institutional fields distinct from criminology).

The depth and scope of our lenses will determine the size of our visual field. If our field of study is narrow, then it is likely we are working with narrowly construed or 'one-sided' concepts (Layder 1993; Frauley 2011) or a one-sided style of social science (Mills 1959). One-sided concepts and styles of enquiry do not allow us to make linkages between the immediate and the remote.[19] We can liken the visual field of the eye to the field of criminology, or more accurately to *the scope and depth of criminological vision*. A criminological imagination will aid in expanding the visual field of criminology. Multiple lenses are often used by social scientists to enable one to 'see' various aspects of something; sometimes theoretical concepts are combined to broaden the scope and depth of analysis. Sometimes they are invented for the same purpose. As the criminological imagination is a meta-theoretical framework that can provide for non-eclectic synthesis of viewpoints (and concepts) on social action and social structure and the relation between the two, it can take two or more theories or sets of lenses (interlinked concepts) and integrate them. This is not simply to increase the number of useful concepts that can be used to think with, but is to facilitate the production of different pictures of our object that can then be integrated to produce more robust, complex, holistic and adequate visualizations. This perspectivalism is what allows for *parallax*. We are not simply producing different pictures of objects or different perspectives on things, but fabricating more complex and higher-quality visualizations that have increased scope and depth. Thus the theoretical-discursive structure of analytic concepts is analogous to the material-anatomical structure of our eyes. It is the structure of the lenses and the structure of their interrelation that gives them their analytic or focal power, and this is what gives the criminological imagination an

---

19   Shearing (1989) makes a similar argument in his rejection of criminology as simply the study of crime. Crime, he says, is a political category, and when criminologists accept this as the object around which criminology is organized it unnecessarily restricts the scope of enquiry. Many have made this argument about the perils and pitfalls of accepting a state definition of crime for criminological enquiry: that it is too legalistic and therefore too narrow to be of use to social scientists.

advance over the predominantly one-sided criminological ways of seeing and understanding currently on offer.

Conceptual Refraction: Mills' Emmetropic Eye

The two conceptions of refraction are directly related to parallax: whether we are dealing with degree of *focal power* of lenses with respect to producing holistic understandings or degree of *dispersion* produced by our lenses with respect to deconstructing complexity, our attention is drawn to how objects may appear to change and how our images and understandings are affected by this.[20] Focal power and dispersion work together to give us a kind of refractive thinking. In unravelling and exposing the layering of our objects of analysis we can identify and describe constituent parts of a more complex whole (i.e., dispersion). In this way the criminological imagination can be employed to reveal complexity through a kind of deconstruction, revealing the impersonal social relations and intimate interpersonal relationships that comprise our object of examination. With this revealing of complexity we can reconstruct our object of concern to produce a more complex or synthetic analytical description and understanding (i.e., focal power).

Mills' prism metaphor suggests a tripartite emmetropic eye. There are three 'sides' or 'surfaces' to the prism or three key parts of the eye that interact to refract and produce a shift in perspective and understanding (i.e., a parallax view). The criminological imagination can be visualized as a multifaceted mechanism for producing parallax. The three sides or surfaces are *the ontological surface*, which has to do with *what* is refracted or *what* we ought to analyse. That is, it sets out the *scope* of criminological analysis. Mills' concepts of 'biography' (including 'personal troubles'), 'personal milieu', 'social-institutional structure' (including 'roles' and 'public issues'), 'history-change' and 'power' together form a model of a society and hence outline the facets of a society that social scientists ought to be concerned with. We are given a *map* that directs our attention to the components and dynamics of a society; *the conceptual surface* or filter makes the mapping we might do possible in that it provides 'sensitizing concepts', such as 'biography' and 'social structure'. These are the analytic tools used for refracting. This conceptual surface reveals *how* we can produce description and sense-making and analyse and draw connections between, for instance, the experiences of criminality and the machinations of social control; *the methodological surface* is the *approach* offered for the study of crime, criminalization and crime control (as well as theoretical

---

20 Our 'lenses' reveal constitutive strands that make up our object (discursive relations, social relations and so on) and in turn enable the production of synthetic and holistic explanations and understandings. This seems empiricist, but if we acknowledge, as realists and Marxists do, that there are necessary or internal relations that make up our object, and that these tether the object to its material place in history and society, we can move beyond the empiricist notion that we are simply or only dealing with what we can see.

and methodological problems internal to criminology and social science). It has to do with how to engage in the use of the conceptual tools offered for refracting. We are directed to continually move back and forth between various strands of thought, between the empirical and the conceptual, and between the interactional (i.e., personal) and structural (i.e., remote).

The criminological imagination, then, building on Mills, can aid in describing criminological problems and issues in a holistic manner through use of the sensitizing concepts discussed above, following along both a vertical and horizontal axis to give the problem breadth and depth (i.e., increased scope). As a conceptual mechanism, the criminological imagination leads us to expand our scope of enquiry by moving between differing points of view (within the conceptual), between the levels of personal experience and social structure (within the empirical), and between the conceptual and the empirical.

Refractive Thinking in Action: Thwarting the Reproduction of the Cheerful Robot

In describing how effective, politically relevant and socially and personally meaningful social science is to be conducted, Mills is also promoting an *approach* for how we might practically transmit a particular 'quality of mind' in the formation of speculative, passionate and holistic thinkers. In large part this approach to enquiry – whether teaching or research – follows on from the tradition of classical sociological thinkers such as Max Weber, Emile Durkheim and Karl Marx. It enables enquiry that moves between problems of milieu and problems of social structure, between small and large, between relationships and relations. The quality of mind characteristic of the sociological imagination, he insisted:

> seems most dramatically to promise an understanding of the intimate realities of ourselves in connection with larger social realities. It is not merely one quality of mind among the contemporary range of cultural sensibilities – it is *the* quality whose wider and more adroit use offers the promise that all such sensibilities – and in fact, human reason itself – will come to play a greater role in human affairs. (Mills 1959, 15)

Although this has been alluded to above, we need to delineate between what Mills (1959, 8) called 'the personal troubles of milieu' and 'the public issues of social structure'. Such a distinction, he stipulates, is an 'essential tool of the sociological imagination'. Personal troubles of milieu are private matters that affect both the 'inner life' and 'external career' of individuals. Milieu designates 'those limited areas of social life of which he is directly and personally aware' (Mills 1959, 8). Milieu is the context of personal troubles. How one expresses or articulates these troubles and resolves them will be in terms of resources immediately accessible – language, material means and so on – in their personal milieu. Some people will have greater capacities to articulate in a more or less sophisticated manner the troubles and their resolution. Public issues, on the other hand, go well beyond the individual, local knowledge and immediate environment. The issues are public or societal rather than private. As personal troubles are individualized experiences of public issues, a wide range of persons may experience in differing ways the same public issues. Thus Mills was keen to advocate that we connect the personal troubles and public issues of modern society, as one cannot exist without the other. However, this connection is often not made, for various reasons. People may not have the capacity to make these connections. Social scientists, likewise, may not have the capacity to make these connections, especially if they are oriented to either abstracted empiricism or grand theory:

> Neither the life of an individual nor the history of a society can be understood without understanding both. Yet men do not usually define the troubles they endure in terms of historical change and institutional contradiction. The well-being they enjoy, they do not usually impute to the big ups and downs of the societies in which they live. Seldom aware of the intricate connection between the patterns of their own lives and the course of world history, ordinary men do not usually know what this connection means for the kinds of men they are becoming and for the kinds of history-making in which they might take part. They do not posses the quality of mind essential to grasp the interplay of man and society, of biography and history, of self and world. They cannot cope with their personal troubles in such ways as to control the structural transformations that usually lie behind them. (Mills 1959, 3–4)

Societal transformation and politics are formative forces for individuals, communities and societies. In addition, individuals are not autonomous selves, but inherently social beings connected to one another in often unrecognized, perhaps unfathomable, ways. Troubles endured might include unemployment, poverty, victimization or simply frustrations, leading to what Merton (1938) called the use of 'illegitimate means' in an attempt to achieve 'culture goals' (i.e., widely disseminated and held cultural values and aspirations). Such troubles are not simply the product of individual failings and are not always resolvable by individuals. Institutional conflict and societal change are important conditions from which public issues emerge and which shape personal troubles. How these will be understood and experienced is largely a product of personal milieu.

The 'foremost political and intellectual task' of social science is to 'make clear the elements of contemporary uneasiness and indifference' (Mills 1959, 13). Threats or perceived threats to what are widely entrenched 'cherished values', he suggested, can lead to experiences of 'uneasiness' and 'indifference', which in turn can lead to 'malaise' and 'apathy' (Mills 1959, 12) and passive acceptance of injustices. These forms of inaction and detachment are the outcome of the play of what Mills (1959, 13) called the 'unruly forces of contemporary society', such as political and economic upheaval. How these unruly forces are connected to and impact our personal experiences is often unclear, he argues (Mills 1959, 11), but must be visualized and made intelligible through the sociological imagination. To illustrate this, Mills offers a few examples, one of which is unemployment:

> When, in a city of 100,000, only one man is unemployed, that is his personal trouble, and for its relief we properly look to the character of the man, his skills, and his immediate opportunities. But when in a nation of 50 million employees, 15 million men are unemployed, that is an issue, and we may not hope to find its solution within the range of opportunities open to any one individual. The very structure of opportunities has collapsed. Both the correct statement of the problem and the range of possible solutions require us to consider economic and political institutions of the society, and not merely the personal situation and character of a scatter of individuals. (Mills 1959, 9)

Crime and delinquency have been linked to the structure of opportunities of which Mills speaks, most famously by Robert Merton (1938). So although Mills does not explicitly speak of crime, criminalization or crime control, these could have easily been utilized as examples of the types of public issues that are embroiled with widespread experiences of uneasiness and indifference. In fact, as criminologists have shown, fear of crime is far more prevalent than crime itself. Crime and delinquency are often experienced as individual or family problems (or as personal troubles), often cast as problems of particular neighbourhoods or workplaces (or problems of milieu), and become targets of populist political campaigns or law reform (i.e., they become public issues). Yet the societal problems and issues associated with crime and delinquency are firstly not intelligible from only an individual or institutional standpoint, and secondly cannot be resolved by only working at one or other of these levels.

Ideas that situate crime and solutions to crime at an individual level can be regarded as simplistic and one-sided. For instance, the prevalent idea that crime is an individual phenomenon caused by people making rational choices to voluntarily violate the criminal law is not adequately contextualized by the variety of viewpoints on the nature of 'social action' or thought explicitly in relation to the structured settings or opportunity structures that frame action. Similar, and equally problematic, is the other prevalent position that crime is an outcome of pathology and can be solved via psychiatric or biomedical initiatives at the level of the individual. For criminologists attempting to employ a criminological imagination, an understanding of criminality or crime control without considering 'historical change and institutional contradiction' will be uni-dimensional and inadequate. Explanations such as 'X *chose* to violate the criminal law' or 'X is biologically *predisposed* to violence' are not social or holistic explanations and are simplistic. Taking into consideration the dynamic entwining of the domain of social action and that of social structure, as well as the crucial role of societal transformation, compels an understanding of individual or group behaviour in terms of the larger context of the political, economic and moral elements or features of social life as embodied in institutions such as the legal system, family, work, education, religion and so on. Particular institutional arrangements and community organization will inflect the character of the public issue in the experiential realm.

In attempting to understand personal troubles by way of public issues, as Mills advocates, we would explicitly connect the level or domain of *biography* with the currents of societal change and organization. According to Mills, we need to attempt to connect these large and general features of societies to the very specific actions and experiences under consideration. In thinking of issues of social welfare, for instance, we might think of the 'institutional contradiction' of privatized public services; public services offered for the benefit of all citizens, but operated by a for-profit corporation that is only concerned with generating profits for shareholders. Here benefits are distributed according to a user-pay model rather than according to need, meaning public services such as policing are offered in an expressly anti-democratic fashion through the market (Bayley and Shearing 1996; Christie 2000; Loader 1999; Rigakos 2002). The contradiction comes from having social entitlements such as safety and security distributed according to market sensibilities that must discriminate on the basis of income or ability to pay. Privatization within the prison system in the USA, for instance, has enabled a booming industry that *requires* crime and mass incarceration in order to produce profits for private shareholders as well as to provide employment for very large numbers of largely unskilled workers (Feeley 2002; Shelden and Brown 2000; Shichor 1993):

> What we experience in various and specific milieux, I have noted, is often caused by structural changes. Accordingly, to understand the changes of many personal milieux we are required to look beyond them. And the number and variety of such structural changes increase as the institutions within which we live become more embracing and more intricately connected with one another. To be aware of the idea of social structure and to use it with sensibility is to be capable of tracing such linkages among a great variety of milieux. To be able to do that is to possess the sociological imagination. (Mills 1959, 10–11)

It is precisely because we may not directly experience or perceive our personal troubles as a manifestation of larger, distant public issues that Mills' sociological imagination is valuable, especially for criminologists interested in social justice:

> Mills also argues that the sociological imagination can liberate us from the bonds of social structure. For him, in fact, understanding the individual's place in the society implied liberation. Once we have learned about the sociological forces that determine our biography, it is possible for us to overcome them and become a spokesperson, as he believed he was, for a more democratic and equalitarian social structure. (Goode 2008, 238–9)

The economic and political changes within Western capitalist states, then – those experienced over the previous three decades – may not seem, for instance to the individual police officer, to be related to the transformation of policing from 'public order maintenance' to 'social service', or the shift from deterrence to management of crime, but they have been shown by Garland (2001) and others to be driving forces. Moreover, with mass incarceration in the USA, for instance, it simply is not plausible or feasible to think of the 'crime problem' in terms of the individual. It is a public issue. Because a public issue 'cannot very well be defined in terms of the immediate and everyday environments of ordinary men' (Mills 1959, 9), one's personal experience and local knowledge acts as a constraint on how one might conceptualize the problem and its resolution. This means that if we are to adequately conceptualize a public issue such as unemployment or crime, or adequately conceptualize the personal trouble of being unemployed, engaging in criminal conduct or being victimized, we have to go beyond our immediate experiences and commonsense knowledge to think about 'the ways in which various milieux overlap and interpenetrate to form the larger structure of social and historical life' (Mills 1959, 8). How, for instance, does the for-profit corporation overlap with the prison, and how does the space of incapacitation overlap with that of the commodity?

Although Mills' text has been read mainly as offering a critique of two differing but limited styles of sociological research, there is an equally important concern for pedagogy. As Kaufman and Schoepflin have recently pointed out: 'the major pedagogical resource of *The Sociological Imagination* has been overlooked for far too long: namely the appendix, "On Intellectual Craftsmanship"' (2009, 20). They stress the benefits for academics and students alike of a pedagogical practice informed by the sociological imagination. Indeed, some scholars have begun to advocate an explicit turn toward 'pedagogy' as an object of criminological analysis (Frauley 2005, 2012; Barton et al. 2010; Pfohl, Chapter 4 in this volume). Just as Mills argued that social science demands that one not split his or her everyday life from work, undertaking critical, non-empiricist and non-theoreticist social enquiry cannot be separated from the *teaching* of social science, as research is a practical endeavour that exemplifies knowledge-production. It is far more likely that a wider population of people will be affected by teaching than research. Pedagogical practice serves to transmit practical knowledge about crime and its control and aids in reproducing the fields of criminology, justice studies and criminal justice administration. Criminology and justice studies are aligned with the 'criminal process' in that they serve to transmit important norms and ideas that support the general acceptance of crime control policies and practices in Western societies (Lacey 1994, 29; Lacey et al. 1990):

> The criminal process consists of a number of institutions, professional groups and practices. These practices operate on the basis of more and less formal systems of norms, which govern the identification, pursuit, prosecution, trial

and sentence of a selection of persons who are alleged to have committed crimes as defined by criminal law. (Lacey et al. 1990, 12)

Lacey et al. (1990, 7), in arguing for a substantive approach to the criminal law and justice administration, argue that we should look beyond these to the ways and means other institutions exercise power and how this might compete with or complement justice administration:

> The education system constitutes a central strategy in society's practice of socialising its members and producing citizens who have internalised many of the norms embedded in criminal law. At school, children encounter for the first time an institutionalised coercive regulatory system, in the form of school rules backed by penalties on breach, and are educated (or indoctrinated?) to have a docile attitude to this kind of disciplinary technique. At school too, we begin to become accustomed to routine and surveillance which prepare us for submission to legal coercion for the rest of our lives. (Lacey et al. 1990, 8)

As education is fundamentally important to how Western societies disseminate and naturalize the norms embedded in criminal law, criminology and justice studies, as they are entrenched within the institution of education, complement and contribute to the criminal process in helping to naturalize political categories such as 'crime' and 'criminal' as well as political processes such as 'criminalization' and 'juridification' (i.e., the expansion of legal regulation). Studying the distinctiveness of education and its institutional parallels with the justice system can tell us quite a lot about what guides and shapes academic criminology, but also how academic criminology contributes to the reproduction of justice administration and how it might be transformative in this regard.

Moreover, as the structure and arrangements within education and the policy process that guides and shapes it operate to enable and constrain academic labour, any attempt to restructure higher education can be seen also as a political attempt to govern the production and dissemination of criminological knowledge, whether intended or not.[21] A critical and self-reflective criminology would endeavour not only to clarify and problematize the practices and discourses of which it is

---

21 White's (2001) commentary on the changes in the conditions under which intellectual work is done in Australian academic institutions, specifically within criminology, is instructive here and is reminiscent of Mills' position. Speaking of the 'commercialization' and 'proletarianization' of knowledge-production at the behest of external pressures from government, 'clients' (such as students, corporations, or the state) and industry, as well as the changes to funding schemes wherein non-utilitarian research is devalued, he argues that intellectual work has taken on the status and character or 'entrepreneurial activity' (White 2001, 130). Pedagogy has been affected by this restructuring of the criminological field as 'there has been a substantial shift in meeting the needs of the private sector for certain types of workers' (White 2001, 128).

composed, but also its institutionalization and alignment with other institutions. Increased attention to what Mills called the 'institutional order' of education will deepen our understanding of how and why 'teaching can become a functional, goal-oriented exercise and the critical, and in this case criminological, imagination can become suppressed' (Barton et al. 2010, 25; see Williams 1999).

Examining the transmission of knowledge and practice within our fields and the intellectual formation of future correctional officers, police officers or administrators will contribute to our understanding of how academics contribute to operations within the criminal justice sector. As graduates from criminology and justice studies are far more likely to have an impact on the delivery of criminal justice services and on policy formation and implementation than graduates from other fields, and because some of them will continue their education and perhaps become part of a future professoriate, it makes sense to direct explicit attention to the institution of education and to pedagogy for how criminology and justice studies support or impugn the production of cheerful robots and all that that entails. Given that criminology and justice studies are entrenched within the political institution of higher education, and that this institution is aligned with the criminal process, it makes sense for criminologists and justice studies scholars to attend to pedagogy and look beyond what may seem self-evident about the role and place of higher education, including criminology and justice studies, in contemporary capitalist societies in order to clarify the relationship with the 'criminal process' and other forms of regulation.[22] At issue is the degree to which justice studies and criminology contribute to the reproduction of the criminal process or other forms of domination: that is, how it is that education as a bureaucratic and political institution conditions sensibilities and supports or impugns the practices and policies found within the criminal justice system and those within the wider society that are sympathetic to the norms and values that underpin the justice system.

If a dominant approach to research is animated by an 'engineering imagination' and bureaucratic ethos, course delivery will likely be topic-centred and informational (Barton et al. 2010; Frauley 2005, 2010). As it is pedagogical practice that infuses or strips a seminar or lecture course of passionately curious research and intellectual puzzlement, it is pedagogical practice and enquiry which will ultimately impugn or foster the (re)production of cheerful robots within and outside the academy.

Asking questions about our positioning, both structural and experiential, within contemporary power dynamics involves what Pfohl (Chapter 4 in this volume) has described as 'rites of unlearning': 'The rigors of unlearning and reflexive relearning', he suggests, 'are not lessons taught to future criminologists at most

---

22   Sears (2003) has offered extensive treatment of the regulatory and reproductive aspect of higher education and how it is implicated in promoting three forms regulation: *market discipline*, *labour discipline*, and to a lesser extent the acceptance of the legitimacy of *coercive discipline*. See also Frauley (2012) and Guebert (2015).

elite academic institutions.' Krisberg spoke of something similar in his discussion of breaking with doctrinaire scholarship:

> to cast off the educational indoctrination which has been our experience in programs of professional training. When one realizes that the material which he or she learned in order to pass exams, get good grades or to butter powerful professors is of little or no value in attacking problems of real human concern, then the first steps toward the integration of one's political, moral and intellectual life can be successfully accomplished. (Krisberg 1974, 158)

It stands to reason that criminology and criminal justice studies should be engaged in promoting this reflexive relearning as a craft practice rather than simply relaying information about the justice system. When we use textbook descriptions of how the justice system operates, for example, we remain complicit with crimes of power, domination and the infrastructure of our colonial past. Why? Because the authoritative text legitimizes a cut-and-dried simplistic depiction of criminal justice administration (see Frauley 2004, 2005). A criminology infused with the quality of mind advocated by Mills would be in the business of promoting 'reflexive relearning'. In Chapter 4 in this volume Pfohl discusses what he terms 'power-reflexive pedagogies', arguing that 'a critical criminological imagination challenges us to dismantle barriers dividing our way of scholarship from our *way of living*'. Pfohl argues, as does Mills, that our scholarly practice cannot be divorced from our lifestyle as it is part of our existence. To 'cultivate' the practice of intellectual craftsmanship that is animated by a criminological imagination we must 'deliberately present controversial theories and facts, and actively encourage controversy' (Mills 1959, 191). Our 'foremost job' as educators, Mills argues:

> is to reveal to them as fully as he can just how a supposedly self-disciplined mind works. The *art of teaching* is in considerable part the *art of thinking* out loud but intelligibly. In a book the writer is often trying to persuade others of the result of his thinking; in a classroom the teacher ought to be trying to show others how one man thinks – and at the same time reveal what a fine feeling he gets when he does it well. The teacher ought then, in seems to me, to make very explicit the assumptions, the facts, the methods, the judgments. (Mills 1959, 79; emphasis added)

Echoing Gramsci (1957), Mills states: 'The question is whether he faces this condition and makes up his own mind, or whether he conceals it from himself and from others and drifts morally' (1959, 79). A social scientist who practices reflexivity 'will try and do his work in awareness of its assumptions and implications, not the least of which are its moral and political meaning for the society in which he works and for his role within that society' (Mills 1959, 77).

Mills here is speaking of the 'intellectual craftsman' as one who participates in and attempts to develop the arts of teaching and thinking.

The formation of future leaders and administrators of the crime control apparatus (including those sectors of the private sphere that contribute to this regulatory process) is one area in which we can make a direct and tangible contribution. That is, we are deeply involved in forging the 'habitus' of people who will occupy key positions in the various bureaucratic intuitions that need to be mobilized to realize positive social transformation.[23] Favouring the criminological imagination as an approach for both research and teaching facilitates the role of 'social scientist' over that of 'research technician' and works against reproducing the bureaucratic ethos necessary to 'science machines'.

Conclusion

As Flight of the Conchords (2008) articulate in their satirical song 'Robots':

> There are no more humans.
> Finally, robotic beings rule the world.
> The humans are dead.
> The humans are dead.

The parodying duo and their absurdist humour speak of a fictitious robotic uprising that has led to the extermination of humans. Humans had become destructive and oppressive task-masters, leading to a widespread 'robo depression' that could only be remedied through the elimination of all humans. However, since the source of this robo depression was structural and not simply psychological, the uprising did not eliminate the conditions of the society under which the extermination had been legitimized and under which robots were forced to live. Thus robots simply replaced humans and continued to reproduce their subordination. Perhaps the greatest irony, though, is that robotic beings had already ruled the world prior to the robotic uprising.

Defeating the cheerful robots is not the plot of a low-budget science fiction film. It is a principal objective of a politically engaged creative (pedagogical and research) practice explicitly informed by the criminological imagination. The criminological transmission of knowledge can either reproduce (i.e., conserve) or thwart the (re)production of cheerful robots. A Millsian approach can help criminologists diagnose, critique and reformulate the differing and perhaps contradictory view points on crime and its control that one must move between, and it can also promote a continual movement of observation and theorization

---

23   I use 'habitus' following the work of Bourdieu. Habitus is the actor's internal cognitive structure, which is shaped by participation in structured social fields of practice. See Frauley (2012).

between the structural-institutional level and the interactional-experiential level of criminal activity, criminalization and the pluralistic forms and strategies of crime control and governance at work within contemporary Western societies. The criminological imagination can facilitate a lateral and vertical speculative imagining, one that is reflexive, comparative, synthetic and synthesizing.

In our enquiries Mills advocates that '[w]e study the structural limits of human decision in an attempt to finds points of effective intervention, in order to know what can and what must be structurally changed ...' (1959, 174). The criminological imagination then, building on Mills, promotes a form of enquiry, aiding in describing criminological problems and issues in a holistic, perspectival and synthetic manner through use of the sensitizing concepts of biography (and milieu), social structure (and institutions and politics), history (and change), personal troubles (the experiential) and public issues (broad social problems), giving our problem or object of focus breadth and depth (i.e., increased scope). As a conceptual mechanism, the criminological imagination leads us to expand our scope of enquiry by moving between differing points of view (within the conceptual), between the levels of personal experience and social structure (within the empirical), and between the conceptual and the empirical. Secondly, as a result of this carefully produced picture we can make sense of the experiential and structural features of the problem and what might be done about this, especially as it concerns transforming structural constraints.

In addition, we need today to transmit in practical ways, in exemplary ways, a criminological imagination that promotes reflexive relearning, where intellectual craftsmanship becomes a way of life. The aim is the mobilization of agencies and personnel within the arena of criminal justice and of effecting change from the inside. This seems feasible and likely if future administrators, police officers, parole and probation officers, prison guards and the like import the criminological imagination into those arenas through their professional practice. This will only happen if this quality of mind and pedagogical corollary becomes normalized within criminology and criminal justice studies.

To realize the theoretical and methodological promise of the criminological imagination we must identify and reject scientism, the role of research technician, and an engineering imagination that divides the poetic from the scientific. Importantly, we must actively embrace and consciously and systematically articulate practices indebted to a quality of mind that values perspectivalism, curiosity, passionate enquiry and systematic, deep and holistic conceptualizing. As Mills has argued, biography, history and social structure are intimately connected and mutually constitutive, and any meaningful and valuable contemplation of personal problems or public issues is always double-sided, meaning there are always experiential and personal as well as structural and remote aspects to be identified and connected. The criminological imagination holds the promise of producing parallax views of the politics of crime and criminalization as well as the practices, discourses and structuring of strategies of crime control. The *parallax effect* generated by the use of the criminological imagination is something quite valuable for enquiry and is in keeping with how

Mills understood 'sense-making' as one of the major objectives of social science. Criminology can benefit from syntheses and holistic and more adequate pictures of our social world, as well as theoretically and empirically grounded and politically located understandings of the linkages between the experiential and institutional aspects of social control today. The criminological imagination will prove invaluable as criminology is increasingly called upon to meet new practical and intellectual problems (Haggerty 2004a; Garland and Sparks 2000; Currie 2007).

References

Althusser, Louis. 1971. 'Ideology and Ideological State Apparatuses.' In *Lenin and Philosophy*, 123–73. London: New Left Books.

Alvesson, M. and K. Sköldberg. 2009. *Reflexive Methodology: New Vistas for Qualitative Research*. Thousand Oaks, CA: Sage.

Axelrod, Paul. 2002. *Values in Conflict: The University, the Marketplace, and the Trials of Liberal Education*. Montreal, QC: McGill-Queen's University Press.

Barnes-Svarney, Patricia L. 1995. *The New York Public Library Science Desk Reference*. New York: Macmillan.

Barton, Alana, Karen Corteen, Julie Davies and Anita Hobson. 2010. 'Reading the Word and Reading the World: The Impact of a Critical Pedagogical Approach to the Teaching of Criminology in Higher Education.' *Journal of Criminal Justice Education* 21(1): 24–41.

Barton, Alana, David Scott, Karen Corteen and Dave Whyte, eds. 2007. *Expanding the Criminological Imagination: Critical Readings in Criminology*. Portland, OR: Willan Publishing.

Bayley, David H. and Clifford D. Shearing. 1996. 'The Future of Policing.' *Law and Society Review* 30(3): 585–606.

Bittle, Steven. 2012. *Still Dying for a Living: Corporate Criminal Liability after the Westray Mine Disaster*. Vancouver, BC: UBC Press.

Blaikie, Norman. 2000. *Designing Social Research*. Cambridge: Polity Press.

Bourdieu, Pierre. 1988. 'Vive la Crise!' *Theory and Society* 17(5): 773–87.

Braithwaite, John 2000. 'The New Regulatory State and the Transformation of Criminology.' *British Journal of Criminology* 40(2): 222–38.

Carrier, Nicolas. 2011. 'Critical Criminology Meets Radical Constructivism.' *Critical Criminology* 19: 331–50.

Carroll, William K. 2013. 'Discipline, Field, Nexus: Re-visioning Sociology.' *Canadian Review of Sociology/Revue canadienne de sociologie* 50(1): 1–26.

Castel, Robert. 2003. *From Manual Workers to Wage Laborers: Transformation of the Social Question*. New Brunswick, NJ: Transaction Publishers.

Christie, Nils. 2000. *Crime Control as Industry*. New York: Routledge.

Clark, I., G. Moran, M. Skolnik and D. Trick. 2009. *Academic Transformation: The Forces Reshaping Higher Education in Ontario*. Montreal, QC: McGill-Queen's University Press.

Clark, I., D. Trick and R. Van Loon. 2011. 'Ontario Reticence in Higher Education: Time to Contemplate Major System Reform.' *The Blue and White*. http://theblueandwhite.ca/article/2011/02/09/00/00/04/ontarioreticence-in-higher-education.html (accessed 9 February 2012).

Coleman, Roy, Joe Sim, Steve Tombs and David Whyte, eds. 2009. *State, Power, Crime*. Thousand Oaks, CA: Sage.

Côté, J. and A. Allahar. 2007. *Ivory Tower Blues: A University System in Crisis*. Toronto, ON: University of Toronto Press.

Currie, Elliott. 2007. 'Against Marginality: Arguments for a Public Criminology.' *Theoretical Criminology* 11(2): 175–90.

Edwards, Adam and James Sheptycki. 2009. 'Third Wave Criminology: Guns, Crime and Social Order.' *Criminology and Criminal Justice* 9(3): 379–97.

Ericson, Richard. 1996. 'Making Criminology.' *Current Issues in Criminal Justice* 8(1): 14–25.

——— and Kevin Carriere. 1994. 'The Fragmentation of Criminology.' In *The Futures of Criminology*, edited by David Nelken, 88–109. Thousand Oaks, CA: Sage.

Fattah, Ezzat. 1997. *Criminology: Past, Present, and Future: A Critical Overview*. New York: Macmillan.

Feeley, Malcolm. 2002. 'Entrepreneurs of Punishment The Legacy of Privatization.' *Punishment & Society* 4(3): 321–44.

Ferrell, Jeff, Keith Hayward and Jock Young. 2008. *Cultural Criminology: An Invitation*. London: Sage.

Flight of the Conchords. 2008. 'Robots.' From *Flight of the Conchords*. Seattle, WA: Sub Pop Records.

Foucault, M. 1970/1998. 'Madness and Society.' In *Aesthetics, Method and Epistemology: The Essential Works of Michel Foucault*, vol. 2, 335–42. New York: Free Press.

———. 1974/1997. 'Psychiatric Power.' In *Ethics: The Essential Works of Michel Foucault*, vol. 1, 39–50. New York: New Press.

———. 1976/1980. 'Two Lectures.' In *Power/Knowledge*, edited by Colin Gordon, 78–108. New York: Pantheon.

———. 1977/1980. 'Truth and Power.' In *Power/Knowledge*, edited by Colin Gordon, 109–33. New York: Pantheon.

Frauley, Jon. 2004. 'Race, Justice, and the Production of Knowledge: A Critical Realist Consideration.' *Canadian Journal of Law & Society* 19: 177.

———. 2005. 'Representing Theory and Theorising in Criminal Justice Studies: Practising Theory Considered.' *Critical Criminology: An International Journal* 13(3): 245–65.

———. 2010. 'The Fictional Reality and Criminology: An Ontology of Theory and Exemplary Pedagogical Practice.' *Current Issues Criminal Justice* 21: 437–59.

———. 2011. *Criminology, Deviance and the Silver Screen: The Fictional Reality and the Criminological Imagination*. New York: Palgrave Macmillan.

————. 2012. 'Post-social Politics, Employability, and the Security Effects of Higher Education.' *Journal of Pedagogy* 3(2): 219–41.

————. 2015. 'Fact, Fantasy, Fallacy: Division Between Fanciful Musings and Factual Mutterings.' In *Framing Law and Crime: An Interdisciplinary Anthology*, edited by Caroline Joan S. Picart, Michael Hviid Jacobsen, and Cecil Greek. Madison, NJ: Fairleigh Dickinson UP.

Gane, Nicholas and Les Back. 2012. 'C. Wright Mills 50 Years On: The Promise and Craft of Sociology Revisited.' *Theory, Culture, Society* 29(7/8): 399–421.

Garland, David. 2001. *The Culture of Control: Crime and Social Order in Contemporary Society*. Chicago, IL: University of Chicago Press.

———— and Richard Sparks. 2000. 'Criminology, Social Theory and the Challenge of Our Times.' *British Journal of Criminology* 40: 189–204.

Gibilisco, Stan. 2002. *Physics Demystified*. New York: McGraw-Hill.

Goode, Erich. 2008. 'From the Western to the Murder Mystery: The Sociological Imagination of C. Wright Mills.' *Sociological Spectrum* 28(3): 237–53.

Gramsci, Antonio. 1957. 'The Study of Philosophy and of Historical Materialism.' In *The Modern Prince and Other Writings*, 58–75. New York: International Publishers.

Guebert, Karl. 2015. 'Reimagining the Educational Field: Thoughts on a Critical Criminology of Education. *Societies* 5(2): 442-59.

Guppy, N. and S. Davies. 1998. *Education in Canada: Recent Trends and Future Challenges*. Ottawa, ON: Minister of Industry (Statistics Canada).

Haggerty, Kevin. 2004a. 'Displaced expertise: Three Constraints on the Policy Relevance of Criminological Thought.' *Theoretical Criminology* 8(2): 211–31.

————. 2004b. 'Ethics Creep: Governing Social Science Research in the Name of Ethics.' *Qualitative Sociology* 27(4): 391–414.

Hammersly, Martyn. 2009. 'Against the Ethicists: On the Evils of Ethical Regulation.' *International Journal of Social Research Methodology* 12(3): 211–25.

Jacobsen, Michael Hviid, ed. 2014. *The Poetics of Crime: Understanding and Researching Crime and Deviance Through Creative Sources*. Farnham: Ashgate Publishing.

Jochelson, R., S. Kohm and M. Weinrath. 2013. 'Mitigating the Protective-services Orientation in Criminal Justice: An Opening Salvo at the University of Winnipeg.' *Canadian Journal of Criminology and Criminal Justice* 55(1): 1–32.

Kaufman, P. and T. Schoepflin. 2009. 'Last but Not Least: The Pedagogical Insights of "Intellectual Craftsmanship."' *Teaching Sociology* 37(1): 20–30.

Kemple, Thomas and Renisa Mawani. 2009. 'The Sociological Imagination and its Imperial Shadows.' *Theory, Culture & Society* 26(7/8): 228–49.

Krisberg, Barry. 1974. 'The Sociological Imagination Revisited.' *Canadian Journal of Criminology & Corrections* 16: 145–61.

Lacey, Nicola, ed. 1994. *Criminal Justice*. Oxford: Oxford University Press.

————, Celia Wells and Dirk Meure. 1990. *Reconstructing Criminal Law*. London: Weidenfeld and Nicolson.

Layder, Derek. 1993. *New Strategies in Social Research*. Cambridge: Polity Press.

Loader, Ian. 1999. 'Consumer Culture and the Commodification of Policing and Security.' *Sociology* 33(2): 373–92.

Lyotard, Jean-François. 1979. *The Postmodern Condition*. Minneapolis, MN: University of Minnesota Press.

McShane, Marilyn D. and Frank P. Williams III. 1989. 'Running on Empty: Creativity and the Correctional Agenda.' *Crime & Delinquency* 35(4): 562–76.

Manicas, Peter T. 1987. *A History and Philosophy of the Social Sciences*. New York: Blackwell.

Merton, Robert. K. 1938. 'Social Structure and Anomie.' *American Sociological Review* 3(5): 672–82.

Messner, Steven. 2012. 'Morality, Markets, and the ASC: 2011 Presidential Address to the American Society of Criminology.' *Criminology* 50(1): 5–25.

Michalowski, Raymond J. and Ronald Kramer, eds. 2006. *State-corporate Crime: Wrongdoing at the Intersection of Business and Government*. New Brunswick, NJ: Rutgers University Press.

Mills, C. Wright. 1939. 'Language, Logic, and Culture.' *American Sociological Review* 4(5): 670–80.

———. 1951. *White Collar*. New York: Oxford University Press.

———. 1956. *The Power Elite*. New York: Oxford University Press.

———. 1959. *The Sociological Imagination*. New York: Oxford University Press.

Morn, Frank. 1995. *Academic Politics and the History of Criminal Justice Education*. Westport, CT: Greenwood Publishing.

Mouton, Johann. 1996. *Understanding Social Research*. Pretoria, South Africa: Van Schaik Publishers.

Nelken, David. 1994. 'Reflexive Criminology?' In *The Futures of Criminology*, edited by D. Nelken, 7–43. London: Sage.

O'Malley, Pat. 1996. 'Post-social Criminologies: Some Implications of Current Political Trends for Criminological Theory and Practice.' *Current Issues in Criminal Justice* 8(1): 26–38.

Palys, Ted 2003. 'Ethics in Social Research.' In *Research Decisions*, 80–120. Toronto, ON: Thomson Nelson.

Pearce, Frank. 1989. *The Radical Durkheim*. Winchester, MA: Unwin Hyman.

——— and Laureen Snider. 1995. 'Regulating Capitalism.' In *Corporate Crime: Contemporary Debates*, 19–48. Toronto, ON: University of Toronto Press.

——— and Steven Tombs. 1998. *Toxic Capitalism: Corporate Crime and the Chemical Industry*. Aldershot: Ashgate Publishing.

Pfohl, Steven. 2015. 'The Criminological Imagination in an Age of Global Cybernetic Power.' In *C. Wright Mills and the Criminological Imagination*, edited by Jon Frauley. Farnham: Ashgate Publishing.

Postman, Neil. 2011. *Technopoly: The Surrender of Culture to Technology*. New York: Random House.

Potter, Garry. 1998. 'Truth in Fiction, Science and Criticism.' *Journal of Literary Semantics* 27(3): 173–89.

Rafter, Nicole. 2006. *Shots in the Mirror: Crime Films and Society*, 2nd edn. New York: Oxford University Press.

Ratner, Robert. 1984. 'Inside the Liberal Boot: The Criminological Enterprise in Canada.' *Studies in Political Economy* 13:145–64.

Restivo, Sal. 1988. 'Modern Science as a Social Problem.' *Social Problems* 35(3): 206–25.

Rhoades, G. and S. Slaughter. 1997. 'Academic Capitalism, Managed Professionals, and Supply-side Higher Education.' *Social Text* 15(2): 9–38.

Rigakos, George. 2002. *The New Parapolice: Risk Markets and Commodified Social Control*. Toronto, ON: University of Toronto Press.

Rose, Nicolas. 1996. 'The Death of the Social? Re-figuring the Territory of Government.' *Economy & Society* 25: 327–56.

Rosenfeld, Richard. 2011. 'The Big Picture: 2010 Presidential Address to the American Society of Criminology.' *Criminology* 29(1): 1–26.

Ruggiero, Vincenzo. 2002. 'Moby Dick and the Crimes of the Economy.' *British Journal of Criminology* 42(1): 96–108.

———. 2003. *Crime in Literature: Sociology of Deviance and Fiction.* New York: Verso.

Sawchuck, Kim. 2001. 'The Cultural Apparatus: C. Wright Mills' Unfinished Work.' *The American Sociologist* 32(1): 27–49.

Sayer, Andrew. 1992. *Method in Social Science: A Realist Approach*, 2nd edn. New York: Routledge.

Schlosser, Eric. 1998. 'The Prison-industrial Complex.' *The Atlantic Monthly* 282(6): 51–77.

Scimecca, Joseph. 1975. 'The Implications of the Sociology of C. Wright Mills for Modern Criminological Theory.' *International Journal of Criminology and Penology* 3: 145–53.

———. 1976. 'Paying Homage to the Father: C. Wright Mills and Radical Sociology.' *The Sociological Quarterly* 17(2): 180–86.

———. 2015. 'Implications Revisited: The Sociology of C. Wright Mills for Modern Criminological Theory.' In *C. Wright Mills and the Criminological Imagination: Prospects for Creative Enquiry*, edited by Jon Frauley. Farnham: Ashgate Publishing.

Sears, Alan. 2000. 'Education for a Lean World.' In *Restructuring and Resistance: Canadian Public Policy in an Age of Global Capitalism*, edited by M. Burke, C. Moores and J. Shields, 146–58. Halifax, NS: Fernwood Publishing.

———. 2003. *Retooling the Mind Factory: Education in a Lean State*. Aurora, ON: Garamond Press.

Shearing, Clifford. 1989. 'Decriminalizing Criminology: Reflections on the Literal and Tropological Meaning of the Term.' *Canadian Journal of Criminology* 31: 169–78.

Shelden, Randall G. and William B. Brown. 2000. 'The Crime Control Industry and the Management of the Surplus Population.' *Critical Criminology* 9(1–2): 39–62.

Shichor, David. 1998. 'Private Prisons in Perspective: Some Conceptual Issues.' *The Howard Journal of Criminal Justice* 37(1): 82–100.

Simon, David. 1985. 'Organizational Deviance: A Humanist View.' *Journal of Society and Social Welfare* 12:521–51.

———. 1988. 'Liberalism and White Collar Crime: Toward Resolving and Crisis.' *Quarterly Journal of Ideology* 12(1): 19–30.

———. 1991. 'White Collar Crime, Dehumanization and Inauthenticity: Towards a Millsian Theory of Elite Wrongdoing.' *International Review of Modern Sociology* 21(1): 93–107.

Slaughter, S. and L. Leslie. 1997. *Academic Capitalism: Politics, Policies, and the Entrepreneurial University*. Baltimore, MD: Johns Hopkins University Press.

Taylor, Ian. 1999. *Crime in Context: A Critical Criminology of Market Societies*. Chichester: John Wiley & Sons.

———, Paul Walton and Jock Young. 1973. *The New Criminology*. London: Routledge.

Teeple, Gary. 2000. *Globalization and the Decline of Social Reform*. Aurora, ON: Garamond Press.

Tombs, Steve and David Whyte. 2003. 'Scrutinizing the Powerful: Crime, Contemporary Political Economy, and Critical Social Research.' In *Unmasking the Crimes of the Powerful: Scrutinizing States and Corporations*, edited by Steve Tombs and David Whyte, 3–45. New York: Peter Lang.

Tudiver, N. 1999. *Universities for Sale*. Toronto, ON: James Lorimer.

Walters, Reece. 2003. 'New Modes of Governance and the Commodification of Criminological Knowledge.' *Social & Legal Studies* 12(1): 5–26.

White, Rob. 2001. 'Criminology for Sale: Institutional Change and the Intellectual Field.' *Current Issues in Criminal Justice* 13(1): 123–42.

Williams III, Frank P. 1984. 'The Demise of the Criminological Imagination.' *Justice Quarterly* 1(1): 91–106.

———. 1999. *Imagining Criminology: An Alternative Paradigm*. New York: Routledge.

Wood, Jennifer and Clifford Shearing. 1989. 'Reinventing Intellectuals.' *Canadian Journal of Criminology* 41(2): 311–20.

Wozniak, John. 2009. 'C. Wright Mills and Higher Immorality: Implications for Corporate Crime, Ethics, and Peacemaking Criminology.' *Crime, Law, and Social Change* 51: 189–203.

Young, Jock. 2011. *The Criminological Imagination*. New York: Blackwell.

Chapter 2

The Demise of the Criminological Imagination: Thirty Years Later

Frank P. Williams III

Thirty years ago I wrote what was the first article explicitly focused on the 'criminological imagination' in *Justice Quarterly*. At the time it was meant to be a theoretical essay on criminological theory-production and the changing nature of the field and, of course, it was generically informed by C. Wright Mills' *The Sociological Imagination*. The article itself took from Mills' work not the whole texture, but instead three critical ideas. The first was the necessity of scholars being able to think outside of routine, to think creatively, and to think using alternative perspectives. The second was the role of change and how that might affect the criminological discipline. The third idea was Mills' concept of humans as products of their milieu and explanations of their actions with this in mind. All of these will be discussed later in this chapter.

In one sense that 1984 essay was a forerunner to a metatheory on the emergence of theories and the field's acceptance of those theories. The refined version of this metatheory later went into a 1988 textbook on criminological theory, co-authored with Marilyn McShane. Knowing that instructors and students tended to approach any textbook containing a built-in theory with a rather negative view, we instead buried the metatheory in a discussion of the social and intellectual context of each of the unit theories and perspectives. This was done by arguing that to understand the various theories one had to situate the author(s) and the perspective(s) in their unique historical moment(s). As it turned out, that view of theory took a substantial amount of historical literature research and discussion with, whenever possible, the theorists themselves and/or individuals surrounding them. The result was, in the largest sense, a demonstration of Mills' structural ideas within the context of the criminological sub-field. The treatment was also successful in that virtually every textbook written on criminological theory since 1988 has adopted some version of a situated-context approach to theory.

The purpose of this chapter is both to clarify the original ideas and to assess the state of the 'criminological imagination' at this juncture in time.[1] Before that, though, the question of exactly what a 'criminological imagination' is comes to mind. Clearly, it is not uncommon for the use of a term or phrase to diverge from

---

1 The focus of this chapter is on the relationship of the criminological imagination to theory-production, not the general orientation of the criminological discipline.

the original meaning. Where the term 'sociological/criminological imagination' is concerned, current usage seems to be much like the expansion of the term 'critical' in critical criminology, where any critique of 'dominant' criminology is now described as being critical.[2] In other words, when a term reaches popular status, attribution is in the eye of the beholder. Recently, I have seen 'imagination' used to describe statistical analyses and 'new' multi-mode data collection, as well as to justify coming to conclusions about data analyses which transcend the entire collection of variables. Mills didn't seem to have these usages in mind even though he clearly discussed such subjects, albeit rather 'critically'. I suspect the chapters in this anthology will do a good job of illustrating the divergent uses of what is now meant by a 'criminological imagination'.

If we use C. Wright Mills' own perspective of the sociological imagination, then it must include the ability to see the world in a social fashion without allowing personal experience to colour the factors behind collective experiences in the wider society. It must also include the ability to see the ways these social factors influence and interact with each other. But perhaps most important, a sociological imagination has the ability to understand and appreciate alternative perspectives of situations and social events. In short, the sociological imagination requires a scholar to transcend his or her own experiences and understandings of reality in favour of a view that encompasses the understandings of others derived from their embeddedness in shared social settings and structures. Lest this be misunderstood, it is important to realize that Mills was not using the term 'social' as if it fell directly under the dominant sociological paradigm of his day or ours. To his mind, the purview of sociology was interdisciplinary, encompassing all social fields like political science, history, psychology and economics. In fact, Mills cautions against a narrow view of the field and expressly warns of the danger of working with a single method or theory. And, on the whole, that was the take-off point of my 1984 essay.

So what will the reader find here? The structure of this chapter is first to discuss in more detail, and for the first time, the context behind the 1984 article and the intended messages; second, to discuss some of the reaction to that piece, and lastly, to provide an overview of the context of today's theoretical endeavours and their 'success' in meeting the criteria of a criminological imagination.[3] The first section will require a little patience of readers, especially those not familiar with the period, as the rationale for including some of the elements might not immediately be apparent.

---

2   A truly ironic usage has been to label biological perspectives as part of the 'critical' tradition.

3   I am deliberately not using citations and sources for this chapter: most readers familiar with criminological history will know them anyway. Secondly, for the most part I do not wish directly to call attention to specific individuals when my comments will apply to many others involved in the same work. Some of the reaction to the earlier article taught me that academics tied to a dominant paradigm can view any criticism of that paradigm as a personal attack.

The Demise of the Criminological Imagination: Context and Background

The 1970s were a time of change and, following an old Irish curse, also an interesting time to be in US criminology. In one sense it was a bit similar to the early days of the Chicago School, with a heady feeling that new things were being created. On the other hand, there also were movements that were antithetical to creativity.

Change in Academia

The late 1960s had produced a few interesting theories for more conservatively oriented criminologists to explore, while many in the new generation of scholars were infatuated with the period's emerging radical perspective. Criminology was starting its move away from sociology departments and there was a sense of excitement among those in programmes considered to be 'pure criminology', some of which were developing doctoral programmes. These early days also saw the emergence of criminal justice academic programmes which would ultimately challenge criminology for hegemony over the study of all things crime. The latter part of the 1970s also contributed to a change in the focus of social scientists with the advent of new technologies and availability of data.

Change in Political Agenda

On another front, the US government had taken notice of crime and the administration of justice. Crime rates were high and President Nixon's 'war on crime' served to put crime on the political agenda. Money began to flow to researchers, criminal justice agencies and educational institutions. The concept of programme evaluation, though still rudimentary, involved academics in the search for both rehabilitative programmes that worked[4] and greater efficiency in the management of criminal justice agencies. C. Ray Jeffery's new concept of crime prevention through environmental design (and the architectural version espoused by Oscar Newman) also found favour in governmental circles, primarily in the federal Department of Housing and Urban Development and in the Law Enforcement Assistance Administration (LEAA; soon to become the National Institute of Justice's Office of Justice Programs) as police proactive crime prevention.

Change as a Result of Synthetic Interests

Academia and LEAA interests also combined, essentially resulting in the creation of an academic criminal justice discipline through a programme designed to fund

---

4   In part, this was due to a new politically conservative mindset and the misrepresented findings of Lipton, Wilkes and Martinson's review of correctional programme effectiveness.

higher education for law enforcement officers.[5] The result was the emergence and proliferation of police science and criminal justice (CJ) programmes and departments. These programmes were usually initiated in colleges and universities for the most mercenary of reasons – to cash in on the availability of federal LEEP (forgivable) tuition loans. These schools were almost universally smaller ones with local or regional missions, many of them community colleges. Faculties of prestigious universities, on the whole, declined to participate in what they deemed as a 'technical and training' field.[6] Because there was a dearth of available scholars to teach in these programmes, it was not unusual to see entire faculties with no doctorates among them, and retired police officers (especially those who came from police training academies) with little in the way of academic credentials were frequently hired. In short, the discipline of criminal justice virtually exploded on the academic scene with little in the way of theoretical and research interests. The end of LEEP funding in 1980 also proved to be the end of many small CJ programme startups. By that time academic criminal justice had established doctoral programmes and their graduates were beginning to fill the need for qualified faculty.[7] Even so, a critical difference was created in the training and interests of most criminal justice students compared to criminology students. CJ, as a discipline, tended toward administration, management and legal courses. Criminology tended toward theory and research. While the two certainly blended together and there were exceptions in disciplinary focus, the disciplinary paradigms were well established.[8] Within academic departments, criminology was more involved in federal funding of research and CJ was more involved in training and

---

5   This programme, called the Law Enforcement Education Program (LEEP), was created to fund higher education for law enforcement officers and those planning to work in law enforcement. It was later expanded to correctional officers. The motivating goal behind the programme was the 1967 President's Commission's recommendation to make law enforcement more professional.

6   This academic mindset, which was likely correct in the early days of criminal justice, was still strongly in effect as of the 1990s. In fact, one of the long-lasting missions of the Academy of Criminal Justice Sciences has been to overcome this 'training' view of the criminal justice discipline by encouraging academic qualifications of faculty and theoretical/research aspects in curricula.

7   It should be noted that as late as 2008 there were more open faculty positions announced than CJ doctoral graduates to fill them. Thus, even though there has been a proliferation of CJ and criminology departments over the last forty years, qualified faculty remains an issue.

8   I, and many of my colleagues who were teaching in CJ doctoral programmes during these years, frequently made such observations in our discussions at conferences. Moreover, as a scholar trained as a 'pure' criminologist and teaching in one of the major CJ doctoral programmes, such disciplinary paradigm differences were relatively obvious to me. Another difference we observed was that students coming into CJ doctoral programmes were less likely to have sociology degrees, and those arriving in criminology doctoral programmes were often from sociology.

management 'efficiency' funding. These differences, and the associated dynamic changes, during this period were critical ones for the criminological imagination.

Change in Technology

What else was integral to the situational context of that period? Frankly, it was a historical event that today's generations of scholars can scarcely conceive of. The general availability of computers for academic research simply didn't exist prior to the 1970s. Access to a university mainframe computer was severely limited, and even when available, computing power was substantially less than that of today's smartphones. Much of the statistical analysis was done by hand, and this meant that analysis of large data sets was virtually impossible; therefore, few academics dealt with such research.[9] A paradigm shift in computing power and the advent of the personal computer served to break through these data restrictions. While this may seem of little import, the reader should imagine what would happen when researchers, over a period of only a few years, suddenly had access to computing power capable of analysing ever larger data sets. To say that a paradigm shift in research occurred somehow seems to understate the event.

Two things occurred as a result. First, improved computing power meant better storage of data, and that meant larger data sets could be collected. This prompted the federal government to begin collection of crime data other than the Uniform Crime Reports and make them available electronically. The first such data came in the form of victimization studies funded by the federal government, and almost overnight the criminological focus shifted from crime data to victimization data. This prompted the second thing: criminological interest tended to leave theory construction behind in favour of analysing the new data. Because the existing analytical techniques were essentially based on hand calculation and small data sets, statisticians began developing new approaches to fit the new data reality. This meant that criminologists now had to be more statistically capable than in the past, and doctoral programmes began to cater for those needs with several required statistics courses. In fact, this was the beginning of curricula that in the future would give more emphasis to research and statistics knowledge than theoretical knowledge.[10] This was true for both CJ and criminology programmes.

---

9   I can vividly remember, as late as 1975, having to get permission to run an analysis that would require much of the mainframe's resources of 40 KB of random access memory (yes, that's kilobytes, not megabytes). It could only be done at 2 a.m., when there were no other pressing demands on computer capacity.

10   Many doctoral programmes during this period replaced their language requirements with statistical proficiency. Some even went so far as to declare programming languages (such as BASIC, COBOL and FORTRAN) as preferred substitutes for traditional 'foreign' languages.

Change in Ideological Orientation

One other factor was important in developing the 1984 article. In doctoral criminology theory classes my students frequently expressed sentiments that there were fewer new theories, and new ones seemed somehow to be more limited than older ones. In the ensuing discussions we usually wound up assessing the assumptions and focuses of these new theories. The consensus was that, after 1970 and up to the end of the decade, the only truly popular theories were social control and social learning (this ignores the myriad conflict and feminist approaches that were subscribed to only by a relatively small group of criminologists), both of which were products of mid-1960s perspectives. At the end of the 1970s two other closely related theories appeared: lifestyle theory and routine activity theory. Rather than being explanations of crime or criminality, both of these theories drew from the new conservative directions and were explanations of the new victimization data. In short, they were essentially products of the rather simplistic and descriptive victimization evidence produced to that point. Up to 1984 the only new addition to criminological theory was a rational perspective which was primarily a restatement of conservative economic theories of crime.

The Collective Implications of a Dynamic Context

Putting these contextual features together to examine the notion of dynamic change in the discipline, it appeared that a combination of research funding changes, the arrival of a criminal justice discipline with more interest in agency efficiency, conservative forces, the availability of computers, the arrival of large data sets and the ascendance of quantitative analysis collectively began to drive criminological thinking. In none of these elements could any sense of Mills' 'imagination' be reasonably credited. Moreover, the paradigm shift in graduate education to a computerized and quantitative focus seemed destined to create a technology-oriented discipline which would endow quantitative data with the essence of reality. From this perspective it seemed that any previously existing criminological imagination was in danger of being swept aside in favour of the new quantitatively focused scientism. Thus, the remainder of the 1984 essay was dedicated to a critique of the assumption that quantitative data accurately represent social reality and human experience. That latter issue apparently appealed to those allied with emergent postmodernism while it simultaneously threatened those vested in quantitative pursuits. I am not sure the 'imagination' focus of the essay was paid much attention.

The Intervening Years and the Current State of the Criminological Imagination

Given the conclusions of this earlier analysis of the discipline's theoretical production, the natural question is: What happened over the past thirty years?

Using the methodology of the original analysis, the contextual effect of these years will be explored.

Popularity of Theories

While certainly not new to those intervening years, the separation of criminologists into camps of supporters for various theories became evident. These camps were tied to competition between graduate schools and friends/mentors, and seemed to play a large part in the popularity of theories. Surely, there was little actual difference in the degree of empirical support for the various theories. In fact, I once reviewed ten years of theory-oriented research in the major journals and found the vast majority of those articles arrived at essentially the same correlations no matter what theory was being tested. Given this, the choice of one theory over another devolves into what one is prepared to like, and that choice generally reflects whatever matches an individual's domain assumptions and worldview. Moreover, across the years there seemed to be the equivalent of fads and fashions in criminological theory and in the larger domain of criminology and criminal justice. During the most conservative years, the most popular theories tended to be those associated with assumed rationality, the control of self-interested behaviour, and the importance of correct parenting. More recently, as a touch of liberalism has returned, an explanation of the dynamic nature of the life-course on criminal behaviour has been received favourably, though probably not by a majority of criminologists.

Does this, regardless of nature of the supporting context and how theoretical popularity is assigned, reflect an application of the criminological imagination? We now turn directly to that issue.

The Context of Recent Creativity

From the late 1980s to the early 2000s there seemed to be a feeling of criminological creativity, with new theories appearing. However, there are two ways to look at the criminological imagination issue: the work of individual criminologists and the work of the field. Mills was obviously challenging the sociological field to meet his prescription of what sociology ought to be doing, not asking a few sociologists to do creative work. In another sense, this challenge meets another theorist's (Albert Einstein) observation that problems are not solved by the mindset that created them. To phrase this in yet another person's (Thomas Kuhn) terminology, those within a paradigm rarely resolve the anomalies of that paradigm. For criminology to have a dynamically creative edge, at least a core group of criminologists (if not the majority of the field), not a few individuals, must be willing to routinely participate in such thinking. Clearly, there were indeed new theories proposed, so the issue really becomes whether the field moved in a more imaginative direction during this period.

Popularity and Imagination

I offer the following evidence to suggest that did not happen. Based on surveys of criminologists and the number of articles in criminological journals testing individual theories, the range of theories during this period devolved into, at most, four popular ones: self-control theory, social learning theory, life-course theory and general strain theory. The interesting heritage behind each of these theories is that all of them are based on core work that occurred prior to 1970. Indeed, Travis Hirschi has even 're-explained' self-control theory as a more focused version of his earlier social control theory. Ron Akers' social learning theory has been extended to a structural version, but a close reading of his 1970s works shows that social structure was already an integral part of social learning. Life-course theory – at least the brand espoused by Robert Sampson and John Laub – integrates perspectives from the 1960s and was developed from longitudinal data collected in the 1940s and 1950s by Sheldon and Eleanor Glueck. Robert Agnew's general strain theory is primarily a processual offshoot of Robert Merton's 1938 anomie theory. In each of these cases I am not arguing that the theorists did nothing creative. But the fact is that there is little to show that the essential theoretical ideas were imaginative.[11]

Popularity and Complexity

The more creative and imaginative theories were those with increased complexity designed to match the field's incipient appreciation that human behaviour was more complex than earlier theorists had believed. New theories dealing with ecology, balancing control, reciprocating interaction, cultural and agency feedback and chaos, to name a few, were developed. While some gained a few adherents, none came close to matching any definition of 'popular'. In fact, I would argue that the very reason for referring to these theories as imaginative is the same reason for their failure to gain support: their complexity. When the hallmark of 'good' theory is its fit to evidence, the inability of others to produce evidence dooms a theory. Because today's quantitative analytical techniques are primarily based on assumptions encompassing a linear, proximately causal, non-stochastic and non-interactive world, there are few if any tools available for analysing complexity. Thus, no available tools means no research, and no research mean no evidence to support the theory; thus, methodological paradigms offer support for theories that support their methodological approach. Moreover, if most of the field has evolved in a quantitative direction (a discussion continued below), such theories leave most criminologists with nothing to do, and the best course of action is to simply proceed as if these theories do not exist. Once again, Mills' historical

---

11 I am not arguing that the original works these theories were based on lacked creativity. And in cases where the same theorist was involved in the original work there is certainly evidence of creativity. To label extensions of that work as imaginative, though, is probably not what Mills had in mind.

dynamic helps to explain the lack of interest in certain theories. If the evidence-producing technology of a historical moment is not sufficient to test a theory, that theory will be put aside regardless of its relative truth. Moreover, Mills' conclusion that the elevation of method requires 'measurable hypotheses' for work to carry forward seems to match the evidence that simplicity in theory gains the most supportive research work. Apparently there is a methodologically driven chase for the equivalent of the Holy Grail in criminology (and, to be fair, most other social sciences): a single variable which explains all criminal behaviour, rates of crime and victimization. Here, though, is the telling criticism: *Not one criminological theorist or researcher would attribute his or her own behaviour to something so simple.* Yet how is the construction of dynamic and complex theory, even though much more likely to be suggestive of true reality, to match the power of a dominant ethos of religious scientism?

Popularity and Disciplinarity

Other theories developed during the period in question have incorporated complexity by integrating elements from disciplines other than sociology: primarily psychology, biology and neurology. Because of criminology's inherited disciplinary paradigm – sociology – and the fact that most criminologists are still trained in sociology departments with a specialization in criminology or deviance, criminology as a field is still dominated by the sociological paradigm. Across the years I have heard criminologists exploring alternative disciplinary perspectives remark on the negative comments they receive about their work.[12] While such work is seemingly more frequent in the past decade, the reception has changed little. This has implications for true integrative work, and in particular work that is interdisciplinary. An associated element is that CJ, as a product of its multidisciplinary origins, is more likely to stray from the sociological paradigms and be more accepting of interdisciplinary theory work. Yet, at the same time, the competition between criminology and CJ seems to decrease the likelihood of criminologists accepting, or doing, interdisciplinary work. At present most of that work has come from those trained either as criminal justicians or as psychologists.

The most honest conclusion I can come to at this point is that popularity serves to retain the dominant paradigm and discourage creativity. The most popular criminological theories have older foundations, use traditional sociological variables drawn from social institutions deemed important by sociologists and emphasize the role of socialization. This has been so since the time of Sutherland

---

12   In the 1980s I was listening to panellists at an American Society of Criminology meeting. One of them was C. Ray Jeffery. When it was his turn to speak (his topic was incorporating sociobiology into explanations of crime), members of the audience began to call out 'Lombroso' and fully half of the audience began booing. At first I was taken aback that academics would act like this, but then I realized the nature of the threat Jeffery's new paradigm would create for them if it were accepted.

and Merton. If we want progress in the field, Einstein seems to be correct: Popularity as a judge of the quality of ideas and solutions is not the way to do it.

The Continuing Effect of Scientism

When I originally wrote of a creeping quantification of thought within criminology (what Mills called 'scientism'), it was to express my concern over an imbalance between understanding theory and understanding method. Moreover, I argued that the issue was more than an imbalance. Method and technique seemed to be practised for its own sake, and reputation-gaining seem to be a product of knowing the newest and latest techniques.

Theory Testing

The rationale for the statement above was based on the practice of journal publication. My reading of the content of criminological and criminal justice journals led me to conclude that articles were seemingly being accepted that lacked an understanding of the theory they purported to test. The most common fault was the use of data that only tangentially provided measures of the concepts representing a theory. Indeed, my assessment is that this issue is only magnified today. Other than the obligatory review of the literature to say what others have used as measures (primarily documenting that the use of proxy variables is common), there is little actual discussion justifying measures which are used as appropriate representations of a theory. This appears due in large part both to training that places a greater emphasis on methodological sophistication than on an understanding of theory and to the modern era's ready access to governmentally funded and stored secondary data. As a result, many researchers simply *approximate* theoretical concepts with variables that are handy in the secondary data they have downloaded.

Quantitative Practice and Error

If articles generally demonstrate a lack of understanding of theories and their concepts, then why are they accepted and published? The commonality among them seems to be cutting-edge statistical analysis. In other words, these articles may serve more as demonstrations of statistical techniques than as tests of theory. But here the issue of data raises its head again. These demonstrations seem to pay little attention to the data assumptions behind any statistical technique. On the whole, more sophisticated techniques require rigorous measurement (what is known as interval or ratio level). In other words, they require data with strong numeric properties. Unfortunately, secondary data are originally collected without these requirements in mind. Thus, most sophisticated statistical techniques actually use improper data. Many such techniques also assume linear relationships and normal distributions, while there is substantial evidence that reality features neither. Moreover, the number of variables used in multivariate analyses frequently violates limitations imposed by degrees of freedom issues, producing, among other things, over-estimates of relationships. Other restrictions exist for virtually all sophisticated statistics. Given this, there should be reasonable doubt that the modelling of complex behaviours in complex environments and with complex social relations is easily accomplished by current statistical techniques. Though there are indeed some statistical techniques by which to model such complexity, these are still in development and generally unknown in the social sciences. The conclusion here is that empirical support for theories tends to fall victim to poor conceptualization and measurement, to the use of variables that were never measures of the theory in the first place, to the misuse of statistical techniques, and to a lack of understanding of sources of error. Ergo, I am not sure we can attribute any real evidence to any theory, even those with simplistic logic structures.

Integrative Theory

The foregoing has implications for newer forms of theory referred to as integrated theory. Can these be applications of the criminological imagination? On the whole, the answer is 'no', for the following reasons. Unit theories are constructed with domain assumptions in the background. These are rarely specified by the original theorist, but can be inferred by a close reading of the theory and sometimes from other work by the theorist. Alternatively, the social and intellectual context in which the theorists work can give clues to his or her view of the world.[13] Failure to understand the domain assumptions of a theory can result in its combination with opposed theories, with the end product being a mélange of contradictory elements. There is also a level-of-explanation issue. One has to pay careful attention to what a theory purports to explain. Some theories attempt to explain behaviour, others to explain crime, others to explain crime rates, and yet others to explain victimization. Combining them requires careful attention to the dependent variable. Finally, in today's world it is common to find integrated theories created from empirical tests by adding statistically 'significant' variables to the explanatory mix. This is what is commonly referred to as grounded theory, and while there is certainly a place for this form of theory construction, there are many reasons why it is a poor way to 'add' elements to existing theory. Chief among these reasons are much of what has been discussed above: poorly measured proxy variables in secondary data combined with improper use of, and misunderstanding of error in, statistical techniques. In sum, how would potentially unique and erroneous

---

13 This represents another argument for an understanding of historical context and even the personality of a theorist. Even older colleagues have surprised me with assumptions about theories and theorists that indicate they know little about the person and his or her work that would inform a view of the theory. Indeed, I have heard suppositions expressed about the meaning of a theory that are in direct opposition to the personality of the theorist him/herself.

correlations derived from handy secondary data be viewed as imaginative and creative applications of the criminological mind?

The Historical Mindset

Finally, I have purposefully left until now any discussion of Mills' insistence that imaginative scholars will appreciate the contextual implications of a dynamic, changing social reality. The fact is that the combination of easy availability of secondary data, emphasis on statistical analysis and a reliance on 'objective' science has served to make historical and dynamic elements rather moot to extant knowledge. Longitudinal data sets are rarely collected, and even when available, there is little understanding and use of the necessary analytical techniques required to measure change in behaviour.[14] Moreover, today's criminologists are more likely to see historical context as perhaps mildly interesting, but not relevant to modern society, and in point of fact this view is behind common misunderstandings of criminological theories. The source of most modern understanding of theory is introductory textbooks and essays on the Internet, with the current generation of scholars leaning even more toward the latter.[15] At best these sources are superficial, at worst absolutely erroneous. Absent a reading of the original materials and an understanding of the situational and historical context in which a theory was developed, is it any wonder that contemporary tests of theories see no problem in using barely recognizable proxy variables in questionable data? To further insist that a historical mindset be a routine tool of criminological practice seems rather like folly.

Conclusions: The Criminological Imagination Today

The context for the original 1984 article, as discussed here, was based on a feeling that scientism was impeding development of a criminological/sociological imagination. The question is: Is it still at work? My conclusion is that the use of criminological imagination is certainly no more frequent today, and is probably less likely to be seen than thirty years ago. Mills' will to scientism is even more endemic today, but with less emphasis on the limits of quantitative techniques. I presume this is because hegemony has endowed scientism with all the elements of a religious belief system. Coupled with a failure to understand the limits of objective data, the omnipresence of large federal datasets, grants becoming a critical

---

14   The family of change statistics relies on different assumptions about error than traditional statistics designed for cross-sectional data.

15   From discussions with colleagues, young and old, I believe the result is that new criminologists have little comprehension of the context of previous theories and tend to see them as a collection of variables rather than an explanation based on the world at that time.

resource for university funding rather than a research resource and a linearity of thinking among today's scholars, there is little room for creative work. To this I would add a declining ability in critical thinking, historical unfamiliarity and lack of exposure to original materials, and the situation is ripe for a criminology based on the antithesis of Mills' sociological imagination.

In one sense, I am most concerned by the construction of research terms in an atmosphere that values objectivity, as the subtle implications of using those terms validates the valuing itself. I suspect the overreliance on numbers to express criminological reality is a very powerful piece of this overall conundrum. *Nothing* is more devoid of human feeling and subjectivity than representing thoughts, feelings, actions and actors as numbers. Thus, an artificial new reality is constructed by the use of abstract concepts and measurements designed around the idea of objectivity.

I have tried to present a case for the view that modern criminological theory construction is relatively constrained. If so, is there a way out of this situation? Can adjustments be made? I suspect the best answers to both questions are 'no'. We have maintained the primacy of the same general approaches for so long that we rarely question the way they reflect on reality. Indeed, the extended primacy of the approaches means that we have built up a language around them that, literally, *protects* them from questioning. Because language contains the symbols of thought, as we learn to think in a language it is those very linguistic conventions that shackle us. Make no mistake: quantitative methodology is a language.

Another reason for continuing the status quo is literally that we have too much vested in the current epistemology. Our educational systems are as much to blame here as anything else we do. We train people to think and provide exemplars of the proper ways and methods of perceiving reality. When we create the message that quantitative skills are paramount, we will get graduates who perceive the world in quantitative terms. Education actually creates pseudo-knowledge. We cannot know the truth, but we can learn the 'proper' way to *perceive* it. Indeed, we perceive it in such a fashion as it becomes useful to us. The burning question, of course, is: 'Useful for what?' If the answer is allied to the situational context of today's values, then knowledge, truth and reality become tautological aspects of the new educational and political world. Perhaps the thing to be valued least is a criminological imagination, and we simply don't teach it. And for that reason I sincerely hope the other contributors to this anthology prove me wrong.

Chapter 3

Contemporary Criminology and the Sociological Imagination

Eamonn Carrabine

The metaphor of 'rendezvous subject' is a well used one in criminology, and it is the traffic in multidisciplinary approaches that has sustained post-war British criminology, but which has also left it prone to a bewildering eclecticism and disorganized fragmentation. This chapter will argue that there is a distinct lack of a sociology of criminological knowledge. Part of this lack derives from a striking amnesia about the past and its own disciplinary history. This amnesia is especially troubling given that criminology and its relationship to sociology are now at a crossroads: where once the linkages had been strong – especially in studies of deviance – today that is no longer the case. There is no doubt that the separation has occurred as criminology has successfully established itself as an autonomous, independent academic subject that no longer sees itself as a sub-field of the legal, medical or social sciences. Some regard this remarkable expansion of criminology and move away from the more basic disciplines as a sign of success and a proud achievement, others are more ambivalent and warn of the dangers growing isolation will bring. This chapter will argue that a renewed commitment to C. Wright Mills' vision of the 'sociological imagination' is the way forward at this decisive moment.

Although Mills (1959, 3) famously declared that neither 'the life of an individual nor the history of a society can be understood without understanding both', the more radical implications of his argument over how the sociological imagination can offer liberation from oppressive conditions are largely forgotten. Today practically every introductory sociology textbook routinely invokes the first element of Mills' definition, how individuals relate to society, but ignores the second, which uses the 'concept to *overcome* the ties that bind us to social structure, *critique* the work of American sociologists who do not reach the same conclusions he did, and enable us to radically *transform* the status quo' (Goode 2008, 239; emphasis in original). Something of this critical project can be seen in Jock Young's (2011) recent attempt to subject criminology to the kind of withering attack that Mills delivered upon sociology over fifty years ago. Here he condemns the 'abstract empiricism' of mainstream criminology, which is described as one-dimensional, banal, technocratic and in the deadening grip of quantification, while that which aspires to 'grand theory' is similarly removed from social realities, thriving on trivial, ponderous obfuscation where 'latter-day Foucauldians have taken an outrageous and iconoclastic thinker and turned his writings into some sort of Talmudic parody of contested interpretation' (Young 2011, 6).

These two contrasting tendencies were initially identified by Mills in his scathing assessment of mid-century American sociology, which was ignoring the major issues of the day – how a post-war corporate economy led by a powerful elite, which had forged alliances with the military machine, was corroding social structures and generating profound inequalities. Instead, the profession was content to produce timid, conservative, inaccessible work that lacked any sense of the big picture or the transformative politics required to change the social order for the better. Directing his critique at the leading representatives of each tendency, he condemned the 'abstracted empiricism', exemplified in the work of Paul Lazarsfeld, for how it mistakes technical sophistication in method for having something important to say, while the 'grand theory' of Talcott Parsons is famously ridiculed for its lack of intelligibility and for evading urgent political questions surrounding the nature of power. In these different ways the emancipatory promise of sociology had become tragically distorted in the Cold War climate of the era. Distancing himself from those 'colleagues who were busy "choosing the west", otherwise giving aid and comfort to the witch-hunters, or neutering themselves by hiding behind the ideology of value-free scholarship' (Aronowitz 2003, 5), it is clear that Mills wanted sociology to rediscover the classic European thinkers of the nineteenth century who sought to comprehend the entire social condition. This ambition is not without its own problems, which I discuss in more detail below, such that any attempt to simply apply Mills to the contemporary social science landscape is likely to end up reproducing the assumptions framing his initial critique.

Revisiting Mills

Every text is a product of its times, and *The Sociological Imagination* is no exception, but one of the striking features is just how tame and respectable Mills' indictment has now become. Quotes from it appear so frequently in introductory sociology textbooks that it is as if 'either American sociology had long ago welcomed and favorably absorbed the essence of Mills's critique or, conversely, could stomach only a thimbleful of his tonic' (Dandaneau 2007, cited in Goode 2008, 250). There is no doubt that Mills would have dismissed these books and the courses they support for so passively accepting the tenets of mainstream sociology, which if anything is today even more thoroughly mired in the troughs he originally identified. In these standard textbook accounts the radical and polemical edge of his work is downplayed and Mills is transformed into a somewhat benign figure, sanctified even, where the rebel becomes a martyr. It is as if he had to 'die young to become a hero in sociology' (Brewer 2004, 318). Of course, this is a further irony, as by the time of his death in 1962 he was widely disliked in the profession, having antagonized and quarrelled with most of the prominent members in it, including those who had initially helped him and admired his work.[1]

A number of commentators have noted how the book is emphatically modernist in orientation, where the voices of classical social theory provide the language with which he can critique post-war American society and the sociologists who inhabit it. Some highlight its Weberian focus on the dangers bureaucratic rationalization presents to human dignity and freedom (Binns 1977; Hearn 1985), while others emphasize the influence of Veblen's (1899/1953) searing indictment of the dilettante upper classes on Mills' own understanding of the close ties between analysis, criticism and style (Aronowitz 2003; Kerr 2009). Furthermore, Veblen's satirical reading of the leisure class is firmly rooted in a historical understanding of how conflicts of interest arise macro-sociologically, while giving shape and meaning to an individual's character. This ability to fuse the deeply personal with the larger picture is an approach Mills would deploy throughout his career (Treviño 2012, 9). Yet the book has been denounced precisely because it is so attached to the old grand metanarratives of classical theory that it cannot speak to the postmodern condition. Consequently, it is ill suited to confront the problems facing contemporary sociology, where Mills is accused of writing 'vaingloriously' and producing a 'hypocritical text with dubious ethics' (Denzin 1990, 4).

These last complaints are not new and were aired in early reviews of the book, charging Mills with messianism, describing him as the 'Billy Graham of sociology' travelling the Earth, 'bearing a torch to light our darkness', and finding fault with Mills for his extreme criticisms, which 'lack profundity' and rendering his own proposals 'lamentably thin' (Fletcher 1960, 169). Many in the sociological establishment, on both sides of the Atlantic, were quick to defend the current state of the profession and the leading figures in it. The most vitriolic review was by Edward Shils (1960, 78), who described Mills as a 'sort of Joe McCarthy of sociology, full of wild accusations and gross inaccuracies, bullying manners, harsh words, and shifting grounds', and who had previously fallen out with him over a translation of Weber that would never see publication, for which Shils largely blamed Mills (Oakes and Vidich 1999). Hence the bitter tirade against him, but the review remains among the most malicious denigrations in the history of sociology,

---

1   Goode (2008, 245) gives the example of how Robert Merton had written to a colleague in December 1946 claiming that Mills was 'the outstanding sociologist of his age in the country', yet within a year Merton declined to support Mills' promotion in the sociology department, while much later Zygmunt Bauman claimed that Mills' death was thought to have been caused by 'the merciless campaign of defamation to which he was subjected throughout the whole of his academic career' (cited in Goode 2008, 250). In Becker's (1994) view, he 'was a difficult smart ass' who ended up marginalizing himself and was driven by the desire to become a Professional Big Thinker, while to 'many staid professionals Mills always seemed too big, too political, too productive and too famous' (Jacoby 2000, 155). At root Mills was intent on becoming a major public intellectual, with a distinctive moral vision that clearly strove for a critically minded 'public sociology' to contest post-war American culture and politics.

on one of the finest books to ever appear in it (Becker 1994). The initial reaction to the book was overwhelmingly negative in the leading American sociological journals: George Homans (1960, 517) thought it was nonsense, not least since he 'describes some work that I am familiar with in such loaded terms that I cannot recognize it', while William Kolb (1960, 969) accused Mills of dogmatism, inflexibility and hypocritically generating his own 'abstract mode of sociologism'.

Of course, opinion about the book has shifted drastically over time. His emphatic rejection of American positivist, functional sociology and endorsement of European social theory chimed with the burgeoning New Left (Hayden 2006), and he was a decisive figure in launching the 'political 1960s, the survivals of which are the few progressive movements that remain, such as environmentalism, and ironically, women's liberation and gay rights' (Goode 2008, 251). It must also be said that Mills' early death helped change perceptions. The book came to be seen as a 'valediction' and his studies anticipated the sociological mood of the 1960s, where the discipline became more 'comfortable seeing itself as a form of critique and debunking' (Brewer 2004, 330). His work was increasingly located in part of a broader attack on positivist sociological methods and the structural-functionalist theorizing then dominant, which would be such a key influence on the development of critical criminology in Britain, as we will see shortly. Denzin's (1990) critique of the book is through a postmodern reading that distils feminist, post-colonial and interactionist approaches to lived experience. He takes Mills to task for claiming to speak on behalf of the oppressed, but nowhere in the book do the 'little people and their personal troubles speak', rather Mills 'speaks for them; or he quotes others who have written about them, usually novelists' (Denzin 1990, 4). Even though fault might now be found with the modernist narrative and muscular posturing in the text, sociology is different today from the early 1960s, and much of this can be put down to the way Millsian ideas were taken up later in the decade.

It is equally clear that *The Sociological Imagination* did not call time on either abstracted empiricism or grand theory. If articles in the leading American sociology journals are any indicator, it would seem that 'Lazarsfeldian abstracted empiricism is now even more abstract, more quantitative, more inaccessible to the nonspecialist untrained in statistics, and at least as apolitical as was the case in Lazarsfeld's time' (Goode 2008, 249). There is no doubt that Mills would also have found the pretensions in much postmodern writing a continuation of the high seriousness and utter irrelevance of Parsonian grand theory (Gitlin 2007). Arguably, the real legacy of Mills lies in the way he developed a distinctive blend of perspectives that challenged the competing orthodoxies in the discipline, and it is this critical orientation that needs to be recovered, especially as the relationships between criminology and sociology stand at a crossroads today.

However, it is important to note that in Britain, at least, the close ties between criminology and sociology themselves only really existed from the late 1960s. Such a late marriage requires some explanation, and will be covered in what follows. Efforts to explain crime scientifically began in the late eighteenth century and gathered momentum in the nineteenth century – emerging from an eclectic mix of medico-legal approaches and Victorian social reform movements. Not all of this vast material constitutes a form of 'proto-criminology' (Garland 2002). Some of it is rather a kind of 'shadow criminology' (Rock 1994) older than that found in universities, but prefiguring much later sociological approaches, and it is to such issues we now turn.[2]

Early Criminologies

Across Europe the early decades of the nineteenth century were characterized by major social upheaval, political instability and economic crises. Many states were constructing legal and bureaucratic machinery indebted to the rationalized principles of the Enlightenment project, which inspired the reform of corrupt institutions. The Enlightenment's 'Age of Reason' founded a new era where the radical idea was that knowledge progressed and would bring liberation from the barbarism of the *ancien régime*, encouraging European intellectuals to see humanity afresh. This 'immaculate conception' account of the birth of criminology can and should be disputed (Cohen 1988, 3), but it did shape a set of preoccupations persisting to this day. The legacy of 'classical' thinkers like Cesare Beccaria, Jeremy Bentham and John Howard is the belief that archaic laws, repressive institutions and arbitrary practices can be reformed through enlightened reason and social engineering.

The Industrial Revolution sped up the migratory flows from the countryside to the city and established a pervasive nineteenth-century fear of the seething urban crowd. The free market opened up glaring inequalities, and efforts to contain the social disruptions accompanying rising unemployment and new class divisions intensified in the rapidly expanding towns and cities. These conditions were not unique to the nineteenth century, but what was distinctive was the way that journalists, missionaries, novelists, reformers and others began to analytically document the wretched conditions endured by the urban poor. Henry Mayhew's remarkable investigations of crime in Victorian London, Friedrich Engels'

---

2 Elsewhere I have described in more detail the development of criminology in the UK (Carrabine 2013), and what follows summarizes some of that argument, not least as I want demonstrate how a particular criminological tradition has been invented in a national context. As the social sciences have developed in different countries they have taken on a distinctive national character, which reflects the historically specific problems addressed in each country. These problems are not always universal, but they do share some common themes, because these more general concerns are often investigated through the particularly pressing cases in each society. Of course, this is not an argument advocating what has been termed 'methodological nationalism', where the nation state is problematically understood to be the natural focal point of disciplinary developments (see Chernilo [2006] for a nuanced discussion of these debates in social theory).

depiction of how uncontrolled industrialization, haphazard urbanization and class apartheid were creating the social problems of the day and Charles Booth's pioneering surveys of urban poverty are among the more well known of these pioneering explorations of social life.

By the middle of the nineteenth century a form of 'scientific' reasoning about crime had also become part of the 'emergent culture of amateur social science' thriving in Victorian England (Garland 2002, 21). Here government officials, acting initially in private but then later in a public capacity, began to analyse the mass of data the new state institutions were producing. From the 1830s onwards papers were delivered to the Statistical Society of London drawing conclusions about the moral and social causes of crime from meticulously calculated correlations of the data (Morris 1957). Similar developments were well under way on the Continent, and two French-speaking authors, André-Michel Guerry (1833) and Adolphe Quételet (1835), were among the first to develop a distinctly sociological form of analysis identifying the social forces producing crime. This new 'social physics' applied concepts from the natural sciences to social problems and established a positivist tradition countering the more biological form later popularized by Cesare Lombroso. Guerry and Quételet were both struck by the stability of crime rates regardless of actions taken by courts or prisons, and in this they established themes developed by Durkheim half a century later. Alongside these early studies of crime there also flourished a series of 'cottage industries' (Rafter 2009, xiii) devoted to the very nature of the criminal mind and body.

It is no accident that the growth of private asylums in the eighteenth century led to a new scientific specialism, which was initially termed 'alienism' (in that it addressed alienated minds), then 'morbid psychology', and finally 'psychiatry'. Many superintendents of these asylums also wrote about their patients, especially those who seemed incapable of controlling themselves, repeatedly engaging in violent and dangerous behaviour, often without remorse – suggesting that criminality was rooted in the brain. This practical experience of managing psychiatric disorders from within institutional settings became a defining feature of British criminology. Here medical expertise dominated scientific thinking on crime, and much of it was produced from within the penal establishment well into the twentieth century.

Although Cesare Lombroso's ideas were very influential and inspired major international congresses, rival national schools of thought (the French remained more sociologically inclined and rejected the biological determinism of Italian positivism) and specialist academic journals, their impact in Britain was largely negligible. Leading practitioners distanced themselves from what they regarded as the sweeping generalizations of the Lombrosian tradition, where it was greeted with a 'professional scepticism, based not on upon anti-scientism but upon a rather different scientific tradition – one which was more modest, more acceptable to the institutional authorities' (Garland 1988, 6). It was this pragmatic, medico-legal approach that predominated in Britain for much of the nineteenth century and well into the mid-twentieth century. Over this period the major studies of crime in

Britain were written by doctors with psychiatric training holding positions within the prison service.

Before criminology became a university-based subject in the UK it was regarded as a minor, applied medical specialism practised by a few enthusiasts working in either the penal system or the network of clinics and hospitals that surrounded it. What was decisive to the formation of criminology as a professional academic discipline in Britain was the flight of intellectuals from Nazi Europe in the 1930s. The arrival of three outstanding legally trained émigré criminologists at three elite universities introduced the criminology that had been advancing separately in Continental universities almost overnight and would dominate for the next few decades. The appointment of Leon Radzinowicz at the University of Cambridge in 1941 would lead him to establish the first Institute of Criminology in a British university in 1959; Max Grünhut at the University of Oxford in 1940 laid the foundations for a research unit that later became the Oxford Centre for Criminological Research in 1973; Hermann Mannheim at the London School of Economics (LSE) from 1935 up to his retirement in 1955 pioneered the teaching of the new discipline to undergraduate and postgraduate students alike. Despite important differences between each, they were pivotal figures transforming criminology into a discipline worthy of government funding (Hood 2004).

When the question has been posed as to why the criminologists of this period had such little interest in the sociology of deviance, the following explanation has been given:

> The answer is simple. People were perfectly aware that there were problems about the boundary between criminality and deviance but these were not of immediate concern. The position of sociology itself was not strong. In 1948 the University of London had two Professors – Ginsberg and Marshall, and Marshall was not a member of the sociology department. David Glass was given a personal Chair in 1949. LSE, moreover, was virtually the only place in the country where sociology was taught on a large scale. Then, as later, the department was split between the theoreticians led by Ginsberg and the empiricists led by Glass. Most of the latter were involved in the classic studies of social mobility then under way. Only Mannheim kept an interest in empirical criminology alive .... The intellectual concerns of criminology at the end of the 1940s were dominated by two major themes: capital punishment and psychoanalysis. (Martin 1988, 38)

There are a number of important points to be taken from this passage. The first is that sociology, as an independent academic discipline, was in a somewhat weak and diffuse form. While there are competing explanations as to why academic sociology did not develop and expand along the lines of the American, German or French experiences between 1880 and 1920, it is clear that British universities continued to ignore the academic claims of sociology between the wars. The dominance of the LSE was reinforced by the system of London external degrees 'which carried the LSE definition of the sociology syllabus to the dependent provincial university colleges of Southampton, Nottingham, Leicester, Exeter and Hull' (Halsey 2004, 56). It was only in the 1950s, when these and other colleges were granted independent charters, that different approaches developed alongside new sociology departments at the civic universities of Birmingham, Liverpool, Leeds and Manchester.

Second, the passage identifies the major preoccupations animating criminology. Capital punishment was the defining political issue of the era – the Royal Commission on Capital Punishment was set up and worked from 1949 to 1953. It was the first commission on a criminological topic that included a criminologist, Radzinowicz, among its members. Legislation that would eventually lead to the abolition of capital punishment was introduced in 1965, but it was not until 1969, at the time of the final debate on abolition in Parliament, that Radzinowicz headed the list of signatories of a letter sent to *The Times* supporting abolition, 'which included the name of every academic criminologist in Britain, save one' (Morris 1988, 32). The other main issue is the way psychoanalysis dominated the 'treatment' of juvenile delinquency. A particularly influential approach was the 'maternal deprivation hypothesis', which maintained that early childhood separations from mothers and mother-figures damage a child's mental health and personality development. The assumptions and prejudices informing mother-blaming, and other ideas like 'problem families' that commanded an enormous amount of attention at the time, were subjected to withering critique by Barbara Wooton (1959) in her major assault on the medicalization of social distress.

During the 1950s the new discipline began to take academic shape. A key factor was the founding in 1950 of Britain's first specialist academic journal in this field. The *British Journal of Delinquency* insisted it would be a multidisciplinary journal, despite retaining a strong clinical focus (two of the three editors were leading psychiatrists), but controversy over the title led to its being changed in 1960 to the *British Journal of Criminology*.[3] The British Society of Criminology was established in 1953 as a space where those unhappy with the dominance of psychiatry and psychoanalysis could meet to further develop the academic, rather than clinical, focus of their activities. Over this period the British government began to fund criminological research, giving official and financial backing, further enhancing criminology's scientific status as an academic specialism. Not only did it establish its own in-house Home Office Research Unit in 1957, but government officials and ministers also helped set up the Cambridge Institute of Criminology at the elite university in 1959, under the energetic direction of Radzinowicz. Significantly, he maintained that criminology could only develop in an interdisciplinary direction, and ideally this would involve: '[a] psychiatrist, a social psychologist, a penologist, a lawyer, a statistician joining together on a combined research operation'

---

3   A year later the Howard League for Penal Reform established the *Howard Journal of Criminal Justice*, and for the next four decades these two journals were the main sites of publication for British criminologists, until the remarkable proliferation of journals from the 1990s onwards.

(Radzinowicz 1961, 177). That this list still contained no mention of sociology should not be surprising in the British context, as sociologists of this era remained largely uninterested in crime and deviance, despite the remarkable expansion of the discipline in universities during the 1950s and 1960s.

The reasons for this sociological indifference are complex, but there is much truth in Raymond Aron's assessment of the state of the discipline at the time: 'The trouble is that British sociology is essentially an attempt to make intellectual sense of the political problems of the Labour Party' (cited in Halsey 1985, 151). Sociologists of the boom period were preoccupied with the consequences, limitations and failures of the welfare state, where the pragmatism of the Fabian Society characterized much of the thinking. Fabian principles favoured gradual reform over revolutionary change, and here sociology was essentially concerned with the constraints social stratification imposed on social mobility and the enduring inequalities produced by the British class structure. Consequently, crime and deviance were regarded as somewhat peripheral to mainstream sociology. The criminological work then being produced was also unlikely to attract much interest, dominated as it still was by psychoanalysts, psychiatrists and psychologists rooted in a tradition of predicting delinquency or dedicated to humanitarian penal reform.

This field would never look quite the same again once Barbara Wooton's *Social Science and Social Pathology* (1959) had ploughed through the terrain, demolishing the pretensions to expertise of the medical, psychiatric and social work professions colonizing how anti-social behaviour was understood. On publication, the book provoked defensive reactions from the professions demolished across 400 pages of text, yet it was also greeted as a 'blistering' and 'exhilarating' achievement that 'laid bare the general poverty of criminology, showing it to be a set of rusty clichés and sloppy generalizations' (Downes 1986, 196). Although these words were written much later, David Downes was recalling his own initial response to the book, when he was just starting his own sociological career in 1959. By attempting to situate criminal conduct in a broader social setting, the key insight was that many social problems were produced by cultural conflicts in highly differentiated societies, and in this the book can be regarded as a forerunner of much that followed.[4]

Encountering Sociology

While it is fair to say that before 1965 there was virtually no British sociological work on crime and deviance, it is important to recognize the contribution of

---

4 Wooton's contribution to the developments of the social sciences in Britain does not receive the full attention it deserves, and in many respects she shares with Mills an impassioned commitment to the role of public intellectual, challenging conventional wisdoms and shaping the political landscape (see Oakley [2011] for an extensive account of her achievements).

Terrence Morris, who played a significant role in introducing American approaches that would later be reworked and transformed by sociologists in and around the National Deviancy Conference (NDC). In Morris' study of crime and delinquency in Croydon, a large town in South London, published as *The Criminal Area* (1957), he carefully situated the work in a long tradition of such area studies stretching back to the nineteenth century, and included Guerry, Quételet, and Mayhew among the precursors to his own research. In addition, he set his empirical work in a wide-ranging review of the ecological studies developed by the Chicago School and thereby initiated the rich tradition of distilling North American sociology in distinctively British settings. This was a theme that would last well into the 1970s, only to be partly displaced by a revival of interest in European critical theory. Morris and Morris (1963) also produced the first home-grown sociology of prison life and introduced concepts, debates and methods from Donald Clemmer, Gresham Sykes and Erving Goffman that remain pivotal to this day.

Similarly, Downes (1966) examined how far beyond the US subcultural theory extended to working-class youth growing up in East London in the early 1960s. He found that concepts like 'status frustration', 'alienation' and 'delinquent subculture' did not readily capture how the boys responded to their situation – they neither envied middle-class lives nor resented them. Instead, they dissociated themselves from the middle class-dominated worlds of school and work. Leisure provided a collective solution to their problems of remaining socially disadvantaged in a time of post-war affluence. Discontent arose when their attempts to enjoy leisure were hindered, and their offences were then typically hedonistic, revolving around drinking, fighting, joy-riding and vandalism. Downes (1988, 46) later explained how this 'attentiveness' to American debates 'reflected the marginality of sociology to the criminological tradition in Britain'. Once the expansion of higher education was well under way in the 1960s, sociology was one of the main beneficiaries, with 28 new university departments of sociology created, accompanied by 'a feverish expansion of staffing' throughout the decade (Halsey 1985, 152). This new generation were becoming increasingly disillusioned with the medico-legal character of British criminology, while the sociological profession itself remained largely uninterested in questions of crime and deviance.

The 1960s was a watershed decade. It was an era when established authority came to be challenged: from popular culture to civil rights, revolutionary upheaval was in the air, and academic disciplines also experienced profound changes. As British sociologists began to study such topics as drug taking, youth cultures and mental illness, they found themselves 'doubly marginalized' (Downes 1988, 46) by both their own discipline and orthodox criminology. In his indispensable essay on these developments, Stan Cohen recalls how a more radical approach to crime and deviance was conceived:

> In the middle of the 1960s, there were a number of young sociologists in Britain attracted to the then wholly American field in the sociology of deviance …. Official criminology was regarded with attitudes ranging from ideological condemnation

to a certain measure of boredom. But being a sociologist – often isolated in a small department – was not enough to get away from criminology; some sort of separate subculture had to be carved out within the sociological world. So, ostensibly for these reasons (though this account sounds suspiciously like colour-supplement history), seven of us met in 1968, fittingly enough in Cambridge in the middle of a Institute of Criminology conference opened by the Home Secretary. We decided to form a group to provide some sort of intellectual support for one another and to cope with collective problems of identity. (Cohen 1981/1988, 80)

The National Deviancy Conference was thus formed as a breakaway faction, and while there was no shared view of what it was for, it was very clear what it was against. This opposition transformed the field into the site of exciting, formidable and urgent political questions that remain central to critical criminology.

The seven founding members were Stan Cohen, Kit Carson, Mary McIntosh, David Downes, Jock Young, Paul Rock and Ian Taylor, each of whom have since shaped sociological understandings of crime, deviance and social control in significant ways. One indication of the incredible intellectual ferment is that in the first five years of the NDC, from 1968 to 1973, there were 63 speakers from Britain at 14 conferences, who between them produced just under 100 books on diverse topics (Young 1998, 16), ranging from the phenomenology of suicide to industrial sabotage, as well as a series of classic analyses of class and youth that are among the main legacies of the NDC. The initial aim was to establish a forum including not only academics, but also activists involved in militant social work, radical prisoners' groups, the anti-psychiatry movement and campaigners against state violence. Soon conflict and division would characterize the group as tensions rose over the different directions critical work should take – but not before the approaches pioneered at the NDC became established and institutionalized themselves. By the time of the last conference in 1979 they had fractured along the same rifts as sociology more generally, acrimoniously disputing the merits of Marxist, feminist and Foucauldian approaches then dominant. Ironically, this was just as Margaret Thatcher came to power with a radical right-wing government, which was intent on advancing a free market vision of society while successfully capturing the terrain of law and order politics for the coming decade.

It is also no accident that the NDC was born in that other tumultuous year, 1968, when revolutionary uprisings and street demonstrations forged a utopian optimism among radical political movements. From the beginning the group was a dynamic mix of anarchists, interactionists, Marxists and phenomenologists committed to transforming the field of criminology from a science of social control into a struggle for social justice. Indeed, many defined themselves as anti-criminologists, so strong was the opposition to the establishment orthodoxy. Similar radical approaches also developed across Europe, especially in Scandinavia, and also in North America, most notably at the Berkley School of Criminology at the University of California, where the Union of Radical Criminologists was founded in 1971. Although the sociology of the NDC was at first quite derivative of

American deviancy theory, there was also a strong New Left influence, especially from British socialist historians like Perry Anderson, Eric Hobsbawm, Sheila Rowbotham and E.P. Thompson, each of whom provided a 'history from below' and understood culture as a 'way of struggle' between classes.

While not completely sharing Anderson's (1968) argument on English intellectual culture, Cohen (1981/1988) did find his diagnosis helpful in explaining why sociology in Britain showed little interest in crime and deviance. This was due partly to a certain parochialism characterizing much thinking, but also a more fundamental failure to grasp what sociology is about. In Anderson's withering assessment the conservative, pragmatic and individualistic traditions of British history have not produced a creative or critical intellectual elite:

> To this day, despite the recent belated growth of sociology as a formal discipline in England, the record of listless mediocrity and wizened provincialism is unrelieved. The subject is still largely a poor cousin of 'social work' and 'social administration', the dispirited descendants of Victorian charity. (Anderson 1968, 8)

According to Cohen (1981/1988, 70), the weakness of sociology is overstated here (and has been contested by others), but the accusation that not only is there a lack of a tradition of revolutionary thought, but a lack of any major intellectual traditions at all – resulting in the 'amateur, muddling-along ethos of British life combined with the Fabian type of pragmatism' that conspired to associate the study of crime and deviance with social work and humanitarian reform.

The critique here recalls Mills' (1943/1963) study of the professional ideology of social pathologists, which regarded deviance as a kind of diseased state and unhealthy maladjustment. Here he insisted that those sociologists who focus on deviation from norms as an instance of social disorganization were blinded to the fundamental problems posed by power and the larger historical context. Instead, he argued that the concept of social deviation was rooted in a particular vision of middle-class morality that advocated piecemeal reform and operated as a conservative 'propaganda for conformity' (Mills 1943/1963, 549). He returns to this theme in *The Sociological Imagination* where the field is located in a discussion of 'liberal practicality' that is accompanied by a 'dogma of a pluralist confusion of causes' (Mills 1959, 85) which is both apolitical and un-sociological. For Mills this perspective espoused a narrow-minded ideal of Protestant small-town America that too often focused on individual failings at the expense of social structure.

Yet his interventions were also to expose deep-seated tensions that few wanted to explore further: 'They effectively planted a huge question mark over the emergent sociology of deviance in all its varieties, a mark which was to remain in place for the next thirty years, like a dark inexplicable shadow which everyone duly ignored for fear of touching it' (Sumner 1994, 157; emphasis in original).

I will return to this theme below, but it is important to note that much of the sociology in Britain at this time was in this tradition of social administration that Mills (1959, 84) dismissed as a movement turning the 'troubles of lower-class people into issues for middle-class publics' that later split 'into the limited concerns of social work, associated charities, child welfare, and prison reform' on the one hand, and into various academic specialities on the other. Under these circumstances his work was initially seen as an attack on British sociology, and leading figures sought to defend the discipline while taking the arguments fairly seriously (Brewer 2004, 327–8). To the many who first encountered sociology in the 1960s, during the major establishment of the discipline in higher education, the book articulated a powerful vision of what sociology could be. And it is for this reason that John Holmwood (2010, 655) maintains *The Sociological Imagination* had a much greater impact in the UK than in the USA, helping to give the new discipline a particular sensibility.

However, it is important to recognize that the indigenous sociology developing in the 1960s took two different directions. One sought intellectual credibility and aspired to fit 'scientific, academic, or professional self-images into which certain topics were not responsible enough to be fitted', while to the 'hard radicals ... deviants were not really politically interesting' (Cohen 1981/1988, 78). By the end of the decade, as sociology rapidly expanded in British universities: '[the] great appeal of the NDC was not only to sociologists of crime in search of a congenial forum, but also to younger sociologists who saw in deviance an escape route from the positivist methods and functionalist orthodoxy of much British sociology' (Downes 1988, 47). To a new generation caught up in the heady political and cultural upheavals of the 1960s, the NDC offered a genuinely emancipating setting for those committed to social justice.

Among the rich diversity of approaches, theories and methods developed in and around the NDC, the strand focusing on youth and class is especially influential. In both Cohen (1972/2002) and Young's (1971) work there was an emphasis on the much-publicized conflicts between youth subcultures and Establishment forces in the 1960s. Both were early formulators of the much-used and abused concept of moral panic. Stuart Hall and his colleagues at the Birmingham Centre for Contemporary Cultural Studies (BCCCS) explained how political struggles and ideological coding were integral to the process of defining a social group as deviant. The collection *Resistance through Rituals* (Hall and Jefferson 1975) brought together papers stressing the creativity of subcultures, as opposed to the wooden determinism of earlier American theorization, in a sophisticated understanding of class conflict. Here post-war youth cultures are seen as collective responses to the material conditions posed by structural disadvantage. These and other themes were later developed in *Policing the Crisis* (Hall et al. 1978), the landmark text written at the BCCCS, which developed an explicitly Marxist account of crime initially suggested in *The New Criminology* (Taylor et al. 1973).

It is worth pausing to consider the achievements of *The New Criminology*, as it is the most well known and most controversial product of the NDC. Written by three sociologists, it successfully differentiated radical European analysis from the American study of deviance. It did so by demolishing the orthodox positions in criminology (especially the positivist focus on individual and social pathology), sociology (here the target was the abstract empiricism of post-war British Fabianism and the mandarism that accompanied it, as well as the functionalist, labelling and subcultural traditions of American sociology) and Marxism (the critique concentrates on classical Marxist understandings of crime as a demoralized response by the 'dangerous classes' to their bleak economic situation). In effect, all prior conceptions of crime and deviance were to be abandoned, to be replaced by their vision of a 'fully social theory of deviance' sketched out in the conclusion of the book.

The 'formal elements' of the theory involve 'a political economy of criminal action, and of the reaction it incites, and for a politically informed social psychology of these ongoing social dynamics' (Taylor et al. 1973, 279). Few did attempt to deliver on the radical manifesto, but many were drawn into the collision with the latest developments in European Marxism that the book inspired. Much later, Young (1998, 28) conceded that 'by far the most complete expression of such an approach' is to be found in *Policing the Crisis* (Hall et al. 1978), not because the authors set out to rigorously follow their requirements, but because they explicitly combined deviancy theory with Marxist analysis. The book examines 'why and how the themes of *race, crime* and *youth* – condensed into the image of "mugging" – come to serve as the articulator of the crisis, as its ideological conductor' (Hall et al. 1978, viii; emphasis in original). It draws together the BCCCS's work on youth subcultures, media representation and ideological analysis in a magisterial account of the hegemonic crisis in Britain, which began in the late 1960s and anticipates the victory of Margaret Thatcher's authoritarian 'law and order' programme in the 1980s.

Taking Sides

Critics from all sides quickly highlighted flaws in these radical directions. Socialists worried that the 'romanticism of crime, the recognition in the criminal of a rebel "alienated" from society is, for Marxism, a dangerous political ideology' (Hirst 1975, 218). Others suggested the failings exposed the inability of the Left to produce any compelling solutions to the problems facing Britain (Mungham 1980). Mainstream voices retorted that the radicals had ignored 'the large measure of consensus, even among the oppressed, in condemning the theft and violence that makes up the bulk of traditional crime' (Radzinowicz and King 1979, 87). Faced with these objections, a bitter divide came to split the Left during the 1980s and 1990s along an 'idealist–realist' polarity. Left realists spoke to social democratic principles and emphasized the need to take crime seriously, insisting that left idealists regarded 'the war against crime as a sidetrack from the class struggle, at best an illusion invented to sell news, at worst an attempt to make the poor scapegoats by blaming their brutalizing circumstances on themselves' (Lea and Young 1984, 1). They advocated reformist, not revolutionary, change and were committed to improving social relations in the inner cities.

Among the most damaging was the total absence of women from those committed to a 'fully social theory of deviance' and a lack of any structural analysis of the consequences of male domination. The beginning of feminist scholarship in British criminology is usually dated from Carol Smart's *Women, Crime and Criminology* (1976), which set down an important marker suggesting that 'criminology' was the radical idea, while 'deviance' was beginning to look rather old-fashioned. By the end of the 1980s she could see no room for feminism within criminology and decided to leave the field altogether (Smart 1990). It is conventional now to chart feminist scholarship in criminology through distinct phases, yet feminist perspectives still lie largely outside mainstream criminology.

This brief account only highlights a few of the main directions taken in the 1970s, but it should be clear that this was a turbulent, productive and exciting era. According to one of the central figures, it 'was a dizzying scene, more a paradigmatic kaleidoscope than a clear-cut progression of superior paradigms delivering a knock-out blow to the inferior' (Downes 1988, 49). Not all these changes resulted from the NDC, even though it can rightly claim to have had considerable impact in British sociology. Cohen (1981/1988, 84–6) concludes his review of the then state of play by pointing to other sub-fields of sociology hospitable to new deviancy ideas. These include education, medicine, mass media, welfare and social policy, as well as cultural studies and a revival of interest in the study of law as a social institution. Nevertheless, the mainstream institutional bases of British criminology remained largely untroubled by the theoretical quarrels and political disputes associated with the new perspectives.

If anything, administrative criminology – empirical research funded by and conducted within government – grew in size and significance over this period, most noticeably at the Home Office Research and Planning Unit, but also in the research branches of the Prison Department, Metropolitan Police and related state agencies, which all became more skilled and prolific. The sense of conflict and schism helped to give a 'useful order to an emerging field' (Rock 1988, 191), while the new perspectives themselves became institutionalized and respectable. In a further irony, it was radical, sceptical and critical versions of criminology that fuelled the remarkable growth of the discipline in the decades to come. As Pat Carlen recently put it:

> it was only as result of the advent of critical criminology that, in the United Kingdom at any rate, the discipline of criminology was reinvigorated sufficiently to put up a successful fight to become recognized and institutionalized as a university discipline independent of its parent disciplines of law and/or sociology. (Carlen 2011, 98)

This expansion has been particularly striking in the UK. Although Carlen set up the first undergraduate degree programme in criminology at Keele University in 1991, she would never have predicted that today some 94 universities would teach criminology and criminal justice in single or joint schemes.

Such an expansion would have appeared even more unlikely in the 1980s, when the decade saw major cuts to the level of funding across the social sciences and, at best, consolidation. Academic criminology remained a small social world, while teaching was restricted to a handful of postgraduate courses and specialist options in the final year of law or sociology degrees. On any measure, the rapid expansion of criminology over the last couple of decades has been remarkable. The major stimulus for this growth has been the successful creation of criminology as an autonomous, independent subject that no longer regards itself as a subsidiary of the legal, social or medical sciences (Peters 2006). Criminology has very quickly established itself within mass higher education systems, exhibiting an impressive ability to attract students, scholars and research grants.

In the UK the rapid expansion of academic posts over the last twenty or so years has been accompanied by a publishing boom where handbooks, textbooks, monographs, edited collections and journal articles now proliferate. This is partly due to the pressure of various government research assessment regimes causing academic overproduction across the sector, but the period has also seen increasing internal specialization of the subject as criminology takes on the organizational qualities of an academic discipline (Loader and Sparks 2012, 8). Such institutional forces include the growth of separate departments, new degree schemes, graduate research funding, large annual conferences and the appointment of researchers whose entire higher education experience has only been in criminology. The creation of such specialist journals as *Policing and Society* (founded in 1990), *Theoretical Criminology* (1997), *Global Crime* (1999), *Punishment and Society* (1999), *Criminology and Criminal Justice* (2001), *Youth Justice* (2001), *Crime, Media, Culture* (2005) and *Feminist Criminology* (2006) are indicative of this trend and give a sense of the diverse sub-fields in the discipline.

Indeed, the sociology of deviance had come under sustained attack for its internal contradictions and inability to confront larger questions of power, control and ideology. These issues were exemplified in Alvin Gouldner's scathing critique of the 'zookeepers of deviance' who presented 'man-on-his-back', rather than 'man-fighting-back' (Gouldner 1968/1973, 38–9), which was a major influence on *The New Criminology*. However, the seeds of destruction had already been sown by Mills (1943/1963) in the 1940s, when he demonstrated how the concept of social deviation was derived from a particular vision of middle-class morality, and these arguments were revisited in an influential article by Alexander Liazos (1972). Here he maintained that despite all the advances in the field over the last couple of decades, the focus still remained on the individual deviant, rather than on the larger social, historical, political and economic contexts. In the final analysis, he was left to conclude that 'we should banish the concept of "deviance" and speak of oppression, conflict, persecution, and suffering' (Liazos 1972, 119).

This offer was widely taken up by critics in the 1970s. The demise of the concept is captured in books like Geoffrey Pearson's *The Deviant Imagination* (1975), which argued that the romanticization of crime, deviance and illness in what he called 'misfit sociology' was ultimately a dead end. Although the concept of deviance was further reworked at the BCCCS, it quickly became subsumed under broader debates surrounding culture, ideology and politics. By the 1980s it is clear that cultural studies had moved on to questions of difference, identity and postmodernism, while a major 'obituary' from the 1990s claimed the entire 'field had died' (Sumner 1994, ix). Arguably, the metaphor of transgression has come to replace the central concerns in the sociology of deviance, where old questions are put in a fresh light. These still speak to the relationship between the centre and the margins, identity and difference, the normal and the pathological, order and excess, and ultimately the desire to transcend limits (Jenks 2003, 5). It is also no accident that these ideas have recently resurfaced in cultural criminology (Ferrell et al. 2008), which has done much to emphasize the role of image, style and meaning in subcultures and the mediated processes through which crime and punishment are constructed.

At the same time, cultural criminology becomes yet another instance of the internal specialization and increasing fragmentation of the criminological enterprise, where: '[the] field of inquiry seems at risk of sinking into a set of cliques where criminologists read the work of others who think like them, write for those very same people and publish only in the journals that they and their colleagues are already reading' (Bosworth and Hoyle 2011, 3). A similar point has been made by Dick Hobbs, who identifies the current 'tendency of criminologists to Balkanize themselves, often preaching to the converted via specialist outlets and citation clubs, has drastically reduced the potential impact of their scholarship, exacerbating the retreat from sociology, and severely restricting criminology's range' (2012, 262). Equally, this is a major problem for sociology, where whole sub-fields of the discipline migrate and establish themselves as new areas or applied subjects, as health studies, social policy, media studies and others have done in the UK – at some cost to the overall coherence, institutional reputation and well-being of the discipline (Holmwood 2010).

The rapid expansion of criminology is not just restricted to the UK, it has been especially pronounced in the USA. According to the American Sociological Association (ASA), criminology and criminal justice majors now outweigh those enrolled on sociology programmes by some two-thirds (Hannah-Moffat 2011, 450). In the USA the movement towards independent criminology and criminal justice programmes was already well advanced, and many were vocational rather than academic in orientation. State universities and colleges led the way in providing professional criminal justice education, where sponsorship from the Justice Department's Law Enforcement Assistance Agency has been pivotal, but this poses awkward questions about what criminology is for and whether it is actually an academic discipline at all (Garland 2011). The institutional separation of criminology from sociology has also occurred at graduate level, while the major professional associations have grown much larger than the crime-related sections of the ASA, and these have been instrumental in strengthening the organizational base of their new discipline (Savelsberg and Sampson 2002, 101).

It is not simply that criminology has divorced itself from sociology in the USA. Sociology has also 'pulled away from criminology, particularly as taught and studied at elite institutions' (Short, with Hughes 2007, 632). The expansion of an applied vocational criminology has had an adverse impact on the subject's intellectual status and hastened the demise of the specialism in the sociology departments at the leading research universities (Garland 2011, 311). Despite the centrality of research on crime and deviance in many of these departments in the first half of the twentieth century, a certain disdain for the subject matter has long been in evidence. As the sociologist Gilbert Geis observed: 'scholars at so prestigious an institution as Columbia University barely deign to work in the field of crime' (1974, 287). The tensions between the disciplines were captured much later by Geis (with Mary Dodge), who would write that:

> criminology and criminal justice split off from sociology, where they were regarded – along with marriage and the family – as waifs, tolerated because they kept enrolments high. Their later structural independence demonstrated clearly enough that the problems they addressed often were considerably more significant than the more esoteric menus offered by their parent discipline. Indeed, as sociology has tended to wane, criminology and criminal justice studies have flourished. (Geis and Dodge 2002, xliii)

This passage captures the kind of populist, lowbrow regard in which criminology is held by some sociologists, but important questions remain about the consequences of such 'independence'.

In Europe the pattern is more mixed, but since 2000 the European Society of Criminology has been important in helping to expand criminology across some fifty countries, hosting a large annual conference and publishing the *European Journal of Criminology*. Aside from these developments, criminology departments and degrees have rapidly increased in Canada, Australia, New Zealand and South Africa, with many beginning to appear in India, China and Asia (Loader and Sparks 2012, 9–10). Criminology is now taught around the world, and while the history, character and disposition of the subject varies considerably (Becker and Wetzell 2006), it is important to consider the implications of these changes.

Criminology as a Discipline

From the outset, many of the leading figures insisted that criminology is not a discipline, and the entire NDC movement can be seen as a form of 'anti-criminology', which has gradually had to 'absorb the implications of its own creations' (Cohen 1988, 16). One influential definition has it that criminology is a 'rendezvous subject', where various branches of learning gather around a shared substantive theme, sometimes overlapping, but more often moving past one another in different directions (Rock 2011, 20). On this reading, criminology is simply a meeting point for the traffic in ideas between researchers schooled in the more fundamental disciplines of economics, history, law, philosophy, psychology and sociology. For some, contemporary criminology has all the organizational trappings of an academic discipline, but has no intellectual core around which the diverse approaches and specialty areas can cohere. It has a 'subject matter but no unique methodological commitment or paradigmatic theoretical framework' (Savelsberg and Sampson 2002, 101), and the worry is that an 'independent criminology' will further 'fragment into distinct specialisms' with an increasingly inward focus resulting in 'negative consequences for collective learning' (Garland 2011, 312). Criminology's growing isolation from the more basic disciplines comes with great costs; as it disengages from them it has opened itself up to greater government intrusion and runs the risk of losing academic status as a university subject.

In the US context, Andrew Abbott has noted how 'status differences' work to keep certain hierarchies in place: 'Criminology departments hire from sociology departments, but seldom vice versa' (2001, 134). Here conventional disciplines have been able to maintain their dominance, despite a plethora of applied subject areas growing around them. Abbott explains how a fairly long historical process has shaped a structure of flexibly stable core of disciplines, surrounded by heady blur of interdisciplinarity, where the conventional disciplines stand in superiority, as it is here that the original, transformative work takes place and where reputations are forged through a process of 'settlement', by which he means the 'link between a discipline and what it knows' (2001, 136). Academics compete with one another through redefining each other's work. He gives the example of how English professors claim superiority over anthropologists and sociologists in the interpretation of modern cultural artefacts like advertisements, as they are textual phenomena and ultimately subject to the 'master' discipline of English. This movement is rarely a two-way exchange of ideas, and developments in the applied field are seldom translated back into the primary field. Crucially, the applied areas are not self-reproducing, but rely on the 'continued importation, and, in consequence on the health of the exporter disciplines' (Holmwood 2010, 646). The strong departmental structure of the US university system has helped to sustain the disciplinary status of sociology, but the prospects in the UK are bleaker in John Holmwood's reckoning, due to the twin threats of interdisciplinarity and the audit culture regulating higher education in the country.

These new systems of governance have also been accompanied by a growing political scepticism toward scholarly expertise, which has altered the once close relationships between policy-orientated criminologists and government officials, provoking a 'growing rift between Home Office and academic researchers' (Newburn 2011, 512). If central government is no longer an important patron of criminological research, then other sponsors have rose to prominence (including the police, penal professionals, pressure groups, private security firms and other non-governmental organizations), yet dangers remain over the readiness of criminologists to produce 'serviceable knowledge for rationalizing the operations of the already powerful' (Loader and Sparks 2012, 15). The struggle is a longstanding one, and confronted by every discipline that seeks to main academic integrity while pursuing research funding and some degree of real-world relevance.

On this last point, one of the defining features of British criminology has been a humanitarian commitment to reforming the system, and this aspiration continues to attract many to criminology. Equally, the 'romantic, voyeur-like appeal of the subject matter' (Cohen 1981/1988, 81) should not be underestimated. Indeed, critics of the sociology of deviance concluded that it was simply the tawdry study of exotic difference, which problematically ignored crimes of the corporate economy and the state's own violence (Liazos 1972). This was an important intervention, and drew attention to the limits of state-defined criminality, which then as now is the result of political processes and offers a reminder that legal categories are social constructions. Nevertheless, this titillating quality is another reason why the field is often accused of lowbrow populism, but it is these attractions to 'lives that transgress' that actually makes criminology a powerful stimulus to the 'sociological imagination' (Braithwaite 2011, viii). This is an important point, and one that needs to be emphasized as criminology fragments and loses its 'sociological soul' (Hobbs 2012, 262).

It should be clear that I am against the increasing 'independence' of criminology from sociology, but it is worth asking: Just what should a sociological criminology look like? Here the pioneering American sociologist Edwin Sutherland's (1924, 3) definition of criminology as a body of knowledge that regards crime as a social phenomenon, which studies the 'processes of making laws, of breaking laws, and of reacting toward the breaking of laws', remains unsurpassed. He poses three deceptively simple questions: Why are laws made? Why are they broken? What should be done about this? Yet it is a formulation that calls for an 'intellectual perspective that lies outside the ideology and interests of those who run the crime-control system and the academics they hire to help them' (Cohen 1988, 9). Crime and punishment are bound up with wider social processes, and while there will always be contested views of what criminology is, these are state-defined categories and practices, which intimately tie criminology to government in quite troubling ways (Garland 2011, 305). One of the central tasks of a sociological criminology is to identify these links and the problems that flow from them, even as the relationships change and become more obscure.

None of this is to say that sociology is the only discipline criminology should be seeking a renewed relationship with; there are no doubt productive encounters to be had with its other constitutive disciplines. In the effort to establish its own disciplinary credentials, criminology has lost some of its intellectual energy, and it is worth remembering that it has nearly always been animated and enlivened by ideas imported from elsewhere. As stated at the outset of this chapter, the metaphor of 'rendezvous subject' is a well used one, and it is the traffic in multidisciplinary approaches that has sustained post-war British criminology, but which has also left it prone to a bewildering eclecticism and disorganized fragmentation. Under these circumstances, the growing separation of criminology from sociology is to be resisted; instead, a renewed focus on how dialogues across many disciplines can be facilitated is the way forward.

Conclusion

The importance of *The Sociological Imagination* today is that it offers a particular sensibility that is inevitably bound up with critique. However, the expansion of criminology has 'marginalised critical writing and reduced theory from a live contested quality that ran like a thread through all aspects of scholarship to a niche or specialism' (Hobbs 2012, 262). This tendency was identified over fifteen years ago in the USA, where Elliot Currie (1998, 18) distinguished between three divisions in American criminology: a large, technocratic, 'mainstream' that rarely ventures into the public arena; a small, but extremely vocal and influential right-wing set of commentators, and a slightly larger radical ghetto, which is content to go 'along with the definition of itself as a fringe, or as a kind of sub-specialization within the larger field'. Of course, as I explained at the beginning of the chapter, the great irony is that the force of Mills' scathing assessment of sociology has itself been lost over the years, domesticated and tamed. Few today practise the sociological imagination in the way that Mills intended (Goode 2008, 251), which is fundamentally a critique of the discipline itself and its relationship to others.

The way contemporary commentators on the current state of sociology mourn its decline and fragmentation has been challenged by Michael Burawoy (2005), who points out that what has happened instead is that sociology has been enlivened by new voices. A similar point has been made by Liz Stanley (2005), writing on the UK, who argues that the 'declinists' are really bemoaning their loss of prestige and authority as the discipline has become home to new and radical voices from the margins. For Abbot (2001) this fragmenting is part of the normal 'chaos of disciplines', and rather than being unique to the present and something to worry about, is instead a sign of health and well-being, as disciplines cycle through and around an inevitable pattern of core principles. In his discussion of these positions Holmwood (2010) makes the important point that the fragmentation of sociology in the UK is also driven by the neoliberal commodification of higher education, which has harmful consequences for sociology that problematize these more optimistic assessments of where the discipline is heading. Furthermore, there is rarely any agreement on what constitutes the organizing core of sociology, which means that it constantly 'has to be achieved against an internal tendency to self-subversion', and this might be best seen as 'a particular kind of "dissensus"' (Holmwood 2010, 649–50).

In Mills (1959) the sociological imagination is conceived as occupying the intersection of biography, history and social structure. It is a way of thinking that is not just restricted to those who 'work in Departments of Sociology or to card-carrying sociologists' (Scott 2005, 3.2), but all three dimensions are indispensable if the sociological imagination is to flourish as a unifying force. What is clear is that much sociology, 'core' and otherwise, has proceeded as 'though history and biography are optional extras' (Stanley 2005, 5.5). For Stanley the sociological imagination has the potential to be an organizing principle around which UK sociology can cohere, while remaining open to the different ways in which the term might be developed. By distilling a sense of crisis in mid-twentieth-century sociology, Mills' ambition was to help change it by rescuing it from the combined perils of grand theory and abstracted empiricism, which were thwarting sociology from realizing its real, liberating promise. In this regard, criminology should be seen as a province of sociology, and some of its main concerns lie at the very centre of sociological thinking. It is this core that is in urgent need of rediscovery if criminology is to regain intellectual energy and vitality.

References

Abbott, A. 2001. *Chaos of Disciplines*. Chicago, IL: University of Chicago Press.

Anderson, P. 1968. 'Components of the National Culture.' *New Left Review* 50: 3–59.

Aronowitz, S. 2003. 'A Mills Revival?' *Logos* 2(3): 1–27.

Bauman, Z. 2000. 'The Man from Waco.' *Timesonline*, 7 July.

Becker, H. 1994. 'Professional Sociology: The Case of C. Wright Mills.' In *The Democratic Imagination*, edited by R. Rist, 175–87. New Brunswick, NJ: Transaction Books.

Becker, P. and R. Wetzell, eds. 2006. *Criminals and Their Scientists: The History of Criminology in Historical Perspective*. Cambridge: Cambridge University Press.

Binns, D. 1977. *Beyond the Sociology of Conflict*. London: Macmillan.

Bosworth, M. and C. Hoyle. 2011. 'What is Criminology? An Introduction.' In *What is Criminology?*, edited by M. Bosworth and C. Hoyle, 1–12. Oxford: Oxford University Press.

Braithwaite, J. 2011. 'Foreword.' In *What is Criminology?*, edited by M. Bosworth and C. Hoyle, vii–ix. Oxford: Oxford University Press.

Brewer, J. 2004. 'Imagining *The Sociological Imagination*.' *British Journal of Sociology* 35(3): 317–33.

Burawoy, M. 2005. 'Provincializing the Social Sciences.' In *The Politics of Method in the Human Sciences*, edited by G. Steinmetz, 508–26. Durham, NC: Duke University Press.

Carlen, P. 2011. 'Against Evangelism in Academic Criminology: For Criminology as a Scientific Art.' In *What is Criminology?*, edited by M. Bosworth and C. Hoyle, 95–108. Oxford: Oxford University Press.

Carrabine, E. 2013. 'Criminology, Deviance and Sociology.' In *History of Sociology in Britain*, edited by J. Holmwood and J. Scott, 459–87. London: Palgrave.

Chernilo, D. 2006. 'Social Theory's Methodological Nationalism: Myth and Reality.' *European Journal of Social Theory* 9(1): 5–22.

Cohen, S. 1972/2002. *Folk-devils and Moral Panics: The Creation of the Mods and Rockers*. London: Routledge.

———. 1981/1988. 'Footprints in the Sand: A Further Report on Criminology and the Sociology of Deviance in Britain.' In *Against Criminology*, 67–92. Oxford: Transaction Books.

———. 1988. 'Against Criminology.' In *Against Criminology*, 45–57. Oxford: Transaction Books.

Currie, E. 1998. *Crime and Punishment in America*. New York: Metropolitan Books.

Dandaneau, S. 2007. 'Mills, C. Wright (1916–62).' In *The Blackwell Encyclopaedia of Sociology*, edited by G. Ritzer and M. Malden. Oxford: Blackwell.

Denzin, N. 1990. 'Presidential Address on "The Sociological Imagination" Revisited.' *Sociological Quarterly* 31(1): 1–22.

Downes, D. 1966. *The Delinquent Solution*. London: Routledge and Kegan Paul.

———. 1986. 'Back to Basics: Reflections on Barbara Wooton's "Twelve Criminological Hypotheses."' In *Barbara Wooton: Social Sciences and Public Policy, Essays in Her Honour*, edited by P. Bean and D. Whyte, 195–214. London: Tavistock.

———. 1988. 'The Sociology of Crime and Social Control in Britain, 1960–1987.' In *A History of British Criminology*, edited by P. Rock. Oxford: Clarendon Press.

Ferrell, J., K. Hayward and J. Young. 2008. *Cultural Criminology: An Invitation*. London: Sage.

Fletcher, R. 1960. 'Book Review of the *Sociological Imagination*.' *British Journal of Sociology* 11(2): 169–70.

Garland, D. 1988. 'British Criminology before 1935.' In *A History of British Criminology*, edited by P. Rock, 1–17. Oxford: Clarendon Press.

———. 2002. 'Of Crimes and Criminals: The Development of Criminology in Britain.' In *The Oxford Handbook of Criminology*, 3rd edn, edited by M. Maguire, R. Morgan and R. Reiner, 17–68. Oxford: Oxford University Press.

———. 2011. 'Criminology's Place in the Academic Field.' In *What is Criminology?*, edited by M. Bosworth and C. Hoyle, 298–317. Oxford: Oxford University Press.

Geis, G. 1974. 'Avocational Crime.' In *Handbook of Criminology*, edited by D. Glaser, 273–98. Chicago, IL: Rand McNally.

——— and M. Dodge, eds. 2002. *Lessons of Criminology*. Cincinnati, OH: Anderson Publishing.

Gitlin, T. 2007. 'C. Wright Mills, Free Radical.' *Peace & Conflict Studies*, Institute of Sociology, University of Münster. Accessed 6 June 2015. http://www.uni-muenster.de/PeaCon/dgs-mills/mills-texte/GitlinMills.htm.

Goode, E. 2008. 'From the Western to the Murder Mystery: The Sociological Imagination of C. Wright Mills.' *Sociological Spectrum* 28: 237–53.

Gouldner, A. 1968/1973. 'The Sociologist as Partisan: Sociology and the Welfare State.' In *For Sociology*, 27–68. London: Allen Lane.

Guerry, A. 1833. *Essai sur la statistique morale de la France*. Paris: Crochard.

Hall, S. and T. Jefferson, eds. 1975. *Resistance through Rituals*. London: Hutchinson.

Hall, S., C. Critcher, T. Jefferson, J. Clarke and B. Roberts. 1978. *Policing the Crisis: Mugging, the State and Law and Order*. London: Macmillan.

Halsey, A.H. 1985. 'Provincials and Professionals: The British Post-war Sociologists.' In *Essays on the History of British Sociological Research*, edited by M. Bulmer, 52–69. Cambridge: Cambridge University Press.

———. 2004. *A History of Sociology in Britain*. Oxford: Oxford University Press.

Hannah-Moffat, K. 2011. 'Criminological Cliques: Narrowing Dialogues, Institutional Protectionism, and the Next Generation.' In *What is Criminology?*, edited by M. Bosworth and C. Hoyle, 440–55. Oxford: Oxford University Press.

Hayden, T. 2006. *Radical Nomad: C. Wright Mills and His Times*. Boulder, CO: Paradigm.

Hearn, F. 1985. *Reason and Freedom in Sociological Thought*. London: Allen and Unwin.

Hirst, P. 1975. 'Marx and Engels on Law, Crime and Morality.' In *Critical Criminology*, edited by I. Taylor, P. Walton and J. Young, 203–32. London: Routledge and Kegan Paul.

Hobbs, D. 2012. '"It Was Never about the Money": Market Society, Organised Crime and UK Criminology.' In *New Directions in Criminological Theory*, edited by S. Hall and S. Winlow, 257–75. London: Routledge.

Holmwood, J. 2010. 'Sociology's Misfortune: Disciplines, Interdisciplinarity and the Impact of Audit Culture.' *The British Journal of Sociology* 61(4): 639–58.

Homans, G. 1960. 'Book Review of *The Sociological Imagination*.' *American Journal of Sociology* 65(5): 517–18.

Hood, 2004. 'Hermann Mannheim and Max Grünhut: Criminological Pioneers in London and Oxford.' *British Journal of Criminology* 44(4): 469–95.

Jacoby, R. 2000. 'False Indignation.' *New Left Review* 2: 154–9.

Jenks, C. 2003. *Transgression*. London: Routledge.

Kerr, K. 2009. *Postmodern Cowboy: C. Wright Mills and a New 21st Century Sociology*. Boulder, CO: Paradigm.

Kolb, W. 1960. 'Book Review of *The Sociological Imagination*.' *American Sociological Review* 29(5): 966–9.

Lea, J. and J. Young. 1984. *What is to be Done about Law and Order?* London: Pluto Press.

Liazos, A. 1972. 'The Poverty of the Sociology of Deviance: Nuts, Sluts and Perverts.' *Social Problems* 20(1): 103–20.

Loader, I. and R. Sparks. 2012. 'Situating Criminology: On the Production and Consumption of Knowledge about Crime and Justice.' In *The Oxford Handbook of Criminology*, 5th edn, edited by M. Maguire, R. Morgan and R. Reiner, 3–38. Oxford: Clarendon Press.

Martin, J. 1988. 'The Development of Criminology in Britain: 1948–1960.' In *A History of British Criminology*, edited by P. Rock, 35–44. Oxford: Clarendon Press.

Mills, C. 1943/1963. 'The Professional Ideology of Social Pathologists.' In *Power, Politics and People: The Collected Essays of C. Wright Mills*, edited by I. Horowitz, 525–52. New York: Oxford University Press.

———. 1959. *The Sociological Imagination*. Oxford: Oxford University Press.

Morris, T. 1957. *The Criminal Area*. London: Routledge and Kegan Paul.

———. 1988. 'British Criminology: 1935–1948.' In *A History of British Criminology*, edited by P. Rock, 20–34. Oxford: Clarendon Press.

——— and P. Morris 1963. *Pentonville: A Sociological Study of an English Prison*. London: Routledge and Kegan Paul.

Mungham, G. 1980. 'The Career of a Confusion: Radical Criminology in Britain.' In *Radical Criminology: The Coming Crisis*, edited by J. Inciardi, 19–34. Beverly Hills, CA: Sage.

Newburn, T. 2011. 'Criminology and Government: Some Reflections on Recent Developments in England.' In *What is Criminology?*, edited by M. Bosworth and C. Hoyle, 502–17. Oxford: Oxford University Press.

Oakes, G. and A. Vidich. 1999. *Collaboration, Reputation and Ethics in American Academic Life: Hans H. Gerth and C. Wright Mills*. Urbana, IL: University of Illinois Press.

Oakley, A. 2011. *A Critical Woman: Barbara Wooton, Social Science and Public Policy in the Twentieth Century*. London: Bloomsbury.

Pearson, G. 1975. *The Deviant Imagination*. London: Macmillan.

Peters, T. 2006. 'The Academic Status of Criminology.' *International Annals of Criminology* 44(1): 53–63.

Quételet, A. 1835. *Sur l'homme et le développement de ses facultés*. Paris: Bachlier.

Radzinowicz, L. 1961. *In Search of Criminology*. London: Heinemann.

——— and R. King. 1979. *The Growth of Crime: The International Experience*. Harmondsworth: Penguin.

Rafter, N.H., ed. 2009. *Origins of Criminology: Readings from the Nineteenth Century*. London: Routledge.

Rock, P. 1988. 'The Present State of Criminology in Britain.' In *A History of British Criminology*, edited by P. Rock, 58–69. Oxford: Clarendon Press.

———. 1994. 'Introduction.' In *History of Criminology*, edited by P. Rock, xi–xxix. Aldershot: Ashgate Publishing.

———. 2011. '"What Have We Done?" Trends in Criminological Theorising.' *Acta Criminologica* 24(1):19–43.

Savelsberg, J. and R. Sampson. 2002. 'Mutual Engagement: Criminology and Sociology?' *Crime, Law and Social Change* 37(2):99–105.

Scott, J. 2005. 'Sociology and its Others: Reflections on Disciplinary Specialization and Fragmentation.' *Sociological Research Online* 10(1). Accessed 6 June 2015. http://www.socresonline.org.uk/10/1/scott.html.

Shils, E. 1960. 'Imaginary Sociology.' *Encounter* (June): 77–80.

Short, F. with L. Hughes. 2007. 'Criminology, Criminologists, and the Sociological Enterprise.' In *Sociology in America: A History*, edited by C. Calhoun, 605–38. Chicago, IL: University of Chicago Press.

Smart, C. 1976. *Women, Crime and Criminology*. London: Routledge and Kegan Paul.

———. 1990. 'Feminist Approaches to Criminology, or Postmodern Woman meets Atavistic Man.' In *Feminist Perspectives in Criminology*, edited by L. Gelsthorpe and A. Morris, 453–65. Buckingham: Open University Press.

Stanley, L. 2005. 'A Child of its Time: Hybridic Perspectives on Othering in Sociology.' *Sociological Research Online* 10(3). Accessed 6 June 2015. http://www.socresonline.org.uk/10/3/stanley.html.

Sumner, C. 1994. *The Sociology of Deviance: An Obituary*. Milton Keynes: Open University Press.

Sutherland, E. 1924. *Criminology*. Philadelphia, PA: Lippincott.

Taylor, I., P. Walton and J. Young. 1973. *The New Criminology*. London: Routledge and Kegan Paul.

Treviño, A. 2012. *The Social Thought of C. Wright Mills*. London: Sage.

Veblen, T. 1899/1953. *The Theory of the Leisure Class*. Scarborough, ON: Mentor Books.

Wooton, B. 1959. *Social Science and Social Pathology*. London: Allen and Unwin.

Young, J. 1971. *The Drugtakers*. London: Palladin.

———. 1998. 'Breaking Windows: Situating the New Criminology.' In *The New Criminology Revisited*, edited by P. Walton and J. Young, 14–46. London: Macmillan.

———. 2011. *The Criminological Imagination*. Cambridge: Polity Press.

Chapter 4

The Criminological Imagination in an Age of Global Cybernetic Power

Stephen Pfohl

It is the political task of the social scientist – as of any liberal educator – continually to translate personal troubles into public issues, and public issues into the terms of their human meaning for a variety of individuals. (Mills 1959, 166)

According to Richard Quinney: 'without critical thought we are bound to the only form of social life we know – that which currently exists. We are unable to choose a better life; our only activity is in further support of the system in which we are enslaved' (Quinney 1974, 16). This chapter brings C. Wright Mills' vision of the sociological imagination to bear upon the labour of criminology in contemporary society. In particular, it asks what it means for criminologists to work within the historical confines of what Mills theorized as 'overdeveloped' or 'postmodern' society (Mills 1959, 166). Mills was one of the first sociologists to theorize a transition in Northwestern society from the modern to the postmodern era. While other theorists pointed to the increasing importance of information to the rational organization of 'post-industrial' society, Mills pictured the 'extra-rational' allures of omnipresent technological feedback in less sanguine terms. By the late 1950s Mills used the term 'postmodern' to depict the emergence of a powerful new form of military guided social control in the years following the Second World War. This signifies a 'Fourth Epoch' of Northwest history – a time in which lived human experience enters into interactive loops of feedback with powerful new Web-based technologies of communication (Mills 1959, 166).

Some of these new information technologies amplify modern bureaucratic rationality and expert systems of surveillance, monitoring, data banking, scientific management and high-tech warfare. Others lure the self out of the 'iron cage' of modern instrumentality into fascinating flights paths of phantasm. Either way, according to Mills:

[it is not] merely that we feel we are in an epochal kind of transition, and that we struggle to grasp the outline of a new epoch we suppose ourselves to be entering .... When we try to orient ourselves – if we do try – we find that too many of our standard categories of thought or feeling as often disorient as help us to explain what is happening around us; that too many of our explanations are derived from the great historical transition from the Medieval to the Modern

Age; and that when they are generalized for use today they become unwieldy, irrelevant, not convincing. (Mills 1959, 166)

Where does the science of criminology stand *vis-à-vis* Mills' critique of 'standard categories of thought' unable to grasp the transition from modern to postmodern society? Mills' critique took aim at both Marxism and liberalism, perspectives that each have contributed significantly to the theoretical contours of contemporary criminology: 'Mills had great respect for Marx but asserted that part of his theoretical perspective was simply inapplicable to mid-twentieth century world. He sharply criticized contemporary Marxist traditions for their metaphysical bent, especially their elevation of "labour" to a privileged position in the social pantheon' (Aronowitz 2012, 3). Orthodox Marxism fails, not simply because of its 'economic determinism', but because it unduly emphasizes the rationality of class-based economic interests.[1] This, according to Mills, represents a 'mental lag ... no longer in line' with forms of contemporary power. Amplifying Marx's theorization of 'false consciousness', Mills contended that 'extra-rational' communication technologies lull us into 'indifference' and 'passive' acquiescence, rather than rational, self-interested social action (1951, 324–9).

Liberal thought, with its emphasis on utilitarian calculation, errs in a similar way. Like Marxism, liberalism makes 'the same rationalist assumption' that people 'will naturally come to political consciousness' by comparing the advantages and liabilities of their respective social circumstances (Mills 1951, 325–6). For Mills, this 'rationalist assumption is unwarranted,' particularly 'in light of a seductive culture of consumption which thrives on privatism and escapism and generates a pervasive indifference toward political life' (West 1989, 135). Viewing human history through the lens of calculated rationality also hinders Marxism and liberal discourse from reckoning more complexly with the material dynamics of history. As a result, there appears a 'gap' between everyday awareness and what is actually happening: 'This gap was filled by the media of communication, which, ... to compress the volume of communication into short hand slogans, created a pseudo-environment of stereotypes that stood for the unseen political world and to which the citizen reacted' (Mills 1951, 324).

Although adrift in the circuitry of media, the masses are not simply 'insensitive clogs' dulled by 'apathy'. Nevertheless, Mills speculates about fascinations induced by media that can make people vulnerable to (the pleasures and dangers of) becoming 'inactionaries' – virtual spectators of worlds to which they actually belong. Sheltered by 'indifference' and 'a sort of numbness', Mills pictured masses of people, particularly 'white-collar' middle-class American people, as living in a

---

1   While critical of orthodox approaches to Marxism, Mills' later work aligned itself with what he referred to as a 'plain' or 'open' form of historical materialism, emphasizing historical specificity and the concomitant force of culture, politics, and the military in structuring of economic life. See, for instance, Mills' *The Marxists* (1962). For a discerning discussion of Mills' relationship to Marxism, see Aronowitz (2012).

kind of suspended reality. Suspended reality of this sort impairs 'awareness' of 'the magnitude and depth' of world historical events taking place around us. One result is the prevalence of 'reasoned cynicism'. Another involves the frenzied 'pursuit' of 'private ecstasies' and 'immediate gratification' (Mills 1951, 327). Either way, for Mills a primary effect of fascinations induced by communicative media was 'somnambulance' – a suggestive state of waking dreams in which it becomes increasingly difficult to distinguish what's imaginary from what's real (1951, 328). In this way, the networked fascinations (and fears) produced by contemporary media enable power to operate more magically than during modernity, capturing attention by 'remote control' and modulating streams of affect with enchanting displays of 'glamour' (Mills 1951, 330, 338).

Criminology in an Age of 'Fascinated Receptivity'

What does being schooled in a techno-culture of 24/7 communicative media hook-ups mean for the practice of criminology today? In 1951 Mills wrote: 'Between consciousness and existence stand communications .... The forms of political consciousness may, "in the end," be relative to the means of production, but, in the beginning, they are relative to the ... communication media' (1951, 51). Alert to far-reaching transformations in the 'cultural machinery' of 'overdeveloped' societies, Mills warned of that electronic media were increasingly capable of producing a 'kind of scheme for pre-scheduled, mass emotions', wherein it is often 'impossible to tell the image from the source' (1979e, 407). Mills pictured the electronic media as a mesmerizing *cultural apparatus* that meld 'first-hand contact' with the fascinations of prefabricated signs. The media, he suggested, 'seep into our images of self, becoming that which is taken for granted, so imperceptibly and so surely that to modify them drastically, over a generation or two, would be to change profoundly modern ... experience and character' (Mills 1951, 334):

> So decisive to experience itself are the results of these communications, that often men do not really believe what 'they see before their very eyes' until they have been 'informed' about it by the national broadcast, the definitive book, the close-up photograph, the official announcement. With such means, each nation tends to offer a selected, closed-up, and official version of world reality. The cultural apparatus not only guides experience; often as well it expropriates the very chance to have experience that can right be called 'our own.' (Mills 1979e, 407)

This colonization of the psyche by media technologies signals the emergence of a 'new society' dominated by the electronic circulation of 'mythic figures and fast-moving stereotypes' (Mills 1951, 334). In this image-intensive world, we are often adrift in captivating sensory waves of fascination and fear, not the least of which involve sensate images of crime and crime control. In Mills' words:

> We are so submerged in the pictures created by mass media that we no longer really see them …. The attention absorbed by the images on the screen's rectangle dominates the darkened public; the sonorous, the erotic, the mysterious, the funny voice of the radio talks to you; the thrill of the easy murder relaxes you. In our life-situation, they simply fascinate. And their effects run deep: popular culture is not tagged as 'propaganda' but as entertainment; people are often exposed to it when most relaxed of mind and tired of body; and its characters offer easy targets of identification, easy answers to stereotyped personal problems. (Mills 1951, 333, 336)

Mills pictured the psychic-sensory effects of electronic media in terms of 'fascinated receptivity' (1951, 339). This results in far-reaching historical amnesia, free-floating anxiety, the manipulative trafficking in stereotypes, including stereotypes about crime, and an inability to grapple responsibly with complex social issues (Mills 1956, 310–20). Here we enter a dreamy twilight zone of images, where watching 'the thrill of the easy murder' relaxes us and our 'deepest convictions' become 'fluid as water' (Mills 1951, 328, 336). In this new cultural terrain, confidence in the future erodes as we are engulfed in waves of 'apprehension, pessimism, tension and "spiritual disillusion"' (Mills 1951, 329):

> It was as if the expert angle of the camera and the carefully nurtured, pompous voice of the commentator had expropriated the chance to 'take it big.' It was as if the ear had become a sensitive soundtrack, the eye a precision camera, experience an exactly timed collaboration between microphone and lens, the machines thus taking unto themselves the capacity for experience. And as the world of this mechanically vivified experience was expanded a hundredfold, the individual became a spectator of everything, rather than an experiencer of what he [or she] earned by virtue of what he [or she] was becoming. There were no plain targets of revolt; and the cold metropolitan manner had so entered the soul of overpowered men [and women] that they were made completely private and blasé, deep down and for good. (Mills 1951, 329)

Mills wrote about the invasion of our minds and bodies by communicative technologies near the beginning of the cybernetic age. Six decades later, the high-speed precession of suggestive media images is far more intensive, trance-like and enveloping. This poses significant challenges for the social and behavioural sciences, including criminology. Indeed, in 'overdeveloped' or media-saturated societies, the criminologist must grapple, not only with new technologies of crime and crime control, but also with the systemic effects of new cybernetic modulations of power (and resistance). This is because fascinating and fearful media images of crime hover close to the hearts and minds of nearly everyone all the time. And, for the most part, the stereotypical glamour and lurid voyeurism crime dramas on TV – whether as news or entertainment or a 'reality TV' hybrid between the two – not only distract attention from structural forces affecting the actuality of law-breaking, but may keep us from 'calling a mine "disaster" a mass murder even if 10 men were killed, even if someone is responsible for the unsafe conditions in which they worked and died' (Reiman and Leighton 2013, 76–7).

In addition to directing attention to some forms of danger to the exclusion of others, popular media images of crime also disproportionately represent 'the *types* of crime committed by poor people', even when committed by the rich (Reiman and Leighton 2013, 77). This results in 'the doubled-edged message that the one-on-one crimes of the poor are the typical crimes that rich and poor criminals alike commit' (Reiman and Leighton 2013, 77). It also creates an erroneous impression that 'the pressures of poverty', patriarchal dominance and racialized hierarchy have little to do with routine expressions of aggression '*and* that the criminal justice system pursues both rich and poor criminals' in an even-handed manner (Reiman and Leighton 2013, 77).

Although this *virtual reality* is broadcast day and night, in truth it is the poor who are primarily targeted by law enforcement. 'In other words, what is most important about' typical media images are:

> the *kinds* of crimes that are shown, not *who* is typically shown to be guilty ....
> The effect is to magnify the risk of lower-class crime to middle-class individuals [and] create the image that it is the poor who pose the greatest danger to law-abiding Americans. Is it any wonder that fear of crime has persisted even as crime rates have gone down? (Reiman and Leighton 2013, 77)

With C. Wright Mills, this is to take seriously the ways that high-speed feedback loops of stereotypical media images impact on the public's imaginations of crime and what should (or should not) be done about it. Sometimes the effects of cybernetic media are decidedly more delusional. As I am writing, I hear the voice of a leading member of the so-called 'Tea Party' on television. This man is picturing half-hearted liberal efforts to extend healthcare benefits to the uninsured as totalitarian big government 'crimes' comparable to the 'evils' of the Nazi holocaust. Do you hear this man's voice calling? It's as if 'the pompous voice of the commentator' has 'expropriated the chance to "take it big"' (Mills 1951, 329).

Fascinating and fearful media images of crime (and virtually everything else) circulate today within a dynamic global cybernetic ecology of power. Cybernetics here denotes the interdisciplinary study of communicative control processes in humans, other animals and machines. The word 'cybernetics' derives from the Greek term *kybernesis*, and refers to mechanisms of steering, governing or control. During the Second World War, Norbert Wiener, the MIT mathematician and pioneer in the application of nonlinear mathematics to problems of *circular causation* and *self-adjusting feedback*, made extensive use of cybernetic logic to help link the eyes and hands of human operators to the firing mechanisms of anti-aircraft guns and precision bombing equipment. Soon thereafter, cybernetic technologies spread throughout society (Pfohl 1993, 2005).

By the early twenty-first century computational exchanges between humans and high-speed networks of media feedback have become the stuff of everyday life (and death). Command, control, communication, simulation, biometrics and prediction – these are among the code words for the cybernetic society in which criminology today performs its *cultural work*. Racialized hyper-incarceration hovers at the outer edge. These new forms of power are altering the social-psychic and historical-material landscape of both crime and efforts to control crime.

Ultramodern Power and New Technologies of Victimization and Control

> Mills views the vocation of being an intellectual as the only alternative to an emaciated liberalism, a traduced communism, and an impotent tragic viewpoint. His conception of the intellectual vocation is value-laden; that is it is shot through with … ideals of critical intelligence and creative democracy. (West 1989, 136)

This chapter tells a short sociological story about the disciplinary practices and displacements of criminology in ultramodern society. Although Mills uses the term *postmodern*, I prefer the word *ultramodern* to depict media-intensive circuits at the helm of cybernetic society. This is because cybernetic forms of power amplify, rather than transcend, what modernity has for centuries subordinated, marginalized or sentenced to death. Governed by a fateful convergence of militarized economic rationality and electronic media that enchant the senses, ultramodern technologies intensify modernity's whitened patriarchal will to power, profit and control. This is a society of omnipresent surveillance and the security state – a society of databanks, captivating illusions and cataclysmic violence. In this society, unprecedented flows of wealth, privilege and armaments are networked together with vast wastelands of poverty, crime, ill health, madness, hunger, fear, contagious paranoia and resentment. Tweet, twitter, tweet; scan, copy, scan. In ultramodern society there is increasingly little difference between what's private and what's not. This lack of distinction also applies to the oscillating boundaries between what's criminal and what's not. It depends, it seems, on who commands the drones.

Ultramodern forms of power are rooted in high-speed loops of fascinating and fearful feedback between our selves and machines of various sorts – market-driven, religious, legal, therapeutic and punitive machines; gendered, racialized and class-specific machines; dream machines and bio-power machines; fantasy machines and confessing machines; visual machines and sound machines, machines that keep us asleep and machines that turn us on; seductive machines that mesmerize us and others that police the globe; machines that meld flesh with data, infecting us with ambivalent desires for both profit and loss; and machines steeped in a continuing *coloniality of power* (Quijano 2000) and *the resistances that power begets* – some criminal, some conscious, some overtly political, but all virtual gateways into the future.

Mills' meditation on media in 'overdeveloped' society resembles aspects of Jean Baudrillard's later portrait of the power of media-intensive 'simulacra and simulations'. Baudrillard (1983) pictures cybernetic media as both a constitutive feature of contemporary life and an mode of intensified social control. Accordingly, the 'implosion' of historical awareness into media-screened memories and forgetting represents, for Baudrillard, a kind of *sign crime*. This signals the emergence of *hyperreality* – a media-engineered reality, governed less by modern representational technologies of copy and capture than by the digital enchantments and terrors of simulated realities generated from pre-modelled stereotypical schemas, and accompanied by ceaseless loops of interactive feedback, modification and mutation. Hidden in plain sight (or hyper-visible), Baudrillard, like Mills, pictures mesmerizing media images as blurring experiential differences between reality and fantasy. As such, writes Baudrillard: 'Disneyland is there to conceal the fact that it is the "real" country, all of the "real" America, which is Disneyland (just as prisons are there to conceal the fact that it is the social in its entirety; in its banal omnipresence, which is carceral' (1983, 25).

Like Mills and Baudrillard, Donna Haraway (1991) also theorizes cybernetics as an 'informatics of domination'. So does Arthur Kroker, who suggests that we today 'live at the historical apex of the triumph of technology and, with it, the penetration into the deepest layers of human subjectivity of the cold logic of instrumental rationality and technical reason' (2014, 104). But cybernetics is no one-way street. As such, Haraway and Kroker each imagine contemporary cyber-culture as also a site for subversive system jamming and innovative struggles for justice. Related assessments of the dangers and transformative potential of cybernetic technologies are found in the work of Arthur and Marilouise Kroker (2013), Jackie Orr (2009), Alondra Nelson (2002), Patricia Clough (2000), Michael Hardt and Antonio Negri (2000), N. Katherine Hayles (1999), William Bogard (1996) and Ron Eglash (1995).

Gilles Deleuze's theorization of 'control societies' likewise reckons with the double-sided character of cybernetic power. Deleuze charts a fateful historical shift from (modern) 'disciplinary societies' – where prison serves as a 'panoptic' model for individual containment – to 'free floating' information-based networks of 'control' – where power's model is the digital code (1995, 178). In control societies, self-contained individuality (Foucault 1979) mutates into market-based modulations of 'dividuals' – oscillating 'statistical' configurations governed, less by fixed identity than by fluid principles of sampling, computational tracking, profit-driven data-banking and viral informational contagion. This is a 'new system of domination' where 'control is based on floating exchange rates, modulations depending on a code setting sampling percentages for various currencies', bodies and desires (Deleuze 1995, 182, 181). But control society is also the locus for creative new struggles for freedom and justice – provided, that is, that movements for change become better attuned to the serpentine technological complexities of our cybernetic present. 'It's not a question of worrying or hoping for the best,' contends Deleuze, 'but of finding new weapons .... A snake's coils are [after all] even more intricate than a mole's burrows' (Deleuze 1995, 182).

Hyper-incarceration in the Global Cybernetic Realm

While digitally modulated ultramodern control technologies may be fast replacing disciplinary social technologies at the core of capitalist/colonialist and modern patriarchal formations of power, this does not mean that disciplinary control practices have disappeared entirely. Quite the opposite! Ramped-up disciplinary technologies remain the norm in many domains, not the least of which are education, militarized policing and low-paid service work. But nowhere is the continuation of disciplinary modern power more apparent than in 'the prison-industrial complex' with its racialized programme of 'hyper-incarceration'. This is made clear by Loïc Wacquant (2009), who documents a troubling shift over several decades from *social welfare* to *prison-fare* as a means of regulating the colour-coded poor. The numbers are staggering. In 1973 380,000 people were imprisoned in the USA (125 per 100,000). By 2009 the number had grown exponentially to 2.3 million (750 per 100,000). Shifts in the racial composition of incarceration are equally dramatic. In 1950 30 per cent of those imprisoned were Black or Latino, while at present, and despite annual decreases in the rate of serious black crime, the figure is 70 per cent (Wacquant 2009). Together these dreadful statistics, and the suffering they connote, make hyper-incarceration one of the most pernicious effects of today's global cybernetic economy.

This new 'penal state' derives in large measure from a systemic intensification of 'social insecurity' and the racialized fragmentation of global wage labour. Of specific importance are: (1) the 'off-shoring' of industrial jobs to regions of the world where labour is more cheaply procured; (2) the 'post-industrial' prevalence of low pay service work, and (3) significant decreases in the power of labour unions. In conjunction with unequal access to quality education, discriminatory drug laws, 'zero tolerance' policing and a deep-seated cultural politics of racialized resentment, hyper-incarceration signifies the bleak downside of ultramodernity and the vengeful punishment of the poor (Wacquant 2009).

Although ballooning rates of incarceration may contribute little to the general public's safety and sense of well-being, one thing about mass incarceration is certain – it 'marks the boundaries of social exclusion in terms that blame the excluded for their plight' (Castells 1998, 149). Pre-empting focused manifestations of social unrest and 'potential rebellion', hyper-incarceration sentences complex social problems to solitary confinement within 'a customized hell' (Castells 1998, 149). Mass incarceration is also key to what Michelle Alexander calls 'the New Jim Crow' – 'a new form of racialised social control' and a 'damaging manifestation of the backlash against the Civil Rights Movement' (Alexander 2010, 21–2, 11). With impoverished African American males composing approximately 53 per cent of the burgeoning US prison population, and nearly one in four under the control of the criminal justice system:

> The racial dimension of mass incarceration is its most striking feature. No other country in the world imprisons so many of its racial or ethnic minorities. The

United States imprisons a larger percentage of its black population than did South Africa at the height of apartheid. In Washington, D.C., the nation's capital, it is estimated that three out of four young black men (nearly all in the poorest neighborhoods) can expect to serve time in prison. Similar rates of incarceration can be found in black communities across America. (Alexander 2010, 6–7)

Mass incarceration thus perpetuates and deepens pre-existing patterns of racial segregation and isolation, not just by removing people of color from society and putting hem in prisons, but by dumping them back into ghettos upon release. Youth of color who might have escaped their ghetto communities – or helped to transform them – if they had been given a fair short in life and not been labeled felons, instead find themselves trapped in a closed circuit of perpetual marginality, circulating between ghetto and prison. (Alexander 2010, 191)

In addition to reckoning with systemic amplifications in economic inequality and the 'New Jim Crow' of hyper-incarceration, critical criminology in the digital age must also attend to a variety of new technologies of both victimization and social control. The manipulation of global financial markets by elite investment bankers represents, perhaps, the cutting edge of new predatory cybernetic technologies (Martin 2007). Other emergent digital technologies of harm include a rapid expanse in electronic identity theft, cyber-bullying, the cynical manipulation of affect, and 'state-of-the-art' military operations of many sorts. Think only of the recent proliferation of predatory drone attacks by the USA and its allies against suspected terrorists in sovereign states the globe over. One common result of such ramped-up control technologies is the 'collateral' death of innocent civilians. An amalgam of technological and military 'intelligences', this is a tragic effect of the (lawless) deployment of high-tech (and high-testosterone) remote killing machines against stereotypical, objectified and dehumanized targets.

Digital innovations in crime march hand-in-hand in history with amplified new technologies of control. As so clearly documented by the revelations of 'criminalized' whistleblower Edward Snowden, the widespread use of high-tech surveillance and data-mining (Staples 1997; Parenti 2003) today represents a concerted assault upon our rights to privacy and unimpeded communications. But digitally enhanced control technologies do much more than spy upon suspected terrorists, criminals and dissidents. Mesmerizing media technologies – many of which target unconscious fascinations and fears – also enhance pre-emptive forms of social control, including efforts aimed at the *engineering of consent* and the *management of contagious collective moods* (Van Ginneken 2013). Think, for instance, of the suggestive media campaign waged by the Bush administration about the imagined dangers of (non-existent) 'weapons of mass destruction' in the lead-up to the 'criminal' invasion and occupation of Iraq. This exemplifies what C. Wright Mills (1960) long ago imagined as a dangerous conflation of military, corporate and communicative forms of power. This, Mills suggested, would result in a widespread 'military metaphysics' and a 'permanent economy of war'. Add to these what is arguably the most determinate of all cybernetic control initiatives – biotechnological efforts aimed at the *unnatural selection* of some genetic pathways into the future, to the exclusion of others (Rifkin 1998; Kroker 2014).

Critical Criminology in the Digital Age

> The lens of orthodox criminology not only distorts, it leaves out. It has a narrow focus [that] … leaves out much more than it sees. These omissions are of as great an interest as the inclusions. In particular it omits all those acts and activities [that] … would suggest that there are wider structural forces involved in the generation of social harms …. It was out of this background that *The New Criminology* emerged. It was heavily influenced by C. Wright Mills, stressing individual actors placed in immediate predicaments set in a wider social structure and historical period combined with … the need to explain both the deviant action and the action against it. (Young 2011, 189)

Inspired by C. Wright Mills' prescient reflections on the emergence of 'overdeveloped society,' this chapter raises questions about the restrictive economy of contemporary criminological expertise. It also inquires about the prospects for enacting a critical criminological imagination in the digital age. What pleasures and dangers accompany criminology, and for whom does the discipline amplify pain? Who benefits most by criminological knowledge, and who loses? Is criminology today so thoroughly enmeshed in global cybernetic networks of power that, intentionally or not, the knowledge produced by criminologists tends to reinforce, rather than challenge, long-standing modern systems of structured inequality? But if this need not be the case – at least not entirely – then how might critical approaches to criminology reckon with, rather than disavow, the profession's own shadowy relations to power? What sort of pedagogical practices might help nurture the intellectual, affective, aesthetic and ethical-political sensibilities necessary for a critical criminological imagination? And how might those who acquire such a *quality of mind* best contribute to struggles for justice, peace and social security the globe over?

Critical approaches to criminology are rooted in both *theoretical and practical* concerns. *Theoretically*, critical criminologists labour to make sense of the relationship between unequal structures of power and the policing of state-administered boundaries between what's criminal and what goes unpunished by law. *Practically*, critical criminologists ally themselves with struggles by people everywhere against what systemic practices of injustice, insecurity, victimization and suffering practices bring about, whether at the hands of outlaws or the state. This is not to suggest that critical criminologies are singular in focus, method or style. They are not. While some attend most to class differentials in crime and crime control, others focus more on gendered, racialized, age-specific or sexual differences in the organization of the law and its transgression. None of these ways of imagining unjust configurations of power, however, exist independent of the others. They are, instead, 'intersectional' and operate in keeping with an interlocking 'matrix of domination' (Hill Collins 1990). But even when addressing but a 'portion of the 'intersecting social relations that are fundamental to the study of crime and justice', together 'the many critical criminologies' insist on 'the liberative potential' of critical scholarship (Michalowski 1996, 15).

Mills makes an incisive distinction between two key forms of intellectual work. The first 'divert[s] attention from structures of power'. The second combines 'criticism' of unjust social structures with efforts to 'create' or 'facilitate' justice-oriented practices of inquiry (Mills 1951, 143). 'Grand theories' that glorify 'the wondrous achievement of harmony' while 'magically' distracting attention from social conflict and suffering are typical of the first style of cultural labour. So is the 'abstracted empiricism' of 'specialists in method' – researchers whose 'economies of truth' ignore the institutional landscapes of power in which social science is practically situated (Mills 1959, 42, 59).

Conventional – or mainstream – practices of criminology also distract attention from the agonistic contests between law-breakers and law enforcers from which criminologists extract their data. This is particularly the case for thinking about crime produced by 'expert technicians', whose 'ascendency ... over the intellectual in America is becoming more and more apparent' (Mills 1951, 157). Mills was a relentless critic of the 'tunnel vision' of experts who provide technical information about 'social problems' to their elite governmental or corporate patrons. According to Mills, such 'hired men' routinely turn a blind eye to the fields of power which spur the conflicts they study (1979c, 605). Following Mills, we might ask whether we can responsibly study the causes of crime without also asking why it is that some types of harm are ritually ignored or even blessed as lawful, while other behaviours, harmful or not, are labelled as criminal. Inattention to such matters is, unfortunately, an unspoken norm within much of conventional criminology.

'In the absence of studies of [power-charged] specific norms,' contends Mills, 'this [expert] mode [of knowledge production] ... shifts the responsibility of "taking a stand" away from the thinker', creating the impression that research is itself an 'apolitical' or 'value-neutral' activity (Mills 1979a, 532). Applying Mills' critique to criminology can be eye-opening. For Mills, practising a sociological imagination requires that we confront three core questions:

> (1) What is the structure of this particular society as a whole? ... (2) Where does this society stand in history? ... (3) What varieties of men and women now prevail in this society and this period? ... Whether the point of interest is a great power state or a minor literary mood, a family, a prison, a creed – these are the kinds of questions the best social analysts have asked. (Mills 1959, 6, 7)

Conventional criminology routinely ignores each of Mills' core concerns. This is made plain when reading published accounts of mainstream criminological inquiry. Consider, for instance, Jock Young's discerning observations about recent state-of-the-art quantitative research on 'drug dealing' published in the prestigious refereed journal *Criminology*. Here 'there is no history' as:

> the scenario depicted is an empty stage upon which the actors – police and drug dealers – appear from nowhere. They have no past, and their future is a mundane world structured by the pushes of deterrence or the lack of it. The war against drugs, the most poignant overarching history, is not even mentioned – the history of the area, the vicissitudes of employment, of neighbourhood, of poverty, ethnic identity, migration and adaptation not even hinted at. (Young 2011, 14)

This results in 'social ... and epistemological exclusion' and the 'rejection and marginalization' of 'dangerous' forms of knowledge that raise 'uneasy' questions about the position of the criminologist in society. It also points to 'social blindness', 'self-censorship', and a 'stifling of the sociological imagination' on the part of mainstream criminology (Young 2011, 177). As Kathleen Ferraro remarks, in also commenting upon Mills, this underscores 'the limitations of theories of crime that focus on individual commitment to a moral order without examining the nature of that order' (2006, 212).

Committed to scholarship in pursuit of a just society (DeKerseredy 2011), critical criminologists pursue Mills' second path of inquiry – directing attention to systemic relations between crime, crime control and social inequalities. But given the constraints of criminology as a modern social science discipline, how might this commitment be best realized in practice? How, in other words, are critical criminologists able to deconstruct, rather than habitually reproduce, professional criminology's institutional complicities with unjust assemblages of power? And how might critical scholars not only make analytic connections between crime, crime control and historical contexts of power, but also contribute, if modestly, to the realization of more just, compassionate and peaceful forms of planetary social existence?

Questions such as these arise when putting C. Wright Mills' provocative vision into conversation with challenges facing critical criminology today. Drawing upon lessons culled from critical approaches to social science, including criminology, in this chapter I try to supplement and stretch some of the boundaries of Mills' otherwise inspiring imagination. In the remaining pages, attention is directed to two interrelated concerns: (1) the relation between biographical and historical specificity in the study of crime and criminal justice, and (2) *power-reflexive ritual approaches* to the criminological imagination in an era of ramped-up cybernetic power. The chapter concludes with a brief discussion of strategies aimed at preventing, reducing, repairing and/or providing reparations for systemic injuries caused by both crime and unjust practices of crime control.

Biography, History and 'Subject Position' in Criminology

> Neither the life of an individual nor the history of a society can be understood
> without understanding both .... No social study that does not come back to the
> problems of biography, of history and of their intersections within a society has
> completed its intellectual journey .... The sociological imagination enables us
> to grasp history and biography and the relations between the two in society ....
> For that imagination is the capacity to shift from one perspective to another –
> from the political to the psychological; from examination of a single family
> to comparative assessments of the national budgets of the world; from the
> theological school to the military establishment; from considerations of an oil
> industry to studies of contemporary poetry. It is the capacity to range from the
> most impersonal and remote transformations to the most intimate features of the
> human self – and to see the relations between the two. (Mills 1959, 5, 6)

The sociological imagination is enacted at the analytic crossroads between the
intimacies of biography and the intricacies of structured history. As Mills states,
the 'first fruit' of *the sociological imagination* 'and the first lesson of the social
science that embodies it ... is the idea that the individual can understand his own
experience and gauge his own fate' by locating oneself within a specific period of
historically structured power and knowledge (1959, 5). This is a 'terrible lesson
and magnificent' – 'the capacity to range from the most impersonal and remote
transformations to the most intimate features of the human self – and to see the
relations between the two' (Mills 1959, 5, 7).

Making connections between the singularity of biography and the fields of
power in which one's life is historically situated was, for Mills, both a valuable
form of *cultural work* and an embodied *quality of mind* (1959, 15). As such, the
sociological imagination requires much more than collecting factual information
about the statistical counters of social life. In this 'age of fact', declares Mills:

> it is not only information that people need, information often dominates their
> attention and overwhelms their capacities to assimilate it. It is not only the skills
> of reason that they need – although their struggles to acquire these often exhaust
> their limited moral energy. What they need; and what they feel they need, is a
> quality of mind that will help them use information and to develop reason in
> order to achieve lucid summation of that is going on in the world and what may
> be happening within themselves – the sociological imagination. (Mills 1959, 5)

What characterizes the embodied *quality of mind* imagined by Mills, and what
does this imply for the epistemological standpoint of critical criminology? Two
things are of particular importance – the historical specificity of all knowledge
claims, and a 'transvaluation' of everyday cultural symbols, values and viewpoints
(Mills 1959, 15). Mills viewed history as 'the organized memory' of humankind
and its comparative study as 'an indispensable' resource for sociological inquiry

(1959b, 149). Without historical specificity, sociology operates in a vacuum of 'abstraction' that 'unnecessarily violates social reality' and freezes the movement of time (Mills 1959b, 150). A nuanced sense of history, on the other hand, enables social science to 'balance the immediacy of the knife-edge present with the generality needed to bring out the meaning of specific trends for the period as a whole' (Mills 1959, 153–4).

Mills alerts us to the falsity of equating today's common sense with timeless truth. As an antidote, the sociological imagination urges critical reflection on what common sense overlooks or takes for granted. Together with historical specificity, the transvaluation of common sense is key to critical inquiry and requires methods of subtle analytic discernment. At issue is how biographical action at once shapes and is shaped by the structures and stories in which it is historically situated. For an example resonant with a critical criminological imagination, consider the opening pages of Patricia Williams' *The Alchemy of Race and Rights* (1991).

Williams, an African American law professor and critical theorist, writes: 'Since subject position is everything in my analysis of law, you deserve to know that it's a bad morning. I am very depressed' (1991, 3). Williams then alerts us to haunting historical matters that bear upon her mood. She is preparing, she tells us, a lecture on laws pertaining to *redhibitory vice* – 'a defect in merchandise which, if existing at the time of purchase, gives rise to a claim allowing the buyer to return the thing and to get back part or all of the purchase price' – and the example she has chosen raises troubling questions about the racialized history of law (Williams 1991, 3). At stake is not some cut-and-dried legal issue, but a case evoking a complex mix of cognitive, affective, moral and bodily responses. This complexity resonates with Mills' picture of the sociological imagination as not merely a theoretical perspective on social life, but an *embodied* quality of mind.

The 'redhibitory vice' Williams examines stems from an 1835 Louisiana court decision concerning the alleged 'craziness' of a slave named Kate. Kate had been purchased for $500. But after judging his newly acquired property to be insane, Kate's master demands his money back. Legal conventions pertaining to the meaning of property and racialized ideas about who counts as a human converge in this case and together haunt Williams' tale. 'I would like to write', she declares, 'in ways that reveal the intersubjectivity of legal constructions, that force the reader to participate in the construction of meaning and to be conscious of that process' (Williams 1991, 7). While Kate's captivity would today be widely viewed as a crime, at the time of her enslavement white supremacist law dictated simply that she was a unit of property. Hence, after being 'satisfied that the slave in question was wholly, and perhaps worse than useless', the court ruled that the plaintiff had a right to get his money back.

With this in mind, it is hardly surprising, that on the day of her lecture Professor Williams finds herself 'very depressed'. In foregrounding the biographical/ historical lens through which she reads (and critically re-reads) the 1835 case in question, Williams invites us to ponder how it is that her historical subject position relates to ours: 'It always takes a while to sort out what's wrong, but it usually starts with some kind of perfectly irrational thought such as: I *hate* being a lawyer' (1991, 3). Like C. Wright Mills, Williams asks how it is that socially instantiated power penetrates the inmost fibres of our being, shaping our beliefs and desires, perceptions and misrecognitions, remembrances and what we forget.

This suggests that biography can never truly be understood in strictly psychological or physiological terms, but only in 'close and continual reference to ... social context' (Mills, 1959, 162). 'Within the broad limits of the physiology,' observes Mills, 'our very perception of the physical world, the colors we discriminate, the smells we become aware of, the noises we hear, are socially patterned and socially circumscribed' (1959, 162). This became crystal clear to me when teaching a seminar on 'Crime and Social Justice' in the spring of 1991, following the trial of Los Angeles police officers charged with brutally assaulting Rodney King, an African American man stopped for a routine traffic violation.

After viewing a widely broadcast video of the beating recorded by a witness to the assault, most Americans viewed the violence against King as indefensible. But this was not the case for the all-white Simi Valley jury who exonerated the police in the first of two trials. During the trial defence attorneys repeatedly played the video in slow motion, freezing key frames, while instructing jurors in how to 'see' the danger King posed to the police as they pummelled him. The jurors concurred, concluding that it was King who had 'endangered' the officers, and not the other way around. One juror went so far as to suggest that King was in 'total control'. Three white male students in my class at Boston College expressed related thoughts. The students repeatedly played a copy of the video used in the Simi Valley trial, freeze-framing key sequences, in a sincere effort to convince the rest of us that Rodney King authored his own assault.

Although nobody else in the class was persuaded, the three students who 'saw' King in charge remained convinced. 'Look how big he is!' they stated, unfazed by the muscular bodies of the officers striking the defenceless motorist. Although it is tempting to characterize such judgements as racist, what shaped the perceptions of the Simi Valley jury and the students in my class was no simple racist mindset that prejudiced them against King. Something more systemic was involved (Bonilla-Silva 2001), something more material – 'a contest within the visual field, a crisis in the certainty of what is visible' (Butler 1992, 16). This renders the field of vision decidedly 'not neutral to the question of race' (Butler 1993, 17). In keeping with Mills' (1959, 162) observation that even 'our very perception of the physical world' is 'socially patterned and socially circumscribed', this represents stark evidence of how 'sociality gets into the flesh' (Brennan 1993, 10).

Social inquiry of the sort imagined by Mills demands that we interrogate the *social personas* we identify with, as well as those we condemn as 'other', deviant or criminal. This makes the social scientist, and the criminologist in particular, no mere student of external facts, but an active participant in the making (and remaking) of history. This is also to envision 'the present as history' – a history that changes 'not merely because more detailed research later introduces new facts', but 'because of changes in the points of view and the current framework'

(Mills 1959, 145). As such, for Mills (1959, 145), sociology's engagement with history is imagined as a process of 'continual rewriting'.

In situating biographical experience within the folds of history, it is important to recognize that the weight of history may be different for those at society's commanding heights than it is for those pushed to the bottom. While powerful elites commonly champion history as a triumphant story of progress (Mills 1959), for people battered by power, history may feel like a constant state of emergency. This we are taught by the 'tradition of the oppressed' – 'that the state of emergency ... is not the exception but the rule. We must attain a concept of history that is in keeping with this insight. Then we shall clearly realize that it is our task to bring about a real state of emergency' (Benjamin 1969, 257).

Critical Criminology, Symbolic Interaction and Social Psychoanalysis

Mills drew upon two general traditions of thought in analysing the relations between history and biography – symbolic interaction and social psychoanalysis. Concerning the first, Mills made extensive use of philosophical pragmatism, particularly the social psychology of John Dewey and George Herbert Mead, Dewey's colleague at University of Chicago. Mead is well known within sociology for his theories of anticipatory 'role-taking' and the social self. Acquiring a sense of self (or biographical identity) was, for Mead, a thoroughly social phenomenon. We become ourselves, Mead suggests, by imagining how 'significant others' view us and adjusting our actions in anticipation of others' expectations. The importance Mead placed on reflexive role-taking in face-to-face interaction has led many sociologists to view symbolic interaction as a 'subjective' theory of micro-social relations. While *taking the role of the other* in everyday social interaction is clearly important to Mead's theory of the self, focusing exclusively on interpersonal role-taking represents a limited reading of Mead's social philosophy.

Equally important to Mead is how historical and linguistic conventions affect people's interpretations of one another, themselves and the world. For Mead, language does more than represent the world. It selectively directs attention to certain matters, while distracting from others. Language, in other words, gives social structure to the worlds within which symbolic interaction takes place. This is its power. Overlooked or underemphasized by 'subjective' approaches to symbolic interaction, this more 'structural' aspect of Mead's thought was key to C. Wright Mills' understanding of the relations between biography and history. For Mills, as for Mead, when taking the role of others in everyday interaction, we simultaneously converse with the 'generalized other' of historical convention: 'The generalized other is the internalized audience with which the thinker converses. ... Imported into the mind, this symbolic interplay constitutes the structure of mentality' (1979b, 426, 427).

This is how power operates in the interstices between biography and the institutional structures of history.[2] Here even the most personal of motives never simply 'denote ... elements "in" individuals'. They are, instead, 'situated vocabularies' given to us in the power-charged conventions of language. In this sense:

> The patterns of social behaviour with their 'cultural drifts,' values, and political orientations extend a control over thought by means of language .... Our behaviour and perception, our logic and thought, come within the control of language. Along with language, we acquire a set of social norms and values. A vocabulary is not merely a string of words; immanent in it are societal textures – institutional and political coordinates. (Mills 1979b, 433)

In addition to asking how our biographies (or subject positions) are situated within the historical conventions of language, the sociological imagination invites us to engage critically with *unconscious* aspects of the social-psychic life of power. Noting that psychoanalytic accounts of the psyche are never strictly individualistic, Mills provides a decidedly sociological twist to Freudian theories of the unconscious. Together, sociology and psychoanalysis are said to link troubling personal dramas to: 'those little family circles in which such dreadful melodrama occur .... In so far as the family as an institution turn women into darling little slaves and men into their chief providers and unweaned dependents, the problem of a satisfactory marriage remains incapable of a purely private solution' (Mills 1959, 160, 10).

Despite gesturing in the direction of an 'important sociological phenomenon', according to Mills, Freudian psychoanalysis was not in itself 'sociologically informed' (Gerth and Mills 1953, 150). This was 'one of Freud's greatest shortcomings' – a tendency to 'overgeneralize ... the psychic impact of particular type of kinship organization – that of the occidental patriarchal family' and to interpret its contours 'as at least quasi-biologically set' (Gerth and Mills 1953, 151). 'The next step forward in psychoanalytic studies', suggests Mills:

> is to do fully for other social institutional arenas what Freud began to do so magnificently for kinship institutions of a selected type. What is needed is the idea of social structure as a composition of institutional orders, each of which

---

2   Together with Hans Gerth, Mills theorizes 'institutions' as selective social pathways that simultaneously constrain and enable particular courses of action. Both institutions and the people they affect depend, however, on reflexive practices of 'role-taking' in everyday 'symbolic interaction'. As such, the model offered by Gerth and Mills (1953) for interpreting the interplay between character and social structure was decidedly 'indeterminate' and shaped by choices made in the 'here and now' of history, rather than being mechanically determined by prior events. Gerth and Mills pictured social life in terms of five sets of mediating institutions – those associated with kinship, politics, religion, economics and the military. Each institutional realm was composed of four interrelated 'spheres' of role-taking – those involving symbols, technologies, education and status (or prestige).

we must study psychoanalytically as Freud studied certain kinship institutions. (Mills 1959, 160)[3]

While underscoring the importance of unconscious dimensions of power, Mills' reflections on psychoanalysis remained underdeveloped. As such, I find it helpful to supplement Mills' foray into social psychoanalysis with ideas drawn from more recent work, such as Avery Gordon's *Ghostly Matters* (1996) and Teresa Brennan's *History after Lacan* (1993). Gordon (1996) deepens Mills' vision of the sociological imagination by reckoning with the 'seething presence' of those uncanny 'structures of feeling' that haunt power's history. Theorizing haunting as a 'constitutive element of modern social life', Gordon explores how 'ghostly matters' can upend social routine, leading us into a 'field that takes the measure of us as much as we take the measure of it' (1996, 7): 'In haunting, organized forces and systemic structures that appear removed from us make their impact in felt in everyday life in a way that confounds our analytic separations and confounds the social separations themselves' (1996, 8).

For better or worse, being haunted means brushing against the ghosts of what power displaces to the margins of consciousness (Pfohl and Gordon 1986). A 'seething presence, acting on and often meddling with taken-for-granted realities', the ghost is then a 'social figure' – 'the sign, or the empirical evidence if you will that tells you a haunting is taking place' (Gordon 1996, 8). Like Gordon, Teresa Brennan is concerned with unconscious dynamics of power and resistance. Analysing distortions, injuries and illnesses ushered into history by an amalgam of patriarchal, capitalist and racist/colonialist systems of power, Brennan pays particular attention to the energetic effects of profit-driven modern technologies of injustice.

Propelled by fantasies of limitless economic accumulation and world mastery, modern technologies fuel aggressive expressions self-enclosed masculinity: 'This is the story of a social psychosis' (Brennan 1993, 1). When coupled with the growth imperatives of capitalism, the effects can be catastrophic. Brennan writes:

> Capitalism can only continue to make a profit through the continuous over-consumption of nature; that is to say capitalism cannot sustain its profit levels and sustain the environment at the same time .... Capitalism, unlike some other forms of market economy [that] replenished the natural environment, [energetically] exploits nature in the same way as it exploits labour. [Capitalism]

---

3   In noting Mills' call for a sociologically informed approach to psychoanalysis, my analysis departs from Stanley Aronowitz's otherwise exemplary depiction of Mills' thought and politics in *Taking it Big: C. Wright Mills and the Making of Political Intellectuals* (2012). Discussing Mills' ambivalence to Freud, Aronowitz states: 'Mills explicitly rejects the psychoanalytic paradigm, even though he acknowledges his debt to *The Authoritarian Personality* and to Max Horkheimer's work in critical theory, to which Mills had access' (2012, 163).

spreads death by turning nature into commodities, without replenishing the life it appropriates in the process, [binding nature ever more quickly into] forms that are not biodegradable, forms incapable of re-entering the life cycles via the reproduction of their own kind or organic decay .... By binding more and more of life in a form which cannot reproduce life, capitalism, and a complicit modernity, disturbs ecological balance, ... producing a more complete and final form of death. (Brennan 2000, 3, 5, 2)

It is easy to picture the imperial aggressions analysed by Brennan as violent forms of crime. But this is not how such violence is typically imagined – except, that is, in the minds of outcasts, malcontents, alienated artists, crazy people, revolutionaries and radical criminologists of various sorts. Buttressed by powerful modern technologies, the victory of the so-called 'civilized' peoples over those condemned to 'underdevelopment' is commonly heralded as a marker of progress. How can this be? Brennan addresses this question through the lens of feminist social psychoanalysis, bringing to light a long-standing 'foundational fantasy' about matter (and mothers) as something destined for 'exploitation' as a 'natural resource' by 'Modern Man' (1993, 167). Kept in check by a constellation of medieval religious, cultural and economic forces, this gendered fantasy is realized in modern/colonial 'era of the Ego'. Here the profit-driven logic of capital combines with new technologies of measurement, manufacture and transportation, permitting world-changing objectification and appropriation of the Earth's energies. In this:

> fantasy is made into reality, as commodities are constructed to serve their human masters, to wait upon them, at the expense of the natural world. These commodities are objects to be controlled: they are nature transformed into a form in which it cannot reproduce itself, nature directed toward human ends. (Brennan 2000, 9)

Psychotic because it is out of touch with material actuality, the technological realization of the foundational fantasy begets a haunting feeling of paranoia – a repressed awareness of the sacrificial violence enacted by modern men of power in the name of economic and scientific progress. This leads to further cycles of aggressive cultural projections and actions aimed at domination, locking the modern Northwest into a self-enclosed culture of death, masculine defensiveness and imperial violence. Brennan describes the dynamic behind this perpetual cycle of technologically fuelled violence in the following way:

> The aggressive imperative involved in making the other into a slave, or object, will lead to territorial expansion (territorial imperialism). This is because the objectification of the other depends on establishing a spatial boundary by which the other and self are fixed. But this fixing of the other leads to the fear that the other will retaliate, which in turn leads to a feeling of spatial constriction.

Moreover, the feeling of spatial constriction is related to the physical environment. These changes have physical effects on the psyche, which in turn alter the psychical perception of the environment, and of one's boundaries. With spatial constrictions, one's boundaries are threatened, and the resultant fear increases the need to control the object. (Brennan 1993, 8)

Brennan's analysis of historically occasioned 'social psychosis' and Gordon's meditation on the haunting complexities of unequal power offer criminology valuable analytic tools for exploring the unconscious of modern law and its transgression. A related use of psychoanalysis is found in Bruce Arrigo and Dragan Milovanovic's *Revolution in Penology* (2009). Arrigo and Milovanovic (2009, 28) interpret 'reactive forces' embedded in modern penal discourse as symptomatic of unconscious historical investments in the collective production of injury and social harm. To counter structured injury of this sort, Arrigo and Milovanovic (2009, 70) call for an ethically informed 'criminology of the shadow', capable of examining 'the depth and breadth' of the structured violence that 'penal harm has come to embody'. Like the work of Brennan and Gordon, *Revolution in Penology* advances Mills' imagination of social psychoanalysis as a valuable tool for the deconstruction of unconscious repetitions of injury and harm, including harms produced by the punishing compulsions of power-charged criminal law and its transgression.

Criminological uses of symbolic interaction and psychoanalysis are given new currency when read through the lens of C. Wright Mills' sociological imagination. More traditional uses of symbolic interaction have addressed other topics of importance, such as role-taking in criminal subcultures, the learned acquisition of definitions favouring crime, the interactional dynamics of labelling, and the stigmatizing effects of being labelled (Pfohl 2005, 351–9). Traditional uses of psychoanalysis, on the other hand, generally conceive of criminality in pathological terms, ignoring the ways that unconscious landscapes of power press upon individual and collective psychology (Pfohl 2005, 117–24). Augmented by recent approaches to the social unconscious of power, Mills' call for mixing psychoanalytic thought with historical understandings of symbolic interaction offers exciting new pathways for a critical criminological imagination. In concluding this chapter, I will explore the implications of Mills' vision for a power-reflexive approach to the criminological imagination.

Power-reflexive Approaches to Criminology in the Cybernetic Age

[T]he sociological imagination is not merely a fashion. It is a quality of mind that seems most dramatically to promise and understanding of the intimate realities of ourselves in connection with larger social realities. It is not merely one quality of mind among the range of cultural sensibilities – it is *the* quality whose wider and more adroit use offers the promise that ... human reason itself – will come to play a greater role in human affairs. (Mills 1959, 15)

For C. Wright Mills, as later for Michel Foucault, power and knowledge are reciprocal forces, each recurrently folding back on the other. For Mills, the 'problem of knowledge and power is, and always has been, the problem of the relations of men of knowledge with men of power' (1979c, 606). Foucault states it this way: 'there is no power relation without the correlative constitution of a field of knowledge, or any knowledge that does not presuppose and constitute at the same time power relations' (1979, 27). Mills, however, was particularly worried about the warping of knowledge by 'men of power' in the emerging postmodern age. In 1955 he wrote:

> Knowledge and power are not truly united inside the ruling circles; and when men of knowledge do come to a point of contact with the circles of powerful men, they come not as peers but as hired men. [At the same time, people] are encouraged to assume that, in general, the most powerful and the wealthiest are also the most knowledgeable, or as they say, the smartest .... Such assumptions also reveal something of what has happened to the kind of experience that knowledge has come to be. Knowledge is no longer widely felt as an ideal; it is seen as an instrument. And in a society of power and wealth, knowledge is valued as an instrument of power and wealth, and also, of course, as an ornament in conversation, a tid-bit in a quiz program. (Mills 1979c, 605–6)

Despite this despairing tone, Mills never relinquished hope that discernment promised by the sociological imagination might reflexively right the balance between knowledge and power. Mills' vision poses uneasy questions for criminology. If criminology is itself implicated in the networks of power it studies, how is it possible for criminologists to *work through* the historical situation in which we find ourselves? And how might this be achieved in ways that are neither strictly determined by, nor free of, the cybernetic webs of power in which we are situated? Is it possible, in other words, to imaginatively double back upon the theoretical stories we tell, the methods we use, and the crime control policies we support (or oppose) so as to more adequately reckon with how our own rituals of knowledge are, for better or worse, also practices of power?

Inspired by C. Wright Mills' sustained attention relationship between biography and historical context, I invite you to imagine the *cultural work* of criminology as performed at the intersections of three interdependent vectors of force: *natural historical materiality*, *social psychic subjectivity* and the *systemic complexities of power*. These forces impact the *knowledge rituals* by which criminologists produce ideas about crime, the criminal and the criminal justice system. Together, these reciprocal vectors of influence point to antagonisms at work in the imagination of criminology. Situating criminological knowledge at the intersection of these several realms raises questions about the selective character of the criminological expertise and what the discipline commonly overlooks, hides, disavows or sacrifices.

Natural Historical Materiality

This first vector of influence locates criminology within the material confines of history. Expanding upon Mills' thesis about the emergence of 'overdeveloped' or 'postmodern' societies, I have argued throughout this chapter that criminology must reckon with its location within fast-moving networks of ultramodern power. This is necessary today, if for no other reason than that so much of what people understand about crime comes to them as pre-modelled images, stereotypes and simulations transmitted by the media. Given this predicament, how might we best distinguish between the virtual realities of crime and law enforcement and their agonistic actualities?

One way is to supplement conventional forms of inquiry – quantitative or qualitative – with an intensive use of historically informed ethnography. While thick ethnographic description might enable a more nuanced understanding, it is equally important to recognize that the fields in which ethnographies of crime and crime control take place are themselves saturated by cybernetic feedback. As such, although important, it is insufficient to simply observe that criminal acts performed by gangs – whether on the street or in corporate offices – involve ritual displays of masculinity. While this is true, it is also necessary to inquire into how specific models of manhood enter the flesh of those who enact them. With Mills, this is to recognize that people are often 'so submerged in the pictures created by mass media that we no longer really see them' (1956, 333). Thus, when making field notes about what people do and say they do, it is also crucial for ethnographers to discern how it is that even someone's most intimate concerns may be symptomatic of exposure to parasitic loops of electronic communicative feedback (Pfohl 1992).

It is not easy to discern how media influences criminals, criminal justice agents and we ourselves. But in the appendix to *The Sociological Imagination* Mills makes some helpful suggestions. These include 'stimulating' our imaginations by maintaining a reflexive research journal. Journal writing of this sort permits personal troubles to cross paths with public issues while mixing analytic work with a sense of play. This is a key aspect of what Mills means by 'intellectual craftsmanship'. This encourages scholarship, not simply as a way to earn a living, but as a 'way of living' itself (Mills 1959, 196). As such, I often use my own journal to meditate upon issues raised by a given day's news, or a book I am reading, or what captures my attention on TV or the Internet. Sometimes I jot down notes about conversations with students or colleagues at work or with family members and friends. Concurring with Mills about the social importance of unconscious matters, I also write down my dreams and make analytic associations to visual or sonorous images that come to me through the media. To make reflexive use of a journal in this way, of course, requires time, and this something that, for many of us, is often in short supply. Nevertheless, in an era of digital speed-up, slowing down to reflect on something one has read, or on a daydream, conversation or media image, can help nurture the *quality of mind* necessary for critical criminological inquiry.

Mills repeatedly calls for historical specificity when it comes to matters of knowledge and power. I use the term *natural historical materiality* to expand upon this idea. By adding the word 'natural' to 'historical materiality' – a term associated with Marx – I hope to draw attention to how the social worlds we study are themselves part of the wider realm of living, energetic nature to which we all belong. This means that human history is also, for better or worse, natural history. I find inspiration for this idea in George Bataille's distinction of *restrictive economies* of human use (more or less what Marx meant by a 'mode of production') and the *general economy* – the wider ecology or cosmos that encompasses life in all its complexity (Bataille 1988). Both types of economy are crucial to the study of social life and history. Marxist criminology directs attention to inequalities in the restrictive economy that foster crime and repressive strategies of crime control. As it is said: *The Rich Get Richer and the Poor Get Prison*. But in an era characterized by catastrophic global climate change, reflexive attention to crimes against the general economy is today vital to the sustainability of planetary life itself.

Social Psychic Subjectivity

This is again about the relations between biography and history. I have already commented extensively about Mills' historical approach to symbolic interaction and social psychoanalysis. As such, I will write little more about these matters, except to remind criminologists that attention to *the psychic life of power* is crucial to social studies of law and its transgression (Butler 1997). Coupling questions about crime with an analysis of 'the subject positions' from which crime and attempts to control arise offers several important lessons.

First, all forms of behaviour – law-abiding and criminal – are unconsciously mediated by imaginary projections or phantasms. This means that social psychic experience is never entirely conscious or transparent. It also means that criminology would be wise to supplement other methodological approaches to the study of crime by exploring what lies beneath or at margins of consciousness.

Second, cultural understandings of crime are mediated by systems of language, or what Jacques Lacan (1977) calls the 'Symbolic Order'. This idea is common to both symbolic interaction and social psychoanalysis. As a child, I was repeatedly told: 'Sticks and stones will break your bones, but names will never hurt you.' This is not true. Just try getting a job once you've been labelled as a felon.

Third, whether imaginary or symbolic, the subjectivity of actors in the drama of crime is inevitably haunted by what is repressed in the ritualized shaping of subjectivity itself. These lessons resonate with Mills' vision of the sociological imagination and are crucial for critical efforts to excavate the psychic contours of power affecting both law-abiding and criminal actors.

The warping of subjectivity by ideology is also important to the critical study of crime and criminal justice. This is evident in the Marxist psychoanalytic theories of Louis Althusser. Althusser (1971, 162) defines ideology as 'the imaginary relationship of individuals to their real conditions of existence'. We are 'hailed' into imaginary relations to the world, contends Althusser, in the rituals of everyday life. This provides us with psychic pathways into some types of subjectivity, but not others. Ideological rituals, we are told, 'transform ... individuals into subjects ... by *interpellation* or hailing' (Althusser 1971, 174). The relevance of Althusser's thought for criminology is particularly evident than in the most salient example he provides of ideological 'hailing' – a police officer calling out to someone in the street. Althusser here (1971, 174) asks us to 'imagine' a 'most commonplace everyday' event – a police officer barking, 'Hey, you there!' How would you respond? It depends, I suspect, on whether you view the police as friend or as foe. And this, in turn, depends on the *psychic life of power* (Butler 1997).

Power, Crime, Crime Control

A third vector of influence on critical reflexivity concerns power. Sociology's predominant viewpoint on this matter derives from Max Weber, who defined power as the ability of one set of actors to exert influence over others, despite resistance by others (1964, 152). Weber's definition is useful, particularly when studying situations of structured social inequality. According to C. Wright Mills, who shares Weber's perspective:

> Power refers to the realization of one's will, even if this involves the resistance of others .... Power is simply the probability that men [and women] will act as another ... wishes. This action may rest upon fear, rational calculation of advantage, lack of energy to do otherwise, loyal devotion, indifference, or a dozen other ... motives. (Gerth and Mills 1953, 307, 195)

The Weberian perspective, adopted by Mills, has significantly influenced criminological theory, where power is typically understood as a tool in the battle between criminals and those who would control them. The unequal distribution of power is also a central to Mills' inspired analyses of the 'power elite' – an interlocking network of economic, political and military actors, bound together by convergences in family background, education, employment and worldview. Mills' thesis about the threats to democracy posed by the unchecked power of elites resonates with critical studies of corporate and governmental crime (Kramer et al. 2002). While both analytically and politically important, this is also a limited imagination of power, one that assumes that power is a resource or weapon that can be wielded against others.

In the interests of a more complex approach to power, I find it helpful to supplement, without negating, Weber's (and Mills') instrumental approach in several ways. In this regard, it is important to also conceive of power as a dynamic field, an intersectional matrix of overlapping gendered, racialized and class-based social forces (Hill Collins 1990). A related conception of power as a field of forces is found in Foucault (1979). This perspective helps criminology to analyse tactical struggles between criminals and control agents within the strategic fields of force to which both belong. It also challenges criminology to imagine justice-oriented interventions aimed at altering the structural dynamics of fields, rather than merely the behaviour of individuals.

Second, while coercive practices of power – by both criminals and the state – will forever remain a concern, it is important for criminology to consider how power also operates to win the consent of those it governs. This is the meaning of hegemony. Coercive expressions of power may be brutal, whether occurring in domestic settings, back alleys, public venues or in abject places of confinement, such the prisons at Abu Ghraib, Guantánamo Bay or Pelican Bay. Hegemonic forms of power operate more seductively. Writing from prison, Antonio Gramsci (1971) conceived of hegemony as the ritual production of common sense – a contestable consensus, or moving equilibrium, between people divided by unequal economic and cultural resources. When most effective, hegemony draws us into imaginary spaces where things appear 'as if' natural and can be taken for granted. In this sense, hegemonic power limits our imagination and can make other ways of doing things, including other ways of doing criminology, unthinkable.

The importance of hegemony for theoretical understandings of crime is evident in Stuart Hall et al.'s *Policing the Crisis* (1978). This study examines a 'campaign' by the British police and media during the early 1970s, alerting the public to a supposed epidemic of 'mugging'. A term imported from US media, mugging arrived in Britain saturated with racialized connotations linking crime with blackness. Creating a 'moral panic' and false 'common sense' about Britain's 'crime problem', the crusade against mugging deflected attention from racialized economic conditions associated with an increased likelihood of crime. It also provided cultural legitimacy for the aggressive policing of black neighbourhoods while provoking widespread fear (on the part of whites) about Caribbean immigrants. In constructing a new hegemony about Britain's 'crime problem', this pernicious war on poor immigrants furthered divisions between white and black segments of the British working class, reinforcing tensions rather than providing the grounds for potential economic and political alliance.

Attention to what Anibal Quijano (2000) theorizes as a global *coloniality of power* also supplements Mills' analysis of power in ways that facilitate critical analyses of crime and the justice system. Quijano, a Peruvian sociologist, contends that no aspect of contemporary culture is free of the lingering shadows of colonial domination. A such, the haunts of 'coloniality' continue to impact upon a wide swath of social life – from definitions of success, pleasure and beauty to phantasms about exotic sexualities, cost effectiveness, pre-emptive warfare and the information value of torture. This is because while colonialism has formally ended, the intricacies of decolonization remain incomplete. This results in the continued 'privileging of Eurocentric forms of knowledge', cultural support for exploitive 'core–periphery relations', and the ritual reproduction of the insistent vicissitudes of 'racial/ethnic hierarchies' (Grosfoguel 2009, 497).

Biko Agozino's *Counter-colonial Criminology* (2003) brings related concerns to the study of criminal justice. Agozino underscores criminology's historical blindness to colonialism's 'punishment of the innocent', particularly the brutal crimes of slavery and its aftermath. Noting that 'criminologists have failed, or refused, to interrogate how much they are implicated by their discipline in imperialist reason', Agozino traces the theoretical origins of criminology to early modern ideas about a 'social contract'. According to the social contract worldview, 'rational principles' guiding ideas about crime and punishment provided the 'best possible foundation for civic democratic rule …. Yet under the slave trade and colonialism, democracy was completely denied, the social contract was nonexistent, and whole populations were treated as criminals without any human rights' (Agozino 2003, 171, 14). Claims to a social contract aside, when applied, the colonized or enslaved, hegemonic practices of criminology typically bask in the 'power of European men to punish others, … especially when they were completely innocent' (Agozino 2003, 14).

Systematic punishment of the innocent represents a form of 'judicial terrorism' and is a reason why critical Third World scholars often demand collective 'reparations' for historical acts of mass victimization (Agozino 2003, 16). It is no wonder, then, that so many so-called 'underdeveloped' countries:

> [even those] that have entered the nuclear arms race shy away from the institutionalization of criminology as an autonomous discipline, despite their huge crime problems. [Indeed,] criminology is concentrated in former colonizing countries, and virtually absent in former colonized countries, because criminology is a social science that served colonialism more directly than many others. (Agozino 2003, 1)

This troubling underside of criminology continues today in the 'internal colonialism' of overdeveloped societies, where social and economic insecurities are paired with a military-like policing of the racialized poor (Pinderhughes 2011).

Criminology's failure to reckon with its complicity with the systemic violence of slavery and colonial domination raises troubling questions for the discipline. Indeed, there is something hauntingly unreal about scholarship that focuses almost exclusively on individual violations of the law while ignoring the systemic terrorism imposed upon innocent people by colonialism, the Atlantic slave trade and their continuing legacies, including the 'New Jim Crow' of mass incarceration. Drawing upon writings of Franz Fanon, Walter Rodney, Patricia Hill Collins and other critical scholars, writers, poets and artists, Agozino's work adds nuance to Mills' ideas about the sociological imagination while providing an important corrective to Mills' own relative blindness to colour-coded practices of power (Aptheker 1960, 82).

For conventional criminologists, questions posed by the discipline's complicity with a continuing legacy of coloniality may sometimes be unnerving. But for scholars committed to impassioned struggles for peace, safety, justice and a radically democratic future, the challenges presented by critiques of coloniality and imperial reason invite a reflexive reckoning with the tragic actualities of history. To further such reckoning, Agozino (2003, 171) calls for *committed objectivity*. Guided by an 'identification ... with all oppressed people everywhere' and 'a desire to contribute to the amelioration of all sufferings through a better understanding of avoidable problems', *committed objectivity* is vigilant about the situated character of its own claims to knowledge, exchanging the illusions of 'complete detachment' and 'pretentious value-neutrality' for 'the ability to take a position and argue it logically without concealing or distorting opposing positions' (Agozino 2003, 172).

Power-reflexive Rituals of a Critical Criminology Imagination

Produced at the intersections of natural historical materiality, psychic social subjectivity and complex fields of power, criminological knowledge participates in the realities of everyday life while inevitably reducing life's complexities to what it can imagine about them. This is because, like all forms of knowledge, the rituals of criminological knowledge are selective or sacrificial. If the term 'ritual' carries religious connotations, this is no accident. When most forceful, hegemonic rituals tend to 'super-naturalize' the historical worlds they symbolize, blessing certain forms of artifice with a feeling of common sense while denigrating or excluding others. In 'overdeveloped' cybernetic society, where knowledge is mediated by dense, high-speed communicative technologies, the issue is even more complex. Here the tissue of sociality itself becomes inextricably linked to the flow of 'knowledge objects, rhetorical mechanisms, writing technologies, ... expert systems, even machine agencies other than human agencies' (Clough 2000, 180).

None of this is either good or bad for criminology. It depends on how we situate our own practices of knowledge. Power-reflexive attunement to the technological environment in which criminology is practised helps upend the virtual reality of media-imagined criminality by returning us to the embodied landscape in which crime and crime control actually take place. Nevertheless, even the most power-reflexive forms of knowledge will remain partial and provisional. This is not to advocate relativity, although Mills occasionally did just that. Nothing, however, is simply relative: 'Relativism is a way of being nowhere while claiming to be everywhere equally, ... a denial of responsibility and critical inquiry' (Haraway 1991, 191). Power-reflexive attunement views knowledge as not simply relative, but relational and complexly systemic. As such, power-reflexive criminology strives to optimize its 'situated objectivity' by making at least partially visible the scenes of power within which it performs its analytic labour.

Toward a Power-reflexive Practice of Criminology

In closing, I invite you to consider three general guidelines for a power-reflexive criminological imagination. The first asks us to discern how our biographical positions in global cybernetic circuits of power impact upon what we see (or are unable to see) about the problem of crime. Typically, this means risking discomfort. For those of us who are men, this requires, for instance, that we regard gender as much more than just a contributing factor to our analysis, the statistical variance of which we labour to reduce. Gender is also a place of systemic privilege for men, whether we consciously recognize this or not. It is thus important to ask how the blinders of our acquired masculinities often channel our attention toward certain types, aspects and explanations of crime, but not others. Is it possible that what fascinates us most about crime may occasionally seem strange, weird or even threatening to women? To gain insight about such matters, we must labour to glimpse how it is that women may view crime differently than ourselves, as diverse as women's own imaginative standpoints and relations to power are from each other.

Related challenges ask that we reckon with how our criminology is potentially influenced by the ways we inhabit *subject positions* embedded in systemic regimes of race, class, sexuality, nation and religion. Typically, this involves rites of unlearning that sometimes make us feel awkward, even embarrassed. While a difficult task, believe me, the rigours of unlearning and reflexive relearning are not lessons taught to future criminologists at most elite academic institutions. As such, acquiring a power-reflexive *quality of mind* may require non-standard sorts of pedagogy, such as the nurturing of scholarly communities committed to research aimed at social justice and the development of a *critical criminological imagination*. This makes a power-reflexive education in criminology not simply a gateway to the job market, but preparation for scholarship in the service of social justice and a sustainable 'way of living' (Mills 1959, 196).

Other power-reflexive pedagogies include ethnographic immersion in the troubled social geographies in which the crime and crime control take place; the study of histories and cultures other than own; learning additional languages; stimulating our imaginations by engaging creatively with various forms of art, literature, music, theatre, film, video, poetry and dance; making alliances with justice-oriented social movements; engaging in a discerning manner with the many new digital communicative technologies that populate the cybernetic worlds we inhabit – from YouTube, Twitter, and Facebook to websites and blogs of many sorts, and, as mentioned previously, making the time to write regularly in a reflexive personal/political journal.

A second guide to power-reflexive criminology involves asking how our own specific research relates to more general configurations of power. Whether we studying corporate price-fixing, cross-border sex trafficking or the relation between madness and crime, a power-reflexive sensibility challenges us to make connections between local crime dramas and the global fields of power in which they are staged. How, for instance, might pressures felt by financial traders in the workplace – including emotional and heart-palpitating pressures – not only foster the likelihood of corporate malfeasance, but also feed back into other systemic phenomena, such as changes in the rate of taxation, variations in the price of oil, or support for the latest war in the Middle East? Might pressures favouring price-fixing, insider trading or armed robbery be felt differently in economic systems other than the capitalist system of which most of us are today a part? What about prostitution and other forms of 'sex work'? Would sex work exist in the forms that it does – or even exist at all – if women had greater social and economic control over their own lives? What about mental illness and its relation to crime? Outbreaks of extreme and psychotic-like violence are undeniably frightening. But doesn't thinking about such violence in strictly individual pathological terms distract us from attending to the possibility the madness is also sometimes a twisted response to the pains of powerlessness? Thinking about complex criminological matters in systemic ways requires that we make imaginative theoretical connections between otherwise isolated events. It also represents a step toward integrating what we study with how we live.

A third guide to power-reflexive criminology involves applying what we learn in our studies to the pursuit of a more just society. This need not occur at some grandiose society-wide level. Perhaps our research will better attune us to injustices much closer to home. It is therefore important to remember that even modest efforts to combat local injustices can help reduce suffering. Most criminologists don't have to travel far to learn such a lesson. Think only of the epidemic of underreported sexual assaults taking place on the college campuses where so many of us work, or of the possibility of racial profiling by police in the communities in which we reside. When thinking about such troubling concerns, we should remember that even small changes or minor reforms sometimes spark imaginative transformations of a systemic sort. This may be particularly the case in societies, such as our own, that are increasingly governed by high-speed electronic swells of informational feedback. Power-reflexive pedagogies alert criminologists to such prospects, asking that we labour to make connections between local and global scenes of crime and crime control.

By linking our scholarship to efforts aimed at the realization of social justice, power-reflexive rituals encourage the development of a critical criminological imagination. In an age of cybernetic power, this demands a *quality of mind* attuned to omnipresent feedback loops of power – both cognitive and sensate – in which the criminal justice system is structurally situated, reproduced, resisted or changed. This calls upon us to ally our efforts, if modestly, with people everywhere trying to break free of the haunting shadows of criminal injustice. Practising reflexivity about power likewise reminds us that the making of a just society begins repeatedly in the here and now. This, after all, is where criminology is practised. As such, and inspired by C. Wright Mills, a critical criminological imagination challenges us to dismantle barriers dividing our way of scholarship from our *way of living*. I leave you with this challenge.

References

Agozino, Biko. 2003. *Counter-colonial Criminology: A Critique of Imperial Reason*. London: Pluto Press.

Alexander, Michelle. 2010. *The New Jim Crow: Mass Incarceration in the Age of Colorblindness*. New York: The New Press.

Althusser, Louis. 1971. 'Ideology and Ideological State Apparatuses.' In *Lenin and Philosophy and Other Essays*, translated by Ben Brewster, 121–76. New York: Monthly Review Press.

Aptheker, Herbert. 1960. *The World of C. Wright Mills*. New York: Marzani and Munsell.

Aronowitz, Stanley. 2012. *Taking it Big: C. Wright Mills and Making of Political Intellectuals*. New York: Columbia University Press.

Arrigo, Bruce and Dragan Milovanovic. 2009. *Revolution in Penology: Rethinking the Society of Captives*. Lanham, MD: Rowman & Littlefield.

Bataille, Georges. 1988. *The Accursed Share: An Essay on General Economy*, translated by Robert Hurley. New York: Zone Books.

Baudrillard, Jean. 1983. *Simulations*, translated by Paul Foss, Paul Patton and Paul Beitchman. New York: Semiotext(e).

Benjamin, Walter. 1969. 'Theses in the Philosophy of History.' In *Illuminations*, translated by Harry Zohn, 253–64. New York: Schocken Books.

Bogard, William. 1996. *The Simulation of Surveillance: Hypercontrol in Telematic Societies*. New York: Cambridge University Press.

Bonilla-Silva, Eduardo. 2001. *White Supremacy and Racism in the Post-civil Rights Era*. Boulder, CO: Lynne Rienner.

Brennan, Teresa. 1993. *History after Lacan*. New York: Routledge.

———. 2000. *Exhausting Modernity*. New York: Routledge.

Butler, Judith. 1993. 'Endangered/endangering: Schematic Racism and White Paranoia.' In *Reading Rodney King: Reading Urban Uprising*, edited by Robert Gooding-Williams, 15–22. New York: Routledge.

———. 1997. *The Psychic Life of Power*. Stanford, CA: Stanford University Press.

Castells, Manuel. 1998. *The Information Age: Economy, Society, and Culture, Volume 1. End of the Millenium*. Malden, MA: Blackwell.

Clough, Patricia Ticineto. 2000. *Autoaffection: Unconscious Thought in the Age of Teletechnology*. Minneapolis, MN: University of Minnesota Press.

DeKerseredy, Walter S. 2011. *Contemporary Critical Criminology*. New York: Routledge.

Deleuze, Gilles. 1995. 'Postscript on Control Societies.' In *Negotiations 1972–1990*, translated by Martin Jay, 177–82. New York: Columbia University Press.

Eglash, Ron. 1995. 'African Influences in Cybernetics.' In *The Cyborg Handbook*, edited by Christ Hable Gray, 17–27. New York: Routledge.

Ferraro, Kathleen J. 2006. *Neither Angels nor Demons: Women, Crime, and Victimization*. Boston, MA: Northeastern University Press.

Foucault, Michel. 1979. *Discipline and Punish: The Birth of the Prison*, translated by Alan Sheridan. New York: Vintage Books.

Gerth, Hans and C. Wright Mills. 1953. *Character and Social Structure: The Psychology of Social Institutions*. New York: Harcourt, Brace and World, 1953.

Gordon, Avery F. 1996. *Ghostly Matters: Haunting and the Sociological Imagination*. Minneapolis, MN: University of Minnesota Press.

Gramsci, Antonio. 1971. *Selections from Prison Notebooks*, translated by Quinton Hoare and Geoffrey Nowell Smith. London: Lawrence and Wishart.

Grosfoguel, Ramon. 2009. 'Geopolitics of Knowledge and the Coloniality of Power: Thinking Puerto Rico and Puerto Ricans from the Colonial Difference.' In *Culture, Power, and History: Studies in Critical Sociology*, edited by Stephen Pfohl, Aimee Van Wagenen, Patricia Arend, Abigail Brooks and Denise Leckenby, 479–506. Chicago, IL: Haymarket Press.

Hall, Stuart, Charles Critcher, Tony Jefferson, John Clarke and Brian Roberts. 1978. *Policing the Crisis: Mugging, the State, and Law and Order*. London: Macmillan.

Haraway, Donna J. 1991. *Simians, Cyborgs, and Women: The Reinvention of Nature*. New York: Routledge.

Hardt, Michael and Antonio Negri. 2002. *Empire*. Cambridge, MA: Harvard University Press.

Hayles, N. Katherine. 1999. *How We Became Posthuman: Virtual Bodies in Cybernetics, Literature, and Informatics*. Chicago, IL: University of Chicago Press.

Hill Collins, Patricia. 1990. *Black Feminist Thought*. Boston, MA: Unwin Hyman.

Kramer, Ronald C., Raymond Michalowski and D. Kauzlarich. 2002. 'The Origins and Development of the Concept and Theory of State-corporate Crime.' *Crime and Delinquency* 48: 263–82.

Kroker, Arthur. 2014. *Exits to the Posthuman*. Cambridge: Polity Press.

——— and Marilouise Kroker, eds. 2013. *Critical Digital Studies: A Reader*, 2nd edn. Toronto, ON: University of Toronto Press.

Lacan, Jacques. 1977. Écrits: *A Selection*, translated by Alan Sheridan. New York: W.W. Norton.

Martin, Randy. 2007. *An Empire of Indifference: American War and the Financial Logic of Risk Management*. Durham, NC: Duke University Press.

Michalowski, Raymond J. 1996. 'Critical Criminology and the Critique of Domination.' *Critical Criminology* 7: 9–16.

Mills, C. Wright. 1951. *White Collar*. New York: Oxford University Press.

———. 1956. *The Power Elite*. New York: Oxford University Press.

———. 1959. *The Sociological Imagination*. New York: Oxford University Press.

———. 1960. *The Causes of World War Three*. New York: Ballantine Books.

———. 1962. *The Marxists*. New York: Dell.

———. 1979a. 'IBM Plus Reality Plus Humanism = Sociology.' In *Power, Politics and People: The Collected Essays of C. Wright Mills*, edited by Irving Louis Horowitz, 568–76. New York: Oxford University Press.

————. 1979b. 'Language, Logic, and Culture.' In *Power, Politics and People: The Collected Essays of C. Wright Mills*, edited by Irving Louis Horowitz, 423–38. New York: Oxford University Press.

————. 1979c. 'On Knowledge and Power.' In *Power, Politics and People: The Collected Essays of C. Wright Mills*, edited by Irving Louis Horowitz, 599–613. New York: Oxford University Press.

————. 1979d. 'Situated Actions and the Vocabulary of Motives.' In *Power, Politics and People: The Collected Essays of C. Wright Mills*, edited by Irving Louis Horowitz, 439–52. New York: Oxford University Press.

————. 1979e. 'The Cultural Apparatus.' In *Power, Politics and People: The Collected Essays of C. Wright Mills*, edited by Irving Louis Horowitz, 405–22. New York: Oxford University Press.

————. 1979f. 'The Professional Ideology of Social Pathologists.' In *Power, Politics and People: The Collected Essays of C. Wright Mills*, edited by Irving Louis Horowitz, 525–52. New York: Oxford University Press.

Nelson, Alondra. 2002. 'Introduction: Future Texts.' *Social Text* 71 (special issue on Afrofuturism): 1–15.

Orr, Jackie. 2009. 'The Militarization of Inner Space.' In *Culture, Power, and History: Studies in Critical Sociology*, edited by Stephen Pfohl, Aimee Van Wagenen, Patricia Arend, Abigail Brooks and Denise Leckenby, 379–409. Chicago, IL: Haymarket Press.

Parenti, C. 2003. *The Soft Cage: Surveillance in America from Slave Passages to the War on Terror*. New York: Basic Books.

Pfohl, Stephen. 1992. *Death at the Parasite Café: Social Science (Fictions) and the Postmodern*. New York: St. Martin's Press.

————. 1993. 'Twilight of the Parasites: Ultramodern Capital and the New World Order.' *Social Problems*, 40(2):801–27.

————. 1997. 'The Cybernetic Delirium of Norbert Wiener.' In *Digital Delirium*, edited by Arthur and Marilouise Kroker, 114–31. New York: St. Martin's Press.

————. 2005. 'New Global Technologies of Power: Cybernetic Capitalism and Social Inequality.' In *The Blackwell Companion for Social Inequalities*, edited by Mary Romero and Eric Margolis, 246–592. Cambridge, MA: Blackwell.

————. 2009. *Images of Deviance and Social Control: A Sociological History*. Long Grove, IL: Waveland Press.

———— and Avery Gordon. 1986. 'Criminological Displacements.' *Social Problems* 33(6): S94–S113.

Pinderhughes, Charles. 2011. *Socialism and Democracy* 25(1): 235–56.

Quijano, Anibel. 2000. 'Coloniality of Power, Ethnocentrism, and Latin America.' *NEPANTLA* 1(3): 533–80.

Quinney, Richard. 1974. *Criminal Justice in America: A Critical Understanding*. Boston, MA: Little, Brown.

Reiman, Jeffery and Paul Leighton. 2013. *The Rich Get Richer and the Poor Get Prison: Ideology, Class, and Criminal Justice*. Boston, MA: Pearson.

Rifkin, Jeremy. 1998. *The Biotech Century: Harnessing the Gene and Remaking the World*. New York: Jeremy P. Tarcher/Putnam.

Staples, William G. 1997. *The Culture of Surveillance: Discipline and Social Control in the United States*. New York: St. Martin's Press.

Van Ginneken, Jaap. 2013. *Mood Contagion: Mass Psychology and Collective Behavior in the Internet Age*. The Hague: Eleven International Publishing.

Wacquant, Loïc. 2009. *Punishing the Poor: The Neoliberal Government of Social Insecurity*. Durham, NC: Duke University Press.

Weber, Max. 1964. *The Theory of Social and Economic Organizations*. New York: The Free Press.

West, Cornel. 1989. 'C. Wright Mills and W.E.B. Du Bois.' In *The American Evasion of Philosophy: A Genealogy of Pragmatism*, 124–50. Madison, WI: University of Wisconsin Press.

Williams, Patricia. 1991. *The Alchemy of Race and Rights*. Cambridge, MA: Harvard University Press.

Young, Jock. 2011. *The Criminological Imagination*. Malden, MA: Polity Press.

PART II
The Criminological Imagination, Theoretical Insights, Empirical Implications

Chapter 5

The Implications of the Sociology of C. Wright Mills for Modern Criminological Theory Revisited

Joseph A. Scimecca

In 1975 I published an article entitled 'The Implications of the Sociology of C. Wright Mills for Modern Criminological Theory'. There I argued that, with the exception of his classic article 'The Professional Ideology of Social Pathologists' (1943), Mills was not noted for any substantive contribution to the field of criminology. However, a comprehensive model of a social system Mills had developed to understand human beings, society and their interrelationship in history could provide the basis for a comprehensive theory of criminal behaviour.[1]

My premise was that Mills produced a 'working model of a social system' – an integrative model that sought to correct Pragmatism's essentially inadequate conception of social structure and Max Weber's deficient notion of personality-formation. Mills used this working model in the same manner, as did the classical theorists – as a basis upon which theories are constructed. The assumption here is that if the theory is found wanting, this need not detract from the model because it can be corrected and made more useful as an analytical tool. For example, Mills' famous 'power elite' thesis is best understood as a theory of stratification concerning weights and relations of elements of a model comprising a social system. Along these same lines, a theory of crime could be extrapolated from this model.

C. Wright Mills' Working Model of a Social System

Although Mills' 'working model' is implicit in almost all of his works, his most precise articulation of the model is found in *Character and Social Structure* (Gerth and Mills 1953) and in *The Sociological Imagination* (1959).[2] In the former work, Mills grafted a conception of social structure as an articulation of institutional

---

1   That Mills was a systematic sociological theorist who developed an integrated model of human behaviour and social structure is described in detail in Scimecca (1977).

2   The fact that Mills' working model of a social system was first set out in a co-authored work does not lessen its importance for an understanding of Mills' sociological

orders onto pragmatism's essentially social structureless notion of personality formation. He focused on the roles individuals played in various institutions orders, how personality was moulded by these various institutional orders, and how these various institutional orders were combined in any given society to form historical types of social structures. *The Sociological Imagination* is essentially a reformulation of the framework worked out in *Character and Social Structure*. The major difference between the two works is that *The Sociological Imagination* has less of an emphasis on personality formation, and more of an emphasis on the historical integration of particular social structures. Content that he had worked out a viable system of personality-formation in *Character and Social Structure*, Mills, in his subsequent works, could concentrate more on objective factors, what he referred to as 'the main drift' of those historical and structural forces that were often impersonal and unrecognized by those who were affected by their impact.

At the core of Mills' working model is a modified version of social behaviourism. Briefly stated, Mills saw the development of personality rooted in four key concepts: *organism*, *psychic structure*, *person* and *character structure*. Organism refers to human beings as biological entities and invites attention to structural mechanisms and undefined impulses. These elements are anchored in the organism, but their specific integration into emotional perceptions and purposes can only be understood by focusing upon one's psychic structure. According to Mills, person refers to the individual as a player of roles. Humans are social actors, and should be analysed in terms of their social actions. In this view, behaviour is best understood in terms of motives rather than explained in terms of stimuli and response. Character structure, the fourth concept, is the most inclusive term for the individual as a whole entity. It refers to the relatively stabilized integration of one's psychic structure and the various social roles played. Basically, those differences found among human beings are attributable to the constitution of their organisms; to the specific role configurations incorporated in their persons and to the idiosyncratic integration of their perceptions, feelings and will within a psychic structure. An adequate portrayal of an individual's personality formation thus involves the analysis of the four concepts within the limits of a given organism and the institutional confines of a specific social structure (Gerth and Mills 1953).

The bridge between individuals and their social structure and the central concept of Mills' working model approach is that of *role*. Roles are by definition interpersonal – that is, they are oriented to the expectations of others. These others are also playing roles, and our mutual expectations set up patterns of social conduct. The individual's psychological functions are thus shaped by specific configurations of roles that he or she has incorporated from society. The most important aspect of personality is the individual's conception of self, or one's idea

---

theory because fragments of it can be seen in Mills' works prior to *Character and Social Structure* and can be extrapolated for the general corpus of his writings.

of what kind of person one is (Gerth and Mills 1953, 22). The image of self one holds is formulated through an interpersonal context by taking into account what people think of us: 'Their attitudes of approval and of disapproval guide us in learning to play the roles we are assigned or which we assume. By internalizing the attitudes of others toward us and our conduct, we not only gain new roles, but in time an image of ourselves' (Mead 1934). The roles one plays and the image one holds of one's self are thus entrenched in the social context. It should be noted that Mills uses the concept of roles in the same manner as did George Herbert Mead – as a mechanism through which individuals develop a reflexive self which enables them to question their roles and the influence of institutions on their role expectations, thereby providing varying degrees of freedom (Mead 1934).

The psychology of an individual and the controls of a society are linked by the concept of role to *institution*. An institution, for Mills, is defined as 'an organization of roles one or more of which is understood to serve the maintenance of the total set of roles' (Gerth and Mills 1953, 13). The roles to be analysed are selected according to two criteria: (1) they must be of pivotal significance in the maintenance and transformation given types of institutional orders, and (2) they should represent the polar or extreme types within given institutional orders. A main focus of the model is upon the type of person selected and formed by the enactment and internalization of these roles. Roles make up the social person; institutions make up the society.

Institutional orders in Mills' working model are defined according to function – that is, an institutional order consists of all those institutions that have similar consequences and ends or which serve similar functions. For Mills, there are five major institutional orders which form the skeletal structure of the total society: the political, the economic, the military, the kinship and the religious orders. There are also several spheres of conduct, which characterize all of the institutional orders. Mills considered symbols, technology, status and education to be the four main spheres. They are called spheres because they are 'rarely or never autonomous as to the ends they serve and because any of them may he used within any of our five orders' (Gerth and Mills 1953, 29).

A social structure, therefore, is composed of institutional orders and spheres; its unity depends upon the relative importance of each institutional order and sphere, and their relation to each other.

A major concern of Mills was the integration of total social structures. He postulated four ideal type models of integration: (1) *correspondence* (several institutional orders develop in accordance with a common principle); (2) *coincidence* (various institutional developments lead to similar resultant ends; (3) *co-ordination* (one institutional order becomes dominant over the others and manages them), and (4) *convergence* (in their development, one or more institutional orders blend). *Correspondence* was best exemplified by the classic liberal society that prevailed in the USA during the first half of the nineteenth century. An example of *coincidence* is the Calvinistic society described by Max Weber (1958) in his treatise on Protestantism and Capitalism. Modern theocracies such as Iran, typify *co-ordination*. And the USA in the mid-twentieth century, as portrayed by Mills in *The Power Elite* (1956), is an example of *convergence*. Today, over a half century later, it would be difficult to argue that convergence in the form of the blending of two of Mills' institutional orders – the political and economic – does not characterize the USA.

Mills' theoretical framework is thus an important contribution to sociological theory in general because it offers a historical social psychology that can explain how human conduct assumes the form it does in any epoch. In short, Mills offers us a model that still can be used to analyse the manner in which psychological regularities are affected and shaped by historical social structures. In Mills' model the institutional orders act in an integrative manner according to the particular legitimization mechanism at work, and those individuals who assume positions of power within the institutional order may be said to constantly manipulate and coerce those who are powerless. Mills emphasizes the differential causal influences of various elements of a system, with the primary influence being power as it is located in the interaction of institutional orders.

This, then, is the general working model of a social system implicit in the works of C. Wright Mills, and in my 1975 article I spelled out its implications for criminological theory in four specific areas: (1) the formulation of criminal law; (2) the question of freedom and determinism; (3) the process by which an individual develops behavioural patterns which are labelled criminal, and (4) the mechanisms through which the society communicates that which it deems criminal. In the ensuing years I have slightly revised Mills' original model to incorporate those changes in the social structure that have occurred – a process that is well within the framework of Mills, who saw different eras influencing the integration of institutional orders (Scimecca 1994).

I therefore now revisit these four areas in light of recent history in the USA in relation to my revised model of Mills, and then conclude by looking at how this revised model can have implications not only for the four areas, but also as for such recent important critical criminology theoretical perspectives as *left realism, feminist criminology* and *peacemaking criminology* which have come to some prominence since Mills' death. I choose these three theoretical frameworks because their adherents not only want to understand society, they want to radically change and bring about a more humane and equitable society – a society that would radically alter the way crime is dealt with. This is in line with what Mills wanted to do, only his scope was much broader than crime.

A Modification of Mills' Model

My modification of Mills' model is fairly simple. As previously stated, Mills' model consists of five institutional orders – the political order, the economic order, the military order, the religious order and the kinship order (the family) – and four spheres of influence – symbols, technology, status and education. First, I drop the military institutional order as one of Mill's major institutional orders, viewing the military as subsumed in the USA under the political order. Obviously, this is not the case in other nations, such as Egypt and numerous Latin American countries. However, I question the autonomy of the military in the USA, and even President Dwight Eisenhower's us of the term 'military-industrial complex' in his 1961 farewell address points to the subservience of the military to the political and economic institutional orders. I add education as an institutional order in its own right, and not a sphere. I do this because I see it as more in line with Mills' Weberian emphasis on the importance of legitimacy holding the society together. I also add the mass media as an institutional order based on what Mills (1964) called 'the cultural apparatus', which was just coming to prominence when he was writing, and for the same reason I add education – the importance of legitimacy. Lastly, I divide the now six major institutional orders into *dominant institutional orders* and *subordinate institutional orders*. The major decisions – what Mills called the 'life and death decisions' of a nation – are made in the dominant orders, and these decisions are legitimized via the subordinate orders. My revised model, then, sees the political and the economic institutional orders in the USA as the dominant institutional orders, and the family, religion, education and mass media as the subordinate or legitimating orders (Scimecca 1994).

Mills' Revised Model and the Four Basic Areas of Concern for Criminological Theory

The Formulation of Criminal Law

A theory based on the revised model would be in agreement with those criminologists who in the mid-1960s and early 1970s began to question the then widely held assumption that the law is an instrument of justice.[3] However, it needs to be pointed out that Mills' original model did not, and the revised model also does not, embrace an instrumental Marxist perspective concerning the formulation of law. Rather than viewing the law purely as a mechanism for maintaining control by a ruling class, the revised model instead sees the law as an instrument of legitimization and integration dependent on what type of system integration mechanism best describes the society at the time. For example, seventeenth- and eighteenth-century America was a society integrated around the mechanism of *co-ordination*; the law was formulated to secure religious interests and values. Contemporary American society is integrated via the *convergence* of two dominant institutional orders: the political and economic. Therefore the law would seek to protect the political and economic interests rather than purely economic ones. This can be seen at work in the laws passed in the USA after September 11th, which gave broader powers to the government to deal with threats or perceived threats

---

3   See in particular, Quinney (1970, 1974).

to the society, and in those laws on the books which did not truly regulate the financial institutions, causing an economic recession in 2008.[4]

Freedom and Determinism

The question of freedom versus determinism can be traced to criminology's earliest beginnings. In short, although criminal law still adheres to the doctrine of free will postulated by Beccaria and his followers, most criminologists, I contend, subscribe to what Dennis Wrong (1961) has called an 'oversocialized conception of man', a position in criminology whose origins are in the Lombrosian School. While there are exceptions, I hold that most contemporary theories of crime in sociology espouse one form or another of determinism. If we look to the discipline of psychology, this is even more prevalent as psychology, in its rush to be seen as a science, is becoming more and more genetically based, with subsequent theories of crime embracing biological causation models.[5] The revised model, on the other hand, offers the very real possibility of freedom. Mills never ceased to adhere to the ideal of the Enlightenment *philosophes* that reason leads to freedom (Mills 1959, esp. ch. 9). Freedom lies in an individual becoming aware that structural problems are the keys to individual malaise. For Mills, individuals can alter institutions, institutional orders, and by extension the society. Although reason does not necessarily lead to freedom, the individual in Mills' (1959, 166–75) scheme is a rational being capable of transcending structural determinants and who is capable of exercising free choice. Power, in the form of those who control the dominant institutional orders, limits the freedom of individuals not holding power. The revised model would mirror these assumptions and provide an alternative to an over-socialized conception of man in criminology.

The Process through Which an Individual Develops Behavioural Patterns which are Labelled Criminal

The revised model starts with the basic premise of 'labelling theory' that those who have been defined as criminals eventually begin to conceive of themselves as criminals, and as they adjust to the definitions forced upon them, learn to play the role of criminal (Lemert 1964, 40–64; Tannenbaum 1938, 3–81). Although the probabilities that an individual will develop action patterns having a high potential of being defined as criminal would have to be spelled out, little if any attention has been given to the actual psychological process involved in the acceptance of a deviant criminal label. Offering an institutional model of where power lies and

---

4   Although this bears resemblance to structural Marxism, Mills' emphasis that the particular epoch defines the integration mechanisms at work supports his Weberian orientation.

5   See, in particular, Andrews and Bonta (2010), Cashmore (2010) and Raine (2002).

how the integrated character structure of the individual relates to his or her social structure provides a more nuanced take on labelling theory.

The revised model could map out just how a deviant image of self becomes accepted. This process would involve an analysis of the manner in which institutions select and reject their members; the institutional formation of person *vis-à-vis* the circle of significant others within the institution; the theory of premiums and traits of character, and the role of anxiety within a given social structure (Gerth and Mills 1953, ch. 6). Also, by looking to dominant institutional orders as the locus of power, we can see that those with more resources are more likely and able to reject the label of criminal.

Given that labelling theory has not progressed much since Mills wrote and still lacks an adequate notion of the psychological processes by which an individual accepts a deviant label, Mills' theory of personality-formation, combined with self-reflexivity and where power lies, could prove to be a valuable addition to labelling theory in general.

The Mechanisms through Which a Society Communicates that Which it Deems Criminal

Societies define diverse behaviours as criminal. Specific definitions are conveyed to the public via personal and mass communication. As Richard Quinney points out: 'the more the power segments are concerned about crime, the greater the probability that criminal definitions will be created and that behavioural patterns will develop in opposition to criminal definitions' (1970, 21). How the definitions are conveyed should therefore be of major concern to the criminologist. The relevance of the revised model to this aspect of criminological theory concerns a modification of Marx's famous dictum that the ideas of the ruling class are the dominant ideas of their epoch. Mills offers the concept 'master symbols' – those 'symbols that justify the institutional arrangement of the order' and their dissemination via the cultural apparatus/mass media (Gerth and Mills 1953, 276). Ideas, are not, in Mills' scheme, the ideas of an economic ruling class, but are those ideas which are best suited to the preservation of the status quo integrated around the particular integrative mechanism at work in a society – in the case of the twentieth-century USA, *convergence*.

For Mills, the cultural apparatus/mass media lies between an individual's existence and consciousness. It provides, via the management of symbols, the interpretation of reality an individual is dependent upon. It is the observation centres, the presentations depots of any given society (Gerth and Mills 1953, 276). The cultural apparatus/mass media is the source of an individual's identity, be he or she a law-abiding citizen or a criminal. As an important mechanism of identity, the cultural apparatus is established and used by dominant institutional orders. Behaviour which most threatens the integration of a society needs to be singled out for special attention. In order to fully understand the formulation and dissemination of criminal definitions, we must understand how and why these definitions are communicated and accepted by the general public. The revised model enables us to do just that.

Contemporary Theories and the Revised Model

Left Realism

Left realism grew out of a group of English criminologists' concern in the mid-1980s that criminologists, specifically those on the left, had neglected inner-city, lower-class crime. Positioning itself against both the right, which stressed an overly strict punishment orientation to crime, and the left, which viewed the offenders as victims of systematic exploitation, left realism saw the poor as victimized both by the capitalist system and by those criminals who were part of their own social class. Perhaps, though, left realists' harshest criticism was reserved for those Marxist criminologists whose primary concern was opposing the criminal justice system rather than providing support for the victims of crime.

The revised model is applicable here, in that the left realists were very cognizant of the process of criminalization. They stressed that the criminal justice system dealt with individuals rather than social groups, but didn't provide a model of personality development – something that Mills offers. Furthermore, the manner in which criminal behaviour is defined can be explained by the revised model. The cultural apparatus/mass media plays a huge role in describing and then helping to formulate definitions of crime and what form the law should take.

Finally, left realists were also more radical than other criminologists on the Left, whom they saw as 'armchair sociologists', criminologists who, rather than taking action against the conditions of crime, seemed content to just criticize it. Instead, left realists wanted to change the conditions of structural poverty as they simultaneously worked for justice for the under-classes. As Mills states, sociologists must 'study the structural limits of human decision making in an attempt to find points of effective intervention, in order to know what can and what must be structurally changed if the role of explicit decision in history-making is to be enlarged' (1959, 174).

Feminist Criminology

Although there are numerous variations of feminist criminological theory, such as liberal, radical or Marxist, they all share common assumptions. First, although biological differences are acknowledged, gender, as a socially constructed concept, is seen as being more important than biology. Gender differences are attributed to the social and cultural values that define gender roles. In particular, society is seen as male-dominated and patriarchal, which produces a male perspective on the social world.

Like many sociologists of his generation, Mills overlooked the importance of gender in favour of social class and power, and his ideas have had little or no impact on feminist theory in general or feminist criminology in particular. Still, this should not preclude the use of the revised model for feminist criminological concerns. What Mills' revised model offers is a way of taking biology into consideration. As historical creatures, more than biology shapes women. By focusing on the structural constraints, a broader picture of women can be seen, and with an understanding of the institutional constraints and role expectations, a blueprint for change, for achieving equality, can be fashioned. By concentrating on the integration of character structure – the interrelationship of biology, personality and role expectation – numerous hypotheses can be generated to help understand how the socially constructed concept of gender affects women's behaviour. For the most part, feminist theories had ignored the importance of biology, whereas the revised model considers biology as a variable in the formation of personality as well as seeing roles as a choice to be accepted or not depending on one position in the structure of power, be it paternalistic or institutionally formulated.

From the start, feminist criminological theorists have criticized the methods of analysis of criminal behaviour – methods that have been predominantly quantitative. Mills always claimed the problem should define the method of research, and not vice versa. The best example of this is found in *The Power Elite* (1956), where Mills, for all intents and purposes invented a new method of research, the sociology of leadership approach, when he questioned the decision-making models of power used by political scientists prevalent at the time because he noted that political decisions are made away from the eyes of social scientists (see Dahl 1961; Polsby 1963). The same can be said about crime.

Also, as women become 'emancipated' through changing gender roles, will there be support for what Freda Adler (1975) and Rita Simon (1975) postulated – that women would commit more crimes as they became more like men? Mills' revised model can help to investigate this hypothesis by asking the question of whether, for example, convergence of the political and economic institutional orders has affected the types of crimes committed by women.

Finally, feminist criminologists want to change society to ensure equality of the sexes. Mills' revised model offers a mechanism that can help usher in this change, in particular by focusing on the legitimacy that comes from the subordinate institutional orders – something that feminist criminologists have already begun to do by questioning patriarchal roles in the family.

Peacemaking Criminology

Peacemaking criminology arose as a theoretical perspective in the past two decades. Harold Pepinsky and Richard Quinney provided an initial foundation for studying crime through a peace-oriented perspective. Pepinsky maintained that the aim of the peacemaking approach to criminology is to 'figure out how we can get along without criminalizing and victimizing one another' (1989, 6). Similarly, Quinney stated that peacemaking involves 'a criminology that seeks to end suffering and thereby eliminate crime' (1991, 110). Peacemaking criminology, however, does not address why people commit crimes, except to imply that a non-peaceful society is conducive to crime. Peacemaking criminologists propose alternate methods for achieving peaceful solutions to the problem of crime. Methods such as reconciliation, restorative justice and alternative dispute-resolution, for example, are offered as processes for potentially limiting crime. Obviously, such peaceful alternative processes would entail an almost complete restructuring of society. For as Barak points out: 'for positive peace to exist as a prevailing social reality, the dominant sources of violence – alienation humiliation, shame, inequity, poverty, racism, sexism and so on – would have to be substantially reduced, if not done away with' (2005, 92). Mills' revised model can provide a means for achieving a peaceful society. By linking crime to the structure of society, the model would not only help to explain how the integration of institutional orders shapes the types of crime, but also show how to change the society.

To its credit, peacemaking criminology moves us away from looking at crime as the result of a dysfunctional and deviant individual. Mills' (1956) revised model, by focusing on the social structure and not on a dysfunctional individual, shows how what he called 'the higher immorality' is a structural phenomenon. While the cliché so often used is 'one rotten apple spoils the barrel', for Mills it is the barrel that is rotten because of the power arrangements in the society and the role expectations attached to those individuals who hold positions of power in the institutions.

Focusing on the formation of one's personality, the role expectations one encounters and the integration of the major institutional orders, provides a blueprint both for understanding crime and for changing society, as the peacemaking criminologists seek to do, and in this a revised Millsian model proves applicable today.

Conclusion

In this chapter I have argued that Mills' model of social systems still has relevance today. By looking at how the individual is shaped by his or her society, Mills offered not only a blueprint for understanding society (and by extension crime), but also a way of changing the society to lessen the impact of crime. Given that three major theoretical frameworks, left realism, feminist criminology and peacemaking criminology, all seek not only to understand crime, but to create a better society via a focus on crime, Mills' revised model can offer a relevant and comprehensive model for understanding how the individual is connected to his or her society. And even more importantly for the critical criminologist, the model shows how social change in the form of a more equitable and humane society can be brought about. This is something that is missing from so much of contemporary criminology today.

References

Adler, Freda. 1975. *Sisters in Crime: The Rise of the New Female Criminal*. New York: McGraw-Hill.

Andrews, D.A. and James Bonta. 2010. *The Psychology of Criminal Conduct*, 5th edn. New York: Elsevier Science.

Barak, Gregg. 2005. 'A Reciprocal Approach to Peacemaking Criminology: Between Adversarialism and Mutualism.' *Theoretical Criminology* 9: 131–52.

Cashmore, Anthony. 2010. 'The Lucretian Swerve: The Biological Basis of Human Behaviour and the Criminal Justice System.' *Proceedings of the National Academy of Sciences* 107(10): 4,499–504.

Dahl, Robert. 1961. *Who Governs? Democracy and Power in an American City*. New Haven, CT: Yale University Press.

Gerth, Hans and C. Wright Mills. 1953, *Character and Social Structure: The Psychology of Social Institutions*. New York: Oxford University Press.

Lea, John and Jock Young. 1984. *What is to be Done about Law and Order*. London: Penguin Books.

Lemert, Edwin M. 1964. *Human Deviance, Social Problems, and Social Control*. Englewood Cliffs, NJ: Prentice Hall.

Mead, George Herbert. 1934. *Mind, Self, and Society*. Chicago, IL: University of Chicago Press.

Mills, C. Wright. 1943. 'The Professional Ideology of Social Pathologists.' *American Journal of Sociology* 49(2): 165–80.

———. 1956. *The Power Elite*. New York: Oxford University Press.

———. 1959. *The Sociological Imagination*. New York: Oxford University Press.

———. 1964. 'The Cultural Apparatus.' In *Power, Politics, and People: The Collected Essays of C. Wright Mills*, edited by Irving Louis Horowitz, 405–22. New York: Oxford University Press.

Pepinsky, Harold. 1989. 'Peacemaking in Criminology.' *Critical Criminologist* 1:6–10.

Polsby, Nelson. 1963. *Politics and Social Life: An Introduction to Political Behaviour*. Boston, MA: Houghton Mifflin.

Quinney, Richard. 1970. *The Social Reality of Crime*. New Brunswick: NJ: Transaction Books.

———. 1974. *Critique of Legal Order*. Boston, MA: Little, Brown.

———. 1991. 'The Way of Peace: On Crime, Suffering, and Service.' In *Criminology as Peacemaking*, edited by Harold Pepinsky and Richard Quinney, 3–13. Bloomington, IN. University of Indiana Press.

Raine, Adrian. 2002. 'The Biological Basis of Crime.' In *Crime and Public Policy*, edited by James Q. Wilson and Joan Petersilia, 43–74. Oakland, CA: Institute for Contemporary Studies Press.

Scimecca, Joseph A. 1975. 'The Implications of the Sociology of C. Wright Mills for Modern Criminological Theory.' *International Journal of Criminology and Penology* 3: 145–53.

————. 1977. *The Sociological Theory of C. Wright Mills*. Port Jefferson, NY: Kennikat Press.

————. 1994. *Society and Freedom: An Introduction to Humanist Sociology*, 2nd edn. Chicago, IL: Nelson-Hall.

Simon, Rita. 1975. *Women and Crime*. Lexington, MA: Lexington Books.

Tannenbaum, Frank. 1938. *Crime and Community*. New York: Columbia University Press.

Weber, Max. 1958. *The Protestant Ethic and the Spirit of Capitalism*. New York: Charles Scribner & Sons.

Wrong, Dennis. 1961. 'The Over-socialized Concept of Man in Modern Sociology.' *American Sociological Review* 26: 183–93.

Young, Jock. 1987. 'The Tasks Facing Realist Criminology.' *Contemporary Crisis* 11: 337–56.

Chapter 6

Sympathy and the Criminological Imagination

Melanie White

It is impossible not to marvel at the scope of C. Wright Mills' argument in *The Sociological Imagination* (2000; first published in 1959). The book diagnoses the challenges that confront the social sciences and delivers a manifesto for their revival. To this end, Mills encapsulates their task and promise in what he terms the 'sociological imagination'. It is a perspective that examines the experience of the individual and the structure of society together as problems of history. Herein lies Mills' legacy for the social sciences: to understand the biography of the individual as always already intertwined with the history of society. As such, the sociological imagination involves an appreciation of how affective experiences such as happiness, well-being, uneasiness, anxiety and malaise are structurally organized. In most accounts of the sociological imagination, however, its structural features tend to be stressed at the expense of its affective or emotional dimensions. This chapter responds to this oversight. It argues that it is necessary to appreciate the affective dimensions of the sociological imagination as a condition for understanding how structural forces shape individual human experience. In so far as a concern for affect must be central to any consideration of the sociological imagination, it must also be a core feature of a 'criminological imagination'.

This chapter begins with a consideration of the affective dimensions of Mills' argument in *The Sociological Imagination*. The chapter draws attention to the capacities of emotional and conceptual awareness. It argues that these two dimensions of 'awareness', along with what Mills terms a 'moral sensibility', are constitutive of the sociological imagination. Accordingly, the chapter claims that together they make up the quality of mind that can translate the 'present as history' for the individual and the 'future of responsibility' for society. My main point is that this quality of mind is a *sympathetic* one – it aspires to create meaning for the inner life (at the level of the individual) and to generate a transvaluation of values (at the level of society). I press this argument into service in the next section of the chapter. Here, I consider the argument presented by the French sociologist and criminologist Gabriel Tarde in his masterpiece *Penal Philosophy* (1912; originally published in French as *Philosophie pénale* in 1890, and translated into English as *Penal Philosophy* in 1903). I claim that this classic social science text offers an early example of the 'criminological imagination'. To this end, I demonstrate that Tarde's conception of 'moral responsibility' exhibits the kind of sympathetic orientation that, according to Mills, is necessary to translate personal troubles into public issues. In closing, I consider the prospects of this 'sympathetic' quality of mind for the criminological imagination.

Emotional Awareness and Moral Sensibility

Mills argues that the sociological imagination is a hallmark of all classic works in the social sciences to the extent that they characteristically attend to the interplay between individual biography and the history of a society. Writing in 1959, Mills observes that the twentieth century has undergone such profound changes – from technological innovations that have transformed communication and transportation networks to manufacturing changes in consumption and warfare – that people have lost the capacity to orient themselves in the world. Mills observes that we can no longer trust our instincts or habits to guide us because they are grounded in '[o]lder ways of feeling and thinking [that] have collapsed and ... newer beginnings are ambiguous to the point of moral stasis' (2000, 4). In other words, the 'style of reflection' that traditionally characterizes this era is no longer adequate to the joint tasks of understanding our place in the world and deriving meaning from it (Mills 2000, 13). Mills observes that it was the traditional vocation of academics, specifically social scientists, to generate new ways of thinking to help people navigate the pitfalls and challenges of a given historical moment. The problem is that contemporary scholars have not stepped up to the challenge and have ignored the intellectual heritage of the sociological imagination. They have betrayed its promise by cultivating tendencies toward 'grand theorizing' or 'abstract empiricism' at the expense of a focus on the historical roots of individual and social life.[1] Accordingly, Mills warns of a burgeoning crisis in the social sciences because neither tendency can account for the 'foremost political and intellectual task of the social sciences', namely 'to make clear the elements of contemporary uneasiness and indifference' (2000, 13). For Mills, then, the sociological imagination is necessary, perhaps now more than ever, to demonstrate how our collective feelings of uneasiness and indifference are symptoms of the disjuncture between our most cherished beliefs and values on the one hand, and the rapid rate of technological, environmental and political changes in post-industrial life on the other. The stakes are significant. Individuals cannot appreciate the connection between their personal experiences and broad social structures, and consequently are confronted with a world that they

---

1   Both tendencies reinforce a 'liberal practicality' that increasingly substitutes 'pecuniary and administrative action' for morally and politically meaningful problems (Mills 2000, 72, 102). In general, Mills worries that academic life has become increasingly bureaucratized, such that social scientists ignore 'the nature of power and its relations to knowledge, the meaning of moral action and the place of knowledge with it, the nature of history and the fact that men are not only creatures of history but on occasion creators within it and even of it' (2000, 113).

do not have the tools to understand. Social scientists have access to these tools, but have failed to put them to use. And so, where individuals have lost sight of their moral calling, social scientists have betrayed theirs.

The two basic problems of the contemporary era, namely a lack of understanding and the loss of meaning, are grounded in shared feelings of uneasiness and indifference. The prevalence of these feelings suggests to Mills that individuals increasingly live their realities as a 'series of traps' – they feel disoriented and retreat from the world. Consequently, feelings of worry, anxiety and uneasiness make up more and more of their affective universe, and undermine their sense of security and well-being (Mills 2000, 3,165). We might say that this feeling of entrapment is both cause and effect in narrowing our field of obligations. We maintain our obligations to those who occupy our immediate field of interest (e.g., family, friends and colleagues), but we no longer have the means to sympathize with those who exist beyond it. Toward these others we may feel indifference and/or apathy (Mills 2000, 11–12). For instance, Mills suggests that we may feel *indifference* to pressing social problems – such as homelessness, poverty, unemployment, climate change – if we do not experience them at first hand. This feeling of indifference may turn to *apathy* if we feel we can do nothing to address these problems. Furthermore, we may experience *uneasiness* or *anxiety* that, if unchecked, can develop into a pervasive *malaise* (Mills 2000, 12).

The value of the sociological imagination is that it helps us to see the extent to which these feelings, both individual and collective, are socially organized. Here, an individual's affective experiences are conditioned to greater or lesser extent by structural transformations in society. Mills argues that '[w]ithin the broad limits of the glandular and nervous apparatus, the emotions of fear and hatred and love and rage, in all their varieties, must be understood in close and continual reference to the social biography and the social context in which they are experienced and expressed' (2000, 161). The social, moral and political complexity of our affective experiences cannot be understood, in other words, without examining their manifestation in the life of the individual and the history of society. We need to appreciate 'social structures and structural changes as they bear upon more intimate scenes and experiences' (Mills 2000, 162; see also 186). If our aim is to understand the nature of contemporary 'uneasiness and indifference', then we must use what Mills refers to as the 'primary analytic tool' of the sociological imagination: the distinction between 'personal troubles' and 'public issues'. Personal troubles are those experiences that 'occur within the character of the individual and within the range of his immediate relations with others; they have to do with his self and with those limited areas of social life of which he is directly and personally aware' (Mills 2000, 8). Public issues 'have to do with those matters that transcend these local environments of the individual and the range of his inner life' (Mills 2000, 8). Both personal troubles and public issues occupy similar affective ground insofar as they both stem from the perception of a threat, whether real or imagined, to one's value structure. Mills argues that '[i]t is the *felt* threat to cherished values … that is the necessary moral substance of all significant problems of social inquiry' (2000, 175; my emphasis).

The interplay between the sense of disorientation associated with a feeling of entrapment, the inability to understand the connection between our own lived experiences and the perception of threatened values, illuminates what Mills identifies as the basic moral dilemma of our time: 'the difference between what men are interested in' – their personal lives, their families, their careers – and 'what is to men's interest' – the future of our planet, our commitment to future generations and so on (Mills 2000, 193). He argues that contemporary social scientists should attend to this basic dilemma in order to fulfil the legacy of the classical founders, namely the pursuit of morally and politically meaningful problems. The difficulty is that – and this is Mills' ultimate worry – we have become so inured to the presence of threat that we no longer appreciate in it a real, genuine dilemma that we must and should care about. In other words, we may understand the terms of the distinction, but we fail to appreciate it as a choice that we are capable of making, no less one that we *must* make. The efforts of contemporary social scientists offer a prime example of this tendency. They tend to forgo the 'tough' problems and take refuge in mundane questions; consequently, they sacrifice the reforming spirit of the social sciences. Mills argues that we must resuscitate the sociological imagination so that we can embrace this dilemma as a basic *moral* responsibility of the social sciences. Not only does he argue that it is necessary to cultivate the requisite emotional awareness that can tackle the pervasive ennui that separates our interests from what is in our best interests, but it can also engender the moral responsiveness necessary to stimulate other commitments and attachments. Thus, the task of the sociological imagination, in short, is not strictly an intellectual one – it is also an emotional one.

I want to argue that the sociological imagination is a perspective that seeks to convert – or to use Mills' language, to *translate* – the general malaise associated with feelings of uneasiness and indifference into 'personal troubles' and 'public issues' as a problem for social scientists (Mills 2000, 9). In passing, Mills suggests that the sociological imagination involves 'translation' as a key methodological technique. I want to tease out what translation might mean for appreciating the role of affective experience in practising the sociological imagination. I want to suggest that translation involves both 'interpretation', in so far as it involves a shift from one language into another, and 'transformation', in so far as it involves a change in form, appearance and structure.[2] As a *technique of interpretation*, translation involves an appreciation of the interplay between theory and method, or rather between 'broader conceptions' and 'detailed information', to generate appropriate problems for social scientific analysis (Mills 2000, 66). This involves substituting concepts with social and historical specificity for universal formulations. As Mills

---

2   We might also posit other forms of translation such as 'normative' and 'synthetic' translation. Normative translation involves eliminating evaluative biases in the formation and solution of problems (Mills 2000, 78), and 'synthetic' translation involves translating grand universalizing narratives, as exemplified by Talcott Parsons, into a common vernacular. For an example, see Mills' (2000, 31) efforts in this regard.

argues, '[s]uch translation, of course, is what all working social scientists do', but what makes it part of the sociological imagination is its emphasis on the level of interpretive work required to 'solve or clarify problems of structural significance' (2000, 66). Put differently, the sociological imagination encourages us to select problems that 'include explicit attention to a range of public issues and of personal troubles; and they should open up for inquiry the causal connections between milieux and social structure' (Mills 2000, 130). Interpretive strategies, in short, help us to translate layers of conceptual abstraction or elements of empirical information into clear problem statements. As a *technique of transformation*, translation seeks to convert the emotional experience of indifference and uneasiness into conceptual problems that the social scientist can address. Indeed, Mills argues that:

> By our choice and statement of problems, we must first *translate* indifference into issues, uneasiness into trouble, and second, we must admit both troubles and issues in the statement of our problem. In both stages, we must try to state in as simple and precise a manner as we can, the several values and threats involved, and try to relate them. (Mills 2000, 131; my emphasis)

These two stages are accompanied by a third, which is the translation of public issues into meaning for human beings. Mills argues that this is the political task of the social scientist '– as of any liberal educator – continually to *translate* personal troubles into public issues, and public issues into the terms of their human meaning for a variety of individuals' (2000, 187; my emphasis).

The effect of this process of translation, this conversion if you will, is not simply to produce a framework for modern society that can help us to define our problems in light of the historical development of our social institutions (not to mention their political and economic dimensions). It also fosters meaning in individuals for their inner life. Translation invites an emotional awakening that brings to mind a sense of translation that has all but slipped away in contemporary usage, namely the sense of being transported by the strength of feeling. It is an emotional state akin to being captivated by the very fact of living in the world. This observation allows us to suggest that the sociological imagination seeks to effect in the individual nothing less than a conversion from 'entrapment' to 'enrapture'. Here, Mills' language captures this sense of translation when he observes that the 'capacity for astonishment is made lively again', and as 'they acquire a new way of thinking, they experience a transvaluation of values: in a word, by their reflection and their sensibility, they realize the cultural meaning of the social sciences' (2000, 8). In all its facets, therefore, translation involves the identification of a certain affinity between things, the recognition of a certain connection between people and events that is *sympathetic* in orientation.[3]

---

3   Scholars have noted that Mills' conception of the sociological imagination bears an affinity to Charles Horton Cooley's idea of the sympathetic imagination (Rose 1969, 623). Both require the presence of a 'quality of mind' that studies human experience in relation

I argue that this kind of sympathetic translation is a component of the quality of mind associated with the sociological imagination. It produces the 'emotional awareness' required to translate indifference into issues and uneasiness into troubles. Emotional awareness enables one to identify and respond to *felt* threats. The very existence of public issues and personal troubles presupposes, in other words, that one is able to apprehend a threat to one's values in the first place. The capacity to perceive such threats, to recognize that one's value structure is under siege, requires a level of emotional awareness that can only be cultivated by the sociological imagination. Therefore, if the aim of the sociological imagination is to address feelings of 'uneasiness and indifference', then we must *translate* both (1) the experience of uneasiness by clarifying which values are threatened, and (2) the experience of indifference by identifying the nature of the threat. This requires a degree of emotional awareness that is characteristic of what Mills calls the 'self-conscious thinker' – a person 'at work and aware of the assumptions and implications of whatever he is about' (2000, 121). For Mills, it is the goal of the social scientist to cultivate this level of emotional awareness in oneself and others. To do so, we must transform – indeed, translate – troubles into issues, disaffection into attachment, and masses into what Mills calls 'publics'. In his words:

> Whether or not they are aware of them, men in a mass society are gripped by personal troubles which they are not able to turn into social issues. They do not understand the interplay of these personal troubles of their milieux with problems of social structure. The knowledgeable man in a genuine public, on the other hand, is able to do just that. He understands that what he thinks and feels to be personal troubles are very often also problems shared by others, and more importantly, not capable of solution by any one individual but only by modifications of the structure of the groups in which he lives and sometimes the structure of the entire society. Men in masses have troubles, but they are not usually aware of their true meaning and source; men in publics confront issues, and they usually come to be aware of their public terms. (Mills 2000, 187)

In sum, the sociological imagination involves a series of techniques that translates inattention into awareness, troubles into issues and issues into meaning. It is in this sense that translation is a kind of conversion. It facilitates not simply a transformation of form, but also a transformation of substance. As such, it requires a sympathetic orientation to the world in which one lives. In other words,

---

to the play of historical forces. For Mills, this quality of mind mediates the biographies of individuals with the structural relations of society in order to cultivate an adequate study of social life. For Cooley (1926, 60), this quality of mind is 'introspective' in so far as it seeks to encourage a mutual understanding between self and others by virtue of shared thoughts and sentiments. There are clear resonances, not to mention differences, between these two thinkers. But the comparison is useful for my purposes because it brings out the sense in which the sociological imagination involves a certain degree of sympathy.

sympathetic translation consists in becoming aware of the fact that by living in the world, one contributes to the shaping of society (Mills 2000, 6).

The quality of mind that comprises the sociological imagination requires not only emotional awareness, but also a conceptual awareness of the structural history of society. Both are required to view the *present as history* and the *future as responsibility* (Mills 2000, 165). In so far as we appreciate the extent to which our current experiences are shaped by structural forces, we can grasp the 'present as history'; and in so far as we recognize that we have a moral obligation to future generations, we apprehend the 'future as responsibility'. We might say that the sociological imagination helps us to *interpret* the past into the present and to *transform* the future into the present. First, the interpretive work required to translate the present into the past requires that we recognize that '[h]istorical transformations carry meanings for individual ways of life' (Mills 2000, 158). Second, the translation of the future into the present involves the process of initiating a 'transvaluation of values' that can engender a new system of thinking and feeling (Mills 2000, 8). In sum, this particular brand of emotional and conceptual awareness consists in a moral sensibility that can 'state the values involved' in order to (1) translate emotions of uneasiness and indifference into personal troubles and public issues, and (2) to 'identify the threat to those values' when translating troubles into issues. We need awareness (both emotional and conceptual) and the moral sensibility that this enables in order to produce meaningful intellectual problems. Social scientists can work toward the goal of understanding and appreciating the intimate connection between personal experiences and broad, historically situated social structures, to escape from the entrapment of indifference and apathy, to embrace the transformative spirit of the social sciences, and to move away from the interests of men toward men's interests. As Mills (2000, 175) insists, this will enable us to get at the 'moral substance of all significant problems of social inquiry'. Thus, the social scientist who demonstrates this quality of mind is, according to Mills, an 'intellectual craftsman'. He or she 'will try to do his work in *awareness* of its assumptions and implications, not the least of which are its moral and political meaning for the society in which he works and for his role within that society' (Mills 2000, 76; my emphasis). In short, awareness and moral sensibility will allow us to regain the ability to orient ourselves in the world.

The Criminological Imagination of Gabriel Tarde

Let us consider the implications of the foregoing discussion for the prospect of developing a 'criminological imagination'.[4] So far, I have argued that the affective dimensions of the sociological imagination must be considered as the condition for generating morally and politically meaningful problems. This must also be, I take

---

4   See Frauley (2010), Krisberg (1974), Scimecca (1975), Williams (1984) and Young (2009, 2011) for other attempts to develop a 'criminological imagination'.

it, the baseline for the criminological imagination. To this end, the criminological imagination follows the sociological imagination in its efforts 'to grasp history and biography and the relations between the two within society' (Mills 2000, 6). Consequently, the task of the criminological imagination consists in posing the kinds of questions that we nominally associate with the sociological imagination: (1) What is the structure of the society under investigation? (2) What are the historical mechanisms of the society? (3) What are the society's prevailing forms of conduct? What distinguishes the criminological imagination from the sociological imagination proper, however, is the way it approaches the last question: What are the society's prevailing forms of conduct? Here, the aim is not simply to detail the character and conduct of a particular society; rather, one seeks to distinguish those forms of conduct that are 'normalized' from those that are 'pathologized'. From there, one must work to determine the historical conditions that foster a society's collective ideas about what conduct is considered 'normal and appropriate' as distinct from that which is considered 'abnormal and inappropriate'. As such, the specificity of the criminological imagination consists in examining those forms of conduct that call 'cherished values' into question. In so doing, it seeks not only to explore their meaning for the 'life of the individual' and the 'history of a society', but also to give us insight into which values are under threat and why. The criminological imagination, therefore, is oriented toward the task of viewing the 'present as history' and the 'future as responsibility' by considering how so-called 'crimes' vary historically from the perspective of the individual and of society. The criminological imagination, in other words, understands that crime is socially and historically organized; it recognizes that the normative valence of its positive (the upholding of norms) and negative (the contravention of norms) characteristics can change over time. This historical perspective allows us to appreciate the contravention of social norms as a potential source of innovation and transformation – indeed, as a site for possible 'translation'.

As with the sociological imagination, affect also shapes the form and substance of the kinds of translation performed by the criminological imagination. My overview of the sociological imagination demonstrated how feelings of uneasiness and anxiety can be accompanied by the loss of moral sensibility. From the perspective of the criminological imagination, then, the translation of affects into personal troubles involves asking whether a particular form of conduct contravenes established norms – and if so, under what conditions, and so forth. In cases where one's values are threatened, the criminological imagination can be used to determine the structural conditions that give rise to conduct that contravenes established norms and/or abrogates core values. The criminological imagination also involves the sympathetic translation of personal troubles into public issues, but it pays particular attention to conduct that challenges accepted norms. It offers a perspective that sees order in disorder and innovation in disobedience – at least in principle. The criminological imagination, in sum, uses the distinction between 'personal troubles' and 'public issues' to identify the points of tension between (1) the values that we support as a society (such as freedom of speech) and conduct that we abhor (such as racism), and (2) those values that we have outgrown (such as residential schooling for aboriginal children) and conduct that has been subject to moral and legal revision (such as recreational drug use and gay marriage).

Now let us turn to consider the work of Gabriel Tarde (1843–1904). Tarde is part of what Mills terms 'classic social science' and occupies one of the general 'intellectual universes' that has influenced the development of the quality of mind Mills advocates. Tarde offers an early, interesting example of the criminological imagination in his *Penal Philosophy*.[5] He served as magistrate in Sarlat, France before being called to Paris to serve as the Head of the Bureau of Statistics in the Department of Justice in 1894. Through the 1880s he became a well-known critic of the 'new' Italian school of positivism led by Cesare Lombroso through a series of articles published in the *Révue philosophique*. His first book, *La Criminalité comparée*, published in 1886, presented a preliminary argument for criminality as a sociological phenomenon. His argument in *Penal Philosophy* draws from his judicial experience and extends the sociological ground of his discussion of criminality into a lengthy rebuttal of positivist criminology.

Penal Philosophy opens with a clear statement of an important public issue: the reformation of criminal law. Tarde skilfully translates this issue into an intellectual problem that concerns the question of whether the individual is by necessity *always* responsible for injurious actions to one's fellow citizens. He notes: 'This very simple question, which is the fundamental point of the body of penal law, now seems as difficult of solution as the problem of squaring the circle' (Tarde 1912, 12). He implies that its difficulty stems from the perception of a general amorphous threat to the prevailing value structure. The lens of the criminological imagination enables Tarde to discern the roots of this threat in vague fears of a 'recrudescence of offences'. Such fears suggest the possibility of a general erosion (or, to borrow from Tarde, a 'derangement') of one's internal guiding principles and values (Tarde 1912, 8). But as he digs deeper, Tarde finds this to be a superficial explanation. He argues – and here he would seem to anticipate Mills – that the true cause of the so-called shift in traditional moral values resides in a complement of economic, political, and historical influences. The problem is that 'traditional morality is the only form that survives in our hearts', yet no coherent moral framework has emerged to take its place. He acknowledges that this may produce a feeling of moral anxiety that is 'fostered by the uncertainty of so many things around us'. Consequently, the public interest in reforming criminal law is, he argues, symptomatic of a general, more fundamental shift in morality that warns of an immanent 'revolution affecting laws and customs' (Tarde 1912, 53). But Tarde cautions that this crisis is not so serious as one might be led to believe. His equanimity derives in part from the historical perspective offered by the criminological imagination. It allows him to see the crisis in morality as a

---

5   Tarde's work is undergoing a resurgence as of late, although he is perhaps best known in sociological circles for his debate with Émile Durkheim (see Borsch 2005; Candea 2010; Latour 2002; Latour and Lépinay 2009; Toews 2003; Vargas et al. 2008; White 2012).

function of a basic structural change in society: the traditional interest to uphold familial respect has been increasingly replaced by the valourization of individual honour. To this end, he argues that:

> Morals themselves are becoming modernized. The old rights and duties are seen to dissolve, but one can also see that new rights and duties are in the process of formation, are spreading at a pace unknown to our ancestors, and that, if the sentiment of respect is everywhere undermined, the sentiment of the individual's honour ... as an incentive of actions is everywhere spreading from the middle classes to the working men .... (Tarde 1912, 11)

This brief overview allows us to claim that *Penal Philosophy* offers a perspective that enables individuals to see how their personal experiences are affected by broad structural changes at the level of society in couple of different ways. First, Tarde observes that one of the affective by-products of the so-called moral crisis in penal law is that it produces a feeling of 'despair' in the individual. Such despair may invite moral transgression, to the extent that a person may respond to the lack of meaning in his or her life by participating in conduct that he or she may have once reviled. Here, the specificity of the criminological imagination reveals itself. It explores how so-called transgressive conduct shapes the historical evolution of values. To this end, Tarde remarks that his contemporary moment is a time of transformation because it encourages experimentation as a possible reprieve from the affective experience of 'despair'. He argues, in characteristically florid style, that:

> it is dreaming, with open eyes, that realist dream which has nothing in common with the religious visions of the past; and for want of finding what it is dreaming about it says that the earth is insipid and the sky is empty; it is in despair. However, in order to get rid of its despondency or its boredom, it digs right and left, with fury, into that which has never yet been disturbed, that which has always been repulsed with disgust. (Tarde 1912, 8)

Tarde observes that the relation between despair and transgressive conduct (e.g., digging left and right into that which has not yet been disturbed) is not particular to his era. Rather, it is found in every historical period where one is confronted with new ideas derived from another historical period or adjacent society. It is this insight that allows Tarde to argue that the phenomenon of crime is a basic social reality.

Second, Tarde seeks to translate the public issue of 'penal reform' into a meaningful intellectual problem that can translate the fear of moral devolution. He tackles the reformist spirit of Italian positivists (e.g., Lombroso) for whom criminal behaviour is a hereditary as much as a psychological problem. He argues that such arguments function as an ill-conceived social Darwinism dressed up as 'criminal anthropology' (Tarde 1912, 45). For if one is 'by nature' a criminal, it will shape how we understand moral responsibility – for instance, can someone be responsible for their actions if they are 'born' a criminal? Tarde's primary concern is how to produce a coherent sociological argument that can counter (1) the idea of a natural born criminal, and (2) the idea that responsibility is by necessity connected to the capacity for free will (Tarde 1912, 12). Tarde worries that neither idea can attend to involuntarily injurious acts – such as, for instance, those performed during an attack of madness. As such, neither idea can form the basis of a theory of responsibility. The first eradicates responsibility altogether; the second is untenable because it is 'as outrageous for society as it is dangerous for the individual, for it likens society to a brute which strikes back blindly after a blow without seeking to discover whether it is or is not intentional or excusable' (Tarde 1912, 19, 216). It is on this ground that Tarde seeks to understand the conditions for penal responsibility. He proceeds methodically. First, he seeks to determine whether a criminal act is conditioned by natural causes or social influences. The answer will bear on how we understand, design and mete punishment. The idea that one is born a criminal logically prepares the ground for the elimination of the 'criminal' from society. However, if one 'becomes' a criminal through the entanglement of personal experience and structural factors such as class, profession, surroundings and otherwise, the possibility of rehabilitation presents itself (Tarde 1912, 217).

Tarde considers the problem of moral responsibility from a sociological lens. He asks: 'what is responsibility if it is not based on free will?' and 'how can we develop a conception of crime and the criminal that is based on social causes?' (Tarde 1912, 19). In order to appreciate Tarde's response to these questions, we must understand what he means by the terms 'social' and 'society'. It is helpful to consider his argument in *Les lois de l'imitation*, also published in 1890, and subsequently translated as *The Laws of Imitation* in 1903. As with *Penal Philosophy*, Tarde's primary claim in *The Laws of Imitation* is that social life is essentially imitative. He offers two basic principles in support of this argument. The first is that there is an 'instinctive' imitativeness in social beings. We might think of imitation here as a fundamental tendency of social life: 'the social being, in the degree that he is social, is essentially imitative, and that imitation plays a role in societies analogous to that of heredity in organic life or that of vibration among organic bodies' (Tarde 1903, 11, 56). We must not leap to the conclusion that this instinct is biological. Tarde observes:

> We eat, drink, digest, walk, or cry without being taught. These acts are purely vital. But talking requires the hearing of conversation .... I begin to feel a social kinship with everyone who talks, even if it be in a strange tongue, providing our two idioms appear to me to have some common source. (Tarde 1903, 66)

The sociality of conversation is such that it involves a kind of expressive association with another. This is what he means when he argues that the very nature of sociality is to imitate. For society is in different degrees an association, and association is to sociality what organization is to vitality (Tarde 1903, 69). Tarde's second principle is that imitation tends toward expansion. A social environment, in so far as it is essentially composed of similar elements, expands imitatively until it is checked by a rival tendency (Tarde 1903, 56). Because of this presumption of similarity, any innovation is therefore not 'new' in principle. Rather, it is the composite of imitative tendencies from bygone eras. In other words, they are comprised of ancient inventions rather than new ones. To this end, Tarde observes that:

> Moreover, the social forces of any real importance of at any period are not composed of the necessarily feeble imitations that have radiated from recent inventions, but of the imitations of ancient inventions, radiations which are alike more intense and more widespread because they have had the necessary time in which to spread out and become established as habits [and] customs. (Tarde 1903, 21)

Accordingly, the tendency to imitate particular beliefs and desires facilitates a drive to assimilation that is countered by the appearance of a counter-tendency. Individual members of society will need to weigh the relative merits of one imitative tendency against those of the other, eventually choosing one. This tendency will then proceed much like a contagion, assimilating beliefs and tendencies all the while, until it is confronted by another counter-tendency (Tarde 1903, 62).

Now, from the perspective of our discussion of the criminological imagination, Tarde offers a theory of society that exhibits a structural and historical awareness. Tarde's concern with the relationship between despair and transgression mirrors to some extent Mills' interest in the disjuncture between 'personal troubles' and 'public issues'. For Tarde, the imitation of beliefs and desires is effectively a historical process of transformation – indeed, of translation. Tarde (1903, 49) argues that there is a natural inclination toward imitation that communicates something of the 'continuity, the power and the irresistibility' of the belief or desire in question. The imitation of particular beliefs, for instance, radiates from one person to another, proceeding little by little, developing in intensity, until such time as they become customary for that society. Hence, law is only the 'formalization of mutually determined engagements and agreements, of rights and duties' (Tarde 1903, 61). Put differently, assimilation is an outcome of imitation, rather than a pre-condition for it. Homogeneity is, therefore, not the root of imitation. According to Tarde: 'In fact, all homogeneity is a likeness of parts and all likeness is the outcome of an assimilation which has been produced by the voluntary or non-voluntary repetition of what was in the beginning an individual innovation' (1903, 72). We might put it this way: imitation tends toward homogeneity, but what sparks the desire to imitate is an inventive impulse. It is the radical and innate diversity of an idea or belief that is worth imitating, that drives social life.

If we return to Tarde's argument in *Penal Philosophy*, we can see the extent to which it is also committed to imitation as a basic element of sociality. But what distinguishes *Penal Philosophy* from *The Laws of Imitation*, among many things, is the particular emphasis on crime as an essentially imitative phenomenon. For Tarde, the criminal is a 'social being' in so far as his or her beliefs and desires are imitative, even when inventing, because he or she always 'uses in combination imitations obtained from various sources' (1912, 277). As much as one may speak of imitation as a 'social' contagion, so too can one speak of it in terms of a 'criminal' contagion (Tarde 1912, 279). If we consider the idea of a 'social' imitation, the capacity to imitate a belief or desire implies the ability to resist its pull or sway. Such resistance may take the form of invention, and may be the harbinger of an imitative tendency that may eventually take the form of a counter-current. Such resistance may be perceived to be 'criminal' in so far as it contravenes established social norms that formalize generally accepted beliefs. But in so far as this 'criminality' may offer a counter to these beliefs, one may see them fragment over time. As for the question of moral responsibility, then, Tarde (1912, 277) argues that the extent to which criminality is essentially social means that the criminal is a member of society; as such, he or she must be responsible for any criminal acts he or she commits.[6] Let us pause briefly to consider Tarde's observations about crime as distinct from the criminal. To the extent that the criminal is a social being, Tarde argues that all social beings have an 'elementary moral sense' that is basic to social life. It has existed in all societies and is common to all peoples. What is considered 'moral' may differ from one society to the next, but what remains constant is a basic 'moral sensibility' that enables us to distinguish right from wrong. This elementary moral sense consists in two feelings: pity and probity (Tarde 1912, 71–2). Pity involves the feeling of sorrow and compassion that derives from a concern for the suffering of others. Probity reflects the emotional commitment to moral principles. In so far as the criminal is a social being, he or she will have the capacity to feel pity and probity to greater or lesser extent. This means that the criminal can be made to *feel* morally responsible for any transgressive acts. In so far as feelings of pity and probity are the basis for moral responsibility, Tarde's 'elementary moral sense' exhibits the kind of sympathetic orientation that Mills argues is necessary to translate personal troubles into public issues.

In summary, Tarde defends a conception of the criminal as a social, not a biological, being – one who is pre-disposed, as all social beings are, to imitation. The responsibility for committing a criminal act is borne by the criminal, who, by virtue of his or her basic sociability, must exhibit a minimum moral sense by which one has 'ability to suffer by reason of sympathy for the sufferings of another' (Tarde 1912, 181). Even though crime may be a 'monstrosity' from the perspective of society, it is also possible to conceive of it as a 'triumph of the individual' because it reflects an innovative impulse: 'From the social point of view crime may be a monstrosity, but not from the individual or organic point of view, because it is the absolute triumph of egoism and of the organism over

---

6 According to Tarde, there are some individuals – such as those who are mentally insane – who are not imitative beings, and as such lack the kind of sociality that would render them responsible.

the brakes of society' (Tarde 1912, 221). Society must stem crime, from Tarde's perspective. To do otherwise is to risk the sanctity of consolidated beliefs and practices that have developed over many, many years. In other words, to the extent that society depends on the imitation of social norms and values, if it sought to glorify the criminal, it would hasten its own death: 'The criminal is the man that society, when it is capable of living and is regular, is compelled to eliminate' (Tarde 1912, 222).

Tarde's *Penal Philosophy* offers an interesting example of the criminological imagination. He translates the public issue of penal reform into a meaningful intellectual problem that explores the social roots of moral responsibility. He offers an analysis of the criminal and crime as rooted in social forces of imitation. He argues that the criminal is part of a particular social milieu in so far as social beings exhibit a basic tendency to imitate beliefs and desires. And he demonstrates how the threat to moral sensibility only surfaces if one adopts the views of the Italian positivist school. For them, the criminal cannot be responsible precisely because he or she is born a criminal – and as such, cannot in principle have feelings of pity or probity because such feelings are socially organized. Hence, his argument claims the sociality of the criminal in order to demonstrate that the criminal is morally responsible for his or her acts. A sympathy for another's suffering and feeling remorseful for one's acts – both are affective experiences that root Tarde's conception of moral sensibility. For Tarde, as for Mills, they form the basis for the future of responsibility, both for the individual and for society.

Conclusion

We might say that the 'promise' of the sociological imagination is expressed by the sympathetic quality of mind that can appreciate the importance of history for individual experience and social life. Both Mills and Tarde demonstrate that sympathetic translation depends on the presence of a basic level of emotional and conceptual awareness in addition to a moral sensibility that can state problems in relation to social historical structures and individual biography. Obviously, Tarde's analysis of criminality and moral responsibility reflects his cultural and historical context. But this is precisely the goal of the criminological imagination – for it offers one way of conceptualizing the relationship between social structure and individual conduct to demonstrate that criminality is an important facet of social life, and can be the basis of politically and morally meaningful problems. We must be mindful of Mills' (2000, 145) dictum that every social science – whether it be sociology or criminology – has a history. And it is from this perspective that Tarde can speak to us and continue to have relevance for us. If the criminological imagination is to take hold, we must be consistently bring our history to bear on the choice of our problems and the nature of the work we undertake. Such is the task and the promise of the criminological imagination.

References

Borch, Christian. 2005. 'Urban Imitations: Tarde's Sociology Revisited.' *Theory, Culture & Society* 22:81–100.

Candea, Matei. 2010. *The Social after Gabriel Tarde*. London: Routledge.

Cooley, Charles Horton. 1926. 'The Roots of Social Knowledge.' *American Journal of Sociology* 32:59–79.

Frauley, Jon. 2010. *Criminology, Deviance, and the Silver Screen: The Fictional Reality and the Criminological Imagination*. New York: Palgrave Macmillan.

Krisberg, Barry. 1974. 'The Sociological Imagination Revisited.' *Canadian Journal of Criminology & Corrections* 16:146–61.

Latour, Bruno. 2002. 'Gabriel Tarde and the End of the Social.' In *The Social in Question: New Bearings in History and the Social Sciences*, edited by P. Joyce, 117–32. London: Routledge.

——— and Vincent Antonin Lépinay. 2009. *The Science of Passionate Interests: An Introduction to Gabriel Tarde's Economic Anthropology*. Chicago, IL: Prickly Paradigm Press.

Mills, C. Wright. 2000. *The Sociological Imagination*. Oxford: Oxford University Press.

Rose, Arnold M. 1969. 'Varieties of Sociological Imagination.' *American Sociological Review* 34:623–30.

Scimecca, Joseph A. 1975. 'The Implications of the Sociology of C. Wright Mills for Modern Criminological Theory.' *International Journal of Criminology and Penology* 3:145–53.

Tarde, Gabriel. 1903. *The Laws of Imitation*. Translated by E. C. Parsons. New York: Henry Holt.

———. 1912. *Penal Philosophy*. Translated by R. Howell. Boston, MA: Little, Brown.

Toews, David. 2003. 'The New Tarde: Sociology after the End of the Social.' *Theory, Culture & Society* 20:81–98.

Vargas, E.V., B. Latour, B. Karsenti, F. Aït-Touati, and L. Salmon. 2008. 'The Debate Between Tarde and Durkheim.' *Environment and Planning D: Society and Space* 26:761–77.

White, Melanie. 2012. 'The Social after Gabriel Tarde: Debates and Assessments.' *Journal of Cultural Economy* 1–7.

Williams, Frank P. 1984. 'The Demise of the Criminological Imagination: A Critique of Recent Criminology.' *Justice Quarterly* 1:91–106.

Young, Jock. 2009. 'Moral Panic: Its Origins in Resistance, Ressentiment and the Translation of Fantasy into Reality.' *British Journal of Criminology* 49:4–16.

———. 2011. *The Criminological Imagination*. Cambridge: Polity Press.

Chapter 7

Re-imagining Social Control:
G.H. Mead, C. Wright Mills and Beyond

Nicolas Carrier

> Reality is never given to consciousness as such, but only in the way that the
> operations of consciousness control themselves. (Luhmann 1995, 264)

The Sociological Imagination aimed at nothing less than to (re-)program both
the means and ends of mid-twentieth-century (American) sociological practice
and ethos. Mills (1959b) reproved sociologists seduced either by 'abstracted
empiricism' or 'grand theory', two polar opposites sharing the same vacuity.
As is well known, to possess a 'quality of mind' testifying to the sociological
imagination means the ability to connect milieu-specific troubled biographies
with historical-specific problematized structures. Mills' plea is for sociologists to
nurture this quality of mind and to become cultural workers (to avoid his own
patriarchal notion of 'cultural workmen'). To commit sociology is to cherish and
protect humanism, reason and liberty, and also to guard against threats highly
reminiscent of Horkheimer and Adorno's (1944/1974) horrid nightmares, such
as manipulation, technocracy and 'rationality without reason', 'psychological
illiteracy', and the spectre of a society of 'submissive masses' and 'cheerful
robots'. In the eyes of Mills (1959a, 15), the injunction to muster a sociological
imagination cogently rests on the historical coincidence of urgent intellectual and
political tasks.

Deflem (2013) has argued that *The Sociological Imagination* – in conjunction
with other key sociological contributions equally belligerent towards Parsons' *The
Social System* (1951) – initiated the first of a series of sociological diagnoses of
the crisis of American sociology. These self-diagnosed crises, he suggests, have
now come to a halt since the climactic 'anti-crisis' moment of public sociology
à la Burawoy (e.g., 2004, 2005a, 2005b).[1] This moment would consecrate Mills'

---

1 The continuity between Mills and Burawoy is also suggested by Nickel (2010, 697),
who reads *The Sociological Imagination* as Mills' 'version of public sociology'. Pleas for a
sociological imagination have led to similar ones in other porously bounded spaces of social
scientific practices (such as anthropological ethnography [Atkinson 1990] and criminology
[Young 2011; Barton et al. 2007]), just as calls for public sociology have been followed by
calls for public philosophy, public ethnography, public history, public criminology and so
on (see notably Carrier 2014; Powell 2012; Wacquant 2011).

indelible imprint on American sociology: 'Sociological radicalization has now been accomplished to the point of a full institutionalization of public sociology as an approach that can no longer be objected to without destroying or, at least, attacking the whole of actually existing sociology itself' (Deflem 2013, 160).[2] Whether we find Deflem's analysis compelling or not, it clearly illustrates both the impact and the perennial actuality of Mills' most programmatic sociological work. Even if we find that sociological practices trying to respond to Mills' plea have 'far too often been limited to conceiving very orderly sets of social practices' (Wagner 1994, 73), or even if we agree with Beck (1999, 134) that the paths towards the sociological imagination devised by Mills are no longer adequate to grasp the complexities, 'paradoxes and challenges of reflexive modernity', there is hardly any observable dissensus within the social sciences on the virtues of imagination.

These virtues are praised in the realms of social scientific practices that self-differentiate themselves, at least nominally, from the majestic territory of sociology. This is done in at least three different ways. First, it can take the form of attempts to bring Mills' strategies within other field of studies. As Frauley documents in Chapter 1 in this volume, this is largely what criminologists have done so far, the criminological imagination remaining largely a copycat notion without much criminological specificity, which oftentimes does nothing more than add a layer of branding to practices already described as 'critical criminology' (e.g., Barton et al. 2007) or 'cultural criminology' (Young 2011). Second, it can take the form of Mills' ambitious attempt at (re)programming the means and ends of a particular bounded academic space, not through Mills' language, but in the idiosyncratic terms of this differentiated space. Such is the case, for instance, in Atkinson's *The Ethnographic Imagination* (1990), which notably focuses on the politics of aesthetics and conventionality of the social scientific textualization of reality. The case remains to be made that criminology can pretend to mobilize a language irreducible to the sociological one, allowing for the rigorous exposition of a criminological imagination that could be satisfactorily differentiated from Mills' programme.[3] And third, praising imagination in the social sciences can take

---

2　For Deflem, this is not cause for celebration, for he suggests that in *The Sociological Imagination*: 'C. Wright Mills has little to say about what the sociological imagination would be other than the capacity to relate private troubles with public issues or to bridge biography and history and to do so in a simple language' (2013, 158).

3　To be clear, many criminological practices – such a biosocial criminology, administrative criminology, crime science and much of 'mainstream' aetiological criminology – are irreducible to a properly sociological language, and operate within a research doxa in which the programme of *The Sociological Imagination* is likely to be regarded as either meaningless or 'unscientific'. The criminological mediation of Mills' programme is necessarily done from a sociologically informed (or at least sensitized) mode of criminological practice – a mode which, quite obviously, neither saturates nor dominates the complex set of communications that dynamically constitute academic criminology (i.e., scientifically territorialized practices of communications that are self-differentiated from non-criminological ones, sometimes through the claim that criminology is an autonomous discipline).

the more humble form of an invitation to widen either the points or the means of observation of a given field of study – that is, to add a focus on objects previously neglected, or to revisit the tools through which society is being observed. In this case, the virtues of imagination are to be found in allowing a field of study to problematize and transcend self-imposed boundaries, such as those that nation states present for many criminological practices (Aas 2007; Stanley 2007). This chapter adopts this third approach and limits its ambitions to submitting the project to re-imagine social control.

The chapter is structured around the following lines of argumentation: social control is a foundational concept of American sociology that was severely truncated in the 1960s and 1970s, allowing it to be placed within the relatively exiguous conceptual trophy case of critical criminology. The truncation of the concept of social control, which led to the current criminologically orthodox social reaction to deviance perspective, operated by the indictment of previous uses of the concept for the blind spot they created on issues of power and normative conflicts. But this indictment proceeded by ignoring important and critical uses of the concept, notably by Mills. Returning to his conceptual work on social control might provide studies of the social with a way to go beyond the 'problematic depression' of the concept (Carrier 2006b). In order to do this, we need to clarify the critical twist given by Mills to Mead's approach to social control, which is concerned with processes of symbolic interaction. Mills focuses more on processes of symbolic communication, yet in a way that is not without limitations. Building from Mead and Mills, a re-conceptualization of social control as communicational achievement is outlined.

A last introductory comment: the re-imagination of social control proposed in this chapter is done by mobilizing the complex jargon of social theory, particularly Luhmannian jargon, frequently associated with the unintelligibility of Parsonian grand theory (see Teubner 1989).[4] This might appear quite paradoxical in an anthology on the classic slayer of sociological jargon and grand theorizing.[5] Still, if Mills (1959b, 120) presented 'the classic social analyst' – a figure with which he self-identified – as someone 'repelled by the association and dissociations of Concepts', he added that the complexity of a conceptual discussion is appropriate when the analyst believes it can 'enlarge the scope of his sensibilities, the precisions of his references, the depth of his reasoning'. As such, the discussion that follows is approached in Mills' spirit of developing a 'parallax view' (Frauley, Chapter 1 in this volume; Kemple and Mawani 2009). This is much needed given the stasis of social scientific visions of social control since Foucault's concerns with anatomo-politics (which largely informs the criminological critical use of social control

---

4   This chapter builds on and expands previous contributions (Carrier 2006b, 2008a, 2008b, 2011).

5   Obviously, it is for the reader to decide whether this chapter is 'drunk on syntax and blind to semantics', as Mills (1959b, 34) characterized vacuous 'grand theory'.

since Cohen's *Visions of Social Control* [1990]) and with bio-politics (which informs many social analyses of 'governmentalized' modes of regulation).[6]

The Expunction of Mills from the Criminological History of the Concept of Social Control

In the USA, the concept of social control was from the outset the architectonic concept upon which a nascent institutionalization of a science of society could rely to decipher the mechanisms underlying the dynamic (re)production of society – a society in which, following Tönnies' foundational *Gemeinschaft und Gesellschaft* (1887), order could no longer be thought of as resulting from natural or communal processes. E.A. Ross (1901), to whom the paternity of the concept of social control is frequently attributed, proposed his infamous and capacious list of modes of social control (including public opinion, law, art, beliefs, social valuations, education, custom, illusion, religion, personal ideals and enlightenment), which together constituted 'the system of social control' responsible for the constitution and reproduction of the artificial order sustaining American modernity. The artificial nature of social order in the context of modernity led Ross to emphasize the political quality of many modes of social control, responsible for the manufacture of individuals' will, sense of duty, self-control, judgement and sentiments. For Ross, sociology can help society to identify and to steer modes of social control founded in Reason – that is, operating a useful domination over individuals.[7] Moreover, sociology can help prevent two potential authoritarian drifts of modernity. The first is the transformation of social control into 'class control', whereby dominant forces leech upon society and use its institutions to their own benefits, imperilling the commonwealth. The second is a system of social control which 'succeeds only too well' in the 'domestication of human beings', taming the strength of

---

6   This fixity has been denounced by Lianos (2003, 2010, 2012; Lianos and Douglas 2000) and Bogard (1996, 2006), who are the only authors I know of to have proposed original and daring ways to re-imagine social control in contemporary society. For a thorough engagement with their own reworking of the concept of social control, see Carrier (2008a).

7   For instance, Ross insists that 'each increment of social interference should bring more benefit to persons as members of society than it entails inconvenience to persons as individuals' (1901, 419). Sociological knowledge on the domination of society over individuals would come with great responsibilities: 'The secret of order is not to be bawled from every housetop. The wise sociologist will show religion a consideration it has rarely met with from the naturalist. He will venerate a moral system too much to uncover its nakedness. He will speak to men, not to youth. He will not tell the "recruity", the street Arab, or the Elmira inmate how he is managed. He will address himself to those who administer the moral capital of society – to teachers, clergymen, editors, law-makers, and judges, who wield the instruments of control; to poets, artists, thinkers, and educators, who guide the human caravan across the waste. In this way he will make himself an accomplice of all good men for the undoing of all bad men' (Ross, 1901, 441).

Americans – the 'last descendants of the German race' – and imperilling the development of human nature and civilization by 'canceling natural advantage'.[8]

The contributions of Ross, Park and Burgess (1921), Lumley (1925) and Mead (1925), as well the incremental influence in the USA of Durkheim's *De la division du travail social* (1893/2007), fastened work on social control to preoccupations with social unity produced through the domination of society over individuals, as well as to the attendant lurking threats of 'social disintegration' (Castel 1988). The culmination of this intellectual path is Parsons' *The Social System* (1951), which was particularly targeted in the claims that social control, as it has been used until the 1960s, suffered from an a-critical normative monism, that it could not support a strong critique of power and domination (particularly when exercised by the state), that it could barely be distinguished from socialization processes, and that it led, as Gibbs (1994, 50) advanced, to nothing more than the tautological statement that 'social order maintains social order'.[9]

The onslaught on a concept of social control articulated to a theorization of society, solidarity or social order successfully established the narrow conceptualization proper to the social reaction to deviance perspective, which is now orthodox in criminological productions. The narrowness of the concept is deliberate so as to enable criminological analyses of processes through which humans are constituted as deviants or criminals, and are acted upon on such grounds. This great post-Parsonian transformation of the concept enabled positivistic projects to measure and predict social control (e.g., Black 1984), but mostly stimulated a massive, multipronged and ongoing critique, focused on objects such as labelling strategies, classificatory schemes, moral panics and moral entrepreneurs, medicalization processes, police repression, crime prevention strategies, exclusionary policies, net-widening, correctionalism, ontologized conceptions of crime, carceralization, the prison-industrial complex, surveillance, penal populism and criminology itself.

Spotlighting all social processes constituting and reacting to deviance and crime, the narrow concept of social control provided a foundational element through which the very identity of critical criminology could be delineated and secured. Notwithstanding the crucial and often tremendously influential critiques

---

8   Ross notably wrote: 'the art of domesticating human beings may succeed only too well. Something of the mournfulness and even disgust with which we look upon the shrivelling of the female breast with the advent of the patent baby food, the decay of the teeth with the perfecting of dentistry, the degeneration of the eye with the improvement of spectacles, and the dermal decadence that follows in the train of scientific clothing, – something of this seizes us when we contemplate the great agencies of Law, Public Opinion, Education, Religion, and Literature speeded to their utmost in order to fit ignoble and paltry natures to bear the moral strains of our civilization, and perhaps by the very success of their work cancelling the natural advantage of the noble over the base, and thereby slowing up the development of the most splendid qualities of human nature' (1901, 438).

9   See, among others, Melossi (1990, 2008), Sumner (1997), Lowman et al. (1987), Cohen (1985), Black (1984), Robert (1984), Cohen and Scull (1983), Meier (1982) and Taylor et al. (1973).

of various mechanics and logics of human sorting that it allowed, the great transformation of the concept of social control is not without costs, as it generates blind spots for social scientific practices of interpretation and analysis. *The New Criminology* (Taylor et al. 1973) and other influential critiques (e.g., Liazos 1972) pointed out that criminology is becoming increasingly blind to wider political contexts and to capitalistic hegemony. Smart's *Women, Crime and Criminology* (1976) indicted not only 'malestream' criminology, but also attempts to make criminology autonomous from sociology, resulting in the inability to place its objects in the domain of sexuality. Other feminists followed suit, suggesting that the narrow concept creates a blind spot on 'the genderized formation of desires, role models and dreams' (Scheerer and Hess 1997, 100). Foucault's call to cut off the sovereign's head (e.g., 1975, 1976, 1997) also inspired many critiques (e.g., Otero 2003; Hunt 1997) which allude to problems stemming from tying social control to formal repressive instruments and activities, imposing a blind spot on capillary forms of power which cannot be observed when mobilizing the 'repressive hypothesis'.[10]

Not only does the narrow concept of social control embraced by criminology generate too many blind spots, the abandonment of a capacious conceptualization, articulated to domination, has been constructed on the basis of a selective reading of classic sociological contributions on social control, from which the work of C. Wright Mills was expunged.[11] It could be suggested that this exclusion was premised on the fact that Mills used G.H. Mead's concept of social control, which was among the conceptualizations of social control attacked in the great transformation of the concept. But Mills critically adapted Mead's conceptualization in a way that is clearly not guilty of an a-critical normative monism, and that is not blind to power.

Mills' Critical Adaptation of Mead's Concept of Social Control

The social psychology of Mead anchors itself in a desire to theorize the interdependence of the dynamic evolution of social organization and human experience. For Mead (as for Mills), the importance of the concept of social control lies in the fact that it enables the theoretical articulation of the biographic with the social, being the principle of the emergence, structuring and evolution of both

---

10 Moreover, many criminological contributions on social control are premised on an epistemological contradiction, suggesting that an increase in crime is at least partially explained by a relaxation of social control – whereas social control is supposedly the means through which crime is socially constituted (Carrier 2006b).

11 Critical theory à la Frankfurt School, in which we find many analyses of debilitating social control mechanisms through non-repressive means (Adorno 1991; Marcuse, 1964; Horkheimer and Adorno 1944/1974), is also pathetically absent from the criminological orthodox history of the concept.

the self and social institutions. Mead's (1925, 276) influential aphorism according to which to be ourselves we must first be others sums up an intricate theorization of the constitution of the self through the organization of the temporally and spatially contingent attitudes, in a first stage, of particular other individuals and, in a second stage, of the 'generalized other', associated with 'the attitude of the whole community' (Mead 1934, 154). The generalized other realizes and instantiates a symbolic and normative community – a community of meaning. This community and its topography are always contingent upon the particular locus of social action entering into the experience of a given individual (Mead 1918, 580), something that Mills (1940/1963) grasped through the notion of 'situated actions'.

Mead insisted on studying consciousness as a conduct through which the complexity of the phenomenal is reduced.[12] The symbolic mediation of a world otherwise inaccessible to social animals – whose societies are organized through communication and irreducible to processes of physiological differentiation – always implies a 'diminution of the reality of the object' (Mead 1925, 254). Mead's social psychology is premised on a temporalized perspectivism; not only are the events in our environment always 'sliced' from a particular standpoint, but this process of meaning-production is dependent upon the 'spatio-temporal plane' on which the objects are located. The attention devoted to the temporal dimension of symbolic mediation allowed Mead to distinguish between the private and social realms of experience,[13] given that a shared social object (e.g., property, crime) will present a meaning that is not totally determined socially, but is contingent upon the interpretation of the present of oneself (Mead 1932, 28). Social control corresponds to this non-totalitarian yet profoundly structuring connection of the act (thoughts, emotions, gestures, practices) of the individual with the social object, which Mead also discussed through the quasi-Freudian figures of the 'Me' expressing itself against the 'I', and of the control exercised by the generalized other (Mead 1934, 1964). Social control is thus not solely repressing or constraining – even though it implies doing violence to the complexity of the phenomenal – but constitutive of the very possibility of social co-ordination. Operating through language, through the social habits carried by social objects, and thus through the experiences of others, social control enables a community by limiting the possibilities of what can be experienced in a given present: 'if we can bring people together so that they can enter into each other's lives, they will inevitably have a common object, which

---

12   According to Joas, Mead 'seeks to discover what is specific to interpersonal problems of action and deduces the basic structures of symbolically mediated interaction from the functional imperatives that lead to their solution' (1996, 132).

13   An experience approached through a philosophy that is not merely visual, but first and foremost tactile (Miller 1980). As such, the theorization of social organization in the work of Mead is not limited to communication (or 'vocal gestures'), but gives a crucial importance to human participation. The attention to the tactile was not maintained in much of the work that Mead's social psychology stimulated or influenced, including Mills' work and Blumer's (1969) de-sociologization of symbolic interactionism.

will control their common conduct' (Mead 1925, 276). The challenges for Mead are thus to overcome the barriers constraining the dimension of the generalized other, of our community, in order to enable the emergence of a truly 'cosmopolitan self' (Aboulafia 2001).

The Meadian conceptualization of social control will be critically revised by C. Wright Mills, but Mead's foundational premises of the inaccessibility of a 'world of solid fact', of the social determination of cognitive operations, and of the linguistic or symbolic manipulation of both discursive and non-discursive practices remained unaltered. For instance, Mills (1939/1963, 433) described language as the 'ubiquitous string in the web of patterned human behaviour', and posited that communication can only exist as communication in so far as it implies an identity of meaning in 'both the utterer and the hearer' – that is, in so far as it generates 'common modes of response'. But, in comparison to Mead, Mills' analysis of symbolic interaction is more clearly done while mobilizing the sociological imagination:

> Language, socially built and maintained, embodies explicit exhortations and social evaluations. By acquiring the categories of language, we acquire the structured 'ways' of a group, and along with the language the value implicates of those 'ways'. Our behavior and perception, our logic and thought, come with the control of a system of language. Along with language, we acquire a set of social norms and values. A vocabulary is not merely a string of words; immanent within it are societal textures – institutional and political coordinates. Back of a vocabulary lie sets of collective action. (Mills 1939/1963, 433)

Mills' adaptation of Mead's work on the generalized other as the locus of social control stems from an alternative standpoint that is both normative and cognitive. Normatively, Mills finds problematic the 'democratic persuasions' of Mead. Cognitively, Mills finds the sociological dimensions of Mead's social psychology to be inadequate, particularly because they fail to narrate, historicize and theorize modernity as a process of incremental enlargement and concentration of power. Such a process has resulted in a shift in the dominant form of the exercise of power in contemporary (American) society: no longer mainly exercised as a form of legitimate authority (in Weber's sense; see Gerth and Mills 1946), power would mostly operate as manipulation:

> The first rule for understanding the human condition is that men live in second-hand worlds. They are aware of much more than they have personally experienced; and their own experience is always indirect. The quality of their lives is determined by meanings they have received from others. Everyone lives in a world of such meanings. No man stands alone directly confronting a world of solid fact. No such world is available. ... The consciousness of men does not determine their material existence; nor does their material existence determine their consciousness. Between consciousness and existence stand meanings

and designs and communications which other men have passed on – first, in human speech itself, and later, by the management of symbols. These received and manipulated interpretations decisively influence such consciousness as men have of their existence. (Mills, 1959a/1963, 405)

Whereas Mead's social psychology was mostly turned towards symbolic transactions involving the 'contact' of the organism with its environment (Miller 1980, 213), Mills devoted greater attention to the 'sequestration of experience' (Giddens 1991) and to the distant, mass-mediated, prefabrication of stereotypical symbolic constructs controlling our cognitive, normative, practical, emotional and libidinal engagements with the world – controlling the very definition and experience of the real – rather than, as the criminological doxa would have it, controlling only the definition of deviancy and crime. To a large extent, *The Sociological Imagination* can be read as Mills' proposed cure to the debilitating impacts of a social control operating mostly outside the realm of legitimate power.[14] It is a social control that incarcerates individuals into 'pseudo-worlds', through problematic stereotypical representations of the environment beyond their 'narrow milieux', and through problematic inculcated modes of relations to themselves, generating a 'loss of sense of structure', and a loss not only of independence, but of the very 'desire to be independent' (Mills 1956, 321–3). As such, Mills' critical twist on Meadian social control is done through a re-description of some aspects of communication or symbolic transactions as being 'coercive and propagandistic practices' (Sumner 1997, 30) through which the power elite maintains and reinforces structural asymmetries, particularly through the policing of the boundaries of legitimate experiences and representations:

> Only certain views are allowed. But more than that, the terms of the debate, the terms in which the world may be seen, the standards or lack of standards by which men judge of their accomplishments, of themselves, and of other men – these terms are officially or commercially determined, inculcated, enforced. (Mills 1959a/1963, 459)

Mills' analysis of social control being mostly expressed as manipulation obviously does not preclude an analysis of the exercise of power through the mobilization of coercion (the repression of dissent or the infliction of pain upon criminalized individuals, for instance). It suggests that domination no longer requires a constant terrorization of those recognized as citizens of the mass society of liberal democracies. It also suggests that a sociological analysis of coercion has first to unearth the socio-historically contingent symbolic assemblages that constitute its conditions of possibility as a form of engagement in the world.

---

14   As such, Mills is a 'social pathologist', but one of a very different kind than the criminologists mobilizing the notion of social disorganization he famously lambasted (Mills 1943/1963; see Carrier 2006a).

Beyond Millsian Social Control

Mills' conceptualization of social control, following Mead, locates its modality of operation in the structuring aspect of symbolic mediation, involving participation into the generalized experiences of others. But Mills liberates this process from material, embodied, forms of sociality, allowing for the examination of non-proximate, inauthentic and ultimately alienating forms of manufacture of the self, associated with militaristic, politico-administrative and economic interests. As such, Mills' critical conceptualization of social control is enabled, at least partly, by moving the point of focalization from symbolic interaction onto the more properly sociological realm of symbolic communication. But Mills' analysis of social control is premised on the assumption of the continuity of the operations of communication and consciousness.[15] Such continuity has been variously criticized, perhaps most forcefully through Garfinkel's (1967) notion of the 'cultural dope' (see Lynch 2012), but also, more externally to the social sciences, through neuroscientific accounts of consciousness and human behaviour. If Mills (1939/1963, 425) suggested that what is needed is a 'concept of mind which incorporates social processes as intrinsic to mental operations', one can further add that what is needed is to go beyond Mills and develop a concept of social control that does not abolish the boundaries between social processes of communication and mental operations. If this can be provided, then we can avoid both working with an 'oversocialized' conception of the individual (Wrong 1961) – which is also quite manifest in the plethora of Foucaultian analyses in criminology and socio-legal studies – as well as with the reductionist biological-behaviourist and neo-Darwinian models of so-called 'scientific' approaches, which are increasingly stepping within the territory of criminology (Carrier and Walby 2014).

One solution can perhaps be found in contemporary social systems theory, which, among other things, theorizes the coupling of consciousness and communication through a concept of communication as a triple synthesis, that of utterance, information and understanding – none of them having any logical or ontological priority (Luhmann 1998, 31).[16] Understanding (as one of the requisites of communication) is not posited as identical with what is being expressed, nor

---

15   Although Mills has showed in much sharper terms than Mead the need to approach human experiences and mental operations socio-historically, Mead was perhaps – because of the importance he gave to time – more sensitive to the impossibility of the identity of symbolic interaction and human experience.

16   For Luhmann, communication 'is always an observational operation because it assumes at least (1) that information and utterance can be distinguished, and (2) that the understanding from which this distinction proceeds does not coincide with utterance but is distinguishable from it' (2013, 27). In this chapter, I use social systems theory in its Luhmannian formulation and do not engage with different manifestations of it. For instance, in relation to law, Luhmann's (2004) analysis is not completely identical to those of Teubner (1993) or Philippopoulos-Mihalopoulos (2011, 2010).

with the factuality of its expression. On the contrary, social systems theory realizes a complete rupture with the unidirectional model of communication mobilized by Mills, instead advancing the thesis of a self-referential manipulation of meaning dependent upon symbolic generalizations, and the thesis of coupled yet differentiated communicational and individual processes of meaning production (e.g., Luhmann 1995, 92).[17]

Social systems theory conceptualizes individuals as observers whose selves are, as in Mead and Mills, dependent upon others. But the theory rests on a radical or operational constructivism that leads to finding Mead's distinction between the private and social dimensions unsatisfactory, as it implies a modality of consciousness escaping the mediation of self-reflection (Luhmann 1995, 260). If 'there can be no self-reference without hetero-reference, for it is not clear how the self can be indicated if it excludes nothing' (Luhmann 2000a, 167), the process of hetero-reference is itself taken as a self-referential achievement. Through reference to others (or to anything else that is taken as an object for consciousness), the self-referential, paradoxical basis of meaning production is de-paradoxified (i.e., it appears external, premised on a reality 'out there'). Social systems theory observes individuals as uniquely structured self-observational operations of consciousness, coupled with the autopoeisis of life as well as with the communicational operations constitutive of the social. This notably means that selves cannot step outside the operational closure of their consciousness to experience the pain of others, to understand others, or even to adopt and generalize the attitudes of others.[18] This is always done self-referentially.[19]

Unless one misreads social systems theory as positing solipsistic existences (see King 2001; Luhmann 2000b, 107), the operational closure of consciousness, allowing for the self-referential production and mobilization of meaning through which an eminently unique identity is both secured and open to change, does not

---

17   Moreover, social systems theory posits the improbability of understanding in Mills' sense, and tries to account for the social productivity of misunderstanding in fostering communication, which is itself tied to the theoretical architecture through which the dynamic reproduction and evolution of society is grasped.

18   Similarly, the dialectical sociology of Freitag is based on a theory of the symbolic in which 'the content of the experience symbolically shared remains attached to sentient experience [*expérience sensible*], which we cannot share with others otherwise than analogically or metaphorically' (Freitag 2011, 80; my translation).

19   Such a conceptualization does not break the line of thought which, from Marx to Mead and Mills, insisted on the manufactured quality of consciousness. But it makes it appear as doing too much violence to the complexity of individuals, notably because of the limited attention it devotes to the non-social elements involved in the emergence of individuality (see also Žižek 2004, esp. 106–26), but also because it tends to maintain a mesmerizing tradition, made particularly visible and material in Gall and Spurzheim's phrenological speculations (Spurzheim 1815), that arranges 'psychological faculties hierarchically, relegating 'sensuousness' – that is, perception – to a lower position in comparison to higher, reflective functions of reason and understanding' (Luhmann 2000a, 5).

imply an anti-Millsian conception of social control. It displaces the locus of *social* control from consciousness to communication, radicalizing Mills' (1940/1963) admonition not to read expression of motives as mirroring internal (psychic) states and energies, but rather as fulfilling the function of interrupting questions about situated projects of action. Social systems theory provides us with a way to limit social control to the realm of communication, thus finally consuming the break between social control and socialization, but without the costly dissociation of the *problématique* of social order realized in the perspective of the social reaction to deviance. In the same way that symbolic communications can only be meaningful for individuals in so far as they are perceived, which means transformed into self-referential constructions of symbolic communications, the operations of consciousness of individuals can only have a social existence through communicational constructions of the operations of consciousness. The proposed re-imagined conceptualization of social control is thus to examine how the real and the possible are controlled through processes of communication. To modify Luhmann's sentence with which I opened this chapter: reality is never given to communication as such, but only to the way that the operations of communication control themselves. The corollaries of such a shift are numerous.

One of these several corollaries is that social control implies epistemic sites irreducible to human participation, albeit dependent upon human perception. The coupling but differentiation of consciousness and communication implies an autonomization of communication from consciousness, which this very moment (you, now, reading this) illustrates: your understanding of the fact that I am writing (and writing this) realizes communication, and your own understanding can only be socially controlled in so far as you express it, and this in turn is perceived (i.e., understood) by others, whether it takes the form of a rebuttal in scientific networks of communication, of objections shared to colleagues in the corridors of a university department, or even of bodily signs of exasperation perceived by others in your environment. Social control thus refers to the way in which communicational events (meaning produced by the connection of self and other, and not limited to the self-reference of consciousness) are recursively connected to each other, either in the loosely and ephemeral fashion of social interactions, or in the more structured and lasting – thus historicized – fashion of social systems such as science and law.[20] For instance, how do scientific or juridical communications include and exclude communications from their own realms of operations? How are scientific communications organized so that a chapter proposing to re-imagine social control is understood as a belonging to the social system of science? What are the conditions for a claim to justice to be accepted as legally relevant in the context of a society in which a differentiated social system of law claims to be the ultimate arbiter of the just and to prohibit 'the denial of justice' (Luhmann 2004)? The truth of science and the justice of law are socially controlled in the sense that

---

20   This corresponds to the difference between simple and complex social systems in social systems theory, which posit their constant mutual reference (e.g., Luhmann 1981).

they are achievements of scientific and legal operations of communications – with the obvious consequence that non-scientific truths and non-juridical conceptions of justice are scientifically and juridically irrelevant (or relevant as myths to be dispelled and illegal behaviour to be repressed).

Juridical constructs of justice and scientific constructs of truth might certainly be interpreted as participating in broader processes of civilizing offensive (Elias 1939/1984) or as involving truth effects that are consequential for the ethical self-formation of individuals. But a control that is social does not operate in, nor as, consciousness, but through symbolic elements constituted in communication, by the linkage of self and other.[21] As such, another corollary of the re-imagined conceptualization of social control is to totally rupture it from the behaviourist framework mobilized by Mead and Mills, and, more broadly, from a theory (of the social over-determination) of action. Social control is no longer grasping or positing the sources of social action, but rather focusing on the ways in which the realm of practice (involving the perception of others) is made into meaningful events of communication. These processes of meaning-constitution are plural and conflicting. They generate different social objects, largely independent from the intentionality animating the act from the perspective of the actor. Stated otherwise, the meaning attributed by the actor to his or her own action (e.g., righting a wrong through violence or taking to the streets to contest global capitalism) does not determine how the act will be controlled socially.[22] Moving away from a theory of action does not imply negating the 'socializing' or 'disciplinary' effects of meaning[23] mobilized in communication, nor does it imply that the self is not dependent upon

---

21   Another corollary of the present conceptual proposition is thus to move away from the Weberian (e.g., Weber 1971, 1986) legacy connecting the juridical order to beliefs in its legitimacy (see Carrier 2008a). Law can operate irrespective of the respect that individuals show towards its communications, even if law does not and cannot grant the right to disrespect the law – even when law fails to clearly articulate 'reasons' for respecting law other than a general (and empty) deontological obligation (see Nobles and Schiff 2013; Carrier 2007).

22   This leads Clam (1995) to write about a process of 'de-phenomenologization'.

23   Obviously, not only does criminal law self-describe itself as the embodiment of the values constitutive of a nation, but it observes its own communications (an 'exemplary' sentence, for instance) as geared towards informing the behavioural 'choices' of the criminalized subject and of the citizenry. Social scientists inquire into the deterrent effects of law through sophisticated positivistic computations, and others posit a government of the soul based on the observation of legal communications supposedly over-determined by the 'power of the norm'. Yet consciousness *qua* consciousness remains inaccessible to the social scientist, and can only take the form of a communicational representation of consciousness (or perception), leading one to also inquire into the social control of scientific communications by the social system of science: What are the conditions for communicational representations of consciousness to be accepted as scientific communications?

interaction and communication. It only implies limiting the realm of a control that is social to meaning (i.e., reality) produced through communication.

The proposed conceptualization of social control is not blind to the violence of law, whether we refer to the critique of the foundational violence of law formulated by Benjamin (1921/2000), Derrida (1990) and Agamben (2005), or to the criminological critique of repression and of the infliction of pain enabled by law. Social systems theory posits the foundationless quality of legal communications (Luhmann 2004), and points out that it is only through a symbolic mediation achieved socially – that is, through communication – that forms of concrete violence can be produced as legal – that is, legally 'legitimate' manifestations of sovereign power (with the usual semantic decoys that critical criminologists target, such as 'keeping the peace' and guaranteeing 'security'; see notably Neocleous and Rigakos 2011). As such, a communicational conception of social control does not neuter critical engagements with manifestation of power (supposing the capitalization of threatening means) and force (see Carrier 2008a, 2011).

Conclusion

The re-imagined conceptualisation of social control outlined above draws its roots from Mead and Mills, yet tries to overcome some limitations of their work on symbolic mediation by mobilizing social systems theory's conceptualization of communication as the triple unity of utterance, information and understanding, troubling the identity of the meaning of social objects in consciousness posited by Mills. The outlined conceptualization is also a deliberate attempt to avoid the limitations associated with the divorce of social control from questions surrounding the *social* ordering of the real and the possible.

The Sociological Imagination was premised on the diagnosis of a radical impoverishment of (American) individuals' ability to think critically, historically and structurally (read: properly), and on a celebration of the enlightening potential of sociological knowledge. Its normative architecture cannot be dissociated from Mills' diagnoses on the deleterious effects of the manipulation of cultural forms by nefarious interests. It was anchored in a humanist and a modernist form of engagement with the world. Human beings and Reason – as ontologically given and as universalized concept – thus escaped the realm of social control as mobilized by Mills,[24] even if some of his previous work (e.g., Mills 1939/1963) insisted on logic and reason being artefacts of social control. The re-imagination of the concept suggested in these pages implies fully accepting this reflexivity, including social control (as an element in scientific communication, as a tool for scientific observation) being itself socially controlled, yet allowing the observer

---

24 Similarly, criminologists working with the social reaction to deviance perspective are unable to observe how they are themselves constructing deviance in the project to bind social control to social order.

to propose interpretations of multiple, co-occurring, conflicting and historically contingent processes through which the real and the possible are socially ordered.

Perhaps one of the chief tasks awaiting social scientists wanting to keep alive the spirit of *The Sociological Imagination* will be to fight against increasingly influential cultural and scientific reductions of individuals and behaviours (particularly when criminalized or pathologized) to the outcome of biological programmes contingently activated by the environment, but without in turn reducing the complexity of living and conscious individuals to a pale reproduction of dominant forms of symbolic renditions of the world. Such a fight would be premised on analysing the ways in which the meaning and the consequences of being a self are socially controlled, and on an active negation of the possibility for a self to exist – for society and for itself – outside the realm of meaning.

References

Aas, K.F. 2007. 'Analysing a World in Motion. Global Flows Meet "Criminology of the Other."' *Theoretical Criminology* 11: 283–303.

Aboulafia, M. 2001. *The Cosmopolitan Self: George Herbert Mead and Continental Philosophy*. Urbana, IL: University of Illinois Press.

Adorno, T.W. 1991. *The Culture Industry. Selected Essays on Mass Culture*. London: Routledge.

Agamben, G. 2005. *State of Exception*. Chicago, IL: University of Chicago Press.

Atkinson, P. 1990. *The Ethnographic Imagination: Textual Constructions of Reality*. London: Routledge.

Barton, A., D. Scott, K. Corteen and D. Whyte. 2007. *Expanding the Criminological Imagination: Critical Readings in Criminology*. Portland, OR: Willan Publishing.

Beck, U. 1999. *World Risk Society*. Cambridge: Polity Press.

Benjamin, W. 1921/2000. 'Critique de la violence.' In *Walter Benjamin: Oeuvres I*, edited by R. Rochlitz, 210–43. Paris: Folio.

Black, D. 1984. 'Social Control as a Dependent Variable.' In *Toward a General Theory of Social Control,* edited by D. Black, 1–36. Orlando, FL: Academic Press.

Blumer, H. 1969. *Symbolic Interactionism: Perspective and Method*. Englewood Cliffs, NJ: Prentice-Hall.

Bogard, W. 1996. *The Simulation of Surveillance: Hypercontrol in Telematic Societies*. Cambridge: Cambridge University Press.

———. 2006. 'Welcome to the Society of Control: The Simulation of Surveillance Revisited.' In *The New Politics of Surveillance and Visibility*, edited by K. Haggerty and R.V. Ericson, 55–78. Toronto, ON: University of Toronto Press.

Burawoy, M. 2004. 'Public Sociologies: Contradictions, Dilemmas, and Possibilities.' *Social Forces* 82: 1,603–18.

————. 2005a. 'For Public Sociology.' *British Journal of Sociology* 56: 259–94.

————. 2005b. 'The Critical Turn to Public Sociology.' *Critical Sociology* 31: 313–26.

Carrier, N. 2006a. 'Academics' Criminals: The Discursive Formations of Criminalized Deviance.' *Penal Field* 3. Accessed 6 June 2015. http://champpenal.revues.org/document3143.html.

————. 2006b. 'La dépression problématique du concept de contrôle social.' *Déviance & Société* 30: 3–20.

————. 2007. 'The Autonomy and Permeability of Law: The Case of the Canadian Prohibition of Cannabis.' *Canadian Journal of Law & Society* 22: 123–38.

————. 2008a. *La Politique de la stupéfaction. Pérennité de la prohibition des drogues*, Rennes, France: Presses universitaires de Rennes.

————. 2008b. 'Speech for the Defense of a Radically Constructivist Sociology of (Criminal) Law.' *International Journal of Law, Crime and Justice* 36: 168–83.

————. 2011. 'Critical Criminology Meets Radical Constructivism.' *Critical Criminology* 19: 331–50.

————. 2014. 'On Some Limits and Paradoxes of Academic Orations on Public Criminology.' *Radical Criminology* 4: 85–114.

———— and K. Walby. 2014. 'Ptolemizing Lombroso: The Pseudo-revolution of Biosocial Criminology.' *Journal of Theoretical and Philosophical Criminology* 6(1): 1–45.

Castel, R. 1988. 'De l'intégration sociale à l'éclatement du social: l'émergence, l'apogée et le départ à la retraite du contrôle social' *Revue internationale d'action communautaire* 20: 67–78.

Clam, J. 1995. 'Phénoménologie et droit chez Niklas Luhmann: De la déphénoménologisation de la sociologie à la dépolémisation du droit.' *Archives de philosophie du droit* 39: 355–77

Cohen, S. 1985. *Visions of Social Control: Crime, Punishment and Classification.* Cambridge: Polity Press.

———— and A. Scull. 1983. 'Introduction: Social Control in History and Sociology.' In *Social Control and the State. Historical and Comparative Essays*, edited by S. Cohen, S. and A. Scull, 1–14. Oxford: Blackwell.

Deflem, M. 2013. 'The Structural Transformation of Sociology.' *Society* 50: 156–66.

Derrida, J. 1990. 'Force of Law: The Mystical Foundation of Authority.' *Cardozo Law Review* 11: 919–1,046.

Durkheim, É. 1893/2007. *De la division du travail social.* Paris: Presses universitaires de France.

Elias, N. 1939/1984. *The Civilizing Process.* Oxford: Blackwell.

Foucault, M. 1975. *Surveiller et punir. Naissance de la prison.* Paris: Gallimard.

————. 1976. *Histoire de la sexualité I: La volonté de savoir.* Paris: Gallimard.

————. 1997. 'Il faut défendre la société.' *Cours au Collège de France, 1976.* Paris: Gallimard.

Freitag, M. 2011. *Dialectique et société. Tome 2: Introduction à une théorie générale du symbolique*. Montréal, QC: Liber.

Garfinkel, H. 1967. *Studies in Ethnomethodology*. Englewood Cliffs, NJ: Prentice Hall.

Gerth, H.H. and C. Wright Mills. 1946. 'Introduction: The Man and His Work.' In *From Max Weber: Essays in Sociology,* edited by H.H. Gerth and C. Wright Mills, 1–74. New York: Oxford University Press.

Gibbs, J.P. 1994. *A Theory about Control*. Boulder, CO: Westview Press.

Giddens, A. 1991. *Modernity and Self-identity: Self and Society in the Late Modern Age*. Stanford, CA: Stanford University Press.

Horkheimer, M. and T.W. Adorno. 1944/1974. *La dialectique de la raison*. Paris: Gallimard.

Hunt, A. 1997. 'Moral Regulation and Making-up the New Person: Putting Gramsci to Work.' *Theoretical Criminology* 1: 275–301.

Joas, H. 1996. *The Creativity of Action*. Chicago, IL: University of Chicago Press.

Kemple, T. and R. Mawani. 2009. 'The Sociological Imagination and its Imperial Shadows.' *Theory, Culture & Society* 26: 228–49.

King, M. 2001. 'The Construction and Demolition of the Luhmann Heresy.' In *Law's New Boundaries. The Consequences of Legal Autopoiesis*, edited by J. Príban and D. Nelken, 123–56. Aldershot: Ashgate Publishing.

Lianos, M. 2003. 'Social Control after Foucault.' *Surveillance & Society* 1(3): 412–30.

———. 2010. 'Periopticon: Control beyond Freedom and Coercion – and Two Possible Advancements in the Social Sciences.' In *Surveillance and Democracy*, edited by K. Haggerty and M. Samatas, 69–88. New York: Routledge.

———. 2012. *The New Social Control*. Ottawa, QC: Red Quill Books.

——— and M. Douglas. 2000. 'Dangerization and the End of Deviance: The Institutional Environment.' *British Journal of Criminology* 40: 261–78.

Liazos, A. 1972. 'The Poverty of the Sociology of Deviance: Nuts, Sluts and Perverts.' *Social Problems* 20: 103–20.

Lowman, J., R.J. Menzies and T.S. Palys. 1987. 'Introduction: Transcarceration and the Modern State of Penality.' In *Transcarceration. Essays in the Sociology of Social Control*, edited by J. Lowman, R.J. Menzies and T.S. Palys, 1–15. Aldershot: Gower Publishing.

Luhmann, N. 1981. 'Communication about Law in Interaction Systems.' In *Advances in Social Theory and Methodology: Toward an Integration of Micro- and Macro-sociologies,* edited by K.D. Knorr-Cetina and A.V. Cicourel, 234–256. Boston, MA: Kegan Paul.

———. 1995. *Social Systems*. Stanford, CA: Stanford University Press.

———. 1998. 'La société comme différence, Sociétés.' *Revue des sciences humaines et sociales* 61: 19–37.

———. 2000a. *Art as a Social System*. Stanford, CA: Stanford University Press.

————. 2000b. *The Reality of the Mass Media.* Stanford, CA: Stanford University Press.

————. 2004. *Law as a Social System.* Oxford: Oxford University Press.

————. 2013. *A Systems Theory of Religion.* Stanford, CA: Stanford University Press.

Lumley, F. 1925. *Means of Social Control.* New York: Century Press.

Lynch, M. 2012. 'Revisiting the Cultural Dope.' *Human Studies* 35: 223–33.

Marcuse, H. 1964. *One-dimensional Man: Studies in the Ideology of Advanced Industrial Society.* Boston, MA: Beacon Press.

Mead, G.H. 1918. 'The Psychology of Punitive Justice.' *American Journal of Sociology* 23: 577–602.

————. 1925. 'The Genesis of the Self and Social Control.' *International Journal of Ethics* 35: 251–77.

————. 1932. *The Philosophy of the Present.* LaSalle, IL: Open Court Publishing.

————. 1934. *Mind, Self and Society from the Standpoint of a Social Behaviorist.* Chicago, IL: University of Chicago Press.

————. 1964. *On Social Psychology: Selected Papers*, edited by A. Strauss. Chicago, IL: University of Chicago Press.

Meier, R.F. 1982. 'Prospects for Control Theories and Research.' In *Social Control: Views from the Social Sciences*, edited by J.P. Gibbs, 265–276. Beverly Hills, CA: Sage.

Melossi, D. 1990. *The State of Social Control: A Sociological Study of Concepts of State and Social Control in the Making of Democracy.* Cambridge: Polity Press.

————. 2008. *Controlling Crime, Controlling Society: Thinking about Crime in Europe and America.* Cambridge: Polity Press.

Miller, D. 1980. *George Herbert Mead: Self, Language, and the World.* Austin, TX: University of Texas Press.

Mills, C. Wright. 1939/1963. 'Language, Logic and Culture.' In *Power, Politics and People. The Collected Essays of C. Wright Mills*, edited by I.L. Horowitz, 423–38. New York: Oxford University Press.

————. 1940/1963. 'Situated Actions and Vocabularies of Motive.' In *Power, Politics and People. The Collected Essays of C. Wright Mills*, edited by I.L. Horowitz, 439–52. New York: Oxford University Press.

————. 1943/1963. 'The Professional Ideology of Social Pathologists.' In *Power, Politics and People. The Collected Essays of C. Wright Mills*, edited by I.L. Horowitz, 525–52. New York: Oxford University Press.

————. 1956. *The Power Elite.* New York: Oxford University Press.

————. 1959a/1963. 'The Cultural Apparatus.' In *Power, Politics and People. The Collected Essays of C. Wright Mills*, edited by I.L. Horowitz, 405–22. New York: Oxford University Press.

————. 1959b. *The Sociological Imagination.* New York: Oxford University Press.

Neocleous, M. and G.S. Rigakos, eds. 2011. *Anti-security.* Ottawa, QC: Red Quill Books.

Nickel, P.M. 2010. 'Public Sociology and the Public Turn in the Social Sciences.' *Sociology Compass* 4:694–704.

Nobles, R. and D. Schiff. 2013. *Observing Law through Systems Theory*. Portland, OR: Hart Publishing.

Otero, M. 2003. *Les règles de l'individualité contemporaine. Santé, mentale et société*. Québec, QC: Presses de l'Université Laval.

Park, R.E. and E.W. Burgess. 1921. *Introduction to the Science of Sociology*, 3rd edn. Chicago, IL: University of Chicago Press, 1969.

Parsons, T. 1951. *The Social System*. New York: Free Press.

Philippopoulos-Mihalopoulos, A. 2010. *Niklas Luhmann: Law, Justice, Society*. London: Routledge.

———. 2011. 'Giving Guilt: The Aneconomy of Law and Justice.' *Distinktion: Scandinavian Journal of Social Theory* 12: 79–93.

Powell, C. 2012. 'How Epistemology Matters: Five Reflexive Critiques of Public Sociology.' *Critical Sociology* 39: 87–104.

Robert, P. 1984. *La question pénale*. Geneva, Switzerland: Droz.

Ross, E.A. 1901. *Social Control. A Survey of the Foundation of Order*. New York: Johnson Reprint Corporation.

Scheerer, S. and H. Hess. 1997. 'Social Control: A Defence and Reformulation.' In *Social Control and Political Order: European Perspectives at the End of the Century*, edited by R. Bergalli and C. Sumner, 96–130. London: Sage.

Smart, C. 1976. *Women, Crime and Criminology: A Feminist Critique*. London: Routledge.

Spurzheim, J.G. 1815. *The Physiognomical System of Drs. Gall and Spurzheim*, 2nd edn. London: Baldwin, Cradock & Joy.

Stanley, E. 2007. 'Towards a Criminology for Human Rights.' In *Expanding the Criminological Imagination: Critical Readings in Criminology*, edited by Alana Barton, David Scott, Karen Corteen and David Whyte, 168–98. Portland, OR: Willan Publishing.

Sumner, C. 1997. 'Social Control: The History and Politics of a Central Concept in Anglo-American Sociology.' In *Social Control and Political Order: European Perspectives at the End of the Century*, edited by R. Bergalli and C. Sumner, 1–33. London: Sage, 1–33.

Taylor, I., P. Walter and J. Young. 1973. *The New Criminology*. New York: Harper & Row.

Teubner, G. 1989. 'How the Law Thinks: Toward a Constructivist Epistemology of Law.' *Law & Society Review* 23: 727–57.

———. 1993. *Le droit, un système autopoïétique*. Paris: Presses universitaires de France.

Tönnies, F. 1887. *Gemeinschaft und Gesellschaft*. Leipzig, Germany: Fues's Verlag.

Wacquant, L. 2011. 'From "Public Criminology" to the Reflexive Sociology of Criminological Production and Consumption.' *British Journal of Criminology* 51:438–48.

Wagner, P. 1994. *A Sociology of Modernity: Liberty and Discipline*. New York: Routledge.

Weber, M. 1971. Économie et société. ⅼ: Les catégories de la sociologie. Paris: Plon.

———. 1986. *Sociologie du droit*. Paris: Presses universitaires de France.

Wrong, D.H. 1961. 'The Oversocialized Conception of Man in Modern Sociology.' *American Sociological Review* 26: 183–93.

Young, J. 2011. *The Criminological Imagination*. Cambridge: Polity Press.

Žižek, S. 2004. *Organs without Bodies: On Deleuze and Consequences*. London: Routledge.

PART III
The Criminological Imagination, Empirical Insights, Theoretical Implications

Chapter 8

Critical Research Values and C. Wright Mills' *Sociological Imagination*: Learning Lessons from Researching Prison Officers

David Scott

C. Wright Mills' 'sociological imagination' signifies a way of thinking about or interpreting the world. It represents a particular way of conceptualizing and approaching social problems, their implications and resolution. It provides a broad-ranging interpretive framework for locating the individual within structural and social contexts, ultimately providing a new way of understanding the social world that makes intimate connections between individual meanings and experiences, and wider collective and social realities. The 'sociological imagination' facilitates a form of interpretation that places understandings of an individual's biography within the sensibilities of wider historical and structural contexts. When undertaking prison ethnography, therefore, C. Wright Mills' 'sociological imagination' demands that researchers provide clear connections between the actor, the event and the location of the research, and the structural, spatial and historical determinants shaping the penal environment. As such, the 'sociological imagination' can be deployed to challenge existing and dominant ways of thinking about prison life and can help facilitate a new and plausible 'bigger picture' offering new orientating *values*, feelings, motives, understandings and meanings (Barton et al. 2006; Scott 2008).

This chapter seeks to explore one specific aspect of adopting C. Wright Mills' 'sociological imagination' in prison ethnography – the formulation and adoption of *critical research values*. Epistemologically, critical research values insist that knowledge and understandings are firmly connected with the actual situational context. It requires the ethnographer to uncover the real – *the truth* – of that situational context, whatever that may entail. This means making a 'metaphysical choice' when interpreting the 'real' (Mills 1959) of the prison place.[1] While undoubtedly there are moments of genuine warmth, humanity and kindness within prisons, such occurrences are largely the exception to the rule, and it is essential that

---

1   Mills' (1959) 'metaphysical choices' shape what ethnographers prioritize and privilege in their research and analysis. As such, the choices determining what ethnographers write about, focus upon and problematize when undertaking prison research inevitably reflect moral and political values. For further discussion, see Scott (2014b).

an ethnographer's 'metaphysical choice' also recognize that prisons in the main are very dark places: they are dehumanizing institutions characterized by violence and exploitation which exist to deliver suffering, pain and blame (Scott 2008, 2013).

It is sometimes helpful to clarify a position by first detailing what it is not. This is perhaps the case with critical research values. The chapter therefore starts by critically exploring a perspective known as Appreciative Inquiry (AI). AI has been the main research method deployed by a number of academics in the UK when undertaking prison research in the last two decades. Drawing upon the writings of AI's leading advocate, Alison Liebling, it details the strengths and weaknesses of the AI method, including its strength in emphasizing empathetic and caring interview skills. Attention is also drawn, however, to its limitations, including the problematic manner in which AI narratives can reconstruct the 'truth' as a means to promote future positive practice and the potential manipulation of AI as a human resources exercise. For a number of reasons, it is maintained that AI does not effectively deploy C. Wright Mills' 'sociological imagination' to inform its research values.

The chapter then explores the importance of delivering accounts which reflect the real, whether positive or negative, and illustrates this point through a consideration of the application of critical research values when undertaking research on prison officers. This part of the discussion once again starts by contrasting critical research values with AI, for deployment of the AI method also connects to the now classic debate about 'whose side we are on' (Becker 1967; Liebling 2001). Building upon the insights of C. Wright Mills (1959), but also those of Alvin Gouldner (1961/1973, 1967), the discussion points to the central importance of the value of acknowledging human suffering through knowledge gleaned in the research process. The review of critical research values is then deepened further by drawing upon a prison officer ethnography undertaken by the author. Utilizing unpublished reflections from my prison journal written during the ethnography, I detail a number of observations and dilemmas which highlight the importance of adopting *critical research values*. To conclude, I draw together the different strands of the chapter to delineate six critical research values informed by C. Wright Mills' 'sociological imagination' that may be adopted for future prison ethnographies.

Appreciative Enquiry and Research Values

> Values are involved in the selection of the problems we study; values are also involved in certain of the key conceptions we use in our formulation of these problems, and values affect the course of their solution. (Mills 1959, 78)

The aim of this chapter to explore which critical research values derived from the sociological imagination should inform prison ethnography. This is perhaps best approached by first identifying what they are not. In this first section I consider the strengths and weaknesses of the alternative method of Appreciative Inquiry as a means of researching prison life, specifically prison officer occupational culture (Liebling and Price 2001; Liebling et al. 2011). Appreciative Inquiry is intended to be a fair and inclusive research method that tells the 'whole story' (Liebling et al. 2001, 162). It claims to provide a faithful or truthful account of the respondents' positive achievements, survival strategies and success stories, alongside their negative experiences. As the approach is future- rather than present- or past-orientated, outcomes and methodology are intimately tied together. Questioning is appreciative, in that as a mode of inquiry it wishes respondents to dwell on the *best* as well as the worst aspects of their prison experience. Interview questions focus on 'prison values' and are very specific. Answers are required to be evidenced by an example, illustration or story from the respondent's actual experiences. AI claims to provide a more sensitive, nuanced and instructive picture of the prison, and therefore a more valuable approach than the traditional problem-orientated studies. The researcher should represent its subjects fairly, listen, empower and facilitate changes, and foster mutual respect.

Importantly, the research does not seek to expose flaws in the prison place, but rather to accentuate the positive and have an open dialogue about how to achieve good outcomes, secure compliance and treat people with respect. A key outcome is that the respondents will feel more valued, and thus have a more positive orientation towards their role, tapping into the dormant potential of officers. Through focusing on the positive, officers will find new meanings, fulfilment, energy, strength and job satisfaction, which will lead to better practice. It is an approach to organizational transformation that is:

> based on strengths rather than weakness, on visions of what is possible rather than what is not possible. It identifies achievements and best memories, and through this technique, locates 'where energy is' in an organisation …. It is based on the establishment of familiarity and trust with a workgroup in the first instance, on the discovery of that organisation's best practices, memories and achievements. (Liebling et al. 2001, 162, 163)

Through the research process, the respondents' knowledge is uncovered and then generalized to create an idealized vision of best possible practice – something that is just out of reach in the current circumstances. The newly energized officers can go and turn this vision, based partly on their own experiences, into a new reality. No new resources or widespread structural changes are necessarily required, for this approach is about transforming the individual and collective officers' private troubles by boosting morale, transforming the penal values held by officers, and by discovering and then achieving attainable positive goals in the prison. Such an approach is understandably very attractive and useful to the prison service and its managers.

As a methodology and qualitative piece of research, the principles of listening, respect and fairness in the interviewing process are welcomed. The approach could also be defended on ethical and political grounds, for it looks to give something back to the respondents and to transform negative penal environments. However, these principles are not unique to AI, and as a potential method for independent prison research it has a number of serious drawbacks. Any kind of AI research would require massive access to be granted from the prison authorities, considerable funding and a large amount of time and other resources. Such research would require the explicit co-operation, and maybe even participation, of prison service managers. This can lead to problems. Perhaps most damningly, the research can be used merely to support and justify the interests of the powerful and the capitalist state. The ethnographer may become a research technician gleaning knowledge, which can be used to further justify the status quo. Mills puts it well when he argues:

> To *appeal* to the powerful, on the basis of any knowledge we now have, is utopian in the foolish sense of the term. Our relations with them are more likely to be only such relations as they find useful, which is to say we become technicians accepting their problems and aims, or ideologies promoting their prestige and authority. (Mills 1959, 193)

The use of AI could be reduced to a human resources exercise to get better and more efficient outputs, rather than being tied to (critical research) values based on social justice. Questions can also be raised about its status as a method. It is both more and less than research: *more* because it looks to not just observe and discover, but also to change, and *less* because the reality may have to be distorted into a mythical positive construct in order to achieve this. Accurate pictures of the lived experiences of those in the prison – managers, staff or prisoners – are unlikely to arise from such interventionist research.

A major claim of AI is that it provides a fuller account of the prison experience than critical research. Such a claim to 'truth', though, is compromised by both the approach and aims of the 'method'. In AI the reality of the situation is replaced by a projection of what could be, not what is: the mythical rather than the real. Rather than paint a picture which accurately mirrors the real, those undertaking AI must conjure an illusion, distorting penal realities to legitimize progressive reforms. Myths replace the real, for research outcomes produced by AI are not the whole story, but rather realities that have been repackaged and reinvented. By necessary implication, AI cannot focus on the negative, for if it does so, future practice could be distorted so that worst practice is achieved. With clear Orwellian overtones, such a future orientation means that what is being portrayed as the present and past is not *what is* or *what has been*, but *what could be*. But is this genuinely, then, an accurate means of assessing the here and now? Research should uncover the real, the truth, whatever this looks like. Again, as Mills argues: 'any style of empiricism involves a metaphysical choice – a choice as to what is most real' (1959, 67). Mills continues: 'one tries to get it straight, to make an adequate statement – if it's gloomy, too bad; if it leads to hope, fine' (1959, 78). As a metaphysical choice, it seems more appropriate to allow the respondents to detail their stories, whether positive or negative, so that their construction of events and reality can be outlined and critically interrogated. This is not to assume that respondents should be considered 'unproblematic bearers of truth', but that, as discussed below, the moment of judgement and interrogation of what has been said comes later, rather than through distortions in the research process itself (Sim 2003; Scott 2014b). Good or bad, Mills (1959) is insistent that the obligation is upon researchers to accurately document what they have heard, witnessed or participated in, rather than selectively omitting views so that a mythical construction of the prison can be stage-managed.

There should be no great aim to change the prison *through the research process itself*. Independent findings might be negative or positive, but at least they are an account of people's actual lived experiences, which can then be used as evidence to inform changes if appropriate. Prison researchers should aim to identify the lived realities of prison conditions, the monotony of prison daily routine – where days collapse into each other – and the general dragging of time that so painfully engender feelings of wastefulness for prisoners and (though less so) prison staff. AI fails to consider the general failure of prison officials to correctly read the feelings, meanings and actions of those they contain, resulting in further difficulties when attempting to use the *research process* as a conduit for change. Prison officers remain illiterate about how the pains of confinement shape prisoners' experiences, for they can only bear witness to many of the inherent harms of imprisonment, rather than sharing them (Scott, forthcoming). To comprehend and critically interrogate findings and personal field notes requires time and reflection. Ultimately, it is the knowledge of prison realities *gleaned from the research* and its compilation of evidence that should motivate activism and radical transformations of the prison place.

The actual future transformation that AI is trying to achieve through the manipulation of officers' past and present experiences can also be problematized. In this sense, AI seems like a therapeutic and individualized means of building staff self-esteem and morale. The aim is to ameliorate the negative and inherently dehumanizing reality of imprisonment without making any connections with the equally important transformations of inequitable power relations in the prison or in wider society, indicating a distinct lack of a 'sociological imagination' (Mills 1959). AI looks to achieve consensual relationships so that positive, functioning and morally performing prisons can exist. Creating a new mythology of the prison is once again the key intention, yet it fails to adequately take into account the nature of confinement. Because prisons hold conscripted populations, they will forever create false hierarchies between the keepers and the kept, generating false dichotomies between 'us' and 'them', conflict, artificial relationships, exploitation and the likelihood of psychic distancing. Surveillance, regulation and control also seem inevitable, as a prison must always be governed by security and order in one way or another. Further, the violence of incarceration relates to not only the physical coercion underscoring penal confinement, nor even the (often targeted and relatively rare, in the UK at least) physical brutality of staff upon prisoners, but also the emotional and psychological lacerations inflicted through the invisible glass of the structured pains of imprisonment. The structural functionalism of AI fundamentally fails to consider the inherent conflicts, pains or inequitable power relations of the prison. Prisons are all about the loss of freedom. It must be questioned whether prisons, which overwhelmingly punish the poor and vulnerable and deliberately impose hurt, injury and potentially deadly pains, can ever perform morally (Scott 2013; Scott, forthcoming).

Clarifying Values – Whose Side are We On?

The prison place is one of conflicting interests and values, and such realities must be acknowledged in the research process. This can also help us deepen our understanding of the relationship between the sociological imagination and critical research values. For Howard Becker (1967), who famously asked the question 'Whose side are we on?', it is impossible to undertake neutral, objective and value-free research. Becker (1967) argued that the researcher must choose a standpoint reflecting either the interests of the subordinate or superordinates of any given research context. Becker argued that there exists a hierarchy of credibility which legitimizes the definers of reality and truth, de-legitimizing the voice of the disempowered. Implicit in Becker's work is the assumption that the (critical) researcher should adopt the standpoint of the underdog. However, this position has been questioned by one of the leading prison researchers and advocates of AI in the UK. Alison Liebling, in an article also entitled 'Whose Side are We On?', argues that:

> in my experience it *is* possible to take more than one side seriously, to find merit
> in more than one perspective, and to do this without causing outrage on the side
> of officials or prisoners ... why is it less acceptable to offer the same degree
> of appreciative understanding to those who manage prisons. Is it because they
> wield power? [Because] their voices are already legitimated? (Liebling 2001,
> 473, 476)

Rather than identifying with the underdog, we should have empathy for the subject, whoever it is, we are researching. For Liebling (2001, 474), 'research is after all, an act of human engagement', and the fieldwork is more rewarding and fruitful if the researcher is prepared to show sympathy and understanding towards the respondent. This position looks to produce high-quality research findings and facilitates a positive experience for the respondent, but fails to consider the deeply divided roles and exercise of power between prisoner and staff in the penal context. To accept such a position unproblematically is a *political* decision, inevitably reflecting values and sympathies. As Mills (1959) points out, it reflects a 'metaphysical choice'. Acknowledgement of standpoint and its consequences are given greatest clarity in the writings of Alvin Gouldner (1961/1973, 1967). For Gouldner, it is not the differential power relations that shape concern for the underdog, but rather their suffering:

> The essential point about the underdog is that he suffers, and this suffering is naked and visible. It is this that makes and should make a compelling demand upon us. What makes his standpoint deserving of special consideration, what makes him particularly worthy of sympathy, is that he suffers .... (Gouldner 1967, 35, 36)

In prison, and elsewhere, it is not only the prisoner who suffers. It would be unfair to deny the suffering of prison staff, but the key variant in terms of attaching political commitment to prisoner suffering is that through the hierarchy of power relations the reality of subordinates suffering is *denied*:

> [The] dominant conceptions of reality sustained and fostered by the managers of society have one common defect: they fail to grasp a very special type of reality, specifically the reality of the suffering of those beneath them. In failing to see this, what they also fail to see is that those beneath them are indeed very much like themselves, in their suffering as in other ways. (Gouldner 1967, 35, 36)

In the penal context, our critical research values should be determined through an acknowledgement of those who suffer the most in prison: prisoners. In response to the question of why it is less acceptable to have political and empathetic allegiances with prison officers and prison managers, the answer is not just that the prison staff have greater power, or that their voices are deemed more legitimate than prisoners; it is that they do not suffer the same extent as prisoners, and that they fail to identify or *acknowledge* the greater suffering of those below them. A critical ethnography drawing upon the 'sociological imagination' (Mills 1959) then reflects a commitment to uncover the truth and acknowledge the inherent pains and suffering created through confinement. The question is not one of *more or less deserving*, but of *more suffering*.

Critical Research Values and Prison Officers

Critical research values may therefore be relatively straightforward for prison ethnographies focused on prisoners' lived experience,[2] but are not so obvious for those focused on prison staff. Here I will draw upon one such study of prison officer occupational culture in one prison in the North West of England in 2002

---

2 Here, please note the important contribution by Joe Sim (2003), who explores the question 'whose side are we *not* on' when it comes to undertaking critical research in prisons. See also the discussion in Scott (2014b).

to explore how C. Wright Mills' 'sociological imagination' can be deployed to inform the ethnographers' critical research values.[3] The ethnography involved observation and semi-structured interviews with 38 prison officers alongside interviews (formal and informal) with other prison staff and prisoners. I draw upon my unpublished notes from the time (Scott 2002) to illuminate critical research values. What is immediately evident is that the values underscoring the research contrast starkly with Appreciative Inquiry detailed earlier. In the first instance, this is clear in terms of critical orientation, funding and independence. Rather than being employed as a 'technician' of the powerful, the research aimed to independently explore prison officers by looking at their occupational culture 'from outside the penal machine'. The research was unfunded, and the research process itself involved the explicit drawing and clarifying of values derived from the application of the 'sociological imagination'.

Alongside independence, a further important value underscoring the research was a commitment to ensure that the study was both relevant and reflexive to the circumstances. What I had initially intended to investigate was 'the extent of the presence of a language of rights among prison officers and other prison staff'. If I had found a language of rights, I had then planned to determine which 'rights' were included and which 'rights' were excluded. It became very obvious within a matter of days at the start of the study that there were not going to be to be very many officers who had a language of rights. And I kept on getting responses from officers such as: 'Why are you talking about these abstract human rights?'; 'What are you are talking about?'; 'You're on a different planet' (Scott 2002). Human rights language was completely alien to the world of the prison officers. Virtually none of the officers I spoke with had even heard of the European Convention of Human Rights or the Human Rights Act. In short, I found that less eligibility, rather the human rights, was the 'language of most prison officers' (Scott, forthcoming).

The initial focus on human rights therefore proved more controversial than I had anticipated. When it came to the actual prison staff talking about rights, there was considerable resistance. Some officers thought, 'Well what's this outsider doing coming in here talking about prisoner rights'? (Scott 2002), and some officers were flippant, or even unpleasant. I was immediately warned about one particular prison officer on my first day at the prison (Scott 2014b). Initial interactions were hostile – when I was on his wing I would hear him bellowing out: 'Human fucking rights. I'm a sex offender, I've got human rights. I've got the human right to go and beat up an old granny' (Scott 2014b). Other staff were not so antagonistic, but still questioned the focus and intentions of the ethnography: 'Do you really believe in that? It's just part of your job, isn't it?'

Despite this initial hostility and mistrust from officers, as time progressed I began to get a reputation as 'counsellor to the prison' (Scott 2002). This reputation was based on the perception that in the interviews I was listening to staff complaints.

---

3   For further details of the research findings and context, please see Scott, *The Caretakers of Punishment* (forthcoming).

The interview approach was based on a 'receptive' model that was largely passive. I wanted the officers to feel comfortable to say exactly what they wanted, and I did not want to indicate whether I agreed or disagreed with their comments. In this sense, I assumed that if I gave them enough rope I would uncover their true feelings, even if the interview schedule was impaired somewhat by this. I felt that a rapport interview, looking to build a relationship with the subject, was the most effective strategy to get the best and most reliable findings possible. I felt this would increase trust and lead to a more honest account of the prison reality.

In interviews, when officers came out with some extreme points, I tried to say as little as possible. I think what I probably did was I 'appealed to higher loyalties' (Cohen 2001). I was thinking in the back of my mind: 'What's the most important here? Is it this specific interaction, or is it the actual research?' What I wanted was for someone to come out and tell me what they really thought, because there are other forms of intervention that the knowledge could be used for. It was only when I started to undertake more interviews together that I found patterns and realized that a considerable number of officers were saying similar things – in other words, that the denial of prisoner common humanity and the privileging of less eligibility were representative, and not just an extreme view from a small number of officers. In one sense, you can most effectively reflect upon the research findings only when you are nearly finished or have completed a substantial amount of the research. This is the moment, rather than during the process, when it is best to reflect.

The early interviews were in effect hijacked by prison officers who were quite happy to talk, and had much to say, about the prison and their experiences. In the interview schedule, the first issue discussed was staff perceptions of the prison and their own human rights. This was originally intended to be a means of establishing a good rapport with staff, and to demonstrate to officers that the research was more than just a discussion of their attitudes towards prisoners. However, staff would spend a considerable amount of time in the interviews on this issue of 'staff rights' (Scott 2002). Unexpectedly, this proved to be extremely useful, opening up new avenues in the research for theorizing denial and prison dehumanization. The focus on 'staff rights' also meant that in officer networks, the word-of-mouth appraisals of the interviews were that I was looking into both staff and prisoner issues, and this both improved co-operation and led to a higher than anticipated number of volunteers, given the duration of the fieldwork. I was getting something very different from my interviews than what I was originally expecting. By asking the 'human rights question' (and especially quite specific sub-questions concerning prisoners' rights to education, food and rehabilitation), what I was getting was in effect very detailed data on prison officer occupational culture. Although it was also evident that I was uncovering more than one adaptation by prison officers to the prison situational context, a large number of officers seemed to adhere to an authoritarian or disciplinarian ethos.

Like a red flag to a bull, human rights – and indeed, any acknowledgement of the common humanity of prisoners – were vociferously denied, indicating that less eligibility was deeply embedded in the dominant adaptation/working personality of officers. As realization of the changing nature of the ethnography dawned, I felt that the best way forward was to embrace this new emphasis, as this aspect of the research seemed to be most important to the prison officers, and most relevant to understanding how such officers acknowledged or denied prisoner suffering.

As a white heterosexual male, I shared certain similarities with the social backgrounds of many of the prisoner officers. This undoubtedly impacted upon my ability to be (eventually) accepted and gain insights into the dominant 'white male' prison officer occupational culture. In the extract below from my prison journal, in the first few days of the ethnography I expressed my concerns about this hyper-heteronormative, white, male culture:

> I instantly felt like I was in a very male and white environment .... The woman Principal Officer [PO] I spoke to on E2 [then the hospital wing] was helpful and I have negotiated access later in the research. I was introduced by a male senior officer who said to me 'she is the one who must be obeyed' and at the end of the meeting when the same senior officer returned to escort me to the central office he said [laughing] 'did she use the whip' [both comments were made deliberately in earshot of the PO] .... I spoke to an Operational Grade Support [OGS] and she talked to me about how she had been sexually harassed but didn't want to do an interview. She was very shy and timid .... [Name] said that she had had to speak to her superiors to stop the bullying. Some of the officers [also OGS] on the same shift, whom I suspect were the main protagonists, made a point of coming up to me and saying that [name] found it difficult to take a joke. (Scott 2002)

While empathy was important in the interview process – officers told me of great anxieties, nervous breakdowns, marriage breakdowns – I could not fully identify with many of the officers' contributions. I found much of what the officers said problematic, but tried to withhold my critical judgement in the interview process itself, reserving this for later reflection and evaluation. Although I had worked out an interview schedule, interventions were based on close listening. I tried to both look like I was listening, showing encouragement, being supportive and active in the interviews, and *actually listen* at the same time, so that I could follow up interesting comments officers were making. I wanted to learn as much as possible, and I ensured that all respondents were fully aware of the research context and secured context.

It is impossible to know whether the officers were always open and truthful. Perhaps all researchers question whether respondents are saying what they want us to hear, or telling us what they really think. It's perhaps only when you do spend time with people and see how they respond in different contexts that you can gain an insight into the accuracy of what they tell you:

> I was talking on the one of the wings to a prison officer, and we were in the room by ourselves, he was really being open, talking about how difficult

the macho world was and how he found it difficult about prison life, and how prison officers barely cope as well. It's not like they are just these horrible people who just go in there and do this horrible job. You know they barely cope and a lot of them were really struggling to cope and that was obvious from the suffering that they were encountering, it was obvious from that. At this point, six prison officers then walked into the room, and you can almost see a physical change. Suddenly he was back to [the macho identity]. (Scott 2002)

Conclusion: Learning Lessons

Drawing upon the discussion above, I believe six critical research values clearly resonate with the insights of C. Wright Mills' 'sociological imagination'.[4]

1. independence;
2. reflexivity and relevance;
3. recognition of privileged position;
4. acknowledging truth;
5. critical judgement; and
6. generating new meanings, interpretations and sensibilities to facilitate change.

Independence

The research must be independent, at least in terms of how the research programme is formulated and executed, if not also in funding. The aims and focus of the research must also be independently determined. The researcher should not be what C. Wright Mills described as a 'technician of the State', justifying or sympathetically evaluating existing policies. This research benefited from independence because officers were more prepared to participate, but equally importantly, there was freedom in the way which the fieldwork could be interpreted. There was no state agency requiring 'robotic' conformity, quick-fix answers or pressurizing the shape of the focus or findings.

Reflexivity and Relevance

It is important that the critical researcher is profoundly conscious of the research environment and is prepared to adapt and allow C. Wright Mills 'sociological imagination' to take hold. Initial perceptions of the research context may be mistaken or more complex than originally envisaged, so prison ethnography

---

4   This chapter has not attempted to provide a comprehensive analysis of all of C. Wright Mills' political values (such as freedom and reason), but only to emphasize those closely identified with the prison officer ethnography undertaken by this author and/or by contrast with prison officer studies utilizing the AI method.

should always be grounded within, and reflect, the specific historical, structural, policy and situational contexts of the study. This may require ethnographers to be flexible and reflexive about their overarching aims and goals. Further, the research must in some way be relevant to the lived experiences of sufferers here and now. In the case study discussed in this chapter, examination of prison officers was deemed 'relevant' because of their role in shaping prisoners' experiences. As such, prison research should be envisaged as a means of engaging in an independent dialogue with the powerful and should be used to uncover exploitation and/or empower those who are suffering.

Recognition of Privileged Position

Prison ethnographers always have a privileged position. They have greater choices and freedom than all they observe. They have chosen to come to prison and can leave easily. Such self-awareness is essential in determining how the research is undertaken, and will also have an impact on how the researcher is treated in the research setting by prisoners and staff. Different prison ethnographers may well be treated very differently, depending on who they are perceived to be. In a very white and male world, I benefited from being white and a man. While it would be impossible to get 'into the mind' of the prison officers, the experience provided the tools to relate to how prison officers constructed their meaning and their social world. Such openness from staff may not be forthcoming to all researchers. C. Wright Mills' 'sociological imagination' can help us to stand in someone else's place for a little while, but we must always recognize that we are merely visitors in their world.

Acknowledging Truth

Prison ethnography must recognize what prisons are – places of pain, suffering humiliation and degradation. There may well be moments of humour, compassion and positive human interaction, but these brief sparks of light should not blind us to the dark back-cloth that characterizes daily prison life. This acknowledgement of the brutal and dehumanizing prison reality must be the starting point for any critical scrutiny of penal incarceration. For C. Wright Mills (1959), we must always be open about the research context and our experience of it. Prison ethnography must therefore be rooted in values which promote honesty, integrity and accuracy. Critical research is an attempt to uncover the truth – real experiences – whatever the shape or form. Researchers should include an acknowledgement of hostile findings, admitting if things go wrong, or if findings are not as anticipated or do not fit the hypothesis. The picture uncovered in the research must be the true picture of the respondents' lived realities, whatever the researcher standpoint and whether or not it provides a positive or negative account of that reality. The question should always be: 'Does the respondent recognize and relate to the findings?'

Critical Judgement

The aim of prison ethnography should not be reconciliation, to justify state practices, improve human resources management or some further utilitarian goal. Nor must it be to uncritically reproduce or condone dominant ideologies and discourses or naturalize their position. Researchers must retain the right to judge findings based on normative values and principles. While undertaking fieldwork, and in particular during interviews, it may well be easy to become immersed within the social world and moral universe of the respondent. For example, in the case study described above I tried to understand the prison officer position and offer some kind of empathy on a human level for those being interviewed. It was easy to be sucked into the officer interpretation of reality. Once the fieldwork is completed, ethnographers will be more able to reflect on the research experience and, utilizing memories, prison journals and the transcripts of interviews, can use their critical judgement to analyse and theorize the findings. Here, the prison ethnographer should use C. Wright Mills' 'sociological imagination' to expose anti-democratic, unaccountable, unjust, exploitative and abusive penal practices.

Generating New Meanings, Interpretations and Sensibilities to Facilitate Change

Ultimately, for C. Wright Mills (1959) the 'sociological imagination' should create new ways of understanding that make intimate connections between individual meanings and experiences, and wider collective and social realities. Prison research must also be located within wider social and political contexts. The critical prison researcher must not just interpret the world of those who are housed within prisons or those who contain them. They must try to facilitate change – though not, however, through the *research process* itself. By necessity, this may include using evidence from their ethnography to call for immediate humanitarian interventions, but we must not lose sight of wider radical transformations in the name of social justice. Researchers must engage in a manner in which findings and processes adopted can be used as valuable tools for changing social structures, or providing the platform for new meanings and interpretive frameworks for subjugated groups. The sociological imagination allows us the rethink the world. It then inspires us to change it. We should be researchers, then activists.

Prison ethnographies cannot be objective, neutral or value-free. The values of researchers will always have an impact on the research process (Mills 1959; Gouldner 1967). Researchers must be prepared to confess their standpoint, openly acknowledging their values. However, it would be a mistake to assume that acknowledgement itself is enough to achieve objectivity. Awareness of the speaking positions, background and interpretive framework merely place the research project into context (Scott 2014b). More important are the means by which such acknowledgment is used to shape the methodology and interventions in the field. Research can never be value-free. Nor indeed should it be. At the heart of the research process is the *clarification* and *justification* of the values adopted in the study by the ethnographer. While the reasons for undertaking prison research will be diverse, *critical research values* drawing upon C. Wright Mills' 'sociological imagination' should be relatively consistent: independence, an honest attempt to provide an accurate reflection of reality, a willingness to expose inhumanity by the powerful and to uncover links between 'private troubles' and 'public issues'.

References

Barton, A., K. Corteen, D. Scott and D. Whyte. 2006. 'Developing a Criminological Imagination.' In *Expanding the Criminological Imagination: Critical Readings On Criminology*, edited by A. Barton, K. Corteen, D. Scott and D. Whyte, 1–25. Cullompton: Willan Publishing.

Becker, H.S. 1967. 'Whose Side are We On?' *Social Problems* 14(3): 234–47.

Cohen, S. 2001. *States of Denial*. Cambridge: Polity Press

Gouldner, A.W. 1961/1973. 'Anti-minotaur: The Myth of a Value Free Sociology.' In *For Sociology: Renewal and Critique in Sociology Today*, edited by A. Gouldner, 3–26. London: Allen Lane.

———. 1967. 'The Sociologist as Partisan: Sociology and the Welfare State.' In *For Sociology: Renewal and Critique in Sociology Today*, edited by A. Gouldner, 27–68. London: Allen Lane.

Liebling, A. 1999. 'Doing Prison Research: Breaking the Silence.' *Theoretical Criminology* 3(2): 147–73.

———. 2001. 'Whose Side are We On? Theory, Practice and Allegiances in Prison Research.' *British Journal of Criminology* 41(3): 472–84.

——— and D. Price. 2001. *The Prison Officer*. London: HM Prison Service.

———, C. Elliot and D. Price. 1999. 'Appreciative Inquiry and Relationships in Prison.' *Punishment & Society* 1(1): 71–98.

———, C. Elliot and H. Arnold. 2001. 'Transforming the Prison: Romantic Optimism or Appreciative Realism?' *Criminal Justice* 1(2): 161–80.

———, D. Price and G. Shefer. 2011. *The Prison Officer*, 2nd edn. Cullompton: Willan Publishing.

Mills, C.W. 1959. *The Sociological Imagination*. New York: Oxford University Press.

Scott, D. 2002. 'Preston Prison Journal.' Unpublished manuscript.

———. 2008. *Penology*. London: Sage.

———. 2013. 'Unequalled in Pain.' In *Why Prison?*, edited by D. Scott, 301–24. Cambridge: Cambridge University Press.

———. 2014a. 'Prison Research: Appreciative or Critical Inquiry?' *Criminal Justice Matters* 95(1): 30–31.

———. 2014b. 'Walking among the Graves of the Living: Reflections of a Prison Abolitionist.' In *Palgrave Handbook of Prison Ethnography*, edited by D. Drake, R. Earle and J. Sloan. London: Palgrave Macmillan.

————. forthcoming. *The Caretakers of Punishment: Power, Legitimacy and the Prison Officer*. London: Palgrave Macmillan.

Sim, J. 2003. 'Whose Side We are Not On? Researching Medical Power in Prisons.' In *Unmasking the Crimes of the Powerful: Scrutinising States and Corporations*, edited by S. Tombs and D. Whyte, 239–57. Oxford: Peter Lang.

Chapter 9

Neo-liberalism, Higher Education and Anti-politics: The Assault on the Criminological Imagination

Alana Barton and Howard Davis

Every debate about the ideals of education is trivial and inconsequential compared to this single ideal: never again Auschwitz .... If coldness were not a fundamental trait ... of people as they in fact exist in our society, if people were not profoundly indifferent toward whatever happens to everyone else except for a few to whom they are closely bound ... then Auschwitz would not have been possible .... (Adorno 1967, 1, 8)

Introduction

Young (2011, 180) differentiates two competing criminologies: 'one that is the voice of those below and the investigator of the powerful [and] the other, which echoes the white noise of the criminal justice system'. The latter, reductionist and functional, examines crime through a decontextualized lens dislocating individual action from broader structural realities. Conversely, reflecting Mills' (1959/2000) recommendations for a 'sociological imagination', the former critically challenges narrow conceptualizations of crime, promoting an understanding of individual biographies within their wider social structures. Thus the imaginative criminologist, imbued with an inclusionary, socialist consciousness, endeavours to confront hegemonic, exclusionary and individualized discourses around crime *and* social problems (Barton et al. 2007).

Most of this book is dedicated to discussion of how this criminological imagination might be developed and expanded. We strongly support this enterprise, having both contributed to the edited collection *Expanding the Criminological Imagination* (Barton et al. 2007), which explored how criminological research, driven by critical political and theoretical priorities, could advance the discipline. But academics are not only researchers. We are also educators. For our ideas to have social purchase they must endure across academic generations, as do the ideas they contest. While we would like *everyone* to develop a critical criminological imagination, the imaginations of present and future criminologists – that is, our students – present an obvious minimum target. In this chapter we consider the deepening difficulties of educating future generations in a hostile climate.

Deepening and disseminating the criminological imagination are important for two reasons. First, the project is necessary in terms of understanding for its own sake. Narrow notions of crime and criminology, conceived within mainstream administrative thinking, limit rather than enlighten. Only momentary reflection is necessary to recognize the debt owed by criminological thought to academics outwith the benchmarked boundaries of today's discipline. An impetus towards narrow specialisms is not new, and nor are the constraints of 'discipline' upon analytical depth and breadth. Since the fracturing of political economy into an abstracted, mathematized 'economics' on the one hand and distinct, jealously territorial social sciences on the other, these disciplines have serviced rather than critiqued power. As economics has disdained the social (and industrial), so the functionalist social sciences have remained 'above' the deep realities of power and conflict. Today, even among the traditional concerns of administrative criminology the 'marginal[ization of] theoretical questions for the sake of "realism" ... [has] den[ied] the relevance of any consideration of deeper causes' (Reiner 2012a, 32).

Second, expanding the criminological imagination generates 'emancipatory knowledge'. Mills perceived the 'imagination' as a practical contribution to a transformative politics challenging injustice and inequality. As welfare claimants are demonized and the politics of exclusion outlaw, 'other' and vilify the poor as much as the 'criminal', seldom has it been more urgent for criminologists to understand the place of their empathic and politicized 'craft', to know, as Becker (1967) might have put it, whose side we are on.

So what is actually required of a criminological imagination? At a minimum, it calls for an *intellectual* understanding of personal troubles around crime and harm as public issues. It demands a holistic orientation, attending to links, commonalities and determining contexts. One must be able to imagine structure, agency (and the self) and the relationships between them. This is no small intellectual matter in an age of individualism. Further, the imagination should offer transformative potential where the 'object of transformation is the person and not simply the extent of their factual or technical knowledge' (Ransome 2011, 214). Education must explain injustice for students, but 'also help them develop critical affectivities through which they are "moved to change it"' (Amsler, citing Burbules and Berk 2011, 53).

Equally, the criminological imagination requires a critical *empathy*, not only with those commonly recognized as 'victims', but also with those whose life courses are marginalized and disrespected. Having an ear and a respect for subjective meaning goes to the heart of what humanistic education is, or should be. But it is particularly important for the *criminological* imagination because criminologists engage with people placed 'beyond the pale'. To invert the sound-bite of former British Prime Minister John Major, the criminological imagination has to understand more, and condemn less.

The Difficulties of the Task

> Nobody quarrels with the need for imagination ... no-one denies the need to relate the micro to the macro level .... Everyone likes the distinction between personal problems and public issues .... But what seems to be missing in the legacy of Mills is the critique of what is going on within the social sciences. For people will applaud imagination, yet fail to address that which systematically undermines it. They will make a nod of abeyance to the work of Mills, yet ignore what is happening in front of their eyes. (Young 2011, 9)

We now turn to the mounting difficulties of maintaining (let alone expanding) young criminological imaginations. We do so in four stages. First, we suggest that neo-liberal capitalism provides an increasingly destructive context for education. Second, within this context, managerialism has diminished learning to tested 'outcomes' alarmingly remote from real understanding. Third, while these developments have been damaging for many students, the neo-liberal counter-revolution has specific implications for criminology. Escalating hostility towards the marginal saturates media debate. Students come to criminology already soaked in the discourses of populist reaction. Fourth, at just the point where expectations of 'consumer students' have narrowed, universities are required to 'give them what they want'. Learning has become a commodity.

Capitalism in Late Modernity

For Wacquant, neo-liberalism is:

> a *transnational political project* aiming to remake the nexuses of the market, state and citizenship from above. This project is carried out by a new global ruling class in the making .... It entails, not simply the re-assertion of the prerogatives of capital and the promotion of the marketplace, but the promotion of four institutional logics: [economic deregulation, welfare state devolution, retraction and recomposition, the cultural trope of individual responsibility, and an expansive, intrusive, and proactive penal apparatus]. (Wacquant 2009, 306; emphasis in original)

Neo-liberally 'turbo-charged capitalism' (Luttwak 1995; Young 2007) has driven profound social, economic, political and cultural changes. Notwithstanding claims that wealth would 'trickle down', inequality has increased dramatically. Industries and organizations 'expand, shrink, merge, separate, "downsize" and restructure at an unprecedented pace' (Luttwak 1995, 7). Economic crisis has cut wages while raising under-employment and insecurity (Reinert 2012; Standing 2011). Even the 'good years' were profoundly unequal (Dorling 2012; Stiglitz 2013). But as economic circumstances have worsened, this unfairness has accelerated. The burdens of neo-liberal failure have been dumped on the poor. Wealth inequality in the UK has grown fivefold since 2006 (Shaheen 2012). While the top 1 per cent of households now each hold average financial and physical assets of £22 million, for the bottom 1 per cent this value is *minus* £10,000. While the top 1 per cent of households own more than the other 99 per cent put together, five million more people live in inadequate housing now than did in the 1990s, and the percentage of households unable to heat their homes adequately has almost quadrupled since 1999 (Shaheen 2012; Poverty and Social Exclusion 2013).[1]

The significance of the neo-liberal counter-revolution for social and criminal justice has been overwhelming. Following the US model, neo-liberal restructuring combines the withdrawal of welfare, the 'rolling out of the police-and-prison dragnet and their knitting together into a carceral assistantial lattice' (Wacquant 2009, 304). It 'coalesces around the shrill re-assertion of penal fortitude, the pornographic exhibition of the taming of moral and criminal deviancy and the punitive containment and disciplinary supervision of the problem populations dwelling at the margins of the class and cultural order' (Wacquant 2009, xx).

This relentless assault has overthrown social democratic thinking. Three shifts have particular significance here: managerialized re-shaping of public services; increased salience of consumption as driver of the economy and definer of personal identity; and the undermining of collective values and the rise of punitiveness. These shifts have defined the past three decades. During the lifetimes of our students, 'progress', 'reform' and' radicalism' have pointed only to more individualism, inequality and 'toughness'. It has become almost impossible to even *imagine* an alternative (Amsler 2011).

Managerialism, Schooling and Education

Public services, for neo-liberals, are inherently 'bad'. Ideally, they are privatized. Where markets do not exist they are created, with needs being met (or not) by companies selling in (far from 'perfect') markets (Connell 2013). Those agencies remaining 'public' are subject to private sector 'managerialism', disciplining employees from whom obedient 'flexibility' is demanded. Instrumental reasoning, measurement and audit underpin relentless drives towards 'efficiency'. The neo-liberal conviction is that state education fails to instil the skills and attitudes demanded by employers and that teachers, like other public sector workers, are obstacles to meeting the grave challenges of global competition. Reforms made supposedly in the interests of children actually 'have the purpose of wresting key controls over performance from front-line staff to senior managers with other targets in mind' (Mather and Seifert 2011, 29).

---

1   This is, of course, not an issue only for the UK. In 2007 in the USA, the richest 0.1 per cent of households had an income 220 times larger than the average of the bottom 90 per cent, receiving in a day and a half what the bottom 90 per cent receive in a year. As 'recovery' got under way, the gains went to the wealthiest, with the best-off 1 per cent taking 93 per cent of the additional wealth created in 2010 as compared to 2009 (Stiglitz 2013).

Exalting bureaucratized rationality, 'school development plans, policies, schemes of work, planning documentation, bench-marking and so forth' have de-professionalized teaching (Case et al. 2000, 613). 'Accountability' is built on tests, measurement, inspection and the 'transparency' of outcomes. Institutions can stand or fall on their statisticized outputs with improvements supposedly 'leveraged upwards by league tables, competitions between institutions, the achievement of targets and attendant funding rewards' (Mather and Seifert 2011, 27). Schools and the systems of which they are parts become 'almost solely concerned not with the development of curious or engaged learners or even with the "disciplining" of individuals, but with measuring, cataloguing, and producing ever more massive mounds of data' (Robbins and Kovalchuk 2012, 199). Our 'fresher' students are 'products' of this commodified, managerialized schooling (McGregor 2009).

The damage becomes increasingly evident. Teachers are pressured to ensure high pass rates, and are found wanting if they fail. Students take increasing numbers of modularized subjects, sitting examinations from different boards in the same subject, or are 'fast-tracked' to sit examinations too early (Garner 2013). As Walton notes, the resurrection of nineteenth-century '"teaching to the test", the reduction of content and assessment to what [can] apparently be measured and compared, and the hollowing out of everything ... stimulating or creative ... [has] reduc[ed] much learning to bite sized assessment exercises' (2011, 19–20). As the futures of teacher, student and institution each rest upon measured outputs, there is an unspoken temptation towards corruption. Exceptional energies are put into 'guidance', 'support' and the 'revision' of coursework. Research by Beaumont et al. (2011) highlights clearly the potential dangers of this, with students reflecting how they could hand in up to five drafts of coursework before submitting the final copy. One noted 'we could hand coursework in as many times as we wanted', while another admitted 'if you do it too many times, it ends up with the teacher kinda writing it for you' (Beaumont et al. 2011, 676)

The temptation for teachers to 'help' too much – to end up 'kinda writing it for you' – has become the elephant in many classrooms. In the research cited above:

> both teachers and students used the term 'spoon-feeding' to describe aspects of this process, and readily acknowledged the role it plays in the development of a dependency culture, rather than one that promotes autonomous learning ... [But while] teachers acknowledged this dependency as an issue [they] considered the pressure to maintain league-table positions conflicted with the aim of developing independent learning. (Beaumont et al. 2011, 682)

The implication is that schools' focus on high grades produces students whose grades are not their own, who lack the capacity for independent study, but who, as is discussed below, are increasingly empowered as 'customers' when they arrive at university to demand more of the same. Moreover, within a culture of 'grasshopper learning', grades and learning become conflated and study becomes the 'technologically enhanced' acquisition of unintegrated 'pieces' of knowledge, forgotten quickly once tested. Deeper *understanding*, within and between subjects, genuine inquiry and making leaps of imagination are forsaken for the 'quick fix' – the 'bit' to be added to the essay that will turn a B into an A.

Popular Punitiveness, Apathy and Anti-politics

In addition to changes affecting student generally, some developments are particularly significant for those studying criminology. Few study criminology or sociology at school, and their initial understandings of 'crime' are developed from dominant media narratives. Drawing on Mills' (1959/2000) conceptualization of both the 'promise' of social science and the skills of intellectual craftmanship, perhaps the most fundamental personal quality for the fresher criminology student is a genuine concern about the wider world and social justice. But this is increasingly challenging in a neo-liberal age. Neo-liberalism has become a normalized force that 'shapes our lives, memories and daily experiences, while attempting to erase everything critical and emancipatory about history, justice, solidarity, freedom, and the meaning of democracy' (Giroux 2008). It has systematically undermined collectivism and community values (Luttwak 1995), leading to 'the loss of a strong sense of common good, common experience and common troubles' (Nixon et al. 2011, 198). As Tawney articulated nearly a century ago: 'It assures men that there are no ends other than their own ends, no law other than their own desires, no limits other than that which they think advisable. Thus it makes the individual the centre of his (*sic*) own universe, and dissolves moral principles into a choice of expediencies' (quoted in Reiner 2007, 10).

In the context of such forces, individuals are abstracted from their structural and historical contexts and normalized to 'a privatised and individualised way of living' (Furedi 2005, 72). They become 'bounded by the private orbits in which they live [while] in other milieux they move vicariously and remain spectators' (Mills 1959/2000, 3) – the precise antithesis of what Mills advocated for the imaginative craft.

As social fragmentation and diversity increase, so do insecurity and anxiety (Young 2003a). As empathy becomes more selective, particular groups become the targets of fear, contempt and punitiveness (Reiner 2007, 16). Reiner (2012b) argues that social democratic thinking before the 1970s was evident in the unexalted social and political status of crime. While acknowledged, most criminal harms seemed fairly insignificant compared to economic depression, famine, war, poverty and so on. Moreover, sympathy for victims of crime did not exclude offenders as subjects of concern. Rather:

> The intellectual puzzle was how and why someone (presumed to be of the same common human stock as non-offenders) had done wrong. Morally and practically there was the question of how their behaviour could be reformed and future wrongdoings averted, for their sake as well as for potential future victims. (Reiner 2012b, 140)

Neo-liberalism, by contrast, elevated (conventional) crime into a significant, if not *the most* significant, threat to society. Violent and sexual crimes in particular, as a staple of media coverage, are over-reported yet devoid of structural context, facilitating the creation of the inherently deviant and criminal 'other'. Discourses around dangerousness and risk on the one hand and 'soft-touch' liberalism on the other together create an 'unacceptable gap' between violent offenders and their 'holiday camp' prisons (Mason 2006a). Public anxieties and mistrust are intensified, and 'public opinion is pushed in a pessimistic and vindictive direction' (Young 2003b, 41). As Mason notes: 'The bottom up pressure from an angry public, driven onwards by screaming red top headlines, demands more displays of repressive punishment: longer prison sentences, boot camps, ASBOs .... Punishment becomes crueller ... as the late-modern "politics of insecurity" justifies hostility and retribution on the criminal' (2006b, 1).

Simultaneously, the victim has become 'iconically central to criminal justice' (Reiner 2012b, 142). The media perpetuates a politically engineered 'zero-sum' game where harsher penalties are promoted, not only to prevent crime, but also as the only means by which 'justice' for victims can be demonstrated. Within such 'common sense', public support grows for welfare cutbacks and penal expansion (Reiner 2012b).

The language of the popular press is constructed around a particular form of morality. The 'amorality' of an acquisitive society that prioritizes affluence and capital over mutuality, equality and fairness is so pervasive that it becomes invisible. By contrast, vengeful notions of 'moralities' are constructed around 'inappropriate' lifestyles (Reiner 2012b). Indeed, at no time since the nineteenth century have the discourses around poverty, morality and crime been so enmeshed. This 'theatre of cruelty' (Giroux 2008) is founded on a series of binary narratives forging and forged by processes of moral exclusion. The 'respectable', law abiding, hard-working and domestically stable are clearly demarked from the minority who are 'disorganised, welfare dependent, criminal and criminogenic, [and] who live in unstable and dysfunctional families' (Young 2007, 18). In other words, there are 'strivers' and there are 'skivers'. The greatest vitriol is saved for those who, regardless of the extent of their privations, are unembarrassed, unapologetic or seemingly content with their lot. This rage against the 'shameless' is nothing new. To quote Adorno: 'A pattern that has been confirmed throughout the entire history of persecutions is that the fury against the weak chooses as its target especially those who are perceived as societally weak and at the same time – either rightly or wrongly – as happy' (1967, 2).

Those most marginalized have even become sources of popular entertainment as well as public hostility. A plethora of television programmes expose the immoral behaviours and dysfunctional lifestyles of those beyond respectability, clearly demarking the 'deserving' and 'undeserving' poor. Examples from the UK include *Trouble on the Estate* (BBC), *Skint* (Channel 4), *Saints vs Skivers* (BBC), *Benefits Britain 1949* (Channel 4), *Nick and Margaret: We All Pay Your Benefits* (BBC), *The Scheme* (BBC Scotland), *People Like Us* (BBC), *Benefits*

Street (Channel 4), *On Benefits and Proud* (Channel 5) and *Gypsies on Benefits and Proud* (Channel 5), to name a handful. The message is that poverty is the fault of a 'degenerate' underclass. Social problems are private and self-imposed misfortunes (Giroux 2008). Conversely, we are served a helping of programmes recounting the benevolence of the rich and famous who help the 'deserving' or 'contrite' poor through: the benefit of their advice (*7 Days on the Breadline* (ITV), *Duchess on the Estate* (ITV)); passing on their skills (*Gordon Behind Bars* (Channel 4), *Football Behind Bars* (Sky 1)); or, less frequently, giving money (*The Secret Millionaire* (Channel 4)).

Students, we should be clear, are not universally 'brainwashed' by such imagery. Many choose our courses precisely because they reject much of what passes for 'common sense'. However, most have lived their lives in cultures of deepening, sometimes visceral, antipathy towards the criminal, the migrant and the poor, and it would be naive to ignore their impact. There is a real tendency among young people towards conservatism when it comes to the politics of class and social inequality (specifically in relation to welfare and benefits) and race (specifically in relation to immigration) (Harris 2013). In a recent poll, while 70 per cent of respondents born before the Second World War regarded the welfare state as one of Britain's proudest achievements, only 20 per cent of the 'Generation Y' sample (born 1980–2000) agreed. Similarly, nearly 50 per cent of 18–24-year-olds rejected the suggestion that those on benefits were unlucky rather than lazy (Harris 2013).

Mills envisaged the 'imagination' as a way in which individuals could understand and (re-)engage with the political dimensions of their lives at both the micro and macro levels. While student involvement in protests against the war in Iraq and the introduction of university fees indicates a level of continuing political engagement, the real extent of political consciousness among students, and young people generally, is a matter of debate. The Citizenship Foundation (2005) reported a 'high' level of political awareness and activity among young people, noting that 80 per cent of survey respondents would sign a petition, 48 per cent would take part in a demonstration and 39 per cent would campaign for a political party 'if a political issue arose that affected them personally'. However, Ipsos MORI estimated that of the 18–24-year-olds registered to vote, only 37 per cent turned out at the 2005 UK general election (Electoral Commission 2005). White et al. (2000, 42) reported that young people's suggestions for reducing their political disaffection included 'less stuffy' and 'more accessible' attire for politicians, the incorporation of politics into chat shows and soap operas, and the use of comedians or celebrity presenters as political role models: 'Other ideas were concerned with mainly making political coverage less "newsy" ... and not focusing on "boring" politicians "droning" on. However, irrespective of the format it was said that the word "politics" should be avoided as far as possible' (White et al. 2000, 42).

For a generation of students, a sense of political subjectivity and active citizenship has been eroded, and political identity has become understood in relation to the personal self, constructed through 'lifestyle' and consumer choices (Furedi 2005) rather than a broader political or social consciousness. In Millsian terms, we might see the failure to understand personal troubles as aspects of public issues as generative of alienation and political apathy. But perhaps we could go further. 'Political' engagement that is contingent on image, entertainment value, celebrity input and uncomplicated sound-bites, or on matters that have only personal relevance for the individual, is not just *a*political. It is *anti*-political. At the very moment criminology is confronted with intensifying state control and violence, devastating social inequalities, exclusions and punitiveness against those most marginalized and disadvantaged in society, our student body – our next generation of criminologists – is in danger of becoming characterized by 'decomposition of collectivity and erosion of both the desire for, and belief in, social and political change' (Amsler 2011, 53).

The Consumer, the Student and the University

Higher education in a neo-liberal world is seen as 'the handmaiden of the economy' (Boden and Epstein 2011, 485). As discussed elsewhere, this has had dramatic implications for social and criminological research (Boden and Epstein 2011; Walters 2007). In terms of teaching, the neo-liberal university promises to place the consumer at its heart, with consumer demands taking a central place in the design and delivery of programmes (McGregor 2009; Quality Assurance Agency 2012). Institutional audit takes evidence of student influence on 'any aspect of the student learning experience', including application and admission, induction and transition into higher education, programme and curriculum design, delivery and organization, and curriculum content and assessment (Quality Assurance Agency 2012, 2). For managers, the inference is clear: the more evidence of 'influence', the better. And it is increasingly the case, for rational consumer-students 'incentivised through debt' (Ransome 2011, 212), that 'the only conceivable purpose of going to university is to get the right sort of corporate job' (Walton 2011, 20). So it is that as the educational horizons of university entrants narrow towards vocational instrumentalism, the university is becoming incentivized, through 'guidance' and the market, to give them exactly what they want.

But there are fundamental problems with student-driven higher education. Students' wants are far less 'rational' than supposed. Their choices often lack congruence with the demands of high-level 'employability'. This is not necessarily a bad thing in itself, but there are disturbing implications if consumer-students are to become the central drivers of higher education. Consumerism '[allows] us a sense that we can establish our identity *without recourse to lengthy and complicated procedures or activities, but rather through purchasing something*' (Nixon et al. 2011, 199; emphasis added). While for academics universities should be about inquiry and learning, and official characterizations have the student rationally maximizing skills valued in the marketplace, for many students a degree is a voucher to a lifestyle. Gratification through purchase does not necessarily align with painstaking investment in one's skills, even when narrowly conceived in terms of 'employability'. Students, in narrow terms, often misperceive the 'real world' of employment (Haywood et al. 2011). They can be 'romantic daydreamers' more than informed, utility-maximizing consumers.[2] Their daydreams 'are unrelated to education, or even to the skills required in a specific career, but are instead focused on consumer lifestyles supported by "well-paid" jobs' (Haywood et al. 2011, 183). And, Mills might note, such rationality stands in direct conflict with the facilitation of *reason* or what a *critical* pedagogy might demand. Fundamentally, an emphasis on purchase 'represents an intellectual shift from engagement to passivity' and a reluctance to engage in intellectual struggle (Williams 2011, 172).

Crucially, rather than challenging this, universities themselves 'pla[ce] attention so firmly upon the student experience [that] the idea that *the purpose of HE is the creation of satisfied consumers [is enhanced]*' (Williams 2011, 172; emphasis added). An irony of neo-liberal policy is that many universities are incentivized, not to deliver rigorous challenging education, meeting the 'needs' of a modern economy, but 'to pander to fantasies of a leisure-based "good life" whilst actually preparing students for more mundane career outcomes' (Haywood et al. 2011, 183). University teachers, as a consequence, are increasingly caught between consumer-students for whom 'the process of learning is less important than the outcome of a degree', and managements who are happy to indulge this contemporary commonplace (Williams 2011, 175). Career progression, in turn, becomes increasingly dependent on hearing 'the student voice', meeting student 'needs' and prioritizing official distillations of 'the student experience'. Student choice – between subjects, modes of assessment and between teachers – has become a staple of 'good practice'. But what if students choose not immersion in learning, but 'anticipated enjoyment, fun or entertainment value' (Nixon et al. 2011, 203)? Responding to demands for entertainment, for 'soft' tutors and 'safe' alternatives to experiment, universities compete to 'satisfy' while dismantling the academic (critical or otherwise) and discarding the transformative.

Customer satisfaction, moreover, sits in stark, if seldom stated, contradiction to the idea that learning may *require* struggle, discomfort and maybe even 'dissatisfaction'. Any sense of critical consciousness is 'diluted when desire is reduced to gratification, pleasure [is] defined by comfort and transformation [is] exchanged for satisfaction' (Amsler 2011, 58). In Collini's view, indeed, 'a "satisfied" student is nigh-on ineducable' (2012, 185). Marketization encourages collusion with 'daydreams', daydreams that elide what higher education really requires and what it really offers. It also flatters consumers with knowledge and understanding about disciplines they barely know. To draw (loosely) on Collini's analogy, student surveys might be appropriate for shaping some aspects of 'the student experience' (there is so much more, the consumer is told, to being a

---

2   This can be said of most of us in our roles as consumers. Consumption in advanced capitalist economies relies upon the successful sale of goods and services as parts of 'lifestyles' that people don't actually need.

student than studying – it is a whole wraparound 'experience'), but they are clearly not appropriate to determine whether a theory module should include a block on Foucault.[3] Moreover, focus on student wants sidesteps both the heterogeneity of interest between past, present and future students – even in narrow instrumentalist terms – and more fundamentally, the fact that 'individuals often need to be told by someone who knows that a particular line of study is *worth* pursuing whether at the time they *want* to or not' (Collini 2012, 186). This is particularly important in the face of subtle or not so subtle pressures from students (and sometimes management) to 'sex up' or dispense with 'dull' subjects. Ironically, for all the official and institutional emphasis on consumer-students in 'quality' processes:

> students may not spot the weaknesses [that *actually do* exist] as they are not best placed to judge whether or not a lecturer has a complete grasp of their field. You can score highly on student feedback almost entirely on style and entertainment value over substance and erudition. Moreover, if you give out bad grades you run the risk of direct translation into negative student feedback. (Fenton 2011, 105)

Paradoxically, as consumer students are almost harassed by universities to 'influence' curriculum design, programme structures and teaching methods, they are simultaneously constructed as 'vulnerable learners' needing 'support' (Williams 2011). This support, it seems, often needs to extend well beyond that accorded to their peers entering full-time employment, or that accorded to schoolchildren. As Williams notes, rather than properly confronting the idea that 'new (particularly intellectual) experiences are stressful and daunting for students, [universities] often reinforce these notions through the proliferation of institutional mechanisms for providing emotional, practical and academic support' (2011, 179). It is ironic to note the extent to which universities will go – in supposedly preparing students for the harsh, 'dog-eat-dog' world of turbo-charged capitalism – to shield them from failure, or from failure as something for which they might bear responsibility. It is easy to see how an eye to league tables might encourage 'kinda doing the work for [them]' in universities, just as in secondary schooling (Beaumont et al. 2011, 676). Current students might have an interest in easier assessment regimes, for example (a 'supportive' university 'satisfying' its customers), but for past graduates who have little influence over these matters, it is important that the value of their qualifications is not diminished. In a market however, preferences are expressed through purchase, and existing graduates have already spent their money and gone.

---

3   The National Student Survey (NSS) has become a key focus for management in UK universities. All final-year students are invited to complete the survey and 'rankings' of departments and programmes are almost instantly constructed upon their publication. Small, statistically insignificant drops in score from one year to the next or in ranking relatives to other 'competitor' programmes can be taken very seriously.

As (many) students become more narrowly instrumentalist and less socially aware or concerned, higher education has become eager, in return for their custom, to give them an 'experience' that 'satisfies' these limited aspirations. Students are encouraged to become a simple aggregation of those knowledges and skills that they can sell in the marketplace, and to aspire only to a life defined by the consumption that this will enable. As service consumer and producer respectively, students and universities are fast becoming mere numbers in education by spreadsheet, and in the anti-politics of the market. Notions that education should involve learning about society itself – its past, its present or its future, its unfairnesses, its dangers and its brutalities – or about the student's own life and responsibilities within it, are fast becoming eccentric.

Conclusion

> The inability to identify with others was unquestionably the most important psychological condition for the fact that something like Auschwitz could have occurred in the midst of more or less civilized and innocent people. What is called fellow travelling was primarily business interest: one pursues one's own advantage before all else and, simply not to endanger oneself, does not talk too much ....The coldness of the societal monad, the isolated competitor, was the precondition, as indifference to the fate of others, for the fact that only very few people reacted. (Adorno 1967, 9)

We might expect that a student of criminology, or indeed the social sciences generally, 'is likely to be worried about the state of the world', that '[t]he danger of a new war, the conflict between social systems, the rapid social changes which he (*sic*) has observed in his country has ... made him feel that the study of social matters is of great urgency' (Lazarsfeld, quoted in Mills 1959/2000, 100). A social and political consciousness is an imperative motivation for, and aim of, the study of sociological disciplines. Indeed, as Adorno (1967) would argue, it is the fundamental role of education per se. To be truly educated is to be politicized. For education to achieve its ultimate goal – to ensure 'Auschwitz should never happen again' (Adorno 1967, 10) – it must be concerned with the nurturing of a critical consciousness and the 'power of reflection, of self-determination, of not cooperating' (Adorno 1967, 4).

Yet increasingly students arrive at university as 'voyeurs' or 'spectators' of this wider world, its inequalities and injustices. Their imaginations have been imperilled by ubiquitous and pitiless representations of 'crime' and harm and of those deemed responsible. Many have been stunted by schooling where what matters most for the enterprise is the 'success' of the enterprise itself. Despite the best intentions of individual lecturers – and there are many who are dedicated to the transformative values of education and the nurturing of 'defiant' rather than 'compliant' imaginations (Boden and Epstein 2011, 477) – the university is less inclined to challenge this development than to climb above its 'competitors' in the next league table.

Critical imaginations are not fostered by market-led education where students are compliant to, and have their educational experience driven by, the demands of business. Neo-liberal regimes of control have shaped education into the means by which the next generation of producers and consumers is created. The roles of learning establishments, secondary and tertiary, as agents of the state and of capital have deepened and consolidated (Boden and Epstein 2011), with universities in particular becoming positioned as central to the 'knowledge economy'. As university leaders amend their titles from vice-chancellor to chief executive (Shaw 2013), one only has to chart the changes in the government departments responsible for universities over the last twenty years to see the growing expectation of the university's role in 'knowledge capitalism'.[4]

Like any business in a competitive market, the university promotes its product (a degree) as part of a desirable lifestyle, a means by which the individual customer (student) can purchase entry to the coveted 'work and spend' culture (Haywood et al. 2011, 183). Students increasingly share with managers the consumerist idea of 'getting what you pay for' and obtaining 'value for money'. We have seen the transformation over five decades from students as 'change agents, radicals and transgressives' (Morley 2003, 83) to consumers who endorse the ideologies of the neo-liberal orthodoxy. Academic education, now thoroughly pervaded by a bureaucratic rationality that in Millsian terms undermines rather than promotes freedom and reason, has been reduced to the most direct route through which the 'cheerful robots' (Mills 1959/2000, 171) it produces can enter the corporate world. It is ceasing to be a means via which one might challenge the fundamental problems with such a world.

When education becomes focused on the interests of the 'self', and in particular the promotion of the self in the market society, it becomes anti-democratic and anti-political. In an individualized and atomized culture where the objective is the 'pursuit of one's own interests against the interests of everyone else' (Adorno 1967, 8), the ability to imagine the relationship between 'the personal troubles of milieu and the public issues of social structure' (Mills 1959/2000, 8) is lost. Coldness and indifference proliferate while empathy diminishes, especially with those most socially marginalized and excluded. There are crucial matters at stake here for criminologists. There are the obvious risks posed to students and the discipline by constriction and hardening of the imagination. Coldness, moreover, as Adorno (1967, 8) reminds us, is a 'condition for disaster'. And we live in cold times.

Some may view the picture we have sketched here as overly pessimistic. It is often expected that a chapter such as this should end by outlining causes for

---

4   In 1992 universities were part of the Department of Education and Science. This changed to the Department of Education and Employment (1995), the Department of Education and Skills (2001), the Department of Innovation, Universities and Skills (2007), then the Department of Business, Innovation and Skills (2009) (Boden and Epstein 2011).

hope and strategies for resistance. Resistance, it might be held, is crushed by pessimism, while hope, on the other hand, is essential for the defiant imagination (Boden and Epstein 2011). And we would agree with Mills that 'the moral and the intellectual promise of social science is that freedom and reason [*should*] remain cherished values' (Mills 1959/2000, 173; emphasis added). That we do not sketch out an outline of resistance here should not be taken as an indication that we believe the challenges we have outlined to be insuperable. However, it does follow from our conviction that they are so formidable and serious that including a few indicative, ameliorative paragraphs in conclusion would be to trivialize the importance of the task at hand: of resistance in dangerous times. Academia and education have become complicit in undermining Mills' 'cherished values', and it would be naive to place our faith in notions of humanity as naturally reason- and freedom-seeking. Now, more than when Mills wrote: 'it has become evident … that *all* men (*sic*) do *not* naturally *want* to be free; that all men are not willing or not able … to exert themselves to acquire the reason that freedom requires' (Mills 1959/2000, 175; emphasis in original). The consequences of unreason can be grave. The bureaucratic-organizational, cultural and structural pressures toward its elevation are mounting. Unless the situation is reversed, to use the words of Valéry, 'inhumanity has a great future' (cited in Adorno 1967, 7).

References

Adorno, T. 1967. *Education after Auschwitz*. Accessed 6 June 2015. http://ada. evergreen.edu/~arunc/texts/frankfurt/auschwitz/AdornoEducation.pdf.

Amsler, S. 2011. 'From "Therapeutic" to Political Education: The Centrality of Affective Sensibility in Critical Pedagogy.' *Critical Studies in Education* 52(1): 47–63.

Barton, A., K. Corteen, D. Scott, and D. Whyte, eds. 2007. *Expanding the Criminological Imagination: Critical Readings in Criminology.* Cullompton: Willan Publishing.

Beaumont, C., M. O'Doherty and L. Shannon. 2011. 'Reconceptualising Assessment Feedback: A Key to Student Learning?' *Studies in Higher Education* 36(6): 671–87.

Becker, H. 1967 'Whose Side are We On?' *Social Problems* 14(3): 239–47.

Boden, R. and D. Epstein. 2011. 'A Flat Earth Society? Imagining Academic Freedom.' *Sociological Review* 59(3): 476–95.

Case, P., S. Case and S. Catling. 2000. 'Please Show You're Working: A Critical Assessment of the Impact of OFSTED Inspection on Primary Teachers.' *British Journal of the Sociology of Education* 21(4): 605–21.

Citizenship Foundation. 2005. 'Political Apathy amongst Young People is "a Myth", Says New Research.' *Citizenship Foundation.* Accessed 6 June 2015. http://www.citizenshipfoundation.org.uk/main/news.php?n171.

Collini, S. 2012. *What are Universities For?* London: Penguin.

Connell, R. 2013. 'The Neoliberal Cascade and Education: An Essay on the Market Agenda and its Consequences.' *Critical Studies in Education* 54(2): 99–112.

Dorling, D. 2012. 'Inequality Constitutes a Particular Place.' *Social and Cultural Geography* 13(1): 1–9.

Electoral Commission. 2005. *Election 2005: Turnout, How Many, Who and Why?* London: The Electoral Commission.

Fenton, N. 2011. 'Impoverished Pedagogy, Privatised Practice.' In *The Assault on Universities: A Manifesto for Resistance*, edited by M. Bailey and D. Freedman, 103–10. London: Pluto Press.

Furedi, F. 2005. *Politics of Fear*. London: Continuum Books.

———. 2011. 'Introduction to the Marketization of Higher Education and the Student as Consumer.' In *The Marketisation of Higher Education and the Student as Consumer*, edited by M. Molesworth, R. Scullion and E. Nixon, 1–8. Abingdon: Routledge.

Garner, R. 2013. 'GCSE Results 2013: Major Slump in Top-grade Passes Revealed as More Pupils Take Exams Early.' *The Independent*, 22 August. Accessed 6 June 2015. http://www.independent.co.uk/news/gcse-results-2013-major-slump-in-topgrade-passes-revealed-as-more-pupils-take-exams-early-8779232.html.

Giroux, H. 2008. 'Slouching towards Bethlehem: The New Gilded Age and Neoliberalism's Theater of Cruelty.' *Dissident Voice*, 11 March. Accessed 6 June 2015. http://dissidentvoice.org/2008/03/slouching-towards-bethlehem/.

Harris, J. 2013. 'Generation Y: Why Young Voters are Backing the Conservatives.' *The Guardian*, 26 June. Accessed 6 June 2015. http://www.theguardian.com/politics/2013/jun/26/generation-y-young-voters-backing-conservatives.

Haywood, H., R. Jenkins and M. Molesworth, M. 2011. 'A Degree Will Make All Your Dreams Come True: Higher Education as the Management of Consumer Desires.' In *The Marketisation of Higher Education and the Student as Consumer*, edited by M. Molesworth, R. Scullion and E. Nixon, 183–95. Abingdon: Routledge.

Luttwak, E. 1995. 'Turbo-charged Capitalism and its Consequences.' *London Review of Books* 17(21): 6–7.

McGregor, G. 2009. 'Educating for (*Whose*) Success? Schooling in an Age of Neo-liberalism.' *British Journal of Sociology of Education* 30(3): 345–58.

Mason, P. 2006a. 'Lies, Distortion and What Doesn't Work: Monitoring Prison Stories in the British Media.' *Crime, Media, Culture* 2(3): 251–67.

———. 2006b. 'Turn On, Tune In, Slop Out.' In *Captured by the Media: Prison Discourse in Popular Culture*, edited by P. Mason, 1–15. Cullompton: Willan Publishing.

Mather, K. and R. Seifert. 2011. 'Teacher, Lecturer, Labourer? Performance Management Issues in Education.' *Management in Education* 25(1): 26–31.

Mills, C.W. 1959/2000. *The Sociological Imagination*. Oxford: Oxford University Press.

Morley, L. 2003. 'Reconstructing Students as Consumers: Power and Assimilation?' In *Higher Education and the Lifecourse*, edited by M. Slowey and D. Watson, 79–92. London: SRHE and Open University Press.

Nixon, E., R. Scullion and M. Molesworth, M. 2011. 'How Choice in Higher Education Can Create Conservative Learners.' In *The Marketisation of Higher Education and the Student as Consumer*, edited by M. Molesworth, R. Scullion and E. Nixon, 196–208. Abingdon: Routledge.

Poverty and Social Exclusion. 2013. 'Going Backwards: 1983–2012.' *Poverty and Social Exclusion*, 28 March. Accessed 6 June 2015. http://www.poverty.ac.uk/pse-research/2-going-backwards-1983-2012.

Quality Assurance Agency. 2012. *UK Quality Code for Higher Education Chapter B5 Student Engagement: Draft for Consultation*. Accessed 6 June 2015. http://www.qaa.ac.uk/Publications/InformationAndGuidance/Documents/Quality-Code-B5-Student-engagement-draft-for-consultation.pdf.

Ransome, P. 2011. 'Qualitative Pedagogy versus Instrumentalism: The Antimonies of Higher Education Learning and Teaching in the United Kingdom.' *Higher Education Quarterly* 64(2):206–23.

Reiner, R. 2007. 'Neoliberalism, Crime and Justice.' In *Social Justice and Criminal Justice*, edited by R. Roberts and W. McMahon, 8–21. London: Centre for Crime and Justice Studies.

———. 2012a. 'Political Economy and Criminology: The Return of the Repressed.' In *New Directions in Criminological Theory*, edited by S. Hall and S. Winlow, 30–51. Abingdon: Routledge.

———. 2012b. 'What's Left? The Prospects for Social Democratic Criminology.' *Crime, Media, Culture* 8(2): 135–50.

Reinert, E.S. 2012. 'Neo-classical Economics: A Trail of Economic Destruction since the 1970s.' *Real-world Economics Review* 60: 2–17. Accessed 26 June 2013. http://www.paecon.net/PAEReview/issue60/Reinert60.pdf.

Robbins, C.G. and S. Kovalchuk. 2012. 'Dangerous Disciplines: Understanding Pedagogies of Punishment in the Neoliberal States of America.' *Journal of Pedagogy* 3(2):198–218.

Shaheen, F. 2012. 'Why Nick Clegg's One-off Wealth Tax Does Not Go Far Enough.' *New Economics Foundation*. Accessed 16 April 2013. http://www.neweconomics.org/blog/2012/08/29/why-clegg%E2%80%99s-one-off-wealth-tax-does-not-go-far-enough.

Shaw, C. 2013. 'Goodbye Vice-chancellor, Hello Chief Executive.' *The Guardian*, 16 April. Accessed 6 June 2015. http://www.theguardian.com/education/2013/apr/16/higher-education-job-titles.

Standing, G. 2011. *The Precariat: The New Dangerous Class*. London: Bloomsbury.

Stiglitz, J.E. 2013. *The Price of Inequality*. London: Penguin.

Wacquant, L. 2009. *Punishing the Poor: The Neoliberal Government of Social Insecurity*. Durham, NC: Duke University Press.

Walters, R. 2007. 'Critical Criminology and the Intensification of the Authoritarian State.' In *Expanding the Criminological Imagination: Critical Readings in*

Criminology, edited by A. Barton, K. Corteen, D. Scott and D. Whyte, 15–37. Cullompton: Willan Publishing.

Walton, J. 2011. 'The Idea of the University.' In *The Assault on Universities: A Manifesto for Resistance*, edited by M. Bailey and D. Freedman, 15–25. London: Pluto Press.

White, C., S. Bruce and J. Ritchie. 2000. *Young People's Politics: Interest and Engagement amongst 14–24 Year Olds*. Joseph Rowntree Foundation. Accessed 6 June 2015. http://www.jrf.org.uk/system/files/1859353096.pdf.

Williams, J. 2011. 'Constructing Consumption: What Media Representations Reveal about Today's Students.' In *The Marketisation of Higher Education and the Student as Consumer*, edited by M. Molesworth, R. Scullion and E. Nixon, 170–182. Abingdon : Routledge.

Young, J. 1999. *The Exclusive Society: Social Exclusion, Crime and Difference in Late Modernity*. London: Sage.

———. 2003a. 'Merton with Energy, Katz with Structure: The Sociology of Vindictiveness and the Criminology of Transgression.' *Theoretical Criminology* 7(3): 388–414.

———. 2003b. 'Winning the Fight against Crime? New Labour, Populism and Lost Opportunities.' In *The New Politics of Crime and Punishment*, edited by R. Matthews and J. Young, 33–47. Cullompton: Willan Publishing.

———. 2007. *The Vertigo of Late Modernity*. London: Sage.

———. 2011. *The Criminological Imagination*. Cambridge: Polity Press.

Chapter 10

Imagining the Unthinkable: Climate Change, Ecocide and Children

Rob White

Introduction

This chapter explores the implications for children of the present failures on the part of governments and businesses to systematically address the causes and consequences of global warming. It does so by arguing that such lack of concerted action around climate change in effect constitutes a form of 'ecocide'. Climate change is intimately linked to a raft of negative consequences involving significant degrees of social and ecological harm. It is this that makes it of particular relevance to the criminological imagination. More than simply a discreet or new type of 'crime', the magnitude of the problem warrants consideration as equivalent to a form of planetary genocide. This is especially apt given that the ecological destruction is consciously and knowingly being allowed to happen. Global warming is predicted to generate death and suffering on a scale hitherto unheard of, and in which all life forms on Earth are implicated.

The chapter begins by briefly outlining the relationship between climate change and criminology. It then introduces the notions of ecocide and intergenerational equity as conceptual lenses by which we can evaluate and critique present-day affairs pertaining to climate change. The special vulnerability of children is discussed in order to illustrate the inequities flowing from 'do-nothing' policies and practices as these affect human populations now and into the future. The explanations for current (non-)interventions are discussed through reference to state-corporate crime. Climate justice is and ought to be of major concern to criminology as a field (given its focus on crime, criminality and justice), and to criminologists as individuals and parents (given that it is our children and our children's children whose lives are at stake). Our whole world depends upon how we, collectively, respond to challenges posed by climate change in the here and now.

Climate Change and Criminology

Until recently, climate change was of little concern to criminology – due in no small part to the field's own techniques of neutralization (including what Mills [1959] called 'abstracted empiricism') when it comes to 'big picture' issues, and a general contrarian attitude to what are perceived to be non-criminological areas of investigation (see Cohen 2001). Yet global warming and climate change are the biggest and most pressing issues of our age. And, increasingly, the consequences of climate change are leaving little to the imagination, criminological or otherwise.

Leading US criminologist Robert Agnew (2011) recently observed that climate change will become one of the major, if not *the* major, forces driving crime as the twenty-first century progresses. His voice is among a relatively small handful of criminologists who realize and acknowledge the gravity of the present situation (see Lynch and Stretesky 2010; Agnew 2011, 2012, 2013; White 2009, 2011, 2012; Farrell et al. 2012; Halsey 2013). Generally within criminology, what is remarkable is the silence in this area, especially compared to the prolific and concerted efforts of colleagues in cognate areas such as law and international relations. The present concern, however, is not with the criminal consequences stemming from climate change (for this, see Agnew 2011; White 2012; Mares 2013). Rather, this chapter attempts to construct global warming, largely based upon anthropocentric causes, as a criminal matter in its own right. In order to capture this criminality, the chapter focuses on ecocide and intergenerational equity as key concepts denoting culpability and responsibility. Before doing so, a few preliminary observations set the scene.

Global warming describes the rising of the Earth's temperature over a relatively short time span. *Climate change* describes the interrelated effects of this rise in temperature: from changing sea levels and changing ocean currents through to the impacts of temperature change on local environments that affect the endemic flora and fauna in varying ways (e.g., the death of coral due to temperature rises in sea water or the changed migration patterns of birds). *Weather* is the term we use for the direct local experience of things such as sunshine, wind, rain, snow and the general disposition of the elements. It is about the short-term and personal, not the long-term patterns associated with climate in general. As the planet warms up, the climate will change in ways that disrupt previous weather patterns, and will in some places even bring colder weather, although overall temperatures are on the rise (Lever-Tracy 2011).

To put this in slightly different language, C. Wright Mills (1959) made a distinction between the, mainly structural 'public issues' and those based upon the directly experiential, the so-called 'personal troubles' of individuals. The sheer number of people experiencing similar things (such as unemployment) means that such personal experiences are in fact *social*, not merely individual, in nature – they stem from and reveal something about the economic and political institutions of the society as a whole. So, too, climate change is a structural phenomenon linked to dominant forms of production, consumption and pollution. We may experience weather individually in terms of personal preferences (some like it hot, some like it cool, some like rain, some like the dry), but at the end of the day it is climatic systems that determine overall weather patterns. Regardless of personal preferences, we are all affected.

Concern about global warming had been expressed for many years, by many scientists in different disciplines. Even though it had been systematically denied and downplayed by contrarians, many of whom have friends in high places (Brisman 2012; Kramer 2013), climate change is accepted by most people today as a serious and urgent issue. Part of the reason for this is that climate- and weather-related events seem to now touch or affect every person living on the planet. They do this directly and indirectly, in ways that are understandable and threatening to ordinary people. Unseasonal weather (such as droughts), extreme weather events (such as cyclones/hurricanes) and natural disasters (such as tsunamis) bring home the immediate effects of global warming to many millions of people. The longer-term effects, such as rising ocean levels, are also not so far over the horizon for those people living in low-lying countries of the Pacific and Indian Oceans. The experience of specific weather events is variable depending upon how one is situated geo-politically, socially and economically. Yet, as individual biography becomes ever more shaped by such events, it becomes easier to see and to locate personal troubles as manifestations of much deeper societal and ecological problems (Mills 1959). Climate change as a public issue is intimately connected to our personal experiences of weather and the hardships this might entail.

How states, agencies and corporations manage and handle the environment has a direct impact on everyone in some way or another. The lack of concerted global action on climate change can be attributed in large measure to the actions of large transnational corporations, especially those in the 'old energy' sectors such as coal mining. Given that the top private corporations are economically more powerful than many nation states, and given that they own and control great expanses of the world's land, water and food resources, these transnational corporations are individually and collectively a formidable force. On occasion, as well, business competitors may use their collective muscle to influence world opinion or global efforts to curtail their activities. For example, analysis of how big business has responded to global warming reveals a multi-pronged strategy to slow responses down (Bulkeley and Newell 2010). Some of the elements of this have included:

- challenging the science behind climate change;
- creating business-funded environmental non-governmental organizations;
- emphasizing the economic costs of tackling climate change;
- using double-edged diplomacy to create stalemates in international negotiations;
- using domestic politics (particularly in the USA) to stall international progress; and
- directly influencing the climate change negotiations through direct lobbying.

It is only continuous pressure from below by grassroots groups and global activists, and the occasional exercise of political will by enlightened politicians from above (as in some Latin American countries such as Bolivia), that moderate the exercise of this corporate power.

None the less, today most governments acknowledge that there is a problem and that it must in some way be addressed. The divides between North and South, geographically and metaphorically, are already deepening as crises related to food production and distribution, energy sources and pollution, and changing climates re-order the old world order. Social inequality and environmental injustice will undoubtedly be the drivers of continuous conflict for many years to come, as the most dispossessed and marginalized of the world's population suffer the brunt of food shortages, undrinkable water, climate-induced migration and general hardship in their day-to-day lives. Women will suffer more than men, people of colour more than the non-indigenous and the non-migrant, the young and the elderly more than the adult, and the infirm and disabled of all ages.

If anything, most disagreement surrounding climate change today concerns the pace of global warming, rather than whether it is happening. In October 2012, for instance, it was reported that:

- The Arctic was warming twice as quickly as was projected in the worst-case scenarios for the last major international climate science report in 2007.
- In 2012, the rate of loss from the Greenland land ice was an all-time record.
- The global food crisis, with climate change as a major driver, was now in its fifth year, and was set to intensify as the effects of recent drought and flooding in key exporting countries were felt further along the food chain.
- Half the corals of the Great Barrier Reef in Australia had disappeared since 1980.
- The water of the world's oceans carried about double the heat energy it held in 1990.
- Current global emissions trajectory would see surface warming exceed 2°C by 2040, and the catastrophic level of 5°C around 2100 (Boyer 2012).

Even if human emissions ceased right now, this moment, the atmosphere would continue warming for another twenty-five years. Moreover:

> the ocean will continue to store heat from the atmosphere for yet more years, preventing or inhibiting the cooling of the planet until long after we're dead and buried. The only question is, how far will the warming go? The more carbon dioxide we put into the atmosphere, the hotter it will get. (Boyer 2012, 14–15)

Global warming is transforming the bio-physical in ways that are radically and rapidly reshaping social and ecological futures. The latest Intergovernmental Climate Change Panel (2013) reported that:

- Warming of the climate system is unequivocal, and since the 1950s, many of the observed changes are unprecedented over decades to millennia. The atmosphere and ocean have warmed, the amounts of snow and ice have diminished, sea level has risen, and the concentrations of greenhouse gases have increased.

- Each of the last three decades has been successively warmer at the Earth's surface than any preceding decade since 1850.
- Ocean warming dominates the increase in energy stored in the climate system, accounting for more than 90 per cent of the energy accumulated between 1971 and 2010.
- Over the last two decades, the Greenland and Antarctic ice sheets have been losing mass, glaciers have continued to shrink almost worldwide, and Arctic sea ice and Northern Hemisphere spring snow cover have continued to decrease in extent.
- The rate of sea level rise since the mid-nineteenth century has been larger than the mean rate during the previous two millennia.

Scientific data continue to demonstrate the depth and scale of the problem.

Part of the reason why responses to climate change have been so little and so late has to do with the nature of 'slow crises' (White 2012). Floods in Brazil, Australia and Sri Lanka in early 2011 have generally been interpreted publicly as once-in-a-hundred-year phenomena. Much the same was said about 'Super Storm Sandy' along the east coast of the USA in 2012. Cyclones and hurricanes are 'normal' in certain regions of the world, even though the frequency and intensity might be changing. There is no one single earth-shattering event that demarcates the 'crisis' of climate change. Transformation is progressive and longitudinal. It is not abrupt, completed or singularly global in impact. This makes the crisis amenable to the reasoning of liberal practicality (Mills 1959), which emphasizes multiple and tiny 'factors', in the here and now, but which cannot deal with 'the whole picture', nor with epochal changes over time. Such ideas and approaches also make it even more difficult to understand the fundamental structure of the status quo, much less the profound ecological transformations (and the reasons for these transformations) that are occurring.

Nevertheless, the damage caused by global warming is already being felt in the form of extreme weather events, increased competition for dwindling natural resources, outbreaks of disease and viral infections, further extinctions of species, continued pressure to trade off food for fuel – and the list goes on. Exploitation of natural resources is a major cause of armed conflict within and between communities and nation states (Klare 2001, 2012; Le Billon 2012; Homer-Dixon 1999). This is largely due to scarcity of resources, which can arise from depletion or degradation of the resource (supply), increased demand for it (demand), and unequal distribution and/or resource capture (structural scarcity) (Homer-Dixon 1999). What humans do to the environment is directly implicated in the production of scarcity, and hence conflict. For instance: 'Deforestation increases the scarcity of forest resources, water pollution increases the scarcity of clean water, and climate change increases the scarcity of the regular patterns of rainfall and temperature on which farmers rely' (Homer-Dixon 1999, 9). Greenhouse gas emissions, a major cause of global warming, are generated by existing industries, and result in even further pressures on already vulnerable eco-systems. Arable land and potable drinking water are at a premium under such circumstances. The race to exploit increasingly scarce environmental resources has been recognized as a key factor in violence, crime and conflict (Homer-Dixon 1999; Klare 2012; Le Billon 2012). These will be exacerbated under conditions of wide-scale climate change.

Various crimes tied to climate-related events, such as food riots, and trends such as climate-induced migration are likely to become more prevalent. Some of these crimes include looting and blackmarketeering in relation to foodstuffs, illegal fishing and killing of birds and land animals, trafficking in humans and in valued commodities such as water and food, and carbon emission trading fraud. A bifurcation of crime will occur. The rich and powerful will use their resources to dump toxic and radioactive waste on the lands of the less powerful, and to build up their carbon credits by exploiting the financial hardships of others. Crimes of the less powerful will be crimes of desperation generated by falls in rainfall, failure of crops and subsistence concerns. Child soldiers and armed gangs will flourish in conditions of welfare collapse or non-existent government support. People will flee and be criminalized for seeking asylum; others will stay, to fight for dwindling resources in their part of the world. Communities will be pitted against each other, and industries against communities. Law and order will be increasingly more difficult to maintain, much less enforce in other than repressive ways. It does not take much to imagine the nightmare that is unfolding before our very eyes.

The Crime of Ecocide

As will be discussed later in this chapter, there are narrow sectoral interests embedded in present socio-economic arrangements that are driving global warming. Juxtaposed with and contrary to these specific interests is the collectivist ideal of 'ecological citizenship'. The appeal of ecological citizenship as a concept stems in part from recognition of the universal interests that underpin humans' relationship with the environment. Ecological citizenship allows for stepping outside prescriptive patriotism (e.g., 'Australia first') when global ecological health and well-being demand a planetary response (e.g., 'Earth first'). It is also tied to the notion of 'Earth Rights' and the survival needs of all species and biospheres on the planet (see Cullinan 2003; White 2013).

Existing laws and conventions do acknowledge such rights to some extent. For example, Principle 1 of the Stockholm Declaration stressed that: 'Man has the fundamental right to freedom, equality and adequate conditions of life, in an environment of a quality that permits a life of dignity and well-being, and he bears a solemn responsibility to protect and improve the environment for present and future generations' (quoted in Council of Europe 2012, 11). Yet the Council of Europe recently observed that 'Currently, no comprehensive legally binding instrument for the protection of the environment exists globally' (2012, 12). Even the Aarhus

Convention[1] only offers procedural rights, not the right to a healthy environment as such. Moreover, it is the impact of the environment on the individual rather than protection of the environment itself that instruments such as the European Convention on Human Rights and the European Social Charter are concerned with.

In the context of major global shifts in climate change, biodiversity and pollution, this presumption may no longer be warranted. So too, the general and unequal impact of climate change highlights the limitations of more narrowly defined legal remedies based upon existing human rights law. The fact is that those least responsible for, and least able to remedy the effects of, climate change are worst affected by it:

> Peasants, indigenous peoples, and artisans who live outside the industrialized globalized economy, who have caused no harm to the earth or other people, are the worst victims of climate chaos. Over 96 percent of disaster-related deaths in recent years have taken place in developing countries. In 2001, there were 170 million people affected by disasters around the world, of which 97 percent were climate-related. (Shiva 2008, 3)

These vulnerabilities to victimization are not only due to geographical location as such. Many countries have coastal areas that are vulnerable to sea-level rise. But the Netherlands, for example, has the technological and financial capacity to protect itself to a greater extent than Bangladesh. Thus, not only are poorer countries less responsible for the problem, they are simultaneously least able to adapt to the climate impacts that they will suffer because they lack the resources and capacity to do so. This raises matters of justice surrounding three key questions: the question of responsibility (e.g., the North owes the South an 'ecological debt'); the question of who pays for action on mitigation and adaptation, and the question of who bears the costs of actions and inactions (see Bulkeley and Newell 2010). The destruction of the environment in ways that affect humans, eco-systems and non-human animals as well as plants can also be conceptualized in legal terms as evidence of a specific sort of crime. Justice in this case is defined not so much by how we respond to harm, but by how we broadly define it to begin with. Ecocide is an example of this.

Ecocide has been defined as: 'the extensive damage, destruction to or loss of eco-systems of a given territory, whether by human agency or by other causes, to such an extent that peaceful enjoyment by the inhabitants of that territory has been severely diminished' (Higgins 2012, 3). Where this occurs as a result of human agency, then it is purported that a crime has occurred. Ecocide as a concept has also been used to describe 'natural' processes of eco-system decline and transformation, as well as human-created destruction of eco-systems. The former include instances

---

1   The Convention on Access to Information, Public Participation in Decision-making and Access to Justice in Environmental Matters, adopted in Aarhus, Denmark on 25 June 1998.

where, for example, kangaroos denude a paddock of its grasses and shrubs to the extent that both the specific environment and the kangaroo mob are negatively affected. The migration and/or transportation of 'invasive' species, such as the crown of thorns starfish off the east coast of Australia or the introduction of trout into the central highland lakes of Tasmania, can lead to diminishment or death of endemic species of fish and coral – again a form of ecocide.

The term has also been applied to extensive environmental damage during war, as in the case of the use of defoliants (e.g., Agent Orange) in the Vietnam War and the blowing up of oil wells and subsequent pollution during the first Gulf War in Iraq and Kuwait. These actions involved deliberate intent to produce environmental destruction in pursuit of military and other goals.

The notion of ecocide has been actively canvassed at the international level for a number of years, since at least the 1960s (Higgins et al. 2013). For example, there were major efforts to include it among the crimes associated with the establishment of the International Criminal Court, although the final document refers only to war and damage to the natural environment. It has been pointed out that: 'For over a decade, in work undertaken by the United Nations, debates and drafting exercises *included* Ecocide until it was finally removed from the text that became known as the Rome Statute, which codifies the four Crimes against Peace' (Higgins et al. 2013, 258).

Nevertheless, environmental activists and international lawyers have continued to call for the establishment of either a specific crime of ecocide and/or the incorporation of ecocide into existing criminal laws and international instruments (Higgins 2012). Recent efforts, for example, have sought to make ecocide the fifth International Crime Against Peace (Higgins, 2010, 2012). The urgency and impetus for this has been heightened by the woefully inadequate response by governments, individually and collectively, to global warming. Climate change is rapidly and radically altering the basis of world ecology, yet very little substantive action has been taken by states or corporations to rein in the worst contributors to the problem. Carbon emissions are not decreasing, and 'dirty industries', such as coal and oil, continue to flourish.

The call for a new crime, ecocide, is premised on the idea of Earth stewardship. Paradigms of trusteeship, of stewardship, are very different to those based upon private property conceptions of ownership. As Walters points out: 'Ownership implies that you can use land but don't have responsibility to others to care for it' (2011, 266). The Earth is seen as being 'held in trust', and it is humans who have the responsibility to provide the requisite stewardship. Threats to nature rights can be conceptualized as, in essence, a crime of ecocide, and thus punishable by law.

The notion of ecocide invites comparison with other crimes that, at least superficially, bear similarities. For instance, it can be observed that:

- Ecocide is NOT the same as *homicide* – even though foreknowledge of consequences combined with anthropocentric causation imply preventable death.

- Ecocide is NOT the same as *suicide* – even though the agents of harm are themselves included as victims of harm.
- Ecocide is NOT the same as *genocide* – even though there are clear similarities in terms of disregard by perpetrators of the magnitude of the harm and disrespect of specific collectivities/victims (White 2014).

Why ecocide, why now? Ecocide describes an attempt to criminalize human activities that destroy and diminish the well-being and health of eco-systems and the species within these, including humans. Climate change and the gross exploitation of natural resources are leading to our general demise – hence increasing the need for just such a crime. From an eco-justice perspective, ecocide involves transgressions that violate the principles and central constituent elements of environmental justice, ecological justice and species justice (White 2013). The transgressions are not only apparent in relation to environmental victims (human and non-human), but have temporal dimensions that traverse the past, present and future. This is captured in the notion of intergenerational equity.

Ecocide and Intergenerational Equity

Public trust and public interest law have been used selectively worldwide to establish future generations as victims of environmental crime (Preston 2011; Mehta 2009). A vital concept, especially in regard to human interests, is the notion of intergenerational equity. Used in an 'environment' (rather than say an 'economic') context, intergenerational equity has three core ideas. These are summarized by Weiss as follows:

> The basic concept is that all generations are partners caring for and using the Earth. Every generation needs to pass the Earth and our natural and cultural resources on in at least as good condition as we received them. This leads to three principles of intergenerational equity: options, quality and access. The first, comparable options, means conserving the diversity of the natural resource base so that the future generations can use it to satisfy their own values. The second principle, comparable quality, means ensuring the quality of the environment on balance is comparable between generations. The third one, comparable access, means non-discriminatory access among generations to the Earth and its resources. (Weiss 2008, 624)

Elsewhere, Weiss (1992) summarizes these three elements or components of intergenerational equity in the following way:

- *Conservation of options* – Each generation should be required to conserve the diversity of the natural and cultural resource base, so that it does not unduly restrict the options available to future generations in solving their problems and satisfying their own values, and should also be entitled to diversity comparable to that enjoyed by previous generations.

This concept is based on that notion that diversity, like quality, contributes to the robustness of eco-systems and cultural systems alike.

- *Conservation of quality* – Each generation should be required to maintain the quality of the planet so that it is passed on in no worse condition than that in which it was received, and should also be entitled to planetary quality comparable to that enjoyed by previous generations.

This concept relates to ecological sustainability and the importance of maintaining balances as part of ongoing change.

- *Conservation of access* – Each generation should provide its members with equitable rights of access to the legacy of past generations, and should conserve this access for future generations.

This concept relates to not degrading what is available, and ensuring effective non-discriminatory access among the human generations to the Earth and its resources. But this is complicated by the expectation that present generations will be sensitive to the interests of people in the future, at which time there may be many more people populating the planet than at present. Current family and fertility policies and population trends therefore have implications for how access might possibly be construed and provided for under quite different demographic conditions (see Schneeberger 2011).

Intergenerational equity is acknowledged in a number of international instruments, such as the UN Framework Convention on Climate Change and the United Nations Economic Commission for Europe's Aarhus Convention. Interest in the concept stems from the Stockholm Declaration on the Human Environment, which in turn led directly to the creation of the UN Environment Programme (Weiss 1992). It is of continuing interest today, as shown by a global conference on 'Implementing Intergenerational Equity: Bringing Future Perspectives to the Status Quo' co-hosted in Geneva by United Nations Environment Programme and the World Future Council on 4–5 July 2012.

It is essential to view intergenerational equity as a temporal concept that points in two directions – to the past, and to the future.

- Past generations
- Present generations
- Future generations

As members of this present generation, we hold the Earth in trust for future generations, while at the same time we are beneficiaries of its resources. Equity must flow to present generations from past generations, while simultaneously present generations must ensure that equity flows to future generations. Moreover, the dynamics of nature (both human and non-human) demand attention to the vagaries of change that naturally occur over time.

The temporal nature of intergenerational equity means there are inherent links between intergenerational equity and intragenerational equity. This is because the obligation is for each generation to pass the planet on in no worse condition than it received it, and to provide equitable access to its resources and benefits. The planet marks out the scale of the obligation. Therefore, equality of rights extends in time as well as space to embrace both generations and geographical regions (and the people who inhabit these). This observation is particularly relevant to the examination of children and intergenerational equity, discussed below.

Weiss (1992) makes the point that intergenerational planetary rights may be regarded as group rights, as distinct from individual rights, in the sense that generations hold these rights as groups in relation to other generations – past, present and future. That is, these are 'generational rights' which must be conceived in the temporal context of generations, rather than rights of identifiable individuals (although there are identifiable interests of individuals that the group rights protect). These generational rights can be evaluated by applying objective criteria and indices to the planet from one generation to the next.

To illustrate how we might measure planetary environmental performance, a range of scientific studies may be drawn upon. So, too, might 'elder knowledge'. Consider, for instance, the following story, told by David Suzuki in his book *The Legacy*:

> A documentary on fishing, *Empty Oceans, Empty Nets*, shown on PBS in 2002, featured an interview with a young skipper on a swordfish boat from Boston who stated that there are still plenty of swordfish. Based in Boston, she travels to Newfoundland, where she reported hearing that a 200-pound swordfish had been caught. 'There are still big ones', she said. The film then cut to an interview with a grizzled fisherman who must have been in his eighties. He recounted that he used to fish just 5 or 6 miles out of Boston and would throw back anything under 200 pounds! Two fishers with radically different baselines. To the young skipper, a trip all the way to Newfoundland was standard procedure, while a 200-pounder was a big fish. (In fact, the average size of swordfish before 1963 was 266 pounds; it had fallen to 133 pounds in 1973, and to 90 pounds in 1996). (Suzuki 2010, 61)

Substantial changes have occurred across a range of environmental indices. Many of these are and have been measured using scientific methodologies. However, as the above story indicates, 'commonsense' thinking may require a jolt of elder knowledge to put things into broader perspective at the level of everyday practices.

From a contemporary point of view, certain actions can be identified as likely to infringe upon intergenerational rights. These include wastes that cannot be confidently contained, either spatially or over time, damage to soils such that they are incapable of supporting plant or animal life, and air pollution and land transformations that contribute to significant climate change on a large scale. Some of these activities are covered by existing international agreements, such as the Montreal Protocol, the Basel Convention, the Antarctic Treaty and the Kyoto Agreement. These are all designed to minimize, reduce or prevent certain activities that damage the atmosphere, plant and animal species, and land and eco-systems.

Mares (2010) argues in favour of the notion of 'carrying capacity' of the planet (i.e., its ability to sustain a given amount of human, plant and animal life) as setting criteria against which harm can be measured, and criminalized. This makes sense if framed within the twin concepts of ecocide and intergenerational equity. That is, intergenerational equity considerations can be gauged according to the strength of the carrying capacity at any one time, and fundamental or serious diminishment of this can be construed as a form of ecocide. Indeed, Schneeberger (2011), in discussing the reverence afforded the Earth by indigenous cultures and their strongly embedded equity considerations (related to the passing on of environmental goods and services to the next generations), suggests that this can be linked to climate science and climate modelling into the next few centuries. To put it differently, if intergenerational equity is indeed the goal, then action is justified now in addressing cumulative emissions. Failure to enact scientific and evidence-based policy relating to carbon emissions is a failure to protect present and future generations. Present-day scientific evidence also provides the objective basis for charges of ecocide – that is, demonstrable, long-lasting, serious environmental harm.

Children, Vulnerability and Equity

Ecocide as an outcome of the failure to address global warming is not just a theoretical debate about abstract propositions. The casualties of climate change are disproportionately found among the most vulnerable population groups. Intergenerational equity refers to 'vertical equity', which cuts across generations over time, and to 'horizontal equity', in which equality of rights extends across population groups as well as time. As stated above, there is a close connection between intragenerational and intergenerational rights (under the rubric of 'conservation of access'):

- *Children*
- People with disabilities
- Poverty
- Class/caste/socio-economic inequalities   ←——————→
- Gender
- Race/ethnicity

The special concern here is with children. The health and well-being of the next generation is entirely contingent upon how children of the present generation are cherished and nurtured. Climate change challenges the planet's capacity to do this.

The special vulnerabilities of children to environment-related harms are demonstrated in the following observations.

Children are Especially Vulnerable

In her article 'Reflections on Environmental Justice: Children as Victims and Actors', Sharon Stephens observed:

> While acknowledging that childhoods around the world are very different and that children do not comprise a self-evidently unitary group (any more than do 'women' or 'people of colour'), we can still see ways in which the special characteristics of children's biology and development represent a foundation for regarding children as a special category of environmental victims. (Stephens 1996, 75)

Differential Risks

In the use of pesticides to prevent the spread of disease borne by mosquitoes, there are 'hidden' costs that may not be factored in. For instance, children and those with chemical sensitivities will suffer disproportionately if chemicals are sprayed, since they are more vulnerable than others to ill effects arising from the treatment. In such circumstances, the crucial questions are not only 'How many will be harmed?' but also 'Who will be harmed?' (Scott 2005, 56). To appreciate this, we need to be conscious of differences within affected populations.

Constructing Risk

The risk assessment process by which 'safe levels' of exposure to chemicals and other pollutants are assessed is highly problematic, and incorporates a range of ideological and moral assumptions. As Field comments: 'The use of the apparently reasonable scientific concept of average risk, for example, means that data from the most sensitive individuals, such as children, will not be the basis for regulation, but rather data from the "statistically average" person' (1998, 90). Thus, science provides grounds upon which we may base judgements, but these grounds are not necessarily neutral in terms of social impact.

Bigger Risks

The World Health Organisation has declared: 'Special attention should be devoted to children because they are generally more vulnerable than adults to environmental hazards. They breathe more air and consume more food and water relative to their size than adults, their bodies are still developing and they have little control over their environment'. The message is that children are not 'little adults', and are especially vulnerable to environmental hazards, to the extent that 'Recent estimates suggest that almost 90% of the global burden of disease from climate change is borne by children' (World Health Organisation 2009, 12).

All Children are Vulnerable, but Some are More Vulnerable than Others

In his book *In the Public Interest*, M.C. Mehta observes:

> Each day, the scale of injustice occurring on Indian soil, is catastrophic. Each day, hundreds of thousands of factories fire up without pollution control devices, thousands of Indians go to work without adequate safety protections and over 12 million children between the ages of five and fourteen, spend their days doing labour instead of going to school. Millions of litres of untreated raw effluents are dumping into our rivers and land and millions of tonnes of toxic hazardous waste are simply dumped onto the Earth. (Mehta 2009, xviii–xix)

While conventionally it is understood that children are more vulnerable to a variety of ailments and environmental risks, rarely are they considered specifically as environmental victims. On the other hand, the need for special protection for children has been acknowledged at the international level for a number of years, in particular through the UN Convention on the Rights of the Child, which emphasizes protection, provision and participation. As Stephens puts it: 'Children have the right to be protected from harm, to be provided with services necessary for their healthy growth and development, and to participate in decisions that affect them according to their evolving capacities' (1996, 80).

The Declaration of the Rights of the Child proclaimed by the UN General Assembly in 1959 states: 'the child, by reason of physical and mental immaturity, needs special safeguards and care, including appropriate legal protection, before as well as after birth'. Principle 2 declares:

> The child shall enjoy special protection, and shall be given opportunities and facilities, by law and by other means, to enable [him or her] to develop physically, mentally, morally, spiritually and socially in a healthy and normal manner and in conditions of freedom and dignity. In the enactment of laws for this purpose, the best interests of the child shall be the paramount consideration.

The Convention on the Rights of the Children reinforces these sentiments. From the point of view of children and the environment, a number of convention articles are relevant. For example, the following have application to the present discussion on children and ecocide.

Article 6 – Right to life
States Parties recognize that every child has the inherent right to life.

States Parties shall ensure to the maximum extent possible the survival and development of the child.

Article 24 – Right of the child to the enjoyment of the highest attainable standard of health

States Parties shall pursue full implementation of this right and, in particular, shall take appropriate measures:

  (c) To combat disease and malnutrition, including within the framework of primary health care, through, *inter alia*, the application of readily available technology and through the provision of adequate nutritious foods and clean drinking-water, taking into consideration the dangers and risks of environmental pollution;

Article 27 – Right of every child to a standard of living adequate for the child's development

States Parties recognize the right of every child to a standard of living adequate for the child's physical, mental, spiritual, moral and social development.

Article 29 – Education

States Parties agree that the education of the child shall be directed to: (e) the development of respect for the natural environment.

Yet, as highlighted by Mehta's comment about children in India, children are not being protected in practice at all. When it comes to matters specific to the rights of children in regard to intergenerational equity, there are occasionally instances when children's interests (both as vulnerable and as the future generation) have come to the fore. For example, in *Minors Oposa* v. *Secretary of State for the Department of Environment and Natural Resources*, the issue of intergenerational equity was considered by the Philippines Supreme Court. Two issues in particular had to be decided: whether future generations should have standing, and how to respond to the claimants, who in this case were a group of children, and who sought an order to the government to discontinue existing and future timber licence agreements: 'The claimants alleged that deforestation was causing environmental damage which affected not only young but also future generations and they sought to establish standing for both present and future generations' (Schneeberger 2011, 26). The Supreme Court held that standing be granted to the claimants and that they had adequately asserted a right to a balanced and healthful ecology.

Beyond this specific case, however, there is little evidence of any serious shift toward protecting children's 'group rights' to intergenerational equity at the international level concerning environmental matters. The International Criminal Court is not really designed to hear such matters (Hall 2013), and when it comes to environmental victims generally, there are considerable ambiguities over the adoption of a narrow or broad definition of 'victim', including reference to suffering due to immediate harm and the substantial impairment of rights in general (see Skinnider 2011; Hall 2013; Jarrell and Ozymy 2012). Existing laws and court decisions tend to be inadequate for the task of considering generalized harms (such as those stemming from global warming), since they tend to be applied in relation to specific victims and specific perpetrators (Brisman 2013). More broadly, international and domestic laws relating to rights matters and to climate change tend to be hamstrung by the political economic context within which they are situated.

Climate Change and State-corporate Crime

The question of justice in relation to climate change inevitably leads to consideration of the nature and dynamics of state-corporate crime. This is because the perpetrators of and responders to global warming tend to be one and the same: namely, nation states and transnational corporations.

State-corporate crime has been defined as:

> illegal or socially injurious actions that result from a mutually reinforcing interaction between (1) policies and/or practices in pursuit of the goals of one or more institutions of political governance and (2) policies and/or practices in pursuit of the goals of one or more institutions of economic production and distribution. (Michalowski and Kramer 2006, 15)

Climate change, it has been argued, provides a classic example of state-corporate crime. Specifically, corporate and state actors in interaction with each other create harms in four ways:

1. by denying that global warming is caused by human activity;
2. by blocking efforts to mitigate greenhouse gas emissions;
3. by excluding progressive, ecologically just adaptations to climate change from the political arena; and
4. by responding to the social conflicts that arise from climate change by transforming themselves into fortress societies that exclude the rest of the world (Kramer and Michalowski 2012).

State-corporate crime relates to both *acts* (e.g., Alberta Tar Sands) and *omissions* (e.g., failure to regulate carbon emissions, reliance upon 'dirty' energy sources). Failure to act *now* to prevent global warming is 'criminal'. Yet things continue much as they have, the status quo is maintained, and the harms mount up. This is the essence of ecocide.

The global status quo is protected under the guise of arguments about the 'national interest' and the importance of 'free trade', which usually reflect specific sectoral business interests. Humanity has certain common interests – universal human interests – such as the survival of the human race in the face of things like global warming and climate change. These common human interests need to take priority over any other kind of interests if humans are, as a species, to survive. Yet this is clearly not happening. In part, this is due to resistance and contrarianism perpetrated by powerful lobby groups and particular industries. This is most evident in state support for risky businesses in countries like the USA, Canada and Australia:

- oil and coal industries and other 'dirty' industries;
- coal-seam fracking and other threats to prime agricultural land;
- deep-drill oil exploration and exploitation; and
- mega-mines and open-cast mining.

Support for these industries is accompanied by resistance from these governments to global agreements on carbon emissions and the use of carbon taxes.

Simultaneously, there is much agreement among powerful interests worldwide to pursue changes in land use, such as deforestation in favour of cash crops, bio-fuels, mining and intensive pastoral industries. Besides being problematic for those immediately affected (like humans and animals living in and off those forests), tropical deforestation is now becoming an international political issue because it is responsible for 20 per cent of global greenhouse emissions (Boekhout van Solinge 2010). Indonesia and Brazil have now become respectively the third and fourth largest carbon dioxide-emitting countries in the world, mainly as a result of clearing rainforest. States have given permission and financial backing to those companies engaged in instigating precisely what will radically alter the world's climate the most in the coming years – greenhouse gas emissions

The exploitation of Canada's Alberta tar sands provides another case in point. This massive industrial project involves the active collusion of provincial and federal governments with big oil companies. The project is based upon efforts to extract and refine naturally created tar-bearing sand into exportable and consumable oil. One result of the project is a wide range of different types of harm to the eco-system, animals and humans. For example, it has been pointed out that tar sands oil production is the single largest contributor to the increase in global warming pollution in Canada. It will lead to the destruction of vast swathes of boreal forest, it contributes greatly to air pollution, and it is having negative health impacts on aquatic life and animals, and on humans who live nearby (see Smandych and Kueneman 2010; Klare 2012).

For those who study this type of environmental degradation, and its associated social and ecological harm, the concept of state-corporate environmental crime is considered an entirely appropriate descriptor (Smandych and Kueneman 2010). Placed within the larger global context of climate change, the scale and impact of the Alberta tar sands project also fits neatly with the concept of ecocide. The role of the federal and provincial governments is crucial to the project, and they are propelling it forward regardless of manifest negative environmental consequences.

There is a close intersection, therefore, between global warming, government action or inaction and corporate behaviour (Lynch and Stretesky 2010) and how these contribute to the overall problem of climate change. In this instance, the state itself is implicated as a perpetrator of harm. Government subsidies for coal-fired power stations and government approval of dams that destroy large swathes of rainforest also constitute substantial crimes against nature. In the light of existing scientific evidence on global warming, continued engagement in and encouragement of such activities represents intentional harm that is immoral and destructive of collective public interest in the same moment when particular industries and companies benefit.

Given the stakes involved, especially for children, the question might well be asked: 'Should the impending destruction of eco-systems, and the human collateral damage associated with this, be thought of as a form of environmental genocide – ecocide?' If so, then it is state leaders and government bureaucrats, as well as corporate heads and key shareholders, who should ultimately be held responsible for this crime.

Conclusion

Among those most vulnerable to the consequences of climate change, now and into the future, are our children. Many children suffer today from polluted air and water, extreme weather events, poverty, exploitive and unhealthy labour conditions, and the effects of toxins in their bodies even before they are born. Current inequities in access to the planet's environmental resources are being compounded by lack of due care for what is left. Meanwhile, the activities of the extraction and waste industries serve to further exacerbate and accelerate global warming. This occurs in a political context within which deregulation and inaction form the essence of the governmental climate change paradigm.

There is an urgent need to hold to account those crimes of today which we know are already impacting upon the adults of tomorrow. Toward this end, this chapter has attempted to set out certain legal principles and agendas that situate the problem of climate change in a criminological and eco-rights context. Our task, collectively, is to protect the future, now. There is a need to do so in the light of that fact that:

- Many children worldwide have not had adequate access to their rightful Earth legacy – present discriminations and environmental injustice constitute violations of intergenerational equity (unequal inheritance from 'past' generations).
- Suffering and harm is evident among children today, as are the heightened risks and vulnerabilities (inequities within the 'present' generation).
- Future harms are already well known, particularly in relation to climate change and threats to biodiversity (putting at jeopardy 'future' generations).

At a strategic and symbolic level, efforts to widen the parameters of legal application and political debate about these issues might be informed by appeal to the UN Declaration of Basic Principles of Justice for Victims of Crime and Abuse of Power (1985). This is essentially a non-binding 'soft law' instrument. Nevertheless, it is concerned with the infliction of harm on individuals and groups, broadly defined, rather than violations of national criminal laws per se. That is, it is concerned with 'those who suffer damage' (see Hall 2013). Tied into the notions of ecocide and intergenerational equity, this notion of victimhood could well provide the grounding for taking the interests and needs of children seriously. However, there is still a need to elaborate and codify the relevant norms of intergenerational equity – in order to reduce the ambiguities about expected behaviour and to distinguish co-operative behaviour from uncooperative behaviour. Here again, the concept of ecocide finds purchase as one means to emphasize the *seriousness* and *urgency* of the problem, and the pressing need for *action* and *redress*.

Addressing intergenerational equity in practice will require much more consideration of specific legal issues – including and especially the crime of ecocide and how best to deal with environmental destruction and degradation. There are also issues relating to how victims and victimhood are to be conceptualized and represented, and how compensation, remediation, rehabilitation and restoration are to be accomplished. There is much work yet to be done – for our children's sake.

References

Agnew, R. 2011. 'Dire Forecast: A Theoretical Model of the Impact of Climate Change on Crime.' *Theoretical Criminology* 16(1): 21–46.

———. 2012. 'It's the End of the World as We Know It: The Advance of Climate Change from a Criminological Perspective.' In *Climate Change from a Criminological Perspective*, edited by R. White, 13–25. New York: Springer.

———. 2013. 'The Ordinary Acts that Contribute to Ecocide: A Criminological Analysis.' In *Routledge International Handbook of Green Criminology*, edited by N. South and A. Brisman, 58–72. London: Routledge.

Boekhout van Solinge, T. 2010. 'Equatorial Deforestation as a Harmful Practice and a Criminological Issue.' In *Global Environmental Harm: Criminological Perspectives*, edited by R. White, 20–36. Cullompton: Willan Publishing.

Boyer, P. 2012. 'Wake Up Call From Real World.' *The Mercury* (Tasmania, Australia), 23 October, 14–15.

Brisman, A. 2012. 'The Cultural Silence of Climate Change Contrarianism.' In *Climate Change from a Criminological Perspective*, edited by R. White, 41–70. New York: Springer.

———. 2013. 'The Violence of Silence: Some Reflections on Access to Information, Public Participation in Decision-making, and Access to Justice in Matters Concerning the Environment.' *Crime, Law and Social Change* 59(3): 291–303.

Bulkeley, H. and P. Newell. 2010. *Governing Climate Change*. London: Routledge.

Cohen, S. 2001. *States of Denial: Knowing About Atrocities and Suffering*. Cambridge: Polity Press.

Council of Europe. 2012. *Manual on Human Rights and the Environment*, 2nd edn. Strasbourg, France: Council of Europe Publishing.

Cullinan, C. 2003. *Wild Law: A Manifesto for Earth Justice*. London: Green Books in association with The Gaia Foundation.

Farrell, S., T. Ahmed and D. French, eds. 2012. *Criminological and Legal Consequences of Climate Change*. Oxford: Hart.

Field, R. 1998. 'Risk and Justice: Capitalist Production and the Environment.' In *The Struggle for Ecological Democracy: Environmental Justice Movements in the US*, edited by D. Faber, 69–94. New York: Guilford Press.

Hall, M. 2013. *Victims of Environmental Harm: Rights, Recognition and Redress Under National and International Law*. London: Routledge.

Halsey, M. 2013. 'Conservation Criminology and the 'General Accident' of Climate Change.' In *Routledge International Handbook of Green Criminology*, edited by N. South and A. Brisman, 107–19. London: Routledge.

Higgins, P. 2010. *Eradicating Ecocide: Laws and Governance to Prevent the Destruction of Our Planet*. London: Shepheard-Walwyn.

———. 2012. *Earth is Our Business: Changing the Rules of the Game*. London: Shepheard-Walwyn.

———, D. Short and N. South. 2013. 'Protecting the Planet: A proposal for a Law of Ecocide.' *Crime Law and Social Change* 59(3): 251–66.

Homer-Dixon, T. 1999. *Environment, Scarcity, and Violence*. Princeton, NJ: Princeton University Press.

Intergovernmental Climate Change Panel. 2013. *Working Group I Contribution to the IPCC Fifth Assessment Report Climate Change 2013: The Physical Science Basis Summary for Policymakers*. Geneva, Switzerland: Intergovernmental Panel on Climate Change.

International Institute for Sustainable Development. 2013. 'UNEP Hosts Conference on Intergenerational Equity.' *Sustainable Development Policy & Practice*, 7 July. Accessed 6 June 2015. http://sd.iisd.org/news/unep-hosts-conference-on-intergenerational-equity/.

Jarrell, M. and J. Ozymy. 2012. 'Real Crime, Real Victims: Environmental Crime Victims and the Crime Victims' Rights Act (CVRA).' *Crime, Law and Social Change* 58: 373–89.

Klare, M. 2001. *Resource Wars: The New Landscape of Global Conflict*. New York: Owl Books.

———. 2012. *The Race for What's Left: The Global Scramble for the World's Last Resources*. New York: Metropolitan Books.

Kramer, R. 2013. 'Public Criminology and the Responsibility to Speak in the Prophetic Voice Concerning Global Warming.' In *State Crime and Resistance*, edited by E. Stanley and J. McCulloch, 41–53. London: Routledge.

——— and Michalowski, R. 2012. 'Is Global Warming a State-corporate Crime?' In *Climate Change from a Criminological Perspective*, edited by R. White, 71–88. New York: Springer.

Le Billon, P. 2012. *Wars of Plunder: Conflicts, Profits and the Politics of Resources*. New York: Columbia University Press.

Lever-Tracy, C. 2011. *Confronting Climate Change*. London: Routledge.

Lynch, M. and Stretesky, P. 2010. 'Global Warming, Global Crime: A Green Criminological Perspective.' In *Global Environmental Harm: Criminological Perspectives*, edited by R. White, 62–84. Cullompton: Willan Publishing.

Lynch, M., Burns, R. and Stretesky, P. 2010. 'Global Warming and State-corporate Crime: The Politicalization of Global Warming under the Bush Administration.' *Crime, Law and Social Change* 54: 213–39.

Mares, D. 2010. 'Criminalizing Ecological Harm: Crimes against Carrying Capacity and the Criminalization of Eco-sinners.' *Critical Criminology* 18: 279–93.

———. 2013. 'Climate Change and Crime: Monthly Temperature and Precipitation Anomalies and Crime Rates in St. Louis, MO 1990–2009.' *Crime, Law and Social Change* 59(2): 158–208.

Mehta, M.C. 2009. *In the Public Interest: Landmark Judgements and Orders of the Supreme Court of India on Environment and Human Rights*, vol. 1. New Delhi, India: Prakriti Publications.

Michalowski, R. and R. Kramer. 2006. *State-corporate Crime: Wrongdoing at the Intersection of Business and Government*. New Brunswick, NJ: Rutgers University Press.

Mills, C. Wright. 1959. *The Sociological Imagination*. New York: Oxford University Press.

Minors Oposa v. *Secretary of State for the Department of Environment and Natural Resources* [30 July 1993] 33 ILM 173 (1994). Accessed 6 June 2015. http://www.jstor.org/pss/20693894.

Preston, B. 2011. 'The Use of Restorative Justice for Environmental Crime.' *Criminal Law Journal* 35: 136–45.

Schneeberger, K. 2011. 'Intergenerational Equity: Implementing the Principle in Mainstream Decision-making.' *ELM* 23:20–29.

Scott, D. 2005. 'When Precaution Points Two Ways: Confronting "West Nile Fever."' *Canadian Journal of Law and Society* 20(2): 27–65

Shiva, V. 2008. *Soil Not Oil: Environmental Justice in an Age of Climate Crisis*. New York: South End Press.

Skinnider, E. 2011. *Victims of Environmental Crime: Mapping the Issues*. Vancouver, BC: International Centre for Criminal Law Reform and Justice Policy.

Smandych, R. and R. Kueneman. 2010. 'The Canadian-Alberta Tar Sands: A Case Study of State-corporate Environmental Crime.' In *Global Environmental Harm: Criminological Perspectives,* edited by R. White, 87–109. Cullompton: Willan Publishing.

Stephens, S. 1996. 'Reflections on Environmental Justice: Children as Victims and Actors.' *Social Justice* 23(4): 62–86.

Suzuki, D. 2010. *The Legacy: An Elder's Vision for our Sustainable Future.* Sydney, Australia: Allen & Unwin.

Walters, B. 2011. 'Enlarging Our Vision of Rights: The Most Significant Human Rights Event in Recent Times?' *Alternative Law Journal* 36(4): 263–8.

Walters, R. 2013. 'Air Crimes and Atmospheric Justice.' In *The Routledge International Handbook of Green Criminology*, edited by N. South and A. Brisman, 134–49. London: Routledge.

Weiss, E. 1992. 'Intergenerational Equity: A Legal Framework for Global Environmental Change.' In *Environmental Change and International Law: New Challenges and Dimensions*, edited by E. Brown Weiss, 385–412. Tokyo, Japan: United Nations University Press.

———. 2008. 'Climate Change, Intergenerational Equity, and International Law.' *Vermont Journal of International Law* 9: 615–28.

White, R. 2009. 'Climate Change and Social Conflict: Toward an Eco-global Research Agenda.' In *Eco-crime and Justice: Essays on Environmental Crime*, edited by K. Kangaspunta and I. Marshall, 15–35. Turin, Italy: United Nations Interregional Crime Research Institute.

———. 2011. *Transnational Environmental Crime: Toward an Eco-global Criminology*. London: Routledge.

———. 2012. 'The Criminology of Climate Change.' In *Climate Change from a Criminological Perspective*, edited by R. White, 1–11. New York: Springer.

———. 2013. *Environmental Harm: An Eco-justice Perspective*. Bristol: Policy Press.

———. 2014. 'Ecocide.' In *Shades of Deviance: A Primer on Crime, Deviance and Social Harm*, edited by R. Atkinson, 203–6. London: Routledge.

World Health Organisation. 2009. *Protecting Health from Climate Change: Connecting Science, Policy and People*. Geneva, Switzerland: WHO Press.

Chapter 11

The Criminological Imagination and the Promise of Fiction[1]

Stephanie Piamonte

Introduction

C. Wright Mills, formulator of the sociological imagination, claims that fiction is inadequate for knowing and explicating self and society and the relations between the two (1959, 17–18). A case study of Richard's Wright's novel *Native Son* (2005) demonstrates that fiction can and does help us know and clarify self, society and the relations between the two. The 'criminological imagination', as a quality of mind, analytic framework and method of knowledge-production, is employed here to explore Wright's novel to make sense of social realities at the level of the individual and the societal, as well as the relations between the two. Criminology, it is argued, benefits from the introduction of fiction as an object of study; not only can fiction be utilized to help criminologists conceptualize self, society and the relationship between the two, literature challenges criminological conventions, helps to clarify and critique criminological concepts, and aids in creating and communicating criminological knowledge.

This chapter demonstrates the promise of literature for the discipline of criminology, as well as the potential of the criminological imagination as a quality of mind, an analytic framework and a method of knowledge-production. Before moving into my analysis of *Native Son*, clarification of the term 'criminological imagination' is required.

Recent studies have attempted to adopt Mills' concept into criminology, but the results have been mixed. A survey of texts containing the term 'criminological imagination' shows that it refers to thinking imaginatively about crime, crime control or criminology (e.g., Gabbidon and Higgins 2007; Hallsworth 2006; Mounce 2008), adopting a critical approach to criminology (e.g., Lynch and Stretsky 2003; Hamm 2005; Aas 2007; Girling 2008; McLaughlin 2008) or thinking about old problems in new ways (e.g., White 2003; Green et al. 2007; Hughes and Rowe 2007; see also Frauley, 2011). While the criminological imagination does not preclude these elements, Mills (1959) explicates a specific conception of a quality of mind that is critical and reflexive, offers a meta-framework for

---

1   This chapter is based on the author's master's thesis.

analysing individuals and their relation to society, and also operates as a method of knowledge-production.

The Criminological Imagination: A Method of Knowledge-production

Mills' (1959, 7) test for any proposed study is whether it has relevance and is connected to the social world. This chapter has relevance to criminology because it encourages a more creative and reflexive consideration of criminology, its objects of study and its methods. This section contains a further consideration of the benefits of such studies for criminology.

Mills (1959, 13–14) claims that intellectual ages are characterized by dominant ways of thinking that produce certain types of knowledge. Mills (1959, 78–9) also proposes that the job of the social scientist is to challenge the assumed structure of society, to provide context and meaning for the individual life (1959, 5, 187), and to challenge the status quo of the discipline (1959, 184). The current prevalence of the physical sciences model within criminology is inadequate to explore cultural meaning or to produce creative knowledge. Social science is not a set of techniques (i.e., the scientific method), it is about sense-making, it is creative rather than descriptive; the criminological imagination produces knowledge, rather than deriving or distilling it from a greater truth or reality.

This chapter has epistemological implications for criminology; the prevalence of the natural sciences model, with its standard of objectivity and the belief that the world is knowable, is challenged. In particular, the fact–fiction divide is challenged. Rather than accepting a dichotomy between art and social science, fact and fiction, subjective and objective knowledge, this chapter follows Mills and explores a broader and richer understanding of social reality: one that is premised on an ontology that includes fiction within the realm of criminological possibilities.

Literature and criminological conceptual systems provide maps for exploring social worlds (Sayer 1992, 59). The social scientist is unable to reduce the complexity of social worlds, either 'real' or 'fictional', to a single interpretation; there is room for debate and alternative interpretations. Indeed, in the hermeneutic tradition, the possibility of ongoing production of knowledge from a single text is considered valuable and worthwhile. This study, in following Mills' advocating of 'sense-making', is an exploration of criminological meaning intended to provide greater appreciation of the criminological imagination and the benefits of exploring what Frauley (2010, 2011) has termed, 'fictional realities'. Exploration of fiction can reveal new paths in criminology.

The Criminological Imagination: A Quality of Mind

A social scientist engaging a criminological imagination necessarily challenges traditional boundaries and conventions. Mills' (1959) conception of a social scientist strongly resembles Gramsci's (1967) organic intellectual, or one who thinks consciously and critically, resisting tradition. Whether thinking organically or with a criminological imagination, the idea of revealing traditional systems of thought and new worlds of possibility is ingrained in a critical discourse; criminology stands to benefit from this discourse.

Historically, criminology has been an evolving and expanding discipline devoted to explaining crime and deviance. Paradigms within the discipline (i.e., classical, positivist and critical) adopt particular methods and objects of study. Rather than focusing on the causes, cures or complaints concerning crime, this chapter follows in the newer tradition of cultural criminology, which emphasizes the important cultural aspects of the criminal experience as well as cultural sources of knowledge (Ferrell 1999). Fiction is a significant and pervasive cultural artefact, and crime fiction in particular is popular. A criminological engagement with these types of crime texts, or lack thereof, provides a measure of the discipline's responsiveness to changing realities (including the potential of fictional realities) to explore and make sense of social realities, and encourages reflection both on and within the discipline. According to Mills, social science is about 'human variety, which consists of all the social worlds in which men have lived, are living, and might live' (Mills 1959, 132). I argue that these social worlds can be found in fiction.

In 1959, the same year Mills wrote concerning the sociological imagination, C.P. Snow wrote about the polar cultures in the West: art and science. Unfortunately, this artificial polarization continues within the discipline of criminology. As a discipline, criminology generally maintains a positivist adherence to formal scientific techniques and methods at the expense of exploring creative methods to produce knowledge and to develop criminological understanding (e.g., Sagarin 1981; Kelly 1991; Engel 2003; Rafter 2006). Within the discipline, the diametrical opposition of science and imagination is still presumed; likewise, science presumably produces truth and fact, while imagination produces fiction. In its presumptions about knowledge, therefore, criminology is exclusive.

According to Mills (1959), the exploration of social realities is to be guided by the necessity of helping the individual engage in sense-making. In other words, the goal of social science is to illuminate and explicate social realities so that people can better understand themselves and their worlds. This is the criminological imagination, its essence and its function. The following sections demonstrate the exercise of the criminological imagination as a quality of mind; this exercise, as much as the conclusions drawn, demonstrates the benefits of a criminology that is imaginatively inclusive.

The Criminological Imagination: An Analytic Framework

Having discussed some of the reasons for engaging a criminological imagination, it follows that there is a need for an analytic framework that is consistent with both the object and purpose of analysis, which elucidates the components and scope of the problem to be studied, and which provides the language of analysis. In broad terms, Mills (1959) explains that the sociological imagination considers the individual and the societal, as well as the relations between the two. Only enquiry that shuttles between these levels achieves the goal of social science: sense-making for the individual. The units of analysis are described as *biography*, which includes the inner subjective life and experience of milieu as well as the external careers of individuals, and *society*, which includes structural change and societal transformation (Mills 1959, 3). The problems to be studied are also identified by Mills (1959). He describes them on two levels, corresponding to his units of analysis: *personal troubles of milieu* and *public issues of social structure* ((Mills 1959, 3–4). Personal troubles are private, relating to the individual and the social setting in which the individual exists, while the latter are public and relate to institutions and structures of society.

While Mills provides the general language for a study using a criminological imagination, his framework is enhanced by the incorporation of existing criminological theories that provide a more specific language with respect to both social structure and biography. In my study, for example, Jack Katz's (1988) micro-sociology corresponds to and further develops Mills' (1959) concept of biography. Katz (1988) can be categorized somewhere between symbolic interactionists and cultural criminologists. He believes that traditional studies of crime and deviance focus on the search for background forces or factors, either in the offender's psychological background or social environment, rather than on the seductive, lived experience of criminality. His justification for focusing on the 'foreground', the experience of the commission of crime and what can be learned from this, is that the 'background' positivistic explanations of crime fail on many levels; many who fall into causal categories do not commit crimes, and vice versa, and those who do fall into causal categories may only commit crimes at specific times (Katz 1988, 4). Katz (1988, 4) therefore argues that the primary causal factor of crime is a *seductive* impulse, or an attraction to commit crime. Rather than looking for causes or solutions to crime, he frames crime as an experience that has meaning, often symbolic, for the criminal actor. He argues that every type of crime has a set of individually necessary and jointly sufficient conditions: a *Path of Action*, which includes the practical requirements for successfully committing the crime, a *Line of Interpretation*, which is how the criminal actor understands how he or she is and will be seen by others, and an *Emotional Process* involving those seductions and compulsions that lead the actor to commit crime (Katz 1988, 9). Crime, therefore, is a process wherein external forces (e.g., milieu or social structure) as well as internal drives both seduce and compel the individual to experience acts of deviance. This concern for the significance and seductiveness of crime for the individual is consistent with Mills' (1959) conception of biography and sense-making. It is also helpful in explicating the actions of the protagonist Bigger Thomas in *Native Son*, a novel devoted to the sensual experience of crime.

While Katz (1988) draws on symbolic interactionism to understand social negotiation and construction, this does not correspond well to Mills' (1959) structural understanding of society. The work of the Birmingham School of Cultural Studies (Clarke et al. 2006) offers a materialist conceptualization of social structure, while retaining a commitment to symbolic meanings. According to the Birmingham School's formulation, people are born into and subsequently formed by institutions and structures such as class, not just social relationships or interactions (Clarke et al. 2006, 4). Following its Marxist influences, the Birmingham School conceptualizes the structure of society as unequal and hierarchical; individuals are constrained by fields of possibility and ranked according to productive relations, wealth and power, making struggle and conflict inevitable (Clarke et al. 2006, 5–6). Because the hegemony of dominant interests requires legitimization, the reproduction of dominant ideologies is required in order to manufacture and transmit consent. State apparatuses and institutions including the family, school, church, cultural institutions, law, police, army and courts, provide these legitimizing ideologies for the hierarchical structuring of society (Clarke et al. 2006, 30). Criminal actions therefore cannot be understood solely in terms of social interactions, but must be understood to occur within a specific context. The context refers to macro social organization, and includes structures such as race, class and gender, values and traditions, forms of social and economic organization, as well as power relations (Layder 1993, 72). For example, imagine a law is broken. While the actions that break the law may evoke a social response (i.e., public outrage), this is distinct from, but also related to, the structural response (i.e., a trial). This structural response reacts to a threat to existing power relations – what Mills (1959) called 'cherished values' – demonstrating the power within the setting of the court as an institution and as an embodiment of justice, which also transmits an ideology of justice. Actors are secondary to the efficiency of a social structure that secures reproduction mainly through ideological hegemony. While Bigger Thomas's individual criminal actions were sensual, they also elicited a significant societal reaction that the Birmingham School helps explain at a structural level.

The final step in assembling the analytic framing as guided by Mills (1959) and enhanced by Katz (1988) and the Birmingham School (Clarke et al. 2006) is to describe a method. Instead of formulaic methods, Mills (1959) emphasizes the importance of fluidity in methods and theory. Mills (1959, 122) cautions, however, that neither methods nor theory are the actual work of the social scientist; instead, they are ways of approaching and studying social problems or phenomena, and suggest ways of extracting meaning or significance from data. Mills is critical of what he calls 'grand theory' (which generalizes problems at the historical and structural level and which tends to be unintelligible because it is removed from the experience of the individual), as well as 'abstracted empiricism' (which is dominated by empiricist method and a focus on form, to the extent that no greater understanding or sense-making occurs) (1959, 27, 33, 35). Instead, Mills (1959, 146) argues for an orderly approach to selecting materials, conceptions and methods, all of which are determined by the problem rather than the discipline and which lead to sense-making. For Mills (1959), there is no single method to guide the criminological imagination, but instead a dynamic interplay between micro and macro issues, concepts and frameworks that results in the modification and clarification of ideas and problems. Textual analysis of the novel *Native Son* is most consistent with my purposes; as an inductive method, the findings are derived through interpretation rather than scientific method. Interpretation and meaning-making are the natural choice for literature, which is expected to have meaning inherent within it. Thus Mills' advocating of sense-making and a special quality of mind are exemplified through textual analysis.

Case Study: An Analysis of *Native Son* by Richard Wright

First, a brief word on the novel and its selection might prove helpful. First published in 1940, *Native Son* is an American novel set in Chicago in the 1930s and deals with themes of racism and violence. It remains a controversial landmark in black American and literary culture, and has enjoyed an unusual amount of analytic attention as a result (e.g., Sagarin 1981; Blake 1991; Kelly 1991; Engel 2003; Ruggiero 2003). *Native Son* was (and continues to be) critically acclaimed and widely read; for example, it was the first African American book to be received by a racially mixed audience, and is one of the Modern Library's 100 best novels of the last century (Rampersad 2005; Random House 2007). Its themes of racism and violence in urban America remain relevant, as indicated by the number of criminological studies in these areas. For these reasons, *Native Son* is an interesting opportunity to test the criminological imagination, as well as the criminological relevance of literature.

In terms of the plot, *Native Son* covers a short period during which Bigger Thomas commits two murders, is caught, and is put on trial. Bigger is a young black man on welfare who is pressured into accepting a chauffeuring job with the white upper-middle-class Dalton family in order to support his mother and younger siblings. On his first day Bigger murders heiress Mary Dalton and disposes of her body. He convinces his girlfriend, Bessie Mears, to help him make it seem like Mary has been kidnapped, and the two attempt to extort money from the Daltons. When Bigger's deception is discovered, he kills Bessie during his escape. He is captured and tried.

I will focus on one of these crimes, the murder of Mary Dalton, in order to demonstrate how the language provided by Katz (1988) and the Birmingham School (Clarke et al. 2006) fits within the meta-framework of the criminological imagination, and how Katz's descriptions of the seductions of crime and the Birmingham School's understanding of class culture can be integrated using the criminological imagination as a meta-framework, resulting in greater criminological understanding.

Katz (1988, 14) describes a type of murder called 'righteous slaughter', in which the murderer self-righteously kills to defend some version of the Good, or what Mills (1959) calls 'cherished values'.[2] The features of righteous slaughter include a self-righteous act defending communal values, a lack of premeditation, a spirit of quickly developing rage, and an arbitrary relationship between what the assailant is trying to do and what he achieves (Katz 1988, 18). The process begins when the victim attacks the worth of the aggressor, so that the latter feels that he or she loses control of his or her identity and agency as a result of becoming an object of ridicule (Katz 1988, 22–3). This feeling of humiliation is perceived as being entirely external in origin; because the aggressor does not recognize any failings or inadequacy within himself or herself, he or she feels innocent, and the source of his or her humiliation becomes blameworthy (Katz 1988, 26–7). Humiliation becomes rage when the aggressor believes the way to resolve the problem of humiliation is to reverse the structure of the humiliation through an act of rage (Katz 1988, 27). Rage therefore (re-)establishes the part of the aggressor's identity that is valuable; in other words, there is a correlation between the offence experienced and the ensuing attack (Katz 1988, 31, 36). A sacrificial slaughter of the victim is the means for the righteous killer to transcend both humiliation and circumstance, and also to be symbolically transformed (Katz 1988, 43).

The righteous slaughter is set in motion from the beginning of the novel, when Bigger's mother blames him for the family's meagre existence and criticizes his supposed lack of manhood because he is content to remain on welfare (Wright 2005, 8–9). This causes him to feel shame, which, according to Katz, is distinct from humiliation because it is internalized, and makes Bigger feel powerless to act (Wright 2005, 10). These family expectations constrain him, and he feels that 'he could never have any way of his own' (Wright 2005, 99). This social shame as well as economic pressures propel him to go to the Daltons' house to accept a job as a chauffeur; his options are to work for white people and become part of the economic system that oppresses him, or starve (Wright 2005, 12). His resistance to white society and his rejection of the economic imperative to work is subordinated by the demands of (re)production.

The Birmingham School reminds us that power relations are reproduced and transmitted in institutions; therefore this necessity to engage Bigger in productive work is precipitated by the power of the capitalist context that requires enough workers and that sets up productivity as a virtue of 'manhood'. In Bigger's mind, he is tricked into surrender of black working-class values by entering into white society (Wright 2005, 12). When he gets the job, Bigger is told that he 'ought to work hard and keep it and try to make a man out of' himself (Wright 2005, 101). This is an example of the hegemony of the white capitalist culture that idealizes the working man (Clarke et al. 2006, 5). This hegemonic ideal subordinates Bigger, who is demeaned by having to work as a chauffeur for a white upper-middle-class family and leave behind the black working-class culture with which he identifies.

---

2   For Mills (1959, 130), cherished values are freedom and reason, but he acknowledges a multiplicity of values may be threatened or implicated in private troubles and public issues.

On entering white society, Bigger experiences fear and humiliation; for Bigger, the two are closely linked. In order to ameliorate his fear, he brings a gun to the interview at the Dalton house (Wright 2005, 43). Bigger reasons that because he is entering white society and interacting directly with the generalized other, he needs a gun to be their equal and to feel complete (Wright 2005, 43). This is significant because it shows how vulnerable Bigger feels as he tries to establish new relationships while entering a new milieu. His first experience of humiliation occurs when he tries to figure out how to enter white society; this is a literal dilemma, as Bigger agonizes over whether to use the front or back entrance to the house and worries about what a police officer might do if he is seen wandering around a white neighbourhood (Wright 2005, 44). According to Bigger: 'It would be thought that he was trying to rob or rape somebody' (Wright 2005, 44). These fears play a significant role later; for now, it is sufficient to note that Bigger understands his movements and actions within white society as regulated and hierarchically constrained.

When Bigger finally enters the house, he experiences the first feelings of rage as he feels more black and inferior as a result of sitting in a white house with its strange objects (Wright 2005, 45–6). To cope with these feelings, Bigger adopts a certain posture during the ensuing job interview in order to act the way he believes the generalized other (embodied in the Daltons) expects and desires: 'He stood with his knees slightly bent, his lips partly open, his shoulders stooped' (Wright 2005, 48). This reaffirms Bigger's subordination within white society; he feels and therefore acts as the inferior. Bigger describes these feelings of inferiority in the following passage:

> Every time I think about it [segregation] I feel like somebody's poking a red-hot iron down my throat. Goddamit, look! We live here and they live there. We black and they white. They got things and we ain't. They do things and we can't. It's just like living in jail. Half the time I feel like I'm on the outside of the world peeping in through a knot-hole in the fence .... Every time I get to thinking about me being black and they being white, me being here and they being there, I feel like something awful's going to happen. (Wright 2005, 20)

Bigger goes on to say that he feels like white people live inside him. This passage should not be interpreted as prophetic, but as an integral part of the process of becoming righteous, following Katz. Bigger constructs the relations between himself and white society as unjust, and experiences these relations as humiliating. The humiliation of class exploitation finds a symbolic target in Mary Dalton and her communist friend Jan.

At their first meeting, Mary Dalton asks Bigger if he is in a union, which is a foreign concept to him (Wright 2005, 51). She repeatedly reaches out to Bigger, assuring him that she is his friend and inviting him to eat dinner with her and Jan in a black restaurant (Wright 2005, 64). While chauffeuring her and her boyfriend, Bigger does not feel included, but rather oppressed by 'two vast white looming walls' (Wright 2005, 67–8). In attempting to deconstruct years of hierarchical societal relations organized by categories such as class and race, Mary instead humiliates Bigger, who believes Mary is acting strangely (Wright 2005, 71). The external nature of this humiliation is evident in the following passage, where Jan insists that Bigger shake his hand and not call him 'sir':

> But they made him feel his black skin by just standing there looking at him, one holding his hand and the other smiling. .... He felt naked, transparent; he felt that this white man having helped put him down, having helped to deform him, held him up now to look at him and be amused. At that moment he felt toward Mary and Jan a dumb, cold, and inarticulate hate. (Wright 2005, 67)

Bigger is humiliated because the reactions of Jan and Mary imply that something is wrong with Bigger when he is acting as decades of relations have conditioned him. His experience of racial discrimination is historical; it permeates both his biography and the social structure in which he exists. Mary attempts to deconstruct the public issue of racialized power relations at the level of biography, ignoring the effects of history. As a result, Mary becomes the symbolic target of Bigger's rage. She does not understand the full magnitude of the public issues (following Mills) of institutionalized racism, and Bigger does not understand her attempts to ameliorate it at a personal level (that of what Mills called 'personal troubles').

The process of turning Mary into a sacrificial victim begins when Bigger tries to get her, while she is intoxicated, up to her room without being caught and losing his job. As he helps her out of the car, he again wonders what white people will think if they are seen; remember that Bigger's greatest fears on entering white society were false accusations of rape and robbery (Wright 2005, 81). Bigger turns Mary into a profane object by cursing her (Katz 1988, 37), and also condemns her for her immoral behaviour with Jan in the car as well as her advances toward Bigger as he tries to get her to her room (Wright 2005, 83, 113). While he is still inside Mary's room, Mrs Dalton appears, realizing Bigger's fears. If Mary makes a sound, Bigger will be condemned, so Bigger silences the immoral (or morally blameworthy) Mary in order to maintain his own innocence. Rather than face rape charges, Bigger smothers Mary to avoid detection by the blind Mrs Dalton. This is a righteous slaughter, intended to maintain Bigger's innocence, as well as his identity as a black, working-class man caught in a dangerous situation (as he interprets the reactions of white middle-class America). Having not raped Mary, but unable to prove it, Bigger blames her for his humiliation and for her own death, and in doing so maintains his own righteousness (Katz 1988, 20). Mary becomes the sacrificial victim of institutionalized race relations. In effect, Bigger attributes Mary's death to the oppressive relations of white society, and to his experiences of these relations.

Although Bigger acts as an individual in murdering Mary Dalton, her death galvanizes white society, including the generalized other as well as institutions; five thousand police officers and three thousand volunteers search for Bigger

(Wright 2005, 242). By murdering an heiress, Bigger represents a significant yet perhaps only symbolic threat to the cherished values of white capitalist society. This act of murder therefore cannot be understood solely at the level of biography, but must also be interpreted in light of the interactions between biography and society. Mrs Dalton, with her white hair, clothes and eyes, symbolically represents the hegemonic spectre and omnipresence of white society that contributes to Mary's death (Wright 2005, 61). She is described as a 'white blur ... standing by the door, silent, ghostlike' (Wright 2005, 85). When Mrs Dalton enters Mary's room, trapping Bigger, the latter acts out of fear of being caught in inappropriate relations; the inappropriateness is determined solely by the colour of his skin. His path of action is to smother the helpless and drunken Mary with her bedclothes in order to preserve his innocence. Bigger commits this act of resistance because he understands that the line of interpretation adopted by the generalized other and the criminal justice institutions will label him guilty because he is a black man in a white woman's room. As a result of this desire to maintain his innocence, and his rejection of this social and structural interpretation, Bigger undergoes an emotional process that makes murder a seductive and even compulsory alternative to injustice.

The murder is an allegory of Bigger's symbolically changing relations with white society. He no longer passively accepts his subordination by white society, but instead actively threatens it with a physical but also symbolic act of resistance: the murder of heiress Mary Dalton. After the act: 'The reality of the room fell from him; the vast city of white people that sprawled outside took its place' (Wright 2005, 87). This is an example of Katz's (1988, 8) moment of self-reflection, in which Bigger experiences himself as an object controlled by external forces. In this process, Bigger creates distance between himself or his biography and society in order to reflexively understand himself in relation to this society (Katz 1988, 5). He believes that by killing Mary, white society no longer subordinates him. He reflects on this realization in the following passage:

> The thought of what he had done, the awful horror of it, the daring associated with such actions, formed for him for the first time in his fear-ridden life a barrier of protection between him and a world he feared. He had murdered and created a new life for himself. ... He was outside his family now, over and beyond them .... While sitting there at the table waiting for his breakfast, he felt that he was arriving at something which had long eluded him. Things were becoming clear; he would know how to act from now on. The thing to do was to act just like others acted, live like they lived, and while they were not looking, do what you wanted. ... He felt that they wanted and yearned to see life in a certain way; they needed a certain picture of the world; there was one way of living they preferred above all others. (Wright 2005, 105–6)

Through the act of murder, Bigger, following Katz, transcends his humiliating circumstances. In addition, following Clarke et al., he seemingly resolves ideological contradictions between the values of his milieu and white upper-middle-class values. Bigger believes that to this point white people ruled him through structures and legislation and unequal economic opportunity, and by sowing in black relations seeds of fear and distrust (Wright 2005, 115). Bigger understands white society to be the dominant culture and the creator of the violence he commits. His relations with society are conditioned by fear, and Bigger responds to the ultimate fear (a charge of rape) with ultimate violence (an act of murder). The sacrificial slaughter of Mary Dalton affects Bigger, altering his self-identity so that he no longer feels fear or hate (Wright 2005, 273). Instead, he is described as '[h]aving been thrown by accidental murder into a position where he had sensed a possible order and meaning in his relations with the people about him' (Wright 2005, 274). Symbolically, Bigger has murdered the unequal and unjust social structure, although its material form is unaffected (Clarke et al. 2006, 37). Bigger undergoes a symbolic transformation from subordinate to free man. The righteous slaughter of Mary Dalton holds potential for him, as he sees it as an opportunity to bring blacks together, because with this act of resistance he has done something significant in acting to overcome the humiliating relations legitimized by the hegemony that reproduces hierarchical race and class relations. Therefore, as a result of his criminal actions, Bigger undergoes a significant transformation; his actions alter his understanding of the perceptions (and perceptiveness) of the generalized other and influence his subsequent criminal actions.

Katz (1988) therefore helps to make sense of Bigger's individual actions, including the seductive motivation and symbolic meaning of the murder of Mary Dalton. The Birmingham School contributes a complementary understanding of how institutions such as race and class influence Bigger's understanding of himself and his situation, precipitating the actions that symbolically resist the hegemony of these unjust structures. We clearly see the dynamic interplay between Mills' (1959) milieu and society and the interactions between the two as they play out in the novel *Native Son*.

This interpretation was framed and necessarily limited by the meta-framework of the criminological imagination as well as by the text of Wright's novel. As Potter (2001, 190) explains, meaning exists and is grounded in reality or in the structure of language. Therefore, while the act of reading is creative, producing meaning, that meaning is constrained by the text. My interpretation was guided by Mills' (1959) concepts in order to better understand the social reality contained in *Native Son*, and also to integrate two seemingly opposed analytical frameworks in interactionism and Marxism. The goal was to explicate the biography of Bigger Thomas by drawing on Katz's ideas about the experiential nature of criminality, to discuss the history of his society by drawing on the structuralist orientation of the Birmingham School, and then draw connections between the two (both biography and structure, and also Katz and Marxism). According to Mills (1959, 4), the typical individual is disoriented by, and disassociated from, the reality and complexity of the modern world. This was true in *Native Son*; Bigger was disassociated from the world, and likewise the casual reader might similarly experience a certain disassociation from the criminological possibilities of the text. Rather than accepting the author's interpretation of events or reality, the criminological imagination was used to resist the self-evident truths and rudimentary criminology of the novel. Instead, an analytic framework that considered the biographical elements as well as the societal elements and the relations between the two was engaged to consider the personal troubles and public issues that Bigger encountered, and to restate them clearly in criminological terms. Specifically, this chapter provides relevant criminological insight and not only introduces imaginings of fictional realities, but furthers discussion of Katz's (1988) concept of righteous slaughter as well as the Birmingham School's structural, hierarchical and hegemonic understandings of society as these relate to crime or murder (Clarke et al. 2006).

Conclusion

This chapter was inspired by Mills' (1959) claims, set out in its Introduction, that literature is inadequate to formulate the problems of biography and society and the relations between the two, as well as his conceptualization of the sociological imagination. In challenging his claims regarding the adequacy and usefulness of fiction as an object of study, it was demonstrated that a criminological imagination based on his work in fact provides an ideal meta-framework with which to consider fiction and fictional realities. In so doing, the assumed boundaries of criminology which previously ignored the potential of fictional realities were challenged. By deriving criminological meaning about the biography of an individual, the structure of society and their dialectical effects through an analysis of *Native Son*, Mills' (1959) assertion that the criminological imagination acts as a method of knowledge-production was demonstrated.

Although *Native Son* was selected due to its critical acclaim and public popularity, its relevant criminological themes of violence and racism, its enduring nature and its ability to stimulate criminological thought and debate, the goal of this chapter has not been to study a particular work of fiction. In a broader sense, this chapter has been devoted to issues of methodology and epistemology. Therefore, demonstrating that criminology can adequately access and analyse fiction is more important than the particular conclusions drawn from an analysis of *Native Son*. In this sense, the analysis of *Native Son* has provided fruitful criminological exploration.

First, the analysis of *Native Son* enabled the integration of particular criminological concepts found in the work of Katz (1988) and the Birmingham School (Clarke et al. 2006), guided by Mills' (1959) concepts of biography and society, and the relations between the two. This makes for a methodological contribution, demonstrating the possibility and potential of the criminological imagination. Second, Richard Wright's *Native Son* was used as the empirical referent to test assumptions concerning the legitimacy and value of fiction as an object of criminological study in terms of its analytic and explanatory potential. This is an epistemological issue, and one that is relevant for consideration as criminology continues to wrestle with how we know what we know, and with what is considered to be a valid source of knowledge and study.

Although Mills' (1959) concept of the sociological imagination is more than fifty years old, his commitment to critical thinking, clarity of concepts and the congruence between epistemology and methodology ensure the continuing relevance of imagination within the social sciences, and has great promise for realizing the viability of a criminology that considers fictional realities as valid objects of criminological knowledge.

References

Aas, K. 2007. 'Analysing a World in Motion: Global Flows Meet "Criminology of the Other."' *Theoretical Criminology* 11(2): 283–303.

Blake, C. 1991. 'On Richard Wright's *Native Son*.' In *Rough Justice: Essays on Crime in Literature*, edited by M. Friedland, 187–199. Toronto, ON: University of Toronto.

Clarke, J., S. Hall, T. Jefferson and B. Roberts. 2006. *Resistance through Rituals: Youth Subcultures in Post-war Britain*, 2nd edn. Florence, KY: Routledge.

Engel, S. 2003. 'Teaching Literature in the Criminal Justice Curriculum.' *Journal of Criminal Justice Education* 14(2): 345–54.

Ferrell, J. 1999. 'Cultural Criminology.' *Annual Review of Sociology* 25: 395–418.

Frauley, J. 2010. 'The Fictional Reality and Criminology: An Ontology of Theory and Exemplary Pedagogical Practice.' *Current Issues in Criminal Justice* 21(3): 437–59.

———. 2011. *Criminology, Deviance, and the Silver Screen: Fictional Realities and the Criminological Imagination*. New York: Palgrave.

Gabbidon, S. and G. Higgins. 2007. 'Consumer Racial Profiling and Perceived Victimization: A Phone Survey of Philadelphia Area Residents.' *American Journal of Criminal Justice* 32: 1–11.

Girling, E. 2008. 'Book Review: "The Vertigo of Late Modernity": Metaphors to Live by and the Methodology of Attentiveness.' *Theoretical Criminology* 12(4): 540–43.

Gramsci, A. 1967. 'The Study of Philosophy and of Historical Materialism.' In *The Modern Prince and Other Writings*, translated by L. Marks, 58–75. New York: International Publishers.

Green, P., T. Ward and K. McConnachie. 2007. 'Logging and Legality: Environmental Crime, Civil Society, and the State.' *Social Justice* 34(2): 94–110.

Hallsworth, S. 2006. 'Book Review: Cultural Criminology Unleashed.' *Criminology and Criminal Justice* 6(1):147–50.

Hamm, M. 2005. 'After September 11: Terrorism Research and the Crisis in Criminology.' *Theoretical Criminology* 9(2): 237–51.

Hughes, G. and M. Rowe. 2007. 'Introduction.' *Criminology and Criminal Justice* 7(4): 315–16.

Katz, J. 1988. *Seductions of Crime: Moral and Sensual Attraction in Doing Evil.* New York: Basic Books.

Kelly, R. 1991. 'Mapping the Domains of Crime: The Contributions of Literary Works to Criminology.' *International Journal of Offender Therapy and Comparative Criminology* 35(1): 45–61.

Layder, D. 1993. *New Strategies in Social Research: An Introduction and Guide.* Cambridge: Polity Press.

Lynch, M. and P. Stretsky. 2003. 'The Meaning of Green: Contrasting Criminological Perspectives.' *Theoretical Criminology* 7(2): 217–38.

McLaughlin, E. 2008. 'Book Review: Straining towards Dissolution: Global Merton vs Global Jihad.' *Theoretical Criminology* 12(4): 531–4.

Mills, C. 1959. *The Sociological Imagination.* New York: Oxford University Press.

Mounce, R. 2008. 'Book Review – Expanding the Criminological Imagination: Critical Readings in Criminology.' *Criminology and Criminal Justice* 8(2): 230–32.

Piamonte, S. 2010. *The Criminological Imagination: Mills, Reflexive Analysis, and Richard Wright's Native Son.* MA thesis, University of Ottawa.

Potter, G. 2001. 'Truth in Fiction, Science and Criticism.' In *After Postmodernism: An Introduction to Critical Realism*, edited by J. Lopez and G. Potter, 183–95. New York: Athlone Press.

Rafter, N. 2006. *Shots in the Mirror: Crime Films and Society*, 2nd edn. New York: Oxford University Press.

Rampersad, A. 2005. 'Introduction.' In *Native Son*, by R. Wright, ix–xxii. New York: Harper Perennial.

Random House. 2007. '100 Best Novels.' *Modern Library*. Accessed 12 June 2010. http://www.randomhouse.com/modernlibrary/100bestnovels.html.

Ruggiero, V. 2003. *Crime in Literature: Sociology of Deviance and Fiction.* New York: Verso.

Sagarin, E. 1981. *Raskolnikov and Others: Literary Images of Crime, Punishment, Redemption, and Atonement.* New York: St. Martin's Press.

Sayer, A. 1992. *Method in Social Science: A Realist Approach.* 2nd edn. New York: Routledge.

Snow, C. 1959. *The Two Cultures and the Scientific Revolution.* New York: Cambridge University Press.

White, R. 2003. 'Environmental Issues and the Criminological Imagination.' *Theoretical Criminology* 7(4): 483–506.

Wright, R. 2005. *Native Son.* New York: Harper Perennial.

Chapter 12

Imagining Transnational Security Projects

David Nelken

When C. Wright Mills wrote about the sociological imagination he was mainly concerned with recognizing the connection between individual biography ('personal troubles') and social structure. It was vital, for example, to understand that unemployment was often a product of social forces, and not see it as the responsibility of the person who was unemployed (Mills 1959). Given that the criminal law has exactly as one of its main functions that of bracketing the influence of social factors and pinning responsibility on individual choice, the task for the sociological imagination in criminology is all the more vital – and its political implications especially significant (Young 2011). More generally, however, sociological imagination is needed wherever we seek to explain why a given phenomenon is linked to one level of analysis at the expense of another. At a time of globalization, there is some confusion about the role being played (and the role that should be played) by transnational, national and more local forms of crime control. In this chapter I will explain the sources of these uncertainties and the ways authors struggle to deal with them. I will then go on to discuss critically a proposed solution from Mariana Valverde, who suggests that we study the process by which what she calls 'security projects' go about constructing crime problems according to different scales. I will then apply her ideas to two current areas of transnational regulation: the effort to control transnational crime threats, and the increasing use of global social indicators in dealing with social problems.

Globalization and Levels of Crime Control

With the advent of globalization, there is an increasingly wide gap between the (global) sites where issues arise and the places where they are managed (the nation state). The consequences of globalization for the economic fortunes of countries, cities or parts of them means that the causes of ordinary crime problems, and not only those perpetrated by transnational criminal organizations, often have little to do with the unit in which they are located. This is so even if most crime – and even some so-called transnational crime – remains in other respects a highly local phenomenon (Hobbs 1998). Different kinds of units emerge as objects and as agents of control. As it increasingly blurs the differences between 'units', globalization changes the meaning of place and the location and significance of boundaries (Appadurai 1996; Shearing and Johnston 2010). Likewise, the use of cyberspace requires and generates a variety of new forms of control and resistance. An ever more important role is played by international bodies such as non-governmental organizations and inter-governmental organizations and influential think tanks. These formulate and spread what have been called 'global prescriptions'– including ideas about what to do about crime (Dezalay and Garth 2002; Wacquant 2009a, 2009b). There is growing internationalization of policing or attempts by international courts of justice to enforce on states common minimal standards of conduct. On the one hand, new forms of 'soft law' characterize the way norms are produced, signalled and sanctioned. On the other hand, war-making, peacekeeping and criminal justice come to overlap – and even war is privatized (Klein 2008).

A criticism of much traditional work in comparative criminal justice is that it attributes too much importance to one particular variable, the nation state, at a time when the state is increasingly losing its monopoly over criminal justice (Drake et al. 2009; Muncie et al. 2009; Nelken 2011a). Katja Aas, the author of a superb recent introduction to 'crime and globalization', argues that: 'one can no longer study, for example, Italy by simply looking at what happens inside its territory, but rather need to acknowledge the effects that distant conflicts and developments have on national crime and security concerns and vice versa' (2007, 286; see also Aas 2011). Not surprisingly, therefore, she devotes little energy in her textbook to problems of comparing individual countries, and instead seeks to show us the complex processes by which the 'global' and 'the local' are intertwined. She tells us, for example, how Italy's use of naval patrols to discourage illegal immigration from Africa has important knock-on effects for other countries in Europe, including those in Scandinavia.[1]

More generally, key crime initiatives now link regional or local centres of power (Edwards and Hughes 2005) and are delegated to the private sector. As Muncie likewise argues, state sovereignty in matters of criminal justice is challenged by the likes of international courts, human rights conventions, multinational private security enterprises, cross-border policing, policy networks and flows, and technologies of global surveillance. It is no longer clear what the scope of nation state-specific criminal justice is and who exactly constitutes the subject of its gaze. 'Governance' increasingly replaces government – and power is increasingly shared with other transnational and private actors. Innovation in crime control often happens not at the state level, but below or above it (Muncie 2011).

On the other hand, it would be premature to say that the nation state has had its day as a source of social ordering (Loader and Walker 2007). Nation state boundaries typically coincide with language and cultural differences, and represent the source of criminal law and criminal statistics. The imposition of a common legal code

---

1   Recent events add a bitter postscript. Whereas Italy in turn relied on agreements with Colonel Gaddafi in Libya whereby he used his detention centres to help prevent potential immigrants from entering Europe, this ended when Gaddafi himself became the enemy and Western countries sent in aircraft to support opposition to his regime, whereby he was overthrown and killed.

and the common training of legal officials form part of attempts to achieve and consolidate national identity. And 'borders' continue to play important instrumental and symbolic roles, not least in responding to immigration. Even if sovereignty has become more difficult to exert in fiscal matters, we have recently been seeing a process of de-globalization after the economic crisis beginning in 2008, when national states had to step in to avoid the meltdown of the financial markets.

In addition, even if we accept that the state is – in many respects – losing its centrality, it does not follow that what happens in the field of criminal justice necessarily follows this general logic. Criminal law continues to be a powerful icon of sovereignty, and the nation state persists as a key site where the insecurities and uncertainties brought about by globalization are expected to be 'resolved'. It is even claimed that the state may 'act out' in responding to some crime problems precisely because it has lost power elsewhere (Garland 1996). Other scholars argue that states are obliged to enforce a new, harsher type of order required precisely because of the dismantling of welfare protections mandated by neo-liberalism (Wacquant 2009a, 2009b). In any case, each country may also have its own reasons for increasing punitiveness. If the USA has seen 'governing through crime' in a range of domestic settings (Simon 2007), in many European societies state power has been used mainly to criminalize non-citizen flows. In places such as South Africa, the state has to underline its ability to provide public safety in order to convince the 'global economy' that it is a 'safe place' in which to do business.

Responding to transnational phenomena such as irregular migration has (or can have) profound effects on the provisions, temper and everyday practice of local systems of criminal justice (Karstedt and Nelken 2014). International law and conventions that seek to spread or enforce human rights have obvious implications for matters such as corruption, terrorism and immigration – but they are also relevant to the length of ordinary criminal trials (Nelken 2008). Conversely, for a wide range of questions regarding international relations, human rights, truth commissions, restitutive justice and transitional justice, it is the proper role of international criminal justice compared to more local means of handling conflict that is a matter of debate (Karstedt 2009). All this means that the outcomes of globalization processes are not predetermined, and that further progress in the direction of greater convergence or interdependence is not inevitable – even if it is often talked about as if it is (Nelken 1997).

Leading writers have been trying to develop the implications of this point. Joachim Savelsberg, for example, accepts that:

> globalization is a powerful process that affects criminal justice and penal policies in many countries. Comparative penal studies that treat countries as independent units of analysis can no longer be justified in light of this situation. While the institutional architecture of penal modernity with its courts and prisons may have remained in place, its deployment, strategic functions and social significance were radically altered. (Savelsberg 2011, 82)

He also accepts that 'global and national penal law and practice interact and partially "constitute" each other'. This also makes it complicated to predict outcomes. The key to globalization's effects, he argues: 'lie[s] in nation-specific institutional arrangements through which knowledge about crime and punishment is produced and diffused, and in which legal and political decision-making is embedded. Distinct reactions are further advanced by country-specific historically rooted cultural sensitivities that support some action strategies and delegitimize others' (Savelsberg 2011, 75).

For Savelsberg:

> globalisation occurs along three paths: norms and practices, including those on punishment; change as a consequence of global shifts in social structure and culture, there is a nation-specific processing of global scripts and nation-specific responses to the arrival of (late) modernity; and a new type of international criminal law has been gaining strength at the global level. (Savelsberg 2011, 75)

In particular, he directs our attention to the importance of agents who, acting locally, use their transnational connections in strategic struggles to impose their authority on a particular field. 'Local actors', he says, 'generally interpret and process global challenges through historically-evolved institutions of knowledge production and political and legal decision making and through the lens of local cultural norms and cognitive frameworks' (Savelsberg 2011, 71). Hence the globalization of the 'local' depends on the localization of the (supposedly) global, and is not just a matter of impersonal macro-social forces (Savelsberg 2011).

For John Muncie, too, '[e]conomic forces are not uncontrollable, do meet resistance and have effects that are neither uniform nor consistent' (2011, 100). As he sees it: 'globalisation as an analytical concept appears both seductive and flawed. It is seductive because it seems to offer some valuable means through which sense can be made of some widely recognised shifts in criminal justice policy, such as the retreat from welfare statism and a resurgence in authoritarianism' (Muncie 2011, 99). But we should not expect that policy transfer be direct or complete or exact or successful: 'Rather, it is mediated through national and local cultures, which are themselves changing at the same time' (Muncie 2011, 100). He argues that both the global and the national inform local identities, institutions, economic interactions and political processes. According to Muncie, globalization is 'a combination of macro socio-economic developments, initiatives in international law and processes of policy flow and diffusion' (2005, 36). The key issue to be addressed is how globalization activates diversity, as well as how it produces uniformity. The challenge is to articulate the dialectic between local specificities and transnational mobilities. For him: 'the specificities of punishment remain embedded in specific geo-political contexts. ... Even neo-liberal modes of governance find different modes of expression in conservative and social democratic rationalities and in authoritarian, retributive, human rights, or restorative technologies' (Muncie 2011, 100).

Globalization can produce both more convergence and greater divergence. Savelsberg tells us:

> Convergence in the purely formal sense often coincides with profound differences in the intent, content and, especially, implementation of legal frames and rules. Even where there is evidence of growing commonalities we should not assume that the explanation lies in globalisation. Similar results do not have to be a result of worldwide trends, indeed they may have quite different causes – just as similar causes, whether global or otherwise and may, under different conditions, lead to different outcomes' (Savelsberg 2011, 71)

For Muncie, likewise: 'The argument that criminal justice is becoming a standardised global product can be sustained only at the very highest level of generality' (2011, 100). In particular, he stresses the way globalization can produce 'contradictory' effects. Thus: 'economic globalism may speak of the import, largely US inspired, of neo-liberal conceptions of the free market and community responsibilisation backed by an authoritarian state. However, legal globalism, largely UN inspired, unveils a contrary vision of universal human rights delivered through social democracies' (Muncie 2011, 99) He criticizes globalization theory for being over-general and not recognizing exceptions, and argues that unravelling the impact of the 'global' and the 'exceptional' requires a level of analysis that neither elevates nor negates either, but recognizes that each is realized only in specific localities, through which their meaning is inevitably reworked, challenged, and contested (Muncie 2011, 99).

To explore the role of the agents of globalization, we need to take a broad view of who is involved. The key actors include politicians, non-governmental organizations or pressure groups, regulatory bodies, journalists and even academics themselves, and not only judges, lawyers, police, probation officers or prison officers. They may also be representatives of businesses such as security providers or those who build and run private prisons. Attention needs to be given to the role of institutions, singly, collectively or in competition. In Europe – but also beyond – EU institutions, the Council of Europe and the European Court of Human Rights system are important players. The same crime threat may call forth responses from a variety of inter-governmental and non-governmental organizations, such as the UN Commissioner for Rights, the International Labour Organisation or the International Organisation for Migration, Human Rights Watch and Amnesty. It is essential to study how agreement is achieved among the various signatories to conventions or those subject to regulatory networks (Merry 2006). We also need to examine what it is that is being spread – scripts, norms, institutions, technologies, fears, ways of seeing, problems, solutions, new forms of policing, punitiveness, or conceptual legal innovations such as the 'the law of the enemy', mediation, restitutive or therapeutic justice? Finally, we can also ask where it is being spread: for example, from or to national, sub-national and supra-national levels in Europe, or more widely?

Given all these developments on the ground, it is not surprising that there is considerable uncertainty about how best to integrate the effects of globalization into the traditional classificatory and descriptive schemes of books about comparative criminal justice. Material that fits awkwardly into the normal comparative paradigm is sometimes relegated to a separate book (Reichel 2007), or to an early chapter (Reichel 2008). Titles such as Winterdyk and Cao's *Lessons from International/comparative Criminology/criminal Justice* (2004) also signal that a variety of related topics are being dealt with – but do not say how, if at all, they may be connected. Sheptycki and Wardak (2005) distinguish 'area studies', 'transnational crime issues' and 'transnational control responses'. But they themselves admit that more needs to be said about when our account of a country's criminal justice system should focus more on internal factors or on external influences. Nick Larsen and Russell Smandych (2008) likewise explain that the cross-cultural study of crime and justice has evolved from a 'comparative' or 'international' approach to what is now increasingly referred to as a 'transnational' or 'global' approach to crime and justice. The effects of rapid globalization have changed social, political and legal realities in such a way that comparative and international approaches to crime and justice are inadequate to capture the full complexity of these issues on a global scale (Beirne 2008, xi). In particular, they draw attention to 'global trends in policing and security, convergence and divergence in criminal justice and penal policy, and international criminal justice, war crimes and the global protection of human rights' (Beirne 2008, xi).

But Piers Beirne (2008), in his preface to their collection, warns against going too far down this road. He concedes that globalization and transnational crime do indeed tend to blur the relatively distinct boundaries and mobilities that exist between nations and between sovereign territories. It is thus increasingly moot whether it makes sense to talk of crime in 'Russia' or in 'India' or in 'Northern Ireland' or in the 'USA' (Beirne 2008, xi). Beirne insists, however, that comparative criminology still has a vital role to play, both in its own terms and also adjacent to global criminology and as one of its key constituents. The question of how globalization and transnational crime affect different societies – similarly or differently, both similarly or differently at the same time, or somewhere in between – is first and foremost a comparative one (Beirne 2008, xi). For example, he sees a valuable role for comparative criminology in identifying that (failed) states are more vulnerable to the penetration of transnational organized crime – which he identifies as places where there are corrupt politicians, weak controls, lengthy borders and so on. Francis Pakes (2010) also worries whether comparative criminal justice is now passé. The subject, he argues, is in the process of losing its relevance. Simply put, the reasoning is that the world has changed, and comparative criminology has changed insufficiently with it. The charge against comparative criminology is that it tends to compare and contrast phenomena in distinct cultures or jurisdictions, and that, by doing so, diffuse interrelations and complications brought about by globalization are ignored or understated (Pakes 2010).

Pakes (2010) asks whether global criminology will supersede the field of what we currently think of as 'classic' comparative criminology so that before comparative criminology gets its act together we will have moved on to doing 'international and transnational criminology', and replies that we should not embrace a 'vision of comparative criminology being abandoned as if it were a ghost town after the gold rush'. The comparative method will remain an influential tool in inquiries involving transnationalization, globalization, crime and control (Pakes 2010). Pakes suggests that the comparative approach could be seen as only a matter of methodology, whereas globalization is an 'object of study'. Globalization, he says, concerns the 'what', not the 'how', describing something taking place in the world, such as the trafficking of illegal goods – or people. Hence there cannot really be any contradiction. But he also concedes that the term 'globalizing criminology' can be used as if it related to methodology. He therefore draws a further distinction between two senses of global criminology that are 'subject to conceptual confusion'. 'Strong' global criminology, he claims, should probably take the world as its unit of analysis. It might address questions such as the relation between climate change and civil unrest, transgressions and control. Here, 'global' denotes object. In contrast, globalized criminology frequently refers to relations: those who advocate it frequently argue that we need to take the interconnectedness of the world into account (Pakes 2010, 18–19).

Characterizing 'Security Projects'

A valuable contribution to this debate is that put forward by Mariana Valverde. In a number of recent publications she has sought to build on the recent governmentality literature (and, before that, the earlier work of Foucault) so as to identify the range of current 'security projects'.[2] The definition of 'security' she uses is a broad one.[3] It covers a wide variety of phenomena, ranging from the differences

---

2   There is more to be said about the definition of each of the terms that make up her neologism 'security project', and especially about whether projects have overriding 'logics'. How do these terms relate to (or substitute for) other key terms such as 'gaze', 'discourse' or 'discipline'? Are the four elements she identifies either necessary or sufficient? She tells us that they serve to expand on the governmentality literature, which spoke only of rationalities and techniques. So we would expect that what she means by 'logic' would include less than rationalities. But in fact we are told that logics embrace a variety of matters, 'including the rationale, the objectives, the telos, what some would call the discourse, and also the ethical justifications' (Valverde 2011, 9). She also tells us that they refer to '[t]he aims and the assumptions of a project – that which tells us what counts as relevant information' (Valverde 2014, 383). They have to do with 'the culturally specific fears and moods that pervade the field of security', and include 'the affective and aesthetic dimensions of governance' (Valverde 2014, 383; see also Nelken 2014a).

3   Valverde tells us that '[a]ll that we can know about security is what people do in its name', so we should 'focus on practices of governance that in fact appeal to security'

between Hobbesian sovereignty, Lockean liberal legality and biopolitical security, to the logic-in-action that distinguishes detective work and community policing, to the changing goals served in different historical periods by the lighting of public parks. She even speaks of the logic of the patriarchal nuclear family that is presupposed by many advertisements for security products for the home. We could certainly add many other potential examples of security projects with distinctive logics: situational versus social crime prevention, law versus psychiatry in dealing with mental illness, or civil versus criminal sanctions (as seen in the rise of anti-social behaviour orders in the UK, and methods for confiscating the proceeds of organized crime worldwide) or the conflation of crime-fighting and war, as in 'the war' against crime or against drugs, and the response to the 9/11 attack on the twin towers in New York. Valverde distinguishes between the logics, scale, jurisdiction and techniques involved in such projects (Valverde 2011a, 2011b, 2014). For her, the question of scale is therefore just one aspect of the way 'security projects' constitute their object of attention. Following her lead, instead of seeking to decide whether the source of crime and/or crime control lies at the global or some other level, we could instead seek to describe (following Mills) how a given level is 'naturalized'.

Valverde tells us that it can be particularly interesting to see how spatial and temporal scaling work together. We could think, for instance, of the way surveillance of targeted locations produces an overload so that there is not enough time to view the images registered, or the fact that Italian prison-type structures for holding irregular immigrants used to be called 'Centres of Temporary Stay' (Centri di Permanenza Temporanea). For her, the significance of temporal scale is too often overlooked. The relevance of this dimension is made clear by the current growth of attention to the pre-crime stage seen in actuarial justice and crime prevention more generally. Many more examples could be added of the relevance of time to social control. We could think of cycles of crime and punishment, or trial by media as way of avoiding waiting. Or we could examine the way efforts that are made to turn the clock back or at least stop it – through restitution, reparation, mediation, and in the international area most obviously with truth and reconciliation commissions. Time can also be a resource for under-controlling. By using the same time frame applicable to conventional crime incidents, the frames used for analysing white-collar and business crimes exclude the many earlier steps that could have been taken to avoid accidents and disasters in the sense of delay in criminal procedures and trials that let off certain classes of offenders. Valverde tells us that the third of her elements, jurisdiction, needs to be distinguished from that of space, with which it does not necessarily coincide. She uses the term somewhat ambiguously, as between its legal and sociological meanings, but arguably this corresponds to the complexity of the phenomena

---

(2011a, 5). But, important as this could be for some purposes, might we not, for other purposes, want to think about projects that are not justified in the name of security, but can be theoretically seen as having the same function?

itself, as seen in the domestic setting in the authority exerted over public property settings such as shopping malls or, even more importantly, in efforts to legitimize different types of transnational legal orders. Last (but not least), she signals the significance of techniques, which for her 'includes everything from architectural details characteristic of certain security institutions to bodily habits' (Valverde 2014, 388). To this mix she also adds law's technicalities.

Valverde sees what she is doing as basically a descriptive rather than a normative exercise. She warns us that her analysis 'will not have direct political or normative lessons', yet she does also think that it 'will be useful for those who want to engage in both practical and intellectual work' (Valverde 2014, 383). In particular, she suggests that this kind of work could help us to understand the governance process, and perhaps eventually suggest some procedural changes that may help create the conditions for a better, more rational and more democratic use, for example, of a local city's powers. But, as always, drawing policy conclusions is not straightforward. She is critical (as no doubt Mills would have been) of 'broken-windows criminology' because it excludes (relevant) city and national information about the larger causes of criminality. But this easily begs the questions of who decides what is relevant, when and why. (Is not every way of seeing also a way of not seeing?). She tells us that 'municipal officials and other actors work together, more often than not, in a dysfunctional manner to manage questions of order and disorder' (Valverde 2011a, p. 1). But how can we know what is functional (and functional for whom)? She herself points out that all depends on how information is used. District-specific data about crime rates, she says, can increase urban differentiation, but it can also be used to channel more resources to more deprived areas.

Another link between the descriptive and prescriptive comes in when Valverde discusses what she calls the 'naturalization' of particular responses to social problems. As she puts it: 'who is thought of as the proper authority ... ends up settling the often unasked question about *how* something or some space is to be governed' (Valverde 2014, 389). The aim of her analytic unpacking of security projects (the importance of considering each of the four elements separately) is not to demonstrate that they are in actual fact independent, but rather to seek out their affinities. The logic (or rationality) of any project will often be the master element, somehow conditioning the others. But she also says that jurisdiction is the 'governance of governance' (Valverde 2011a, 14), which would seem to make it more important than logic. In any case, there is nothing deterministic about such relationships – for example, techniques may be subordinated to logics, but they may also run away with a project and undo its logic. She goes on to talk about whether responses built into given projects are appropriate or incommensurable, saying that:

> techniques that are likely to be effective at one temporal scale are often incommensurable with (and possibly in conflict with) techniques that work at a different pace and over a different period of time. And since temporal scale is

often taken for granted and rendered almost invisible, these structural conflicts may only become apparent if problems arise. (Valverde 2011a, 13)

These are interesting claims, but we must also take care not to assume that 'contradictions' in our categories always correspond to tensions on the ground. It is enough to think of the persistence of multiple conflicting backward- and forward-looking justifications for penal sentences.

Border Panics and Cybercrime

Although most of Valverde's examples are drawn from domestic contexts, her approach is particularly valuable in trying to grasp the increasingly complex interconnections among transnational, national and local responses to crime and other social problems. Many, perhaps even most, contemporary security projects result from 'border panics' about how to draw borders more tightly to protect the nation state or groups of states. This is especially true when dealing with immigration, which is too readily transformed into an actual or potential crime threat. But who should be responsible for responding to this challenge? In 2013 a total of 366 people – mostly from Eritrea – died in October when the boat carrying them sank off the shores of the Italian island Lampedusa, near Sicily. In response, the European Commission emphasized the need to launch more Mediterranean-wide search and rescue patrols to intercept migrant boats earlier. This, it was said, would be a way to 'show real European solidarity beyond words'.[4] The Home Affairs Commissioner, Cecilia Malmstroem, told reporters after the meeting that she had asked ministers from the 28 member states to allow a major operation by the EU's Frontex border naval patrol agency to cover the whole Mediterranean, from Cyprus to Spain. According to her, 'this was a moment to show real European solidarity beyond words'.[5] The commissioner's spokesman, Michele Cercone, said: 'It could help prevent tragedies like the one in Lampedusa.'[6]

Yet, from the point of view of those trying to start a new life in more favoured countries, the solidarity being expressed by interrupting migration projects is very questionable. As pointed out by a BBC commentator at the time:

> Much of what EU ministers are discussing has been in the pipeline for some time. ... Similar measures were introduced in 2011 when the Arab uprisings led to an increase in people fleeing Libya and Tunisia. ... [T]the best illustration of how Europe is approaching this problem can be seen in a 'mobility partnership'

---

4   See Matthew Price, 'Lampedusa Wreck: EU Seeks Mediterranean Migrant Sea Patrols', *BBC News*, http://www.bbc.co.uk/news/world-europe-24440908 (accessed 6 June 2015).

5   Ibid.

6   Ibid.

signed by the EU and Morocco, which focuses on ways to limit illegal migration. On the one hand, the EU promises to grant more visas for Moroccan students, business leaders, and the like. On the other, Morocco is obliged to stop migrants leaving its shores for Europe. Human rights groups have pointed to numerous occasions when they say the authorities have broken international law in attempting to do this.[7]

The collective heart-searching about the need to do more for immigrants after the Lampedusa tragedy was in fact short-lived. Only a brief time afterwards, video footage of the holding camp for irregular immigrants there showed people of both sexes being hosed down naked in public in a bid to fight disease. The mayor of Lampedusa, Giusi Nicolini, said the video made the centre look like a 'concentration camp', and that Italy as a whole should be 'ashamed'.[8] The speaker of Italy's Chamber of Deputies, Laura Boldrini (a former UN Commissioner for Human Rights), said that the treatment the migrants were enduring was 'unworthy of a civilized country'.[9] But as long as immigration is treated as a threat to (economic) security matters are unlikely to change.

The same applies to dealing with the challenges of terrorism and transnational organized crime. Take, for example, efforts to control cybercrime, especially where the data to be accessed is held on the Cloud, and is therefore seen to pose special problems to nationally based law enforcement authorities. There are genuine uncertainties about the appropriate procedures to be complied with when carrying out an investigation if they are not to risk the data they obtain being excluded at court (Walden 2011). At a recent confidential meeting I attended in one European country, the questions raised pointed to the significance of many of the elements in Valverde's framework. Should cyberspace be treated as a separate reality from other forms of space? Or is it just a matter of working out where it connects with space as territory? But what, then, if this option leads to results that are arbitrary in terms of who should really bear responsibility for criminal acts? Is it the location of the perpetrator, the host server, the locus of action or the location of the victim that matters?

Speed is also a key aspect of the response here. Dealing with cybercrime is said to be all about urgency and emergency. Law enforcers and policy-makers complain that the time taken to comply with domestic procedures, and even more so requests for international assistance, cannot match the pace of new technologies. They place much stress on the need to help victims of paedophiles or of human traffickers in real time, even if, in practice, they may more often be dealing with financial crimes. At the meeting, some representatives of both

---

7   Ibid.

8   Rosie Scammell, 'Italy Migrant Centre Like a "Concentration Camp', *The Local.it*, 18 December 2013. http://www.thelocal.it/20131218/italy-migrant-centre-is-like-a-concentration-camp (accessed 6 June 2015).

9   Ibid. The situation has been growing steadily worse since these lines were first penned.

state bodies and private computer server operators even expressed a desire– and willingness – to access data which held compromising material even if it was outside their jurisdiction. As far as jurisdiction is concerned, sovereignty can be seen as the result as much as the presupposition of intervention. Certainly, criminal justice officials make no concession to self-policing by hackers themselves (Glenny 2011). Powers given to combat organized crime are in practice often used to develop a more technologically advanced response to traditional 'high-volume crime' (Sheptycki 2002). Dealing with cybercrime involves a series of technical assessments of how data are stored (and made difficult to access), how they are moved and who is responsible for them (though sometimes the difficulties are exaggerated). Methods needed to overcome these difficulties are used to justify the use – and misuse – of highly sophisticated methods of surveillance.

Globalizing Social Indicators

A more complicated case for applying Valverde's framework concerns the role of what have been described as global social indicators. A social indicator has been defined as: '[a] named collection of rank-ordered data that purports to represent the past or projected performance of different units generated through a process that simplifies raw data about a complex social phenomenon' (Davis et al. 2012, 6). Indicators are a crucial part of exercises 'to compare units so as to evaluate their performance by reference to one or more standards' (Davis et al. 2012, 6). These instruments are not always associated with matters strictly defined as crime control. They serve as a way of standardizing, co-ordinating and assessing progress in responding to a variety of matters such as those involving business prospects, financial soundness, the provision of food and medicine, environmental protection, human rights and refugee protection (Davis et al. 2012; Nelken 2014a). Although all these issues may be related to security in a broad sense, indicators also play a part in dealing with the specific challenges of transnational crime, such as attempts to control human trafficking (see, e.g., Nelken 2011b; Zaloznaya and Hagan 2012). And, more interestingly, global indicators are also part of efforts to govern security projects themselves.

The appeal of indicators is not difficult to understand. They claim to translate phenomena such as respect for the rule of law into a numerical representation that is easy to understand and comparable across actors. They are seen as having the legitimacy of science. Their simplicity enables more effective communication with those who are governed as well as the general public, thereby promoting ideals of transparency and accountability, for example where donors are involved. They can promote horizontal accountability between governments, and can form part of a delegation of autonomy or discretion in exchange for providing feedback on decisions taken. They promote collaboration at international levels, and are especially useful where international law obligations are difficult to enforce. Their use facilitates interaction between groups, organizations or 'regimes' that otherwise would have difficulties in doing so by providing a working language for inter-system communication, as when they help development experts talk to human right lawyers.

On the other hand, as Sally Merry (2011), among others, has emphasized, indicators also have controversial 'knowledge' and 'governance' effects. As to the first, indicators, Merry tells us, are 'performative'; naming produces knowledge by announcing categories to be measured as if they were self-evident, open to public scrutiny, simple in conception and readily accessible in a way that private opinions are not. But the labels thus chosen do not necessarily accurately reflect the data that produce the indicators. These numerical measures, she says, 'submerge local particularities and idiosyncrasies into universal categories to produce a world knowable without the detailed particulars of context and history' (Merry 2011, S84). Indicators 'constitute' the phenomena they seek to measure – even as they assert a claim that it is a measurable, pre-existing reality. They also have feedback effects, bringing to life what they purport to be measuring (and sometimes intending to do this), as with notions such as 'better business', 'corruption' and 'fragile states'. In fact, some of those who are the most positive about the indicators they describe are not worried about those indicators constituting reality.

The second set of effects, by contrast, have more to do with the new systems of governance emerging in the post-war period that seek to shape behaviour 'at a distance', encouraging 'governance of the soul' and self-management rather than command and control models. Indicators help to make individuals, organizations and countries responsible for their own behaviour as they try to comply with the measures of performance they measure. Case studies of indicators show us that, in practice, local and international actors make pragmatic use of more parochial and more general standards according to a calculus of political advantages. They therefore remind us that a key issue – also for those involved – is whose standards are being assumed and applied. Sometimes those being relied on are ones already existing, favoured by the most powerful groups involved in the making or monitoring indicators concerned. But it can sometimes be good that we apply 'higher' standards of health and security elsewhere if it counteracts the tendency of globalization to lead to lesser standards. Ideals may be 'found' as well as 'lost' in translation. It may be less easy to justify a 'one size fits all' approach as an attempt to find applicable standards that do not belong to any given society.

Valverde's framework offers an interesting entry point for examining these effects of global social indicators. Their purported 'global' reach, for example, is important in transforming merely 'local' standards into what purport to be more general ones. In terms of time scales, the work of imposing order through indicators usually involves a much slower process of naming or shaming than the speed required to deal with transnational criminals – though they can sometimes involve short time frames, as when rating agencies change their indicators of financial health. In terms of jurisdiction, the way that social indicators treat the 'units' as if they can be ranked independently perpetuates the idea that they exist separately. Indicators sometimes assert authority on the basis of international agreements;

at other times, powerful countries may simply assume the right to act in the name of universal human rights by using their control over important political or economic resources. Social indicators build in quantitative social science methods as a way of homogenizing very different kinds of social problems and social contexts. Yet, however questionable the techniques used for formulating and applying indicators, it can be hard to contest them without access to the same data (or drawing on competing indicators).

Drawing on Valverde's approach can also help in appreciating the extent of overlap in responding to transnational crime challenges and the making of global indicators. Both these developments reflect the increasing interdependence between countries, and involve proactive action by nation states that goes beyond their territory (in the case of immigration, involving the national, the European and international levels). In each case, nation states with different levels of power and hegemonic culture play different roles in policing or being policed, and in spreading, or being obliged to comply with, purportedly common standards as measured by social indicators. But there are also differences. While the attempt to control cybercrime, for example, seems to be guided by the aim to bolster what is still mainly nation state-based enforcement of criminal law, the making of global social indicators is a productive form of power arguably linked to the long-term construction of a new global order.

Conclusion

This chapter has examined the need for sociological imagination in connecting local and global responses to crime and offered an appreciative reading of Valverde's idea of security projects as a contribution to this task. One point (among others) that perhaps needs to be further examined is the role of those being controlled in resisting control. It would be wrong to portray them as merely passive objects. Valverde does speak about what she calls 'jurisdictional games', but she blurs the sense of the game as a social practice with pre-set rules, and 'gaming' as a means by which (either side) outwits the other by *not* following the rules. The targets of indicators, those whose conduct is being measured, may sometimes be able to turn the tables and manipulate or 'game' indicators. Some commentators argue that the possibility of resistance – and contestation – should be built into the operation of global social indicators (Rosga and Satterthwaite 2012). It may, then, be difficult to distinguish gaming on the one hand (e.g., the manipulation of results of social interventions or the actual protection of human rights) from resistance or contestation to controversial standards (such as neo-liberal market orthodoxies) on the other. Going further, building in contestability could even be seen as a way of legitimizing the use of indicators in general by allowing the expertise behind a given indicator to be challenged (Nelken 2014b). Can we ever really guard the guardians (and could this be done without indicators)? No doubt Valverde would wryly remind us that this task, too, is a security project.

References

Aas, Katya Franko. 2007. *Globalisation and Crime*. London: Sage.
———. 2011. 'Victimhood of the National? Denationalizing Sovereignty in Crime Control.' In *International and Comparative Criminal Justice and Urban Governance*, edited by Adam Crawford, 389–412. Cambridge: Cambridge University Press.
Appadurai, Arjun. 1996. *Modernity at Large: Cultural Dimensions of Globalization*. Minneapolis, MN: University of Minnesota Press.
Beirne, Piers. 2008. 'Preface.' In *Global Criminology and Criminal Justice: Current Issues and Perspectives*, edited by Nick Larsen and Russell Smandych, xi. Buffalo, NY: Broadview Press.
Crawford, Adam, ed. 2011. *International and Comparative Criminal Justice and Urban Governance: Convergence and Divergence in Global, National and Local Settings*. Cambridge: Cambridge University Press.
Davis, Kevin E., Angelina Fisher, Benedict Kingsbury and Sally Engle Merry, eds. 2012. *Governance by Indicators: Global Power through Classification and Rankings*. Oxford: Oxford University Press.
Dezalay, Yves and Bryant Garth. 2002. *Global Prescriptions: The Production, Exportation, and Importation of a New Legal Orthodoxy*. Ann Arbor, MI: University of Michigan Press.
Drake, Deborah, John Muncie and Louise Westmarland, eds. 2009. *Criminal Justice, Local and Global*. Milton Keynes: Willan Publishing and Open University Press.
Edwards, Adam and Graham Hughes. 2005. 'Comparing the Governance of Safety in Europe.' *Theoretical Criminology* 9(3): 345–63.
Garland, David. 1996. 'The Limits of the Sovereign State: Strategies of Crime Control in Contemporary Society.' *British Journal of Criminology* 36: 445–71.
Glenny, Misha. 2011. *Dark Market*. London: Bodley Head.
Hobbs, Dick. 1998. 'Going Down the Glocal: The Local Context of Organized Crime.' *Howard Journal of Criminal Justice* 37: 407–22.
Karstedt, Susanne, ed. 2009. *Legal Institutions and Collective Memories*. Oxford: Hart.
——— and David Nelken. 2014. *Globalisation and Crime*. Farnham: Ashgate Publishing.
Klein, Naomi. 2008. *The Shock Doctrine: The Rise of Disaster Capitalism*. Toronto, ON: Vintage Press.
Larsen, Nick and Russell Smandych, eds. 2008. *Global Criminology and Criminal Justice: Current Issues and Perspectives*. Buffalo, NY, Broadview Press.
Loader, Ian and Neil Walker. 2007. *Civilizing Security*. Cambridge: Cambridge University Press.
Merry, Sally Engle. 2006. *Human Rights and Gender Violence: Translating International Law into Local Justice*. Chicago, IL: University of Chicago Press.

———. 2011. 'Measuring the World: Indicators, Human Rights, and Global Governance.' *Current Anthropology* 52(supplementary issue 3): S83–S95.

Mills, C. Wright. 1959. *The Sociological Imagination*. New York: Oxford University Press.

Muncie, John. 2005. 'The Globalization of Crime Control – the Case of Youth and Juvenile Justice: Neoliberalism, Policy Convergence and International Conventions. *Theoretical Criminology* 9(1): 35–64.

———. 2011. 'On Globalisation and Exceptionalism.' In *Globalisation and Comparative Criminal Justice*, edited by David Nelken, 87–109. Farnham: Ashgate Publishing.

———, Deborah Talbot and Reece Walters. 2009. *Crime, Local and Global.* Cullompton and Milton Keynes: Willan Publishing and Open University Press.

Nelken, David. 1997. 'The Globalization of Crime and Criminal Justice: Prospects and Problems.' In *Current Legal Problems: Law and Opinion at the end of the 20th Century*, edited by Michael Freeman, 251–79. Oxford: Oxford University Press.

———. 2003. 'Criminology: Crime's Changing Boundaries.' In *The Oxford Handbook of Legal Studies*, edited by Peter Cane and Mark Tushnet, 250–70. Oxford: Oxford University Press.

———. 2008. 'Normalising Time: European Integration and Court Delays in Italy.' In *Paradoxes of European Integration*, edited by Hanne Petersen, Helle Krunke, Anne-Lise Kjær and Mikael Rask Madsen, 299–323. Aldershot: Ashgate Publishing.

———. 2011a. *Globalisation and Comparative Criminal Justice*. Farnham: Ashgate Publishing.

———. 2011b. 'Human Trafficking and Legal Culture.' *Israel Law Review* 43(3): 479–513.

———. 2014a. 'Afterword: Contesting Global Indicators.' In *Measuring Development, Corruption and the Rule of Law: The Production and Use of Indicators for Global Governance*, edited by Sally Merry, Kevin Davis and Benedict Kingsbury. Cambridge: Cambridge University Press.

———. 2014b. 'The Logics of Security: A Comment on Valverde.' *Criminology & Criminal Justice* 14(4): 405–11.

Pakes, Frances. 2010. 'The Comparative Method in Globalised Criminology.' *Australian and New Zealand Journal of Criminology* 43: 17–34.

Reichel, Philip L. 2007. *Handbook of Transnational Crime and Justice*, 4th edn. New York: Sage.

———. 2008. *Comparative Criminal Justice Systems*, 5th edn. Upper Saddle River: NJ, Prentice Hall.

Rosga, AnnJannette and Margaret L. Satterthwaite. 2012. 'Measuring Human Rights: UN Indicators in Critical Perspective.' In *Governance by Indicators: Global Power through Classification and Rankings*, edited by Kevin E. Davis, Angelina Fisher, Benedict Kingsbury and Sally Engle Merry, 365–91. Oxford: Oxford University Press.

Savelsberg, Joachim. 2011. 'Globalization and States of Punishment.' In *Comparative Criminal Justice and Globalisation*, edited by David Nelken, 69–86. Farnham: Ashgate Publishing.

Shearing, Clifford and Len Johnston. 2010. 'Nodal Wars and Network Fallacies: A Geneological Analysis of Global Insecurities.' *Theoretical Criminology* 14: 495–514.

Sheptycki, James. 2002. *In Search Of Transnational Policing*. Aldershot: Ashgate Publishing.

——— and Ali Wardak, eds. 2005. *Transnational and Comparative Criminology*. London: Glasshouse Press.

Simon, Jonathan. 2007. *Governing through Crime*. Oxford: Oxford University Press.

Valverde, Mariana. 2011a. 'Questions of Security: A Framework for Research.' *Theoretical Criminology* 15: 3–22.

———. 2011b. 'The Question of Scale in Urban Criminology.' In *International and Comparative Criminal Justice and Urban Governance: Convergence and Divergence in Global, National and Local Settings*, edited by Adam Crawford, 567–86. Cambridge: Cambridge University Press.

———. 2014. 'Studying the Governance of Crime and Security: Space, Time and Jurisdiction.' *Criminology & Criminal Justice* 14(4): 379–91.

Walden, Ian. 2011. 'Accessing Data in the Cloud: The Long Arm of the Law Enforcement Agent.' Queen Mary School of Law Legal Studies Research Paper 74/2011. *SSRN Journal*, 14 November. Accessed 6 June 2015. http://ssrn.com/abstract=1781067.

Wacquant, Loïc. 2009a. *Prisons of Poverty*. Minneapolis, MN: University of Minnesota Press.

———. 2009b. *Punishing the Poor: The Neoliberal Government of Social Insecurity*. Durham, NC, Duke University Press.

Winterdyk, John and Lin Cao. 2004. *Lessons from International/comparative Criminology/criminal Justice*. Toronto, ON: De Sitter.

Young, Jock. 2011. *The Criminological Imagination*. Cambridge: Polity Press.

Zaloznaya, Marina and John Hagan. 2012. 'Fighting Human Trafficking or Instituting Authoritarian Control? The Political Co-optation of Human Rights Protection in Belarus.' In *Governance by Indicators: Global Power through Classification and Rankings*, edited by Kevin E. Davis, Angelina Fisher, Benedict Kingsbury and Sally Engle Merry, 344–64. Oxford: Oxford University Press.

Index